January 2023

For George and Phyllis —

In warm friendship
on the occasion of a
welcome Reunion.

Best wishes,

Bruce

Between History and Myth

Between History and Myth

Stories of Harald Fairhair and the Founding of the State

BRUCE LINCOLN

The University of Chicago Press
Chicago and London

Bruce Lincoln is the Caroline E. Haskell Distinguished Service Professor of the History of Religions at the University of Chicago, where he is also affiliated with the Departments of Anthropology, Classics, Medieval Studies, and Middle Eastern Studies.

The University of Chicago Press, Chicago 60637
The University of Chicago Press, Ltd., London
© 2014 by The University of Chicago
All rights reserved. Published 2014.
Printed in the United States of America

23 22 21 20 19 18 17 16 15 14   1 2 3 4 5

ISBN-13: 978-0-226-14092-6 (cloth)
ISBN-13: 978-0-226-14108-4 (e-book)
DOI: 10.7208/chicago/9780226141084.001.0001

Page vi: The epigraph comes from Pierre Bourdieu's *Practical Reason* (Stanford, CA: Stanford University Press, 1998), 40.

The University of Chicago Press gratefully acknowledges the generous support of the Divinity School at the University of Chicago toward the publication of this book.

Library of Congress Cataloging-in-Publication Data

Lincoln, Bruce, author.
    Between history and myth : stories of Harald Fairhair and the founding of the state / Bruce Lincoln.
        pages cm
    Includes bibliographical references and index.
    ISBN 978-0-226-14092-6 (cloth : alk. paper)—ISBN 978-0-226-14108-4 (e-book)
1. Harald Haarfagre, King of Norway, approximately 860–approximately 940.
2. Norway—History—To 1030.   I. Title.
    DL463.L56 2014
    948.1'014092—dc23
[B]   2013050778

For Louise

If the state is able to exert symbolic violence, it is because it incarnates itself simultaneously in objectivity, in the form of specific organizational structures and mechanisms, and in subjectivity, in the form of mental structures and categories of perception and thought. By realizing itself in social structures and in the mental structures adapted to them, the instituted institution makes us forget that it issues out of a long series of acts of *institution* (in the active sense) and hence has all the appearances of the *natural.*

This is why there is no more potent tool for rupture than the reconstruction of genesis: by bringing back into view the conflicts and confrontations of the early beginnings and therefore all the discarded possibles, it retrieves the possibility that things could have been (and still could be) otherwise.

PIERRE BOURDIEU

Contents

Illustrations

Figures

Tables

Synoptic Tables

1

Introduction

I

All institutions, like all groups, tell stories about their beginnings. Such tales are oft repeated, finely wrought, and usually much beloved. They are also eminently useful and always more complicated than their audiences suspect. But were their complexities more evident, they would surely be less useful. And here one must ask: Less useful for what? Less useful to whom?

Sometimes such narratives style themselves "origin myths"; sometimes "histories of foundation." Sometimes they advance no generic claims and defy easy categorization, blurring—indeed, defying—the distinction between history and myth. This interstitial status may produce confusion for analysts and others, but it adds to the stories' fascination. What is more, it makes them more elusive and more effective still. (More effective for what? More effective on whom?)

Among those institutions most in need of an impressive creation account is the state, particularly as it tries to legitimate itself and to manage its inevitable tensions and contradictions by naturalizing itself and its operations, while representing its origins as somehow much greater than natural: heroic, miraculous, divinely graced or inspired. Examples of state-founding narratives on this model are easy to come by, and their close study is always instructive. One thinks of certain books in the Hebrew Bible, for instance (I and II Samuel, I and II Kings),[1] Vergil's Aeneid,[2] or Bishop Weems's *Life of George Washington*.[3] The grade-school textbooks of most nations regularly play this role and fit this pattern.[4]

II

State-founding events supposedly lie behind state-founding stories, and if one could know the former directly, it would be instructive to compare history-as-lived to history-as-recounted so that one could gauge the degree of embellishment, erasure, distortion, and tendentious fantasy operative in the latter. Alas, such experiments are not easily staged, especially for events (and pseudoevents) of long ago, where one has access to the historical real only via the stories. In such terrain, critical method depends on close reading of texts, comparison of one variant to another, and consistently posing irreverent questions (Useful for what? Useful to whom?).

Their admitted limitations notwithstanding, such methods can be revealing, provided one understands what they can—and cannot—do. In general, they shift interest from the moment of action to that of narration (understanding that narration is also an action of sorts); also from the heroism of the actors to the subtlety, hidden interests, and consummate skill of the storytellers. From the gritty process of state formation to the well-polished stories of same.[5]

III

Seeking an example with which to explore these issues, I was drawn—no doubt, for idiosyncratic reasons—to the Old Norse sagas and, more particularly, to the subgenre of *Konunga sögur* ("Kings' Sagas"), which treat the institution of the state as a series of royal lives.[6] And most particularly of all to the stories of Hálfdan the Black (said to have ruled ca. 839–58) and his son, Harald Fairhair (ruled ca. 858–930, as king of a unified Norway from the mid-870s), for these two—and the space in between them—mark the transition from legendary prehistory to that which modern scholars regard as history proper.[7] The distinction between the two figures is not made primarily on evidentiary or epistemological grounds, for we do not know much more of Harald than of his father. Rather, it is the sagas themselves that construe the difference as ontological, even cosmogonic, for they recount how Harald changed existence itself and created a new world by consolidating monarchic power, unifying the Norwegian nation, and establishing a modern state.

IV

Stories of Harald's state-founding activities began to circulate more or less contemporarily with the events themselves. This was not a spontaneous reaction to the unfolding drama, however, for Harald employed a number of skalds as his propaganda corps. He is said to have valued them most highly among his retainers, and he placed them in positions of signal honor.[8] In turn, they were expected to bestow still greater honor upon him, for it was their task to transform the king's accomplishments into unforgettable verse and undying fame. Their poems circulated widely, as did other accounts of royal deeds that gradually took the shape of legends, tales (*þættir*, sing. *þáttr*), and sagas. One of the earliest of the Kings' Sagas gestures toward the abundance of material in circulation, stating, "Many things and wondrous ones are remembered of [King Harald], but now it would take too long to narrate these individually."[9]

All this was oral tradition, however, for literacy came to Scandinavia only with and through Christianity.[10] The first literature produced in the North thus tended to be ecclesiastical and hagiographic. Lives of the saints were particularly popular, first those which originated elsewhere and were written in Latin, subsequently translated into the Old Norse vernacular.[11] In turn, these stimulated local production and lives of the monarch-saints responsible for Norway's conversion start to be written in the twelfth century. Other kings then received attention, beginning with the monarchy's founders.[12] Individual Kings' Sagas and more comprehensive attempts to narrate dynastic history thus blossomed between 1180 and 1240, culminating in Heimskringla, a monument of medieval literature written about 1230–35 and usually attributed to Snorri Sturluson (1178–1241).[13] These developments postdate Harald Fairhair's founding of the Norwegian state, however, by a good three and a half centuries. While they are enormously revealing documents, what they reveal is not history "wie es eigentlich gewesen."[14]

All told, we have fewer than a dozen variants of Harald's story, and we will take these up in subsequent chapters. The chief surviving sources include Theodricus Monachus, Historia de Antiquitate Regum Norwagiensum Chapter 1, Historia Norwegiæ 10–11, Ágrip af Noregskonunga sögum 1–4, Fagrskinna 1–3, the "Tale of Hálfdan the Black" (*Þáttr Hálfdanar svarta*, in Flateyjarbók 1.561–67), the "Tale of Harald Fairhair" (*Þáttr Haralds hárfagra*, in Flateyjarbók 1.567–76), Hálfdan the Black's Saga, and Harald Fairhair's Saga (the second and third sagas included in Heimskringla). Pieces of the narrative and allusions to it are also scattered in other sagas, including Orkneyinga Saga, Egil's Saga, Laxdæla Saga, Flóamanna Saga, Barð's Saga, and others.[15] We should not, however, mistake this dossier for the full body of evidence. As we have seen, all of these sources are relatively late and all drew on prior variants—written and oral, poetic and prose, learned and popular, Norwegian and Icelandic—some of which survive, some of which are known only by name, and many of which are lost altogether.[16] What each version could assume, however, was an audience already familiar with the story and keenly interested in it. They could address themselves to readers (or hearers) who could recognize modifications to the conventional shape of the story and appreciate such nuances as these innovations conveyed. Putting it this way is too crude, however, for the extent of such knowledge, skills, and interest surely varied from one reader to another. Thus, as a given text introduced ever-more-subtle innovations to its version of the story, the fewer and more select would be the number of those who could recognize these shifts and understand their import. And a skillful narrator could make telling use of just such variations.

V

Their disparate sources notwithstanding, the Kings' Sagas are not simple chronicles or haphazard in their organization. On the contrary, recent studies have identified certain typological concerns that motivated these texts and determined their structure. *Grosso modo*, they describe a gradual but inevitable progress toward realization of a transcendent ideal: an ideal that manifests itself in history via the establishment and integration of two key institutions: first the state, and then the church.[17]

To cite an early example, Theodricus Monachus's Ancient History of the Norwegian Kings (written ca. 1180), inscribed this pattern in the nature of time itself. Thus, Theodricus expressed severe reservations about the accuracy of dating and generally preferred to give the length of a given king's reign, without specifying the years in question. There are, however, a very small number of exceptional cases, where he does cite the year, always describing it as "the year [numbered X] from the incarnation of our Lord." The first of these, mentioned in the very first line of the text, is the year of Harald Fairhair's accession.[18] The second is the death of St. Olaf, who accomplished the conversion of Norway.[19] The first date thus marks the establishment of proper kingship, the second, that of the Christian faith, and the phrase *ab incarnatione Domini* identifies both as crucial moments in sacred history, when God's plan for salvation takes large steps toward its fulfillment.

VI

Heimskringla makes a similar point, while expanding on the same structure. Thus, it begins with a race of Asian heroes who migrated from the center of the world to northern Europe (a frozen, uncivilized territory), bringing kingship with them.[20] The first section of the text, known as Ynglingasaga, describes how these invaders established themselves first in Sweden, then suffered defeats and were driven west in disorder. The next two sagas are named for Hálfdan the Black and Harald Fairhair, and they recount how these heroic figures founded a proper kingship in Norway. Subsequent sagas treat establishment of the True Religion (also ultimately imported from Asia, by way of Rome, England, and Germany) as a complement to the royal state, a process that began with two kings who adopted Christianity as their personal faith (Hákon the Good, r. 934–61, and Harald Graycloak, r. 961–70) and culminated in the two who waged aggressive campaigns to convert the Norwegian nation (Olaf Tryggvason, r. 995–1000, and St. Olaf, r. 1015–28).

Within this schema, Harald Fairhair occupies the crucial mediating position. On the one hand, he represents the fulfillment of the political process that produces the royal state. On the other hand, he anticipates the religious process that results in a Christian nation, for Heimskringla depicts him as having intuitively grasped religious truth, even while still a pagan. This is conveyed in a detail this text introduced when reworking earlier accounts of Harald's accession.

Traditionally, these stories center on an oath Harald swore, pledging to make himself sole ruler of the nation or die in the attempt. All accounts of that oath describe the gestures at its center, as Harald vowed never to cut his hair until he realized his ambition. Heimskringla is the first variant, however, to include certain words that Harald spoke or, more precisely, it is the first to place these words in his mouth: "This vow I swear and therefore I appeal to God, he who created me and who rules over all."[21]

This phrasing is meant to convey a simple but profound faith: a natural religiosity that follows when innate reason reflects on the world's wonders, as perceived by the senses, yielding an intuitive understanding of the supreme deity as creator and ruler of the cosmos, and recognition of oneself as a dependent part of his glorious creation. A much more elaborate expression of this point occurs in one version of Fagrskinna. There, after swearing to conquer Norway, Harald goes on to swear a second oath in which he renounces pagan gods, idols, and sacrifices, while showing himself to have absorbed all the truths of natural religion.

> "And I swear this also, that I will make sacrifice to no god whom men now worship, except the one who made the sun and who made and ordered the world. And since I plan that I will be sole king in Norway and will place under me all other kings, those who previously have been both powerful and mighty, I shall do all things with confidence in the one who is mightiest and rules all. And no one will be dear in friendship to me who worships another

god than that one, because I believe I see the truth that a god who has no more power than a stone or a block of wood cannot help me or anyone else. I am only a man and I know that I will die, like other men, and I know I have an ambitious spirit. And if I knew that I would have a life as long as I know that a god lives, then I might not be happy until I had all the world under me and my control. Therefore, it is significant concerning these gods, that if they had any real divinity or power, then they would not have won so small a realm to rule as one stone or a small grove. Therefore shall every man with intelligence let himself be convinced," said the king, "he who knows anything has grasped that the only true god is he who created all things and he alone can give full help to a man, because he has made the man, just as he made all else. Therefore, I will strive for that as long as I live, so that just as my mind strives for him who is mightiest of all, so I also hope that with his support I will become mightier than all the petty kings who now are in Norway."[22]

Even this is not yet the more perfect religiosity of faith in the salvific power of Christ, which requires revelation, scripture, the intervention of the church, and a transformation of the self through conversion. But it is a significant step toward that faith, and these texts assert that a rudimentary religious truth was already present in Harald before he started the process of state formation. Like its founder, the state is thus represented as always already having been rich in religious potential: a potential that awaits a fuller and richer development.

Such readings of the text are certainly accurate. Harald is a state-founding hero and a "Noble Heathen," in Lars Lönnroth's useful phrase.[23] Creation of the state is a monumental accomplishment of vision, political will, and military force. It is religiously informed and motivated *ab origine*, but it is also subject to a process of religious conversion, reform, and perfection that unfolds in subsequent history. All this is said directly and by implication.

And yet there is more.

VII

Within the relatively wide social, political, and narrative field represented by the Kings' Sagas, one finds differing attitudes toward kings, kingship, and the Norwegian state. Some texts and variants are more, and some less, favorably disposed, reflecting—also forming and interacting with—the attitudes of their audiences. Texts also differ in the degree of subtlety with which they advance their views, although the difference is not between those that are subtle and those that are crude, but between the subtle and even-more-subtle. Such distinctions correlate not just with authorial skill, but also with the texts' relations with and attitudes toward royal power, which determined the extent to which they needed to mask their intentions.

Of all the texts, none is subtler than Heimskringla, which regards Harald Fairhair and all he represents with distinct ambivalence. Beneath a celebratory veneer, it harbors other discursive projects, including a critique it advances so skillfully and slyly that most modern critics have failed to perceive it.[24] Never quite explicit, its critique normally remains a subtext, legible to some readers only, while remaining invisible to others. One can become more conscious of it, however, by following seemingly stray narrative threads to their conclusion and drawing inferences from them, or by comparing the details from one variant to another. The chapters that follow—each of which is named for a seemingly minor character in the story—take up this work. Collectively, they show that the story of Harald, his oath, his faith, his kingship, and his state is more complex—also a good deal more fascinating—than has generally been recognized. I would rather not frontload my conclusions, but prefer to let readers share the experience of seeing them gradually take shape as we work through the primary texts, whose subtlety, intricacy, tactical shrewdness, and linguistic and narrative skill are a delight to observe. Let me simply, if briefly, note that my study of these materials has led me to think that the story of Harald's oath sits precisely at that point where the distinction of myth and history breaks down, where the state encounters all that refuses and resists it, and where praise and blame (or, to use a more contemporary vocabulary, propaganda and critique) somehow manage to coexist.

Gyða

I

Our story concerns the founding of a state, or—to be more exact—two states, since one emerged in direct reaction to the other, the first being the unified kingdom of Norway, and the second the emphatically antimonarchic commonwealth of Iceland.[1] A number of surviving sources narrate the events surrounding a peculiar oath sworn by the man who would radically reinvent kingdom and kingship alike. Several of these sources are of Norwegian provenance. The oldest ones date from some three hundred years after the events in question. Among these is an anonymous tract entitled Historia Norwegiæ, written in Latin perhaps as early as 1170, but possibly as late as 1220. The others are in the Old Norse vernacular and include Ágrip af Nóregs konunga sögum ("Epitome of the Sagas of the Kings of Norway," ca. 1190) and Fagrskinna ("Fair Skin," named for its smooth vellum), probably written in Norway around 1220. Each of these draws on its predecessors, as well as other sources—written and oral, Norwegian and Icelandic—that have not survived. For the most part, these are succinct chronicles of events, supplying valuable information but relatively lacking in narrative detail.

The Icelandic sources differ on this score, particularly the account given in the second and third books of Heimskringla, entitled Hálfdan the Black's Saga and Harald Fairhair's Saga. Deceptively simple in its diction, which favors short, crisp descriptive sentences and eschews direct authorial comment, Heimskringla is a masterpiece of medieval history writing, within which thousands of characters and episodes are intricately woven together by subtle cross-references and allusions.

Three other Icelandic sources are preserved in the Flateyjarbók collection, which was assembled in the fourteenth century. The first of these is the "Tale of Harald Fairhair" (*þáttr Haralds hárfagra*), a text that dates from the 1230s or later and draws on Heimskringla, as well as an older, now-lost *Harald Fairhair's Saga, from which it preserves some independent information.[2] Second, predictably enough, is the "Tale of Hálfdan the Black" (*þáttr Hálfdanar svarta*), which draws on a now-lost *Saga of King Harald, Dofri's Foster Son (*Saga Haralds konungs Dofrafostra*), itself of uncertain date. Finally, there is the Greater Saga of Olaf Tryggvason (*Ólafs saga Tryggvasonar in mesta*), compiled in the fourteenth century and based on versions of this saga written by Icelandic monks around 1180–90, to which have been added materials taken from Heimskringla.[3]

All these sources attribute the unification of Norway to a petty district king, whose reign is said to have lasted an astounding seventy years (ca. 858–930). Initially known by a patronym as "Harald Hálfdanarson," he acquired the sobriquet "Shaggy Harald" (*Haraldr lúfa*) when he swore not to comb or cut his hair until he forced all Norway to submit, and he became "Harald Fairhair" when this task was accomplished.[4] By considering the story of Harald's vow, its multiple variants and the multiple stories to which it connects, and paying close attention to the ideological maneuvering carried out via fine points of emplotment and diction, we can get a good idea of the way states described themselves in their moment of emergence. Beyond that, we can also see how subsequent historical reflection modulates and redeploys the stories states tell about themselves.

II

A convenient starting point is the relatively simple account found in the "Tale of Harald Hairfair."

> Then King Harald took [= married?][5] Gyða, the daughter of King Eirik of Hörðaland. But she said this to the king that he should conquer all Norway and bring it under him, as it says in another chapter of the Saga of Olaf Tryggvason. Then King Harald swore this vow: not to let anyone comb his hair or cut it until he became sole king over Norway. For that reason he was then called "Shaggy Harald." He had these sons with Gyða: Guthorm, Harek, and Guðrøð.[6]

For all its brevity, this text delineates a classically gendered division of labor, within which idea and inspiration are represented as female, agency and execution, male. Although the woman possesses a capacity of thought and imagination that permits her to register dissatisfaction with the way things are and to envision novel alternatives, such change can be accomplished only through physical force unavailable to her as woman. Male and female are thus interdependent: she needs his power, he needs her direction. But in contrast to the process of biological reproduction, inception of this enterprise begins with the woman's desire, while the longer, harder task of bringing it to fruition falls to the man.

Another version of this story appears in Heimskringla and the Greater Saga of Olaf Tryggvason, the two of which are virtually identical (See synoptic table 2.1). This variant follows the same pattern but is more complex, giving some psychological depth to the story, while adding many details and reorganizing its temporal structure. Thus, whereas the Flateyjarbók variant does not specify just when Harald and Gyða were married, that of Heimskringla carefully disarticulates the episodes and sets them in sequence. First, Gyða makes her suggestion, which she frames as a precondition for their union. Second, Harald takes his vow, after which follow ten years of military campaigns. These culminate in the battle of Hafrsfjörð, where he quashed all effective opposition within Norway, an event that historians have dated anywhere from 868 to the early 890s but is probably best set in the mid 870s.[7] Only then, when he had consolidated his power over the unified state, were the two finally married.[8]

In ways, then, Gyða plays the role of the female inciter that figures prominently in numerous Old Norse sagas.[9] Hers is, however, a distinctive and atypical performance. To begin, she addresses a man who is no relative of hers, where other inciters direct their suggestions and reproaches to fathers, husbands, sons, or brothers. In doing so, such women understand themselves to be defending the interests of lineages to which they belong by birth or marriage, and whose continued vitality they aim to secure. Toward this end, they remind the family's responsible males of past acts of violence that deprived the group of valued kinsmen, and urge them—particularly when these men are reluctant and waver—to take the requisite vengeance. In this, their goals are conservative and reproductive. They ask their men, sometimes in shrill and abrasive terms, to live up to traditional values and to preserve traditional institutions, defending the group against loss of its personnel, but also its honor.[10]

Gyða, in contrast, speaks of an institution that has never previously existed in Norway, although she can point to precedents in Denmark and Sweden. This is the monarchic state—that is, a geographically extensive polity united under a single ruler (*ein-valdi*)—and she calls on Harald to establish this by military conquest. The project she envisions and articulates is one without basis in tradition or morality, being grounded only in a sense of the possible:

that is, in vision and desire.[11] Gyða's speech is one of political ambition that initiates a project of expansion, conquest, and subjugation; that of the classic inciters, in contrast, is a speech of moral obligation, aimed at defense and preservation of existing institutions. They speak the interests of lineage and family, while she speaks those of the emergent nation and state.

In ways, Gyða thus may have less in common with the inciters than with seeresses and visionaries, like Veleda, the quasi-deified prophetess of the Bructeri described by Tacitus,[12] or the Norns and the völva ("Sibyl") of the Poetic Edda.[13] All of these women were gifted with knowledge of the future and could comprehend how that which will be is made possible, perhaps even inevitable, by the sedimented deeds of the past.[14] Whatever visionary powers they possessed, however, the agency of such women—like that of Gyða—was mediated through males. Thus, for her part, the völva of Völuspá was a dead woman, awakened by Óðinn's necromantic spell, when he sought wisdom to help forestall cosmic disaster. And Veleda, for all her power, was kept isolated in a tower, lest her sacred aura be compromised by mortals' approach. Accordingly, she transmitted her messages always through a trusted kinsman.[15]

III

Not only did her extraordinary powers of perception permit Gyða to envision the conditions of possibility for a new form (and scope) of the Norwegian state, but at a more personal level, she could also anticipate her own future and take steps to reshape it. Along these lines, it is important to note some details in the Heimskringla account of her dealings with Harald, details that go considerably beyond the version found in the "Tale of Harald Fairhair."

> King Harald sent his men after a maiden who was named Gyða, the daughter of King Eirik of Hörðaland—she was in fosterage at Valdres with a powerful landowner—whom he wanted to take as his concubine, because she was an extremely beautiful woman and rather proud. But when the messengers came there and presented his message to the maiden, she answered in this manner. She was not going to waste her maidenhood in order to take a man who, as king, has no more realms than a few counties to manage. "And it seems extraordinary to me," she said, "that there is no king who wants to take possession of Norway and to be sole ruler over it, as have King Gorm in Denmark and Eirik in Uppsala."
>
> Her answer seemed extremely proud to the messengers, and they asked of her speech: what reply should come to this? They said that Harald was so powerful a king that he was a fitting match for her. Although her answer led their mission in a way other than they might wish, they saw they had no

choice, for they could not take her against her will, and they prepared to depart. And when they were ready, she led the men out. Then Gyða spoke with the messengers and bade them to take these words of hers to King Harald. She would consent to become his proper wife if he will first do this for her sake: place all of Norway under him and rule that realm just as independently as King Eirik ruled Sweden and King Gorm, Denmark. "Because then, it seems to me," she said, "he might really be called a sovereign king"[16]

The text is clear, but not blunt, regarding Harald's initially less-than-honorable intentions. It is not as wife (*kona*) that he desired the beautiful Gyða, but as concubine (*frilla*). A feminine substantive formed from the verb *frjá*, "to love," *frilla* most literally denotes a lover. More technically, it is a woman with whom a man has sexual relations but for whom no brideprice is paid, no marriage performed, and whose children, at best, have limited rights of inheritance, being illegitimate in the full sense of the word.[17]

In the Heimskringla version, the story thus begins with a sexual proposition made by a petty king, which his intended inamorata—herself the daughter of a king no lower in status than her suitor—converts into a proper, but conditional, proposal of marriage. Brushing aside the terms of Harald's initial suggestion, she agrees to become "his proper wife" (*eigin kona hans*), but only if he succeeds in making himself sole ruler of the nation, and does that "for her sake" (*fyrir hennar sakir*). The Greater Saga of Olaf Tryggvason makes this point explicit. In the one passage where it does not follow the Heimskringla version, that text has Gyða begin her response to Harald's messengers by saying: "Much less do I want to be his concubine."[18]

The audacious project of state formation is thus construed as something instrumental, being directed toward the ultimate—if deferred—projects of seduction on the part of the male and family formation on that of the female. Here, however, we must note a puzzling anomaly to which we will later return. When discussion moves toward marriage—as it does, for instance, when the messengers tell Gyða that Harald is a "fitting match" (*fullræði*) for her, that is, someone of equal or greater status, as required by the proprieties of marriage—such negotiations ought properly be conducted with Gyða's father, and not with the girl herself.[19]

IV

If Gyða rejects Harald's initial suggestion, the king accepts hers when relayed to him by the messengers. Describing the young woman as "extremely insolent" (*furðudjǫrf*), they urge the despatch of sufficient troops to bring the wench in by force. King Harald, however, is of a different opinion.

King Harald answered that this maiden had not spoken or done anything so
bad as to demand vengeance. Rather, he ordered that she have great thanks
for her words: "She has made me aware of things," he said, "that now seem
wonderful to me and that I had not considered before." And then he said:
"This vow I swear and therefore I appeal to God, he who created me and rules
over all. Never shall my hair be cut or combed until I have taken possession
of all Norway, with its tributes, taxes, and administration, or otherwise to
die."[20]

Once this oath has been sworn, the narrative shifts from a story of love
to one of war with a shocking abruptness. Thus, as the next chapter opens,
Harald has assembled a great army and marched north through the Dales.
What follows is described without euphemism.

When he came down on the settlements, Harald had all the men killed and
the dwellings burned. And when the people became aware of this, everyone
fled who could: some down to Orkadal, some to Gaulardal, and some to the
marches. Some sought pardon and all who came to a meeting with the king
obtained that, and they became his men.[21]

Harald uses his army as an instrument of terror, but also as one of recruit-
ment. Those in his path have three choices: become his victims, flee, or join
up. The structure of the passage might be read to suggest that the last course
of action is the wisest, but the text passes no explicit judgment. Never does
it speak directly against king, kingship, or the Norwegian state; rather, it lets
details accumulate and implicitly invites readers to draw their own conclusions. By organizing the narrative such that the Gyða episode is immediately
transparent to Harald's violence, the text remains legible in different fashions
by the different audiences to whom it was directed. At the most superficial
level, it offers a romantic mystification of state violence for its Norwegian
readers by making a female responsible for the male use of force. At the same
time, it renders this ideological maneuver so obvious as to inoculate Icelandic audiences against it, instructing them, as it were, not only on the behavior of kings, but also on the disjuncture between kings' stories and their
actions.

V

Heimskringla goes on to show how Gyða's concern for proper marriage,
family, and rights of inheritance ironically produces destruction of the very
institutions she sought to defend. Thus, it states that Harald introduced a
key innovation in the territories he conquered: a radical revision of property

laws, especially those applying to rights in land.²² Previously, land had been regarded as óðal (Medieval Latin *allodium*), that is, part of an inalienable patrimony belonging to the lineage (*ætt*) and not to any individual, with the result that land could not be bought, sold, or even owned in the usual sense of ownership.²³ Rather, each generation had usufruct rights over their land for the duration of their lives, but were obliged to transmit it unimpaired and unencumbered to the generation of their heirs. Under such a system, political authorities might have control over people, but never over their land. We are told, however, that as part of his drive to increase his power, Harald proclaimed an end to this system, arrogated the lands as his own, and charged the previous owners rent on the lands that traditionally had been theirs. To collect these rents, he set an earl in each district, who contributed sixty men to the king's army and, for his troubles, was entitled to keep one third of the monies he extracted.²⁴

Quickest to recognize the opportunities present in these new offices and administrative structures was Earl Hákon of Hlaðir, a powerful nobleman who rallied to Harald after the latter's first victories and contributed the troops that let the king prevail in the Trondheim district, which thereafter became his capital. In return for these signal services, the earl received the Strinda district as his administrative domain, and the alliance between the two men was sealed by a marriage between Harald and Hákon's daughter, Ása.²⁵ In the Heimskringla version, this is Harald's first marriage: an event of critical importance for the fulfillment of his ambitions, but—another irony—one that relegated the woman who inspired those ambitions to the position of second wife.²⁶

Harald's legal and administrative innovations let him fill the royal coffers and raise larger armies than was possible for any of his rivals. The system he introduced contains the elementary logic of a dynamic and expansionist state, that is, the symbiosis of revenue and force. Thus, Harald's armies let him enforce his new laws, collect his new taxes, raise bigger armies, and conquer new territories in which to impose his laws and taxes, and from which he could raise bigger armies still. His changes were bitterly resented, however, by those of the old noble families who, less flexible and farsighted than Earl Hákon, did not leap at the opportunity to become Harald's earls and reap the profits. Deprived of their óðal holdings, many of them liquidated such assets as they could and left Norway for territories to the west, especially Iceland, where—according to the stories that constituted the foundation myths of the commonwealth—they sought to construct a society free of the tyranny they perceived in Harald's monarchic institutions.²⁷ Others, however, resisted bitterly, and did so up through the battle of Hafrsfjörð, where Harald crushed the last, desperate opposition to his rule. Heimskringla begins its account as follows:

> The news was reported from the country's south that the men of Hörðaland, Rogaland, Agðir, and Telamark had gathered together and made a rebellion with ships and weapons and many men. The originators were Eirik, king of Hörðaland, Sulki, king of Rogaland, his brother, Earl Soti, Kjötvi the Wealthy, king of Agðir, and Thorir Haklang, his son. From Telamark there were two brothers: Hroald Hrygg and Hadd the Hard.[28]

Here, listed first among the ringleaders is a familiar name: Eirik, king of Hörðaland, none other than Gyða's father.[29] This last irony leads us back to the lingering anomaly in the negotiations for Gyða's hand. Where normally a suitor sought permission from a woman's father to marry her, the logic of this case made such a step impossible. Under ordinary circumstances, the two men would collaborate to produce a marriage and a family that would continue—and reproduce—the old order. Gyða, however, stipulated a condition that made this impossible, for she asked Harald to create a radically new kind of state before she would consent to marriage. In order to do so, he had to destroy the old social, political, and economic institutions of which her father was very much a part. While cast as a drama with profound consequences for specific characters, Hafrsfjörð was more than a victory for Harald and a defeat for King Eirik of Hörðaland: it was also the foundation of the state on the ruins of the family, for just as lineages had lost control over their patrimonial lands, so patriarchs' ability to dispose of their women also diminished. The means of production and reproduction alike were passing toward king and state.

VI

Like other sources, Heimskringla recounts that resistance to Harald ceased after the battle of Hafrsfjörð, as his adversaries were either dead or chose to leave the country. Savoring his victory, the new sovereign then summoned the woman who started him on his path. Although the text avoids describing Gyða as Harald's concubine (*frilla*), its description is hardly that of a legitimate marriage (cf. synoptic table 2.2).[30]

> King Harald had now become sole ruler over all Norway. Then he recalled that which the maiden, the one who was very proud, had said to him. Then he sent men to her and had them bring her to him and he laid her beside him. These were their children: Álof was the oldest, then was Hrœrek, then Sigtrygg, Fróði, and Thorgils.[31]

If indeed this constitutes a marriage, Heimskringla makes clear it was not Harald's first, and in no event was it the last. Rather, marriage was one of the prime instruments through which Harald forged alliances, and sources give him something on the order of ten wives and twenty concubines.[32] Of these, by far the most important was the marriage that joined him to Ragnhild, a Danish princess whom he also wed after the victory at Hafrsfjörð, when he had achieved hegemony within Norway and no longer needed to negotiate for the support of local nobles. This match was one of international diplomacy, securing good relations with the foremost power to the south and confirming Harald's status as a monarch comparable to the Danish kings.

The Danes did not give such recognition to Harald lightly, however, and serious negotiations preceded the match. Heimskringla says that he was obliged to give up his nine other wives before receiving Ragnhild's hand.[33] The "Tale of Harald Fairhair" goes further:

> King Æirek, on the advice of his daughter, sent word to Harald that he would give the maiden to him in marriage if he would renounce his own wives and concubines. This being delivered, the messengers went back. Then the king sent all his wives home to their kinsmen. And after that, King Harald sent south to Denmark for Ragnhild and she was sent to him. Thereafter, he made a wedding for her and she was most noble in appearance.[34]

No source makes explicit mention of Gyða's fate, but both Heimskringla and Flateyjarbók quote a verse from the Haraldskvæði, a poem by Harald's skald Thorbjorn Hornklofi:

The high-born king	who took a Danish wife
forsook the Holmrýgir,	and she of the line of Hölgi,
and the maidens of Hörðaland,	and she from Hedmark.[35]

Here, only the Danish princess is named as Harald's "wife" (*kona*), and as such she stands in contrast to the discarded "maidens" (*meyjum*, from *mær*), who are implicitly dismissed as pleasant playthings perhaps, but inappropriate matches for the "highborn king" (*konungr . . . kynstóri*).[36] That Gyða was among these unfortunates seems clear, to judge from the mention of Hörðaland, her home province. We are thus meant to understand that she who first dared to imagine the unified Norwegian monarchy was among the abandoned: a victim of the state she first envisioned and that her husband—if, indeed, he ever was such—only thereafter created.

One would feel considerable sympathy for this proud, ingenious, and abandoned woman, were it clear she ever existed. Her role in the narrative is to arouse just such sympathy, while undercutting one's respect for Harald and admiration for his accomplishment. That such a character served the critical purpose of Icelandic opposition to Norway and to kingship is made clear by the fact that Gyða does not appear in most of the Norwegian Kings' Sagas, where state-founding initiative is credited to Harald alone.[37] The sole exception—which we will shortly consider—only confirms the sharp critical edge of the Gyða story.

Presumably, the historical Harald did cast off his earlier wives before marrying his Danish princess, as reported by the skaldic verse composed at the time of these events, which constitutes our oldest and best source. That text is quoted in Heimskringla and the "Tale of Harald Fairhair" in such a way that it seems to refer to Gyða. More likely, however, it was this verse that stimulated Heimskringla (or its Icelandic antecedents) to invent this otherwise unknown woman from Hörðaland, whom they made responsible for Harald's inspiration and a prime victim of the royal ambitions that she first awakened. In so doing, their goal was not to give a real woman belated recognition, but rather to diminish the king and the institution he founded.

VII

The Gyða story does occur in one Norwegian text, Fagrskinna, which survives in two manuscripts. One of these—known as the A-Text—contains three passages lacking in the other (the B-Text), and these seem to be later additions.[38] One of the longest and most important is a variant of the narrative we have been treating, in which all names save Harald's have been changed. Gyða here becomes "Ragna," who is otherwise unknown, as is true of the ancestors named in her lineage. The story, however, is immediately recognizable, although many details are changed in ways that make Harald more clearly the hero of the story, while rendering his inamorata less sympathetic.

Thus, when Ragna is first introduced, her wealth is stressed alongside her beauty. Her father has just died, we are told, and as his sole heir, she has gained control of his realm (here Thotn, and not Hörðaland).[39] That notwithstanding, when Harald professes his love to the maiden—and the text makes clear that this love is deep and sincere[40]—she responds by inquiring about his property holdings and inheritance prospects.[41] Scandalized by this expression of material interest, the young king rebukes her sternly.

> Then Harald answered angrily and said: "I thought, Ragna, that you would be led to my bed with great honor for the sake of love, but because you have upbraided me with these reproaches, it is now the case that you should be led to my bed as a poor concubine."[42]

Clearly, this passage is meant to rebut a rival version of the story (see synoptic table 2.3). While granting that Harald spoke in terms of concubinage, it asserts that this was not his original intention, only an angry—and temporary—response to the lady's provocation. Properly chastised, she is made to respond with stereotypically feminine skill, charm, and disingenuousness, disclaiming her earlier words as little more than a joke the king has taken too seriously. It is within the context of such defensive repositioning that she advances her epoch-making suggestion.

> Ragna said this to the king: "Do not be angry, lord King, although we speak
> playfully and it does not exalt your kingship to contend with women, still less
> with little girls like me. Better it is, lord King, to contest with other kings, who
> now take up all the land within. And I want to tell you this, if I have my own
> way, I will become neither your concubine nor that of any other man. I shall
> have for my own man that one who will make all Norway's men his subjects
> or I shall have no one."[43]

Harald's response to Ragna's speech confirms the nobility of his intentions. Straightaway, he swore a vow that had two parts. First, he would have no wife—*kona*, not *frilla*—in Norway, save Ragna. Second, that toward that end he would place all other district kings under his power.[44] Going further, he proclaimed a new law that established the rights of women (*kvenna rétt*). Henceforward, no woman could be taken by force, and any woman who wished to preserve her chastity was entitled to do so.[45]

This is a new addition to the story and its intentions are fairly clear. Within the Icelandic sources, the Gyða narrative cast King Harald in a doubly unfavorable light. Not only was he dependent on a woman for his kingship; he also posed a threat to her, to sexual morality, processes of family formation, and women in general. The earlier Norwegian sources, including the B-Text of Fagrskinna, took no note of this story, but the A-Text added a variant designed to rebut all embarrassing aspects of the tale and to defend Harald's reputation as a thoroughly honorable man and—who would have guessed?—an early feminist hero.

3

Rögnvald the Powerful

I

If Gyða prompts Harald Fairhair's vow in some variants of the story, another figure stands at the end of that story, both in Norwegian and Icelandic accounts. Three sources preserve this narrative, and two of them tell it in virtually identical fashion. These are Fagrskinna and the "Tale of Harald Fairhair," which place Harald's haircut just after the decisive victory at Hafrsfjörð that made him sole ruler of Norway.[1] In order to link this to other pieces of its grand narrative, Heimskringla relocates this scene a year or two later, following a great naval expedition to the west, in which Harald conquered the Orkneys, the Shetlands, the Hebrides, and the Isle of Man.[2] While all three versions of the story agree in most particulars save the timing (synoptic table 3.1), Heimskringla offers the most detail.

> King Harald was at a feast given by Earl Rögnvald in Mæri. By then, he had possession of all the land. The king took a bath there, and King Harald let his hair be dressed and then Earl Rögnvald cut his hair, which previously had been uncut and uncombed for ten years. At that time, they called him "Shaggy Harald," but thereafter Rögnvald gave a nickname to him and called him "Harald the Fairhair." And all who saw him said that was the truest of names, because Harald had hair that was both abundant and fair.[3]

Not only does Earl Rögnvald remove Harald's dreadlocks,[4] thereby transforming him from a wild war leader to a civilized sovereign, moving him from nature to culture; he also gives him the sobriquet by which he is still known to history. And here, one needs to ask why the narrative assigns this role to Rögnvald, rather than to some other character? Answering this seemingly simple question will lead us through four sets of interrelated narratives and different levels of meaning.

The first of these focuses directly on relations between the hirsute king and his barber. According to Heimskringla, Rögnvald was one of the first high-ranking aristocrats who rallied to Harald's cause, after Earl Hákon of Hlaðir and Earl Atli the Slender. And when the two latter worthies slew each other in a jurisdictional squabble, he emerged as the foremost of Harald's supporters among the nobility.[5] Thereafter, we are told that Earl Rögnvald "was King Harald's dearest friend, and the king valued him greatly."[6] The text dates the beginning of this friendship to the period just after the battle of Solskel, where Harald won control of the Mæri and Raumsdal districts on the west coast of Norway. Sizing up prospects in the wake of that victory, Rögnvald pledged himself to Harald's service and received these provinces as his earldom in return (synoptic table 3.2).

Along with this territory and the income it produced, Rögnvald administered the system of laws and taxes that Harald had put in place and led his troops against King Vemund, who had rallied the forces Harald defeated at Solskel. Catching Vemund by surprise, Rögnvald burned him in his own hall, along with ninety retainers. This exploit secured Harald's control of western Norway and won the valuable Fjorð districts for him.[7] Indeed, the earl's military and political talents were considered exceptional, for the epithet giver came to have epithets of his own, being popularly called Rögnvald the Powerful (*Rǫgnvaldr inn ríki*) and Rögnvald the Wise in Counsel (*inn ráðsvinni*). Heimskringla comments, "Men say both were true names."[8]

For more than twenty years after Rögnvald accepted King Harald as his liege, the two men provided an ideal model of collaboration between feudal lord and vassal. At no point is there a hint of friction between them: no surfacing of ambition and resentment on the part of the earl, no suspicion or ingratitude on that of the king. The scene of the haircut captures the perfect quality of their dealings. Rögnvald's position is clearly subordinate to Harald's, but one of high honor, for he is simultaneously the king's servant, name giver, and host. Moreover, the service he performs as royal barber shows the absolute nature of Harald's trust, for no other man is permitted to approach the royal body so close, much less bearing a sharp weapon.[9]

The idyllic nature of this vignette notwithstanding, the possibility of conflict between nobles and kings was ever present in the ninth, tenth, and eleventh centuries. As several generations of scholars have observed, the earls were the key figures in the administrative apparatus of medieval Norway, and they held considerable, quasi-autonomous power. Situated intermediate to king and people, they were able to play both ends of the system against each other, alternately representing themselves as instruments of royal rule or defenders of local tradition, as best served their purposes. Geographic considerations figured prominently in the calculus of power, for the more distant an earldom lay from the king's person, the more difficult it was for the king to control. Some earls challenged kings openly, but others were content to quietly slip from their grasp. Whether open or covert, such conflicts were hardly fortuitous, but the recurrent expression of unresolved structural tensions. Indeed, Halvdan Koht, Gudmund Sandvik, Sverre Bagge, and others have taken the rivalry of nobles and kings to be the implicit central theme of the entire Heimskringla.[10]

II

If the account of Harald and Rögnvald exhibits ideal cooperation between aristocracy and monarchy, the underlying contradiction between the two institutions manifests itself in a second set of stories that focus on Harald's sons, who, as they approached maturity, asserted the claims of the royal family against those of the nobility. In a strictly legal sense, these young men raised several questions of great importance: Does the king own all the land, or do the earls have some independent claim to it? Do the earls serve at the king's pleasure—as his bureaucracy, in effect—or is there some other agency that legitimates their power? What principles of inheritance apply to the royal family, and how do these affect contrary claims by the sons of earls? Finally, the youths raised the question of succession, which opens up instability within kingship itself: Does the realm pass to one royal son only, or can his brothers and half brothers also expect to inherit some portions of the realm? Given the number of Harald's progeny—most sources credit him with twenty sons, by eight different women[11]—these questions acquired some urgency as the princes came of age.

Matters were particularly vexed regarding the rights of Harald's four youngest sons, whose mother was Snæfrið, a Finnish sorceress. She and her father (who was himself famed as an evil magician)[12] tricked the king into accepting a proper marriage ceremony as the price of sharing her bed, after which he stayed in the north for many years, much to the detriment of his realm. So outraged was Harald when finally freed from the Finns' sexual and magic enchantments that he tried to disinherit the products of this union, although he ultimately relented.[13]

Two of these sons do not figure in our story, although one of them went on to found that branch of the lineage from which all Norwegian kings from 1045 to the present trace their line of descent.[14] The other sons have less

long-term importance, but two of them figure prominently in the story
of their encounter with Earl Rögnvald. That narrative is first presented in
Orkneyinga Saga, a text written about 1190–1200, which served as one of
Heimskringla's sources.[15] Both texts also drew on the same older sources
and oral traditions, especially a now-lost text known as *Turf-Einar's Saga.[16]
Orkneyinga Saga voices its criticisms quite openly:

> When the sons of Harald the Fairhair were fullgrown in age, they became ex-
> tremely overbearing and unruly at home. They attacked the king's earls, killed
> some, and drove some off their property. Snæfrið's sons, Hálfdan High-Leg
> and Guðrøð the Radiant, attacked Rögnvald, Earl of Mæri, killed him, and
> took over his realm. But when King Harald learned that, he was very angry
> and attacked his sons.[17]

Although the Heimskringla account parallels this passage closely (synoptic table 3.3), it differs in several ways. Two of these are points where Orkneyinga Saga followed their common source, while Heimskringla softened their
relatively harsh judgment of Harald's sons. Thus, in the first instance, it replaced the description of them as overbearing and unruly with a much more
diplomatic phrase: "They were all precocious in their accomplishments."[18] It
did not abandon the more critical language entirely, however, but reserved it
for use in a later chapter, as we will shortly see. Second, it omitted the statement that Harald was angry with his sons. On a third point, Heimskringla
expanded on the older materials, giving a much fuller account of the young
killers' motives. Thus, where Orkneyinga Saga said Harald's sons "attacked
the king's earls, killed some, and drove some off their property," it reserved
this phrase for later use and at that time explained the cause of their depreda-
tions: "It came about that they were ill pleased with the fact that the king gave
them no realms, but set an earl in each district, and it seemed to them that the
earls were lower born than they were."[19]

We have noted that Heimskringla reserved two phrases from older accounts of Rögnvald's death. To appreciate its skillful use of this material,
we must also note that it inserts a date into the story, saying that Rögnvald
was killed when Harald was forty years old, roughly twenty years after his
conclusive victory at Hafrsfjörð.[20] The saved phrases were then displaced to
a later chapter that begins as follows: "King Harald was then fifty years old.
Many of his sons were grown up, and some were dead. *They became extremely
overbearing within the land* and there were disagreements among themselves.
They drove the kings' earls off their property and even killed some."[21]

What had been a single incident in Orkneyinga Saga thus becomes a
decade-long pattern in the Heimskringla version. The problem is redefined

not just as a matter of two wild sons and one earl's death. Rather, it is a structural issue with perduring effects: a contradiction between monarchy and aristocracy finds expression in jealousy over status, rival claims to territory, and lethal violence of princes against earls. In an attempt to solve this problem, Harald calls a great assembly—unknown in all other variants—where he tries to placate his sons, while fudging issues in such a way that his tilt toward the ambitions of kingship do not constitute a transparent breach with the antithetical interests of nobles.

Toward this end, he is said to have modified the laws such that each son received a district-sized kingdom from his father: a district associated with his mother's natal kin that, as a result, was also construed as an earldom the boy inherited through his matriline.[22] In these utterly ambiguous domains, the sons received half the revenues and held the title of king. Moreover, as the centerpiece of their royal regalia, they occupied thrones precisely calibrated to index their station: one step higher than an earl's throne, one step lower than Harald's (i.e., that of the "real" king, who ruled the nation rather than a district). This solution, however, only succeeded in displacing the problem, for the sons who were kings in name and nobles in practice, seated halfway between aristocrats and monarch, now openly coveted Harald's throne, and each district championed that son it regarded as its own. "As a result of this," the text observes, "there was much new discord among the brothers," discord that built to fratricidal strife.[23]

All this lies ten years and more after poor Rögnvald's death, and it is worth returning to that earlier event, which could be read—particularly by those in the commonwealth of Iceland—as an object lesson in the dangers monarchy posed to an aristocratic order. Not even Rögnvald was safe, the story seems to say. An earl can be powerful, wise, loyal, and trusted; he can make himself the king's best friend and serve him ably for decades, and still be cut down by the king's sons: a victim not just of wild youths, but also of the dynastic principle and the monarchic state.

III

Although Heimskringla suppressed this detail, Orkneyinga Saga described Harald's reaction to Rögnvald's murder as one of anger, and all sources agree that he took quick steps to set matters aright. By declining to focus on personal and emotional considerations, however, Heimskringla left open the possibility that Harald's motives were overdetermined. In particular, one is free to imagine that in this moment of crisis, the king sought to reassure his other earls, whose continued service was necessary to management of the realm.

Whether driven by sentiment, policy, or both, Harald's moves were not difficult to predict. Anticipating his father's forceful response, Hálfdan High-Leg—one of the two killers—fled Norway for the islands, and in a moment we will see what became of him there. In contrast, his brother Guðrøð installed himself as lord over Rögnvald's earldom, only to be undone by Harald's intervention. Heimskringla provides the most detailed version, saying that Harald came down upon Guðrøð with a great army, forced his surrender, packed the wayward boy off to a distant province, and returned Rögnvald's lands to the latter's son Thorir, to whom he also gave Álof, his own eldest daughter (synoptic table 3.4).

In its thematization of Harald's efforts to make amends, Heimskringla dodges a point that Orkneyinga Saga underscored in two different ways. The latter work specifies, first, that Harald gave his daughter as wergild, that is, compensation for Thorir's father (*i fǫðurbœtr*); second, that Thorir received his land as paternal inheritance (*fǫðurleifð sina*).²⁴ In both instances, Orkney-inga Saga asserts that Thorir had these as a matter of law, and not—as Heims-kringla implies—an ad hoc gesture of royal largesse. In the older account, Harald gave *justice*, which entailed the prestation of daughter and earldom. Ensuring justice, of course, is the standard function that legitimates kingly rule according to medieval ideology. In the case at hand, however, to rec-ognize the demands of justice serves the interest of aristocracy rather than kingship, since it acknowledges that the claims of earls against kings have a firm basis in law.²⁵

Understanding Álof as wergild helps us comprehend how this story ad-vanced an aristocratic critique of Norwegian kingship, even in moments when it seems to cast the latter institution in a favorable light. At a deeper level still, the saga also advanced a critique of certain aristocrats, particularly those who remained in Norway and accommodated themselves to kingly rule. Rögnvald represents one example of such nobles, and his death offers an object lesson to others. Thorir is another such example: a man whose fate is less extreme than his father's, but undesirable all the same. Thus, by accept-ing his royal bride, Thorir—acting now as the senior male of his kin—agreed that his family had been amply compensated for Rögnvald's death. Accord-ingly, he was obliged to abandon any thought of vengeance and to regard the matter as settled. Others, however, seem to have questioned Thorir's mo-tives and judgment. A critical perspective permits one to see him as having been bribed and/or intimidated by the king: having struck a dirty bargain, then settled into a comfortable but craven and unfilial inaction. Whence the scornful epithet conventionally assigned to him: "Earl Thorir the Silent" (*þórir jarl þegjandi*).²⁶

IV

No one was more critical of Earl Thorir than his half brother Einar (or Turf-Einar, as he is often called, for having introduced the use of peat for fuel in the Orkney Islands). Just before avenging Rögnvald, Einar composed an oft-quoted poem, singing his own praise and mocking his brother:

> Neither from Hrólf's hand,
> Nor from Hrollaug's do I see a spear
> Fly against the host of our foes.
> It behooves us to avenge our father.
> But tonight, as we press our attack,
> That one sits silent
> Over the stream pouring from his flask—
> Thorir, Earl over Mæri.[27]

Here, in addition to Thorir, Einar names two other brothers, both of whom have their importance, as do all Rögnvald's sons. Turning to them leads us to a third body of narrative, and a third perspective on the questions that Harald's conquests, kingship, and state posed for Norwegian nobles. As various texts that draw their information from the *Turf-Einar's Saga report, Rögnvald had six sons, the first three by concubines and the last three by his wife (synoptic table 3.5). Of these, the first legitimate son was Ívar, who served loyally in Harald's army and was killed during the conquest of the Orkneys. In compensation (í sonarbœtr), Harald then gave these islands to Rögnvald.[28] Being himself occupied in Norway, the earl tried to keep this prize in the family, transfering it first to his brother, then to his eldest son, Hallað. Neither solution took, however, and Hallað returned to Norway in disgrace, where he renounced his status as a noble.[29]

Although there are some differences among the sources, in general they recount how Rögnvald called three of his four remaining sons together to decide who would become earl of the Orkneys (synoptic table 3.6). Hrólf, the oldest surviving legitimate son and the foremost warrior among them, was unavailable. Several years earlier, he had offended King Harald and been banished from Norway, after which he won Normandy for himself and founded the ducal lineage that produced William the Conqueror and all subsequent kings of England.[30] This left Thorir, Hrollaug, and Einar.

According to most versions of the story, Rögnvald assessed his sons' character and prospects in sequence. Thorir—his sole remaining legitimate son, but the youngest of them all—he counseled to stay at home in Mæri, where he would inherit his father's earldom. This came to pass, as we have seen, although not quite as Rögnvald expected. Hrollaug, in contrast, could never hope to become an earl. "Your fate leads to Iceland," Rögnvald explained, "There your lineage may be prolonged and you may become high ranking in that land."[31] Before following this advice, however, Hrollaug served King Harald for a spell. According to Landnámabók (compiled ca. 1280), this served to alienate him from his father, but such is not reported elsewhere.[32] This text also identifies Hrollaug as one of the original settlers (*landnámsmenn*) of Iceland and a leading man of the early commonwealth. This is confirmed in the Íslendingabók of Ari the Wise, the oldest and most authoritative work of Icelandic history (written ca. 1130). There, one finds a passage listing the foremost men in each quarter of Iceland, starting in the east and moving clockwise: Hrollaug's name stands in the very first position.[33]

As the story continues, Rögnvald finally came to Einar, his least favorite son. Knowing the depth of his father's antipathy, the boy made a bold offer, which Rögnvald curtly accepted. Heimskringla reports their conversation as follows:

> Einar said: "I have little respect from you, and I've had little love to share. I will go west to the islands, if you will give me some help. I will promise you this, which should be extremely welcome: I will never come back to Norway."
>
> Rögnvald said it pleased him well he would not return, "because I have little hope that your kinsmen will be honored in you, since your mother's lineage is all thrall-born."[34]

In the above passage, Heimskringla modified its sources slightly to make Rögnvald's speech even harsher and more mean spirited than in other versions, a change that heightens the irony of what is to follow. It also made other, more sweeping changes, and we will return to these shortly, but the upshot in all variants is that Einar sailed west and became earl of the Orkneys, which— as fate would have it—is where Hálfdan High-Leg fled after Rögnvald's murder. At first, Hálfdan met with success and drove Einar into exile in Scotland. Within a year, however, Einar returned, bringing a large army with him. In the battle that followed, he defeated young Hálfdan, then hunted him down, killed him, mutilated his body with the infamous "blood-eagle,"[35] composed a poem celebrating his victory (one stanza of which is quoted above), and reestablished his control over the earldom.[36]

When news of this made its way back to Norway, Hálfdan's brothers were outraged and bent on vengeance. King Harald restrained them, however, by making the cause his own. When the king arrived in the islands with his army, Einar fled to Scotland once more, from whence he sent emissaries to negotiate with the monarch. Ultimately, a peaceful resolution was reached, the details of which bear examination. Two different chapters of Heimskringla describe it. The first of the following passages comes from Harald Fairhair's Saga and follows closely the account of Orkneyinga Saga. The second comes from St. Olaf's Saga, within a summary of the Orkneys' history.

> The earl submitted everything to the king's judgment. King Harald decided against Earl Einar and all the Orkneymen and ordered them to pay sixty marks of gold. It seemed an excessive fine to the propertyholders. The earl announced to them that he would pay it on his own and then he would possess all the allodial lands in the islands. They agreed to this, mostly because the poor ones had little land and the rich ones thought they could redeem their allodial lands as soon as they wished. The earl paid all the fine to the king and afterwards the king went east in autumn. For a long time thereafter, the earls owned all the allodial lands in the Orkneys . . .[37]

> King Harald had the people of the Orkneys swear over to him all their allodial lands. After that, the king and earl settled their differences. The earl made himself the king's man and took the land in fief from the king. He was not obliged to pay any tax on it, because it was very wartorn. The earl paid sixty marks of gold to the king.[38]

Both sources agree that a large fine was paid, which they treat as one-time retribution, and not the basis for ongoing taxation or tribute. They also agree that Earl Einar paid this himself and that he was reconciled with King Harald, in spite of having killed his son. Finally, they agree that the allodial rights to land were reorganized, but they differ markedly in their description of how this was done and what it entailed. Thus, the first account has the earl wind up with title to all the land in the Orkneys; the second gives title to the king and makes the earl his vassal. The former text is obviously more favorable to Einar, who emerges as the hero who avenged Rögnvald against the king's family, in spite of the contempt that his father had for him, and who emerged from conflict with the king not only with his honor intact, but also with greater—and not less—control over his earldom.

This version is probably too good to be true, as it originates in *Turf-Einar's Saga, which was eager to claim that its hero had won an unusually high degree of independence for the Orkneys. This, however, was less due to Einar's personal accomplishments—or Harald's largesse—than it was a function of the islands' location at the outer edge of Norway's sphere of influence, where it would have been difficult for the king to collect taxes under any circumstances. Norwegian sources also acknowledged this state of affairs but sought to put the best face on it. Thus, after narrating Hrólf's conquest of Normandy, Historia Norwegiæ went on to describe what his half brother Einar accomplished.

> "Meanwhile, [Hrólf's] relatives in the Orkneys firmly established their rule. In truth, up to this day, these islands are under the dominion of their descendants. **Having been exempted from tributary laws,** they faithfully serve the kings of Norway.[39]

All this helps us appreciate Heimskringla's strategic handling of these materials. If the story of Rögnvald's life and death permitted the text to dramatize the dangers that kingship posed to earls and other nobles, the story of Rögnvald's sons let it entertain various responses to those dangers, one of which it construed as the most admirable and advantageous. As delineated in other existing traditions, these characters offered three basic responses to Harald's consolidation of power, each with two variations (fig. 3.1). The first of these responses was that of the warrior-noble: the knight who put his strength at the king's service, like Ívar, or the adventurer, like Hrólf, who used that strength to advance his own goals, regardless of the king's wishes.

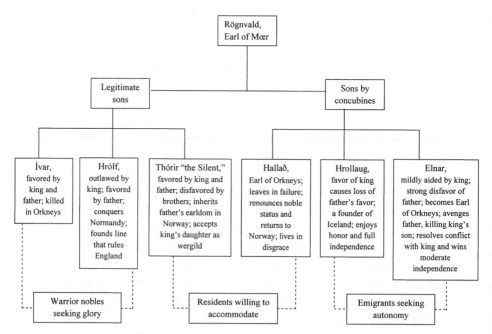

FIGURE 3.1: Rögnvald's sons and their life histories.

The narrative tends to discourage those who would pursue these options, however, for Ívar's story ended in an early death, while Hrólf's demanded such an extraordinary combination of gifts and luck as to be virtually irreproducible.

A second set of brothers tried the possibility of staying in Norway and accommodating to changed circumstances. Again, they offered a better and a worse form of this strategy, but neither of the two is portrayed as appealing. Thus, when Hallað settled down to life on Norwegian soil, he had seen his ambition overseas come to naught. Stripped of noble station, he was a broken man, fit for contempt or pity. Thorir, in contrast, was externally successful: prosperous, noble, and well connected. His success, however, was bought at high cost, and his epithet "the Silent" marked him a figure of shame.

This leads us to the two brothers who represented the optimal strategy: Hrollaug and Einar, both of whom emigrated from Norway and made admirable lives in the islands to the west. Of the two, Hrollaug's life was less problematic. Once in Iceland, he won land, the respect of others, and full independence, while Einar's dealings with the king were much more complex and his freedom somewhat more limited. Periodically, he came into conflict with Harald and his sons, as a result of which he sometimes had to fight, sometimes withdraw, sometimes negotiate, and sometimes compromise. In the end, he was forced to accept the king as his lord, but this acceptance was mostly nominal, since he and his fiefdom remained free of obligation to pay taxes. While Hrollaug may have represented the absolute best case, Einar still cut an impressive figure.

This analysis helps us recognize and understand a major—indeed, a shocking—modification Heimskringla made in its sources. For where Orkneyinga Saga and all other variants give serious attention to Hrollaug before moving on to Einar, Heimskringla radically abbreviates the story and omits Hrollaug entirely.[40]

This choice seems to reflect a view that the course of full Icelandic independence—as represented by Hrollaug and the *landnámsmenn* in general—was becoming less viable in the 1220s and 1230s, when the Norwegian throne sought to assert power over Iceland. Under the strained circumstances in which Iceland found itself as Heimskringla was being composed—a subject we will treat in the following chapter—this narrative seems to have subtly urged Icelanders to entertain the possibility of a path intermediate to futile resistance and docile capitulation: a situation like that of the Orkneys, involving nominal submission, while preserving maximal autonomy. The figure through whom the text imagined and advocated such a path was Turf-Einar, a man who knew how to defend his honor and fight against Norway (as when he avenged Rögnvald and killed Hálfdan High-Leg), but who also knew when to negotiate and how to make a favorable peace (as in his reconciliation with King Harald).

Clearly, Einar was the hero of the story as told in the saga that bore his name. It was he who avenged Rögnvald, and, what is more, the Orkneys looked to him as their founding father. The author of that saga had no difficulty acknowledging the excellence of Hrollaug, there being little danger that Orkneymen would abandon their national hero for a foreigner. For Heimskringla, however, the problem was the reverse. An Icelandic audience would surely identify with Hrollaug, while granting that Einar did well under difficult circumstances. The text seems to imply that increased pressure from Norway made the situation of Iceland in the 1230s resemble that of the Orkneys in the 890s more than its own circumstances in the period of its origins. As a result, a shift of mythic ancestors could seemingly be useful. Insofar as Hrollaug would engage the enthusiastic attention of an Icelandic audience, he would divert attention from Einar, whom the text wished to construe as the story's hero and a worthy model for Icelandic policy. The solution was to erase Hrollaug.

This brings us to a fourth narrative related to the others already discussed, which encodes a still more radical perspective, one even more inconvenient to the text's purposes and thus ignored altogether. Thus far, we have not bothered to explore Earl Rögnvald's genealogy, in part because Heimskringla tells us nothing of it, save the name of the earl's father (Eystein Glumra).[41] Orkneyinga Saga contains more information, however, all of it consistent with its own purposes. Not only does that text speak the interests of the islands rather than that of Norway, it also speaks those of the nobles rather than of the kings. The earliest title by which it is known, in fact, is The Earls' Sagas (*Jarla sǫgur*).[42]

By whatever name, this saga opens with a plainly mythic account quite different from that with which Heimskringla opens, although certain allusions make it clear that the latter text was familiar with this alternate tradition.[43] The narrative starts with a king of the ancient north, who bears the name Fornjótr ("Ancient Jute" or perhaps "Primordial Being").[44] His descendants include "Ocean" (Hlerr), "Flame" (Logi), "Frost" (Frosti), "Snow" (Snær), and Thorri (the name of the month from mid-January to mid-February). The last of these is said to have been a great sacrificer, who instituted the midwinter offerings that were named for him (Thorra-blót). A crisis occurs, however, when this man's daughter, Gói (the month from mid-February to mid-March), absconds, and his two sons go looking for her. The firstborn son, whose name was Nórr, searched by land, working his way from Lappland west to the sea and then south, conquering wherever he went. His brother, Górr, searched by sea, sailing through the Baltic, Oresund, Kattegat, Skagerrak, and out into the Atlantic.[45] Finally, the two brothers met at a fjörð on Norway's western shore. Their sister still missing, they decided to divide the territory across which they journeyed. Nórr became king over the mainland, which thereafter bore his name: Nór-vegr ("Nór's Way"), and the fjörð was also named for him (Nóra-fjörð).[46] In contrast, Górr claimed the islands, and received the title of "sea king," that is, a ruler whose power is based in his fleet and who has a somewhat antagonistic relation to the land. This manifests itself in his sons, of whom we are told: "They were sea kings and extremely overbearing men. They often encroached on the realm of Nórr's sons, and they had many battles. Now one side, then the other was victorious."[47]

The story thus provides us with two models for dealings between the Norwegian king and the rulers of the outlying islands. First, there is the fraternal cooperation between Nórr and Górr, manifested in their joint search for their missing sister and their peaceful meeting at Nórafjörð, which ended this quest in a peaceful division of territory and responsibilities. Second, there is the pattern of inconclusive violence between the two men's sons. Here, a subtle point is worth noting: Nórafjörð more or less divides the district of Sogn from that of Mæri. As such, it marks the limit of Rögnvald's earldom, within which he cut Harald's hair.

One is thus tempted to believe that the idyllic pair of Harald and Rögnvald, in the eyes of some, mirrored the equally ideal relations of Nórr and Górr, while the violence that erupted when their sons came of age similarly replicated the raiding and feuds of subsequent generations descended from the two brothers. This suspicion is confirmed by the genealogy with which Orkneyinga Saga segues from myth to history: a direct patriline that begins with Górr and culminates, six generations later, with the birth of Rögnvald, Earl of Mæri, "the Powerful and Wise-in-Counsel."[48]

By including this story, Orkneyinga Saga made a powerful point, construing the Orkney earls and other inhabitants of the islands as not being Norwegians in any sense and not owing obeisance to Norway. As descendants of Górr, rather than Nórr, the islanders were junior cousins of Norway, who could choose to cooperate but could also choose to defy and compete with those whom they defined as descendants of their ancestor's elder brother. Although the compilers of Heimskringla surely knew this story, given their familiarity with Orkneyinga Saga, they chose to ignore it, conceivably because it interfered with their goal of coming to terms with Norway.

4

Snorri Sturluson

I

The results of the two preceding chapters are clear, but also contradictory. In the story of Gyða, we saw how Heimskringla used this character to dramatize the danger the monarchic state posed to women, the institution of the family, and the property rights associated with it. Given this, and given the irresistible nature of Harald's power, Icelandic sources generally treat emigration to Iceland as the best course of action. Moreover, when read from the perspective of Iceland in the mid-thirteenth century—when the commonwealth was menaced by an increasingly powerful and ambitious Norwegian throne—the voyage of the *landnámsmenn* was easily construed as the prototypic model for their descendants' refusal to knuckle under.

In roughly comparable fashion, the story of Rögnvald and his sons explored the threat the monarchy posed to nobles, the institution of aristocracy, and its associated property rights, including those to territories outside the mainland. Once again the mid-thirteenth-century context is relevant, and this narrative addressed much the same pressing concerns as did that of Gyða. This time, however, Heimskringla not only declined to make the *landnámsmenn* represent an ideal solution; it erased them altogether. In their place, it offered Turf-Einar and a policy styled after the Orkneys: that is, negotiations designed to preserve a high degree of autonomy, while accepting Norwegian hegemony. A federal solution, rather than a nationalist defense of independence.

Inconsistency of this sort is striking and forces the question: Have we an incoherent text, given to indecision, evasion, or self-contradiction on issues of vital importance? If so, how did it come to be this way? Further: What is the text's relation to the situation and interests of its author?

There are four ways to address these questions, none of them mutually exclusive. First, we need to note the text's intertextual relations, its recycling of older materials, and the conventions of medieval historiography whereby fidelity and inclusiveness as regards tradition were valued more highly than originality or a strong authorial perspective.[1] Clearly, Heimskringla works to integrate materials drawn from earlier narrative strains that differ not just in diction and style, but also in their interests, perspectives, and values. Its goal is to absorb, encompass, and supersede them all, and in pursuit of this ambition it sometimes includes materials that sit awkwardly together.[2]

Second, we should understand that a text of this sort probably resulted from the collaborative efforts of scribes and researchers, directed by someone who also served as lead writer and final redactor.[3] Given its composite nature, the text inevitably includes some discontinuities and dissonances between sections drafted by different contributors.

Third, we ought to stress the historical and political context in which Heimskringla was compiled, the split nature of its audience, and the status of international relations. For it is a work about Norwegian kings written in Iceland at a moment when Hákon Hákonarson (r. 1217–63) was pressing to assume control over the Icelandic commonwealth. Such attempts prompted resistance and resentment, which found their prime literary expression in the sagas Icelanders wrote about their heroic ancestors who fled Norway rather than submit to the imposition of royal rule.[4] Kings' Sagas were a different genre, however, intended for a different audience. First written by Norwegians for Norwegians and above all for the royal court, they later came to be written by Icelanders, who were famed for their historical knowledge and literary skill.[5] In some instances, they were commissioned by the throne and reflected the interests of their royal patrons.[6] In Heimskringla, however, there is no overt sign of patronage. Rather, it seems to be a text intended for Norwegian and Icelandic readers alike, monarchs and freeholders, foes and advocates of annexation.[7] As a result, it gestures in different directions at alternate moments, seeking to satisfy incompatible interests in divergent fractions of its audience, while blurring such maneuvers through the use of ambiguity, understatement, reticence, and multilayered subtexts.

A fourth possibility is to consider the man who is usually regarded as Heimskringla's author (taking authorship in the sense noted above): Snorri Sturluson (1179–1241). This involves some measure of risk, however, for no manuscripts of Heimskringla name Snorri as its author. Other sources of the thirteenth and fourteenth centuries name Snorri as an authority on the Norwegian kings, and he was certainly one of the few Icelanders sufficiently learned, ambitious, and able to have produced a work on this scale. Given this—and possibly evidence drawn from now-lost manuscripts—pioneer scholars of the sixteenth century first identified Snorri as its author. This attribution has been widely accepted, but some continue to voice doubts.[8] Absolute certainty is impossible, and barring the discovery of new evidence, one can only say that Snorri remains the most likely candidate. If it is correct to connect him to Heimskringla, what we know of his shifting position in the 1220s and 1230s might help us understand the motives for some of the text's hesitations and ambivalences, while also heightening our appreciation for the exceptional skill with which it develops its critical subtexts.

Conceivably, "Snorri" may be no more than a Foucauldian author-function by which naive readers seek to stabilize and give coherence to an inherently unstable text. If that is so, the first three factors alone—the way the text relates to its predecessors and rivals, the collaborative nature of its production, and the divided audience for which it was intended in the mid-twelfth-century context—are sufficient to account for the text's occasional incoherence and its extraordinary intricacies. But given the likelihood that the traditional attribution is correct, it is worth considering Snorri's situation, which provides an instructive view of Norwegian-Icelandic relations at that historic moment.

II

Snorri was not only an author and intellectual, but also a well-positioned political leader, who had a sizable following and considerable wealth and at times held high office. Although his father was among the foremost chieftains of his era, Snorri was raised in fosterage by Jón Loptsson (1124–97). Thoroughly schooled in poetry, history, and other subjects by his foster father, upon the latter's death Snorri secured his own position in the common-wealth, first by contracting a highly advantageous marriage, then by pursuing lawsuits with uncommon success and making symbolic shows of force while avoiding actual combat.[9] At some point in his thirties he seems to have cast his horizons beyond Iceland, making use of his learning and poetic skills to ingratiate himself with leading men in Norway.

The initial object of his ambitions was Earl Hákon Galin (d. 1214), nephew of King Sverri (r. 1184–1202) and half brother of King Ingi (r. 1205–17). Snorri dispatched an adulatory poem, written in elegant skaldic verse, to this well-placed nobleman and won a rich set of gifts in return, along with an invitation to visit him in Norway. Unfortunately, the earl died before Snorri could take advantage of the offer, but he deferred his plans rather than abandoning them altogether.[10]

After serving a term as lawspeaker, the highest political office in the com-monwealth (1215–18), Snorri renewed his efforts. He now directed these to

Earl Skúli (d. 1240), uncle and regent to King Hákon Hákonarson (r. 1217–63), who acceded to the throne at the age of thirteen just as relations between Norway and Iceland turned more precarious. Thus, Íslendinga Saga recounts how, in the last year of King Ingi's reign (1216–17), Pál Sæmundarson, the son of an important Icelandic chief, voyaged to Bergen, where he was greeted with suspicion. The Bergeners believed he was after an earldom or even meant to raise rebellion and make himself king over Norway. In the face of this, Pál decided to leave Bergen for Trondheim, where he could meet with the king. He set sail with six ships, which sank under mysterious circumstances, and all aboard were lost. Sæmund Jonsson, Pál's father, was outraged and brought a large group of followers to the Assembly Place in Eyr, where he pressed charges against the Bergeners for plotting his son's death. Succeeding by some combination of legal argument and intimidation—the text tells us little—he forced them to pay such heavy compensation that even his brother Orm found it exorbitant.[11]

Even so, Sæmund remained unappeased, and he imposed heavy fines on the next Norwegian ship to arrive at Oddi, his farm in Iceland. Unhappy at this, the merchants conducted themselves in menacing ways, and people suspected they were plotting against Sæmund. Accordingly, he surrounded himself with armed men, but his brother Orm was less cautious, trusting to his status as a priest. To no avail: when he went to buy lumber from the Norwegians, they killed him, his son, and several others of his party, then harassed local shipping before sailing home. In the months that followed, the cycle of vengeance and countervengeance continued, for Orm's son-in-law dragged a Norwegian out of church and had him killed, believing him a kinsman of Orm's slayers.[12]

On both sides tension ran high: Norwegians still resented Sæmund's conduct at Eyr, while Icelanders were scandalized by Orm's murder at Oddi. In this troubled climate, Snorri perceived opportunities, and in 1218 he set sail for Norway. Íslendinga Saga says nothing explicit about his motives but claims he was ignorant of Orm's death, learning of it on arrival.[13] Such protestations suggest bad conscience and probably reflect an attempt to blunt criticism. As the account makes clear, Snorri was much less interested in championing Orm than in courting favor with the new king and Earl Skúli, the latter of whom then held foremost power. These attempts, moreover, were highly successful.

When Snorri came to Norway, King Hákon and Earl Skúli had become the rulers. The earl took remarkably well to Snorri, and he journeyed to the earl. But the men who went abroad with Snorri, Ingimund Jonsson and Árni, the son of Brand Gunnhvatsson, decided on a journey south [i.e., a pilgrimage to Rome]. Snorri spent the winter with the earl. And when the following summer came, he went east to Gautland to visit Askel the lawman and Lady Kristin, who was previously married to Hákon Galin. Snorri had composed the poem about her that is called "Sleeplessness" [*Andvaka*], at Earl Hákon's request. She welcomed Snorri becomingly and gave him many handsome gifts. She gave him the battle standard that Eirik Knutsson, king of Sweden, had had when he brought down King Sörkvi at Gestilsrein. The next autumn, Snorri traveled back to Earl Skúli, and he spent a second winter there in very high favor.[14]

Several points can be gleaned from this passage. First, it seems Snorri's companions disapproved of his purpose and conduct, for they quickly dissociated themselves from him, seeking the grace of the Roman pontiff rather than the favor of the Norwegian king. Second, Snorri's earlier approach to Hákon Galin helped pave the way for his success, having made him known and appreciated among upper circles of the Norwegian nobility, as witness the connection between Hákon's widow and Earl Skúli. Third, at the same time that he courted these nobles, they sought to assess and recruit him. This is suggested by the gift Snorri received from Askel: a royal battle standard around which those committed to a king's cause rallied at a time of triumph. That this particular standard belonged to a Swedish and not a Norwegian monarch gave the object a useful ambiguity. Snorri was not obliged to react in defensive fashion, and the nobles could gauge the way he accepted the staff as an index of his potential usefulness.

Other attempts at co-optation followed. While staying with Earl Skúli, Snorri was made a royal page (*skutilsveinn*), the office of those permitted to wait on the king at table.[15] In Norway, this was a title of honor accorded persons of rank who were trusted and privileged with close proximity to the king. From an Icelandic perspective, however, it had different associations, since it encoded subservience to royal power. Like the gift of the battle standard, proffering this title was part of a feeling-out process. When Snorri accepted, his hosts drew conclusions and pressed the game further.

After two years in Norway (1218–20), Snorri decided to set sail for home at a particularly telling moment. According to Íslendinga Saga 38, many Norwegians still bore a grudge over Sæmund's conduct at Eyr, and they urged a punitive expedition for that summer. Some advised restraint, however, and Snorri—whose departure was scheduled for spring—threw in with this party.[16]

Snorri strongly counseled against the expedition and gave the advice of making friends with the best men in Iceland. He said that as soon as he could bring them his word, men would see fit to turn themselves to compliance with the Norwegian rulers. He also said that there were then no greater men in Iceland than his brothers, who surpassed Sæmund, and he said they would follow his words when he came home. With such arguments, the earl's temper softened, and he counseled the Icelanders to ask King Hákon to intercede for them so there would not be a military expedition. The king was young then, and Dagfinn the lawspeaker, his counselor, was the greatest friend of the Icelanders. And so it was that the king decided there would be no expedition.[17]

A very curious story, in which Snorri can be read as both the savior of his country and its betrayer. The text situates him in a position of complex mediation, associated first with the pro-Iceland faction in Norway, and second with a pro-Norway faction in Iceland, which he offered to organize and lead, thereby pitting himself against Sæmund and the anti-Norwegian champions of independence. Further, it implies that he adopted this position in order to spare his country invasion and bloodshed, insinuating that he was the only man sufficiently knowledgeable and well connected to do so. Evaluation of his conduct ultimately depends on several issues that cannot be resolved, given the state of our evidence. First, was there really a threat of invasion, or were the Norwegians bluffing? Second, what was the actual balance of power: should the Norwegians have undertaken an invasion, would they have succeeded in the military conquest of Iceland? Third, was Snorri sincere or disingenuous in the commitments he made? Did he really intend to work on behalf of his hosts, or was he telling the story he thought they needed to hear in this critical moment?[18] Evidently the Norwegians themselves harbored doubts along this last line, since they sought to ensure their Icelandic friend would be good to his promise. The passage quoted above continues.

> King Hákon and Earl Skúli made Snorri one of the king's barons, and this was mostly the plan of the Earl and Snorri. And Snorri was supposed to convince the Icelanders that they should turn themselves to compliance with the Norwegian rulers. Snorri would send his son Jon, and he would be the earl's hostage to ensure things came out as had been said.[19]

Carrots and sticks. Obviously, giving Snorri the carrot was meant to ensure his loyalty. Going well beyond his earlier rank as royal page (*skutilsveinn*), the title of baron (*lendr maðr*) placed him in the upper ranks of the Norwegian nobility. This was an unprecedented honor for an Icelander, since this title was unavailable at home. From Snorri's standpoint, receiving such recognition distinguished him, gave him influence, and helped advance his ambitions. From the perspective of those more committed to Icelandic independence, however, his new station worked to his discredit, for accepting it made him—and made him legible as—the foreign king's vassal. We are told that becoming a baron was primarily his idea and that of Earl Skúli. Apparently, this was something the two men decided on together, but their purposes surely differed. For his part, Snorri sought to increase his wealth, power, and prestige, while the earl sought to obligate, dominate, and corrupt him. And should this bribe not ensure Snorri would honor his bargain, the crafty earl took his son as hostage (*í gíslingu*), in which moment the stick complements the carrot.

III

To put it mildly, Snorri's position upon return to Iceland was compromised and conflicted. Not surprisingly, he met a mixed reception. We are told he sailed in a ship given him by Earl Skúli and brought with him fifteen treasures the earl had bestowed, which, among their other effects, must have been meant to impress those who met him. The text says Snorri was received "with all honors" (*með hverjum sæmðum*) but also notes that some people were angry with him: most of all, Orm's kinsmen, who suspected him of collusion with the Norwegians.[20] Two praise poems he wrote in Earl Skúli's honor were particularly offensive to their sensibilities, and they produced biting parodies of them (table 4.1).

It is in the years following this decidedly ambivalent homecoming and welcome that Heimskringla took shape, a multilayered history of the Norwegian kings seemingly intended for distribution in Norway and Iceland alike. Although it is ostensibly a celebratory account of the kingship, its subtexts often contain sharp critiques that would have been more legible—and much more appreciated—in Iceland than in Norway.[21]

All the medieval texts that recount Norwegian history position the story of Harald Fairhair's oath and conquests as a virtual myth of creation: the moment and process whereby the nation, state, and monarchy came into existence. In Heimskringla, however, this key narrative is framed by two episodes: that of Gyða at its beginning and that of Rögnvald at its end. As we have seen, these episodes were drawn from different traditions and sources (Haraldskvæði and the lost *Harald Fairhair's Saga, on the one hand, Orkneyinga Saga and the lost *Turf-Einar's Saga on the other), and it may be that different assistants contributed to the research and writing of them, producing certain disjunctures between the two episodes. Even were this so, I would be persuaded that the dissonances are intentional, functional, and revealing. What they reveal is not incompetence or confusion, but an editorial decision

TABLE 4.1. Snorri's praise poem for Earl Skúli and its Icelandic parody

Snorri's Verse (Íslendinga Saga 38)	Southerners' Parody (Íslendinga Saga 38)
Hard-muzzled was Skúli Created far greatest in strong-gleaming [gold] Among earls of the outland. *Harðmúlaðr vas Skúli rambliks framast miklu gnaphjarls skapaðr jarla.*	It looks bad to us to kiss The earl who rules over the land. The lip is sharp toward lords. Hard-muzzled is Skúli! Never has one heaped More filth before wise princes, Coming from a sea raven.* The people find fault in these verses. *Oss lízk illr at kyssa jarl, sás ræðr fyr hjarli, vǫrr es til hvǫss á harra, harðmúlaðr es Skúli. Hefr fyr horska jǫfra hrægamms komit sævar, —þjóð finnr lǫst á ljóðum—, leir aldrigi meira.*

* For eagle shit as a kenning for bad poetry, see Snorri's myth of the theft of mead in Skaldskaparmal 58:

When the Æsir saw where Óðinn was flying, they set his vat out in the yard and as Óðinn came into Asgarð, he vomited the mead into the vat. But Suttung was so close to catching him that he sent some of the mead out his rear and no one took charge of this. Whoever wants it can have it and we call it the portion of the poetaster.

En er Æsir sá hvar Óðinn flaug þá settu *þeir út í garðinn ker sín, en er Óðinn kom inn of Ásgarð þá spýtti hann upp miðinum í kerin, en honum var þá svá nær komit at Suttungr mundi ná honum at hann sendi aptr suman mjǫðinn, ok var þess ekki gætt. Hafði at hverr er vildi, ok kǫllum vér þat skáldfífla *hlut.

to hedge one's bets in a tense situation or, more precisely, to satisfy the incompatible desires and demands of different audiences at different moments in the narrative. Norwegians and Icelanders, kings and commoners could see what they liked by focusing on Gyða and her father or, alternatively, on Rögnvald, Harald's sons, and Turf-Einar.

Further, Heimskringla reshaped the details of these subsidiary narratives such that they spoke to the aggrieved relations of Iceland and Norway in the moment it was written, but with absolutely contradictory results, for as we have seen, the Gyða story implicitly favored Icelandic resistance to Norwegian ambitions, while that of Rögnvald tilted toward accommodation.

Insofar as Snorri had important relations with groups on both sides of the water and hoped to preserve their favor, one can imagine that he permitted

Heimskringla to become a site where their competing interests met and left their imprint, without either one gaining absolute ascendance. Uncertain whether commonwealth or king would prevail, Heimskringla provided something for everyone, maintaining an indeterminate position that may well reflect that of Snorri himself. Ultimately, however, it is not one man who is of prime interest, but a set of narratives that move through multiple texts, the historical contexts and audiences relevant to each text, and the complex relations among them.

Commander Guthorm

I

Heimskringla normally does not advance the harshest criticism of King Harald and what he represents, but its interventions are often extremely subtle, as can be seen from the way several different texts handle the character of Guthorm. All are in general agreement in describing him as Harald's "kinsman" (*frœndi*).[1] More precisely, he is Harald's matrilineal uncle, that is, his mother's brother or—as anthropological theory posits—the "male mother," whose dealings with his sister's son are particularly supportive and affectionate.[2] Some sources also specify that Guthorm was only six years older than his nephew, making their relation particularly close.[3]

A passage included in one version of Fagrskinna makes Guthorm the son of Dag the Wise, a "powerful chief" (*ríkr hersir*) in Haðaland, that is, a local noble of the premonarchic era.[4] Dag also had a daughter, Helga the Well-Mannered, known to some as Helga of the Magnificent Hair, who was famed for her beauty and virtue.[5] Seeing her, Hálfdan fell in love and married the woman, and Harald was born directly thereafter.[6] Heimskringla, in contrast, tells a more elaborate story. Here, Guthorm's sister is named Ragnhild, and their father is Sigurð Hart, king of Hringariki, the biggest, strongest, and most handsome of all men, himself descended (in his matriline) from the foremost kings and heroes of Denmark.[7] This lineage provided royal status and incomparable prestige for those defined as Sigurð Hart's descendants, and it had other advantages which we will discuss in the next chapter, à propos of Ragnhild.

Heimskringla introduces a story unattested elsewhere, in which Sigurð Hart was killed by a berserker who abducted his children, with the intention of marrying the incomparable Ragnhild. That wedding was delayed,

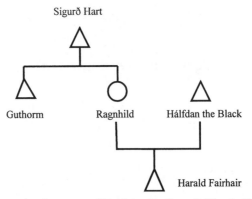

Sigurð Hart

Guthorm   Ragnhild   Hálfdan the Black

Harald Fairhair

FIGURE 5.1: Relation of Guthorm to Harald Fairhair, according to Hálfdan the Black's Saga 5.

however, as the berserker needed to heal from wounds suffered at Sigurð Hart's hands, and this delay permitted Hálfdan to rescure the captives.[8] Inclusion of this episode helped explain how Hálfdan, still a relatively minor district king, could win so illustrious a bride from a family whose status far exceeded his own. In addition, it explained why Guthorm was particularly devoted to Hálfdan, Ragnhild, and their son (fig. 5.1).

II

In addition to its basis in the kinship system and the rescue narrative, Guthorm's extreme loyalty served to characterize the ideal relation of military force to political authority, for when the young Harald took the throne, his uncle Guthorm became commander of his army. One can read this situation of the loyal martial uncle and the promising—but initially weak and needy—royal nephew as a trope for relations between the old war troop and the nascent state. Heimskringla is careful to lavish praise on Harald's innate excellence and great potential, while subtly suggesting that at this historic juncture, real power remained with his uncle:

> Harald took the kingship after his father. He was then ten years old. He was the greatest, strongest, and most handsome of all men, a wise man and a great leader. Guthorm, his mother's brother, became leader of the royal retinue and all the land's government. He was commander of the troops.[9]

Although the passage identifies Guthorm as "leader" (*forstjóri*) of the administrative apparatus and military commander in chief (*hertogi*), it leaves unclear how and from whom he acquired such status, saying only that he "became" leader and "was" commander. The reflexive verb used in the first instance (*gerðisk*) might even imply a certain autonomy, since it most literally means "he made himself" leader.[10] Perceiving the potential danger in such an implication, the "Tale of Harald Fairhair" voiced things differently, making clear that however powerful the martial uncle may have been, his status derived from—and remained dependent on—that of his royal nephew, insofar as "King Harald made his kinsman Guthorm commander of all his troops" (cf. synoptic table 5.1).[11]

"Commander" (Old Norse *hertogi*) is, in fact, the title Guthorm bears in all subsequent appearances.[12] Literally, it denotes the leader who draws up the battle host,[13] and in this military capacity he provides invaluable service in Harald's first struggles with other district kings. Heimskringla treats these early campaigns in the opening chapters of Harald Fairhair's Saga, where Harald and Guthorm work closely together and the text generally does not distinguish between their individual contributions. On three occasions, however, it breaks with this pattern, tilting first to Guthorm, then to Harald, then to Guthorm in the last instance.

Thus, after describing the way local rivals were plotting to take advantage of Harald's youth and weakness,[14] the text shows Guthorm assuming responsibility for military intelligence, planning, and initiative: "When Commander Guthorm learned that, he gathered the troops and he traveled with King Harald and they turned first against Haki up country and they met the enemy in some valley."[15] In the following sentence, however, Guthorm disappears, leaving Harald to take credit for the combat itself: "There was a battle there, and King Harald was victorious."[16]

With this first battle, Harald successfully defended his little kingdom against one invader. Immediately thereafter, Harald and Guthorm moved against the others who had been plotting against them. These campaigns took them to central Norway (fig. 5.2), where they caught their enemies literally sleeping and overcame them all. The prose describing these events generally employs third-person-plural verb forms that avoid distinguishing between the contributions of the two men,[17] but the final summation is different. After initially stressing the king's augmented territory and stature, it credits this to his commander's martial virtues.

> After the death of these four chiefs, King Harald possessed Hringariki and Heiðmark, Guðbrand's Dale and Haðaland, Thotn and Raumariki, Vingulmark, all the northern lands, **by the power and prowess of Guthorm, his kinsman.**[18]

Although this passage passes no negative judgment on Harald's accomplishments, it signals a relation of dependence and identifies a problem

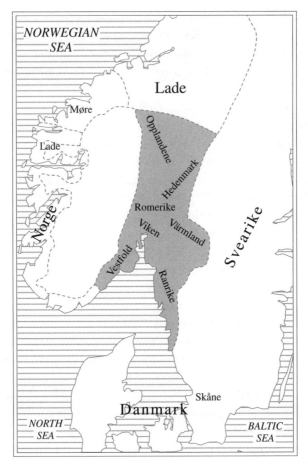

FIGURE 5.2: Harald's initial conquests, ca. 858–68, expanding outward from his inherited territories of Vesfold, Viken, Romerike, and Hedenmark. Map courtesy of Dick Gilbreath, Gyula Pauer Center for Cartography and GIS, University of Kentucky.

inherent in the relation of political and military power, whose potential is greatest when the state is weak and the military is not only strong, but also ambitious and insubordinate. The narrative acknowledges these dangers but obviates them, reassuring the reader that (*a*) King Harald's weakness is temporary only, being an aspect of his youth, and (*b*) Commander Guthorm is absolutely loyal.

Somewhat harsher is the critique offered by Egil's Saga, an openly antimonarchic text and a great champion of Icelandic independence.[19] There, Harald is depicted as having been even more dependent on Uncle Guthorm than Heimskringla ackowledges, and having remained so for much longer.

There was a man named Guthorm, the son of Sigurð Hart. He was the mother's brother of King Harald. He was the king's foster father and manager of
his land, because the king was a child when he first acceded to the kingship.
Guthorm was commander over King Harald's troops when he conquered the
land, and he was in all the battles the king fought when he went about the
land in Norway.[20]

At three different points, this passage goes beyond what Heimskringla—
or any other surviving source—dares to say. First, it characterizes Harald as
having been a child when he took the throne, using a term that emphasizes
the extremity of his youth.[21] Second, it states that Guthorm was Harald's foster father (*fóstrfaðir*), which gives him more authority over the young man
than does an uncle-nephew relation, while it also acknowledges his lower social status.[22] Third, it specifies that Guthorm participated in every one of the
king's campaigns. In contrast, Heimskringla lets his importance fade rather
quickly as Harald matures and takes control of his military.

III

That transition is handled a bit awkwardly, however, and here we need to
revisit the episode we considered in chapter 2. Thus, Harald and Guthorm's
early victories increased not only the young king's holdings but also his confidence, and it is immediately after these campaigns that Harald set his designs on Gyða.[23] As we saw, her rebuff aroused grander ambitions in the king,
prompting him to swear his great oath. What we did not discuss, however,
was the response that Harald's oath elicited, which the text associates with
the character of Guthorm.

> Then [King Harald] said: "This vow I swear and therefore I appeal to God, he
> who created me and rules over all. Never shall my hair be cut or combed until
> I have taken possession of all Norway, with its tributes and taxes and adminis-
> tration, or otherwise to die." For this speech, Commander Guthorm thanked
> him greatly and made it his royal task to fulfill the king's word.[24]

Here, Guthorm ratifies the king's ambitions and presents himself as the
means of their realization. Utterly loyal and fully subordinate, he is also the
man of action who will make these things happen, and will make them happen by force.[25]

What happens next is extremely strange. Having sworn his vow, Harald
launches a northern offensive, which Heimskringla describes as follows:

> After that, the kinsmen gathered a great army and prepared their journey to
> Upland, north through the Dales, and thence north through Dofrafell. When

he came down into the settlements, he had all the men killed and the dwellings burned. And when the people became aware of this, everyone fled who
could: some down to Orkadal, some to Gaulardal, some to the marches, and
some sought pardon from him. And all who came to a meeting with the king
obtained that, and they became his men.[26]

Although the first sentence declines to name Guthorm, his participa-
tion in the expedition is signaled not only in the phrase "the kinsmen" (*þeir
frændr*, in the plural nominative), but also by the actions described—gather-
ing troops and provisioning for a march—which are the sorts of things he
previously has done. In the second sentence, the verbs abruptly shift from the
plural to the singular and the man responsible for these acts—attacking, killing, burning—is Harald and Harald alone.[27] Without explanation, Guthorm
has vanished from the scene, Harald has assumed command, political and
military authority have been united, and the nature of warfare has changed.
It is not necessarily more brutal or vicious, but it has become more ambitious
and more aggressive, martial force having become the means by which one
reduces one's enemies to a position of lasting subordination. Previously, the
role of the military had been to defend one's territory and to launch raids or
preemptive attacks that might yield some gain within the local balance of
power. With Harald's oath, the army—now under his personal command—
has become the prime instrument for constructing the conquest-state: a project of relentless expansion, extraction, and domination.

Chapters 5–19 of Harald Fairhair's Saga describe a decade of constant wars
of aggressive conquest, culminating in the battle of Hafrsfjörð (872), where
the king's forces crushed all opposition. Never once in all these campaigns
does Commander Guthorm appear in combat, nor does he collaborate much
with his nephew. Rather, he is consigned to defensive duties, protecting territories in the rear judged vulnerable to attack. His model of the military
still has its uses, but these are only a part of the new order, within which
Guthorm's role has been eclipsed.[28]

IV

One gets the impression that Guthorm has been put out to pasture, and later
chapters of Harald Fairhair's Saga offer a picture of what he was doing in
semiretirement. Just before the battle of Hafrsfjörð, King Harald began to
have children by his many wives, and the first was a boy named Guthorm,
borne to him by Ása, his first wife (see above, chap. 2).[29] From the start, the
commander took a keen interest in his namesake.

King Harald's children were brought up where their maternal relatives lived. Commander Guthorm sprinkled King Harald's eldest son with water and gave him his own name. He adopted this boy and fostered him, and kept him with him in eastern Vík. He was raised there, with Commander Guthorm. Commander Guthorm had all direction of the land around Vík and Upland when the king was not near.[30]

Much information is transmitted in this brief passage, and four points should be noted. First, King Harald used his sons to reinforce the alliances he contracted with local nobles via his numerous marriages. By sending the boys back to be raised by their mothers' fathers and brothers, he continued the exchange relation with those who had been wife givers to him. As his sons grew up, they were expected to become his agents, assuming administrative control over these provinces and enjoying the status of princes and earls (see above, chap. 3). Second, young Guthorm constitutes an important exception to that strategy and pattern, for he is given to his great-uncle Guthorm (i.e., his father's mother's brother) to raise in Vík, rather than being sent to his mother's family in Hlaðir. Ása's father, as we saw in chapter 2, was the first earl to rally to Harald's cause and helped him win control of Trondheim, but instead of rewarding this support, Harald used his firstborn to reward the even earlier and even more valuable support he received from Guthorm. Third, the text describes Guthorm as having "sprinkled water" (*hafði vatni ausit*) on the boy and having given him his name, these being practices the Old Norse sagas (all written after conversion) construed as the pagan equivalents of Christian baptism.[31] By showing the commander as having performed such rites and his grandnephew as having received them, the text construes them as "noble heathens" and Christians *avant la lettre*.

We are not told much about Commander Guthorm's later years, save that he stayed in Vík, which he protected against attack for at least ten years after Harald fulfilled his vow and become sole king of Norway.[32] Some time thereafter, he died a natural death (*sóttdauðr*), at which point the district passed to his namesake, not as an inheritance, but as an act of royal generosity: "Commander Guthorm died a natural death in Tunsberg. King Harald then gave control of all this realm to his son Guthorm and set him over the chiefs there."[33]

Heimskringla makes this seem an act of benevolence, through which a grateful king carried out his uncle's fondest wish and saw to it that the old man's realm passed directly to his beloved namesake. Gratitude, kindness, consideration, tact, and generosity can all be read into the gesture, and the simplicity of the diction invites unwitting readers to do so. Those who know more—that is, further details and other versions of the story—might well hesitate.

We have already discussed one reason for such hesitation when we noted that Harald is said to have terminated rights of inheritance to lineage-controlled property (óðal) and transferred ownership of all land to the crown. Nothing suggests that Commander Guthorm held any hereditary rights to the Vík, or that he could transmit control to his heirs. Rather, he was charged with steering and defending the district on behalf of the king, from whom he received these charges. With Guthorm's death, it is not the sentimental issues of family continuity, rootedness in place, a sense of home and belonging that are at issue, but the more practical question of how administrative control is to be reproduced. Such control is not transferred to the commander's descendant and heir, moreover; rather, it reverts to Harald, who then bestows it on his own son, who was named for and fostered by dependable Uncle Guthorm.

Had Guthorm any sons of his own, the question of succession might arise in more pointed fashion, manifesting itself in open or latent rivalry between his biological offspring and his foster son. Heimskringla maintains a discreet silence on this, but Egil's Saga gives a fuller account.

> Guthorm had two sons and two daughters. His sons were named Sigurð and Ragnar; his daughters, Ragnhild and Aslaug. Guthorm took sick, and as his time approached, he sent men to meet King Harald, and he asked him to look after his children and his realm. A little later, he died.
>
> When the king learned of his death, he had Hallvarð Hard-Traveler and his brothers called to him. He told them they should go on an errand for him to the east in Vik. The king was then staying in Trondheim. The brothers prepared for their journey in most magnificent fashion. They chose troops and had that ship which was the best they had captured. This was the ship that Thorolf Kveld-Ulfsson had owned, which they had taken from Thorgisl Gjalland.
>
> When they were ready for their voyage, the king told them their errand. They should go east to Tunsberg, where there was a market town. Guthorm had had his residence there. "You will bring me Guthorm's sons," the king said, "and have his daughters raised there until I give them in marriage. I will get men to take care of the realm and to support the girls in fosterage."
>
> When the brothers were ready, they went on their errand, and they got a fair wind. In spring, they came to Vik and went east to Tunsberg, where they carried out their mission. They took Guthorm's sons and much money. When they were ready, they went back on their way. The trip began slowly for them, and there was no news of their voyage until they sailed north by the Sogn Sea, with good wind and fair weather, and they were then very cheerful.[34]

Although this passage draws no explicit moral judgment, it is much less open to an innocent and generous reading than is Heimskringla's account. In the latter case, it would take a very deep and well-informed reading to perceive the text's guarded critique of the way Harald responded to Guthorm's death. Here, only the most superficial reader could imagine the king's sole concern was to carry out the last wishes of his dear deceased uncle by taking good care of his realm and his children.

Numerous clues suggest a raw power grab by a ruthless monarch, including the troops that accompany Hallvarð and his brothers; the warship on which they travel (previously stolen from the saga's heroes);[35] the secretive way the king informs them of their mission; their seizure of Guthorm's money, along with his children; and, most sinister of all perhaps, the fact that the saga never mentions those children again, leaving one to imagine their fate once they have effectively become the king's captives. The crew's good cheer on the return voyage also feels vaguely ominous, and what we are told of Hallvarð and his brothers when they are first introduced only adds to one's disquiet, for they are, in fact, the henchmen and thugs King Harald reserved for his nastiest business.

> There were two brothers named Sigtrygg Swift-Traveler and Hallvarð Hard-Traveler. They were with King Harald and were men of the Vík. Their matrilineage was in Vestfold, and they had a relation of kinship with King Harald. . . . Sigtrygg and Hallvarð tended to all the king's errands, both inside and outside his land, and they had gone on many voyages that were perilous, both to slay [or: abduct][36] men and to seize the goods of those whom the king made them attack. They had a large company about them. They were not friendly with most people, but the king valued them greatly, and they were the best of all men for travels on foot and on skis. So too, they were quicker than other men when traveling by ship. They were big, valiant men and most foresighted.[37]

V

On stylistic and other grounds, most experts now take Egil's Saga and Heimskringla to have been written by the same author, normally understood to be Snorri.[38] If this is so, the same knowledge of Harald's ruthlessness and greed lies behind both accounts of events following Guthorm's death. What the one text spells out in some detail, the other treats with considerable discretion. This is not to say that Heimskringla represents the king as innocent, even noble. Rather, it suggests his questionable conduct ever so slightly, trusting that some of its readers will know enough to fill in the rest of the story.

Ultimately, the question of authorship is less important than that of audience. Egil's Saga is willing to offer a much more open critique because it is a saga of heroes who fled Norway for Iceland as a result of King Harald's offenses against their families, and who continued to battle him and his descendants even after their emigration. As such, it courted an Icelandic readership prepared to think the worst of the king. Heimskringla, in contrast, is the foremost work of the Kings' Saga genre, written by an Icelander to be sure, but written for Norwegians, as well as Icelanders, and for Norwegians including the king and his court.

Both texts use the Guthorm episode to consider the place of the military in the new monarchic national state, and both raise the same fundamental questions: What is the hierarchical relation of king and commander? How firmly is the latter subordinated to the former? How indispensable is the service provided by the commander, and does this change over time? Finally, what is the return on the most loyal service? Egil's Saga provides a radical response, asserting that Guthorm's services were indispensable and this continued for the duration of the conquest period. Apparently, that won him a certain measure of consideration for the balance of his life. Beyond that, however, the king knew no gratitude and showed no mercy. Once Guthorm was gone, his family, fortune, and land were ripe for the picking.

Heimskringla's version is much more reserved. Having treated Guthorm's contributions as initially invaluable, it makes this a temporary state of affairs, constituting Harald's oath as the turning point when he assumed control of the military, shifted it into conquest mode, and became independent of his uncle, whose dated methods were relegated to home-guard service. Still, the king was grateful to the old commander, to whom he entrusted some prime territories and his own firstborn son. In closing Guthorm's story, the text delicately hints that King Harald may have taken advantage of the old man's heirs, but only a portion of its audience would have known enough to recognize the hint and understand its import. The critique is advanced with sufficient discretion to remain invisible to those who might find it offensive, that is, the current Norwegian king, his admirers and supporters.

6

Ragnhild

I

The Norwegian tradition, as represented by Fagrskinna, seems to have been divided regarding the identity of Harald's mother. As we saw in the last chapter, one variant of this text named Helga the Well-Mannered, daughter of Dag the Wise, as the wife of Hálfdan the Black and Harald Fairhair's mother.[1] The other variant of Fagrskinna calls her Ragnhild, as do most other sources, and it connects her to an exceptionally noble lineage: "Her father was Sigurð Snake-in-the-Eye, the son of Ragnar Shaggy-Breeches."[2] These vividly named men were semilegendary Danish kings of the ninth century, members of the fabled Scylding dynasty that figures prominently in Beowulf. A variety of sources, including the Skjöldunga Saga (written between 1180 and 1200), Saxo Grammaticus's History of the Danes (between 1208 and 1218), and the Saga of Ragnar Loðbrók (fourteenth century) preserve the same sequence of Danish kings and add other pieces of information.[3]

Some of these follow from explications of the monarchs' singular epithets. Thus, we learn that Ragnar was known as "Shaggy-Breeches" (Old Norse Loðbrók, Latin Lothbrog) from the hairy trousers he used as rudimentary armor when fighting a dragon.[4] In similar fashion, Sigurð obtained the name "Snake-in-the-Eye" (Old Norse ormr-í-auga, Latin serpentini oculi) when snakes appeared on his face at birth. This portent identified him as a descendant of the most famous dragon slayer of all, confirming his mother's claim that she was the daughter of Sigurð Fafnir's-Bane and, as such, the sole survivor of the great Völsung line.[5]

Fagrskinna is not alone in suturing Harald to the Scyldings via his mother, a move that appropriated some of that dynasty's prestige for the monarchy he founded, while also helping construct Norwegian national identity as the union of a Swedish patriline (the Ynglings, who originally ruled in Uppsala)

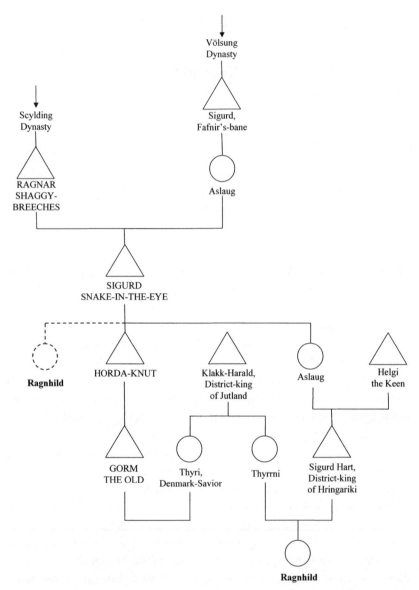

FIGURE 6.1: Two versions of Ragnhild's genealogy. The version in the dotted lines comes from Fagrskinna 1; the version in the solid lines comes from Hálfdan the Black's Saga 5 and Skjöldunga saga, as preserved in "Abridgment of the Saga of the Danish Kings" ("Ágrip af Sögu Danakonunga"), 325.

and a Danish matriline (the Scyldings). Four other sources, all written in Iceland, did something similar, but in ways that differed from the testimony of the Norwegian-authored Fagrskinna (synoptic table 6.1). The texts in question are the Skjöldunga Saga (most probably the source for the others),[6] Flóamanna Saga 1, Hálfdan the Black's Saga, and the "Tale of Hálfdan the Black" (Flateyjarbók 1.562). All three make Ragnhild a daughter of Sigurð Hart, not Sigurð Snake-in-the-Eye, which gave her—and her offspring—a very different status (fig. 6.1).

According to the Icelandic sources, Ragnhild's sole connection to the Scylding line was through her father's mother, a weaker kinship tie, since patrilineal descent determined social identity. Instead of standing in the royal Danish family, this placed her in the line of petty district kings who ruled Hringariki, a province northwest of Hálfdan's base in Vestfold. Hálfdan's union with her was thus less glorious, but more comprehensible within the decidedly local context of his political ambitions.

II

Fagrskinna thus elevated Ragnhild by connecting her to dragon-slaying heroes and Danish kings. In contrast, Heimskringla used her to prophesy Harald's coming greatness, investing his person and his accomplishments with a supernatural aura. Going beyond the other Icelandic sources, it supplied the following information.

> Ragnhild's mother was Thyrni, the daughter of Klakk-Harald, king of Jutland, and sister of Thyri Denmark's-Savior. The latter was married to Gorm the Old, who then ruled the Danish empire.[7]

Although this passage identifies Thyrni as Ragnhild's mother, she is quite unknown elsewhere. Apparently, she serves as the device of a confected genealogy that connects Ragnhild with Queen Thyri of Denmark and her father, Klakk-Harald, both of whom were well-known historical figures (fig. 6.2). Stories about Klakk-Harald and Thyri appear in Saxo's History of the Danes, the Greater Saga of Olaf Tryggvason, and the Jomsviking Saga, an early version of which was a source for Heimskringla. In the surviving but later version, the following information is given.

> Harald was the name of the earl who ruled over Holstein. He was called Klakk-Harald. He was a wise man. The earl had a daughter who was named Thyri. She was prophetically gifted in her intellect, the most beautiful of women to see, and she interpreted dreams better than did other people.[8]

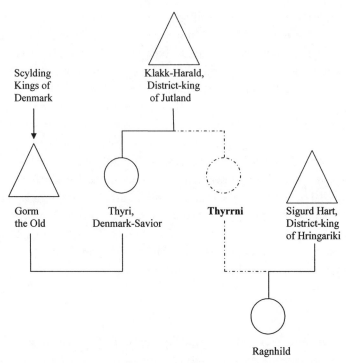

FIGURE 6.2: Genealogical information provided by Hálfdan the Black's Saga 5. Thyrrni occurs in no other source, and the relations in which she figures (marked in dotted lines) are Snorri's invention.

In contrast to Heimskringla, this text and others in the Jomsviking tradition identified Klakk-Harald as the earl of Holstein.[9] Heimskringla elevated him to district king of Jutland, thereby making his daughter Thyrni a more noble and a more geographically appropriate match for Hálfdan.[10] Saxo went further still, replacing Klakk-Harald with King Ethelred of England. He further claimed that Ethelred fostered the sons his daughter Thyri bore to Gorm and bequeathed his kingdom to them.[11] Ignoring this blatant attempt to legitimate Danish claims on the English throne, all other sources focused on the extraordinary wisdom of Klakk-Harald, whom the Greater Saga of Olaf Tryggvason pronounced the wisest of all men in Denmark.[12] Even wiser still was his daughter, however, of whom Klakk-Harald himself said, "She is much wiser than I."[13] (See synoptic table 6.2.)

The wisdom in question was mystic and revelatory. Historia Norwegiæ thus referred to Thyri as *prudentissima*,[14] using the term in its most literal sense to identify her as one who is gifted in foresight, Latin *prudens* being a contraction of the participle *pro-videns*, "fore-seeing."[15] Jomsviking Saga confirms this, describing her as "prophetically gifted in her wisdom,"[16] using a term (Old Norse *spakr*) built on the religiously significant verb *spá*, "to prophesy," which denotes a mystic power of vision that can penetrate dark secrets and peer far into the future (cf. the debased and secularized semantics of its English cognate "to spy").[17] The "Tale of the Jomsvikings" gives the most precise identification of her powers, calling her the most outstanding of dream interpreters, royal dreams being a particularly privileged form of prophesy and revelation.[18]

Both Saxo and the Jomsviking texts recount that before Thyri accepted Gorm's offer of marriage, she demanded he produce dreams for her to interpret, and to this he willingly acceded.[19] Saxo's version of the story is somewhat garbled, but the Jomsviking texts have Gorm dream on three successive nights that oxen came out of the sea, first white ones, then red, and then black.[20] On each occasion these animals stripped the land of its grass, then returned to the sea. Thyri—here cast as Joseph to Gorm's Pharaoh[21]—interpreted these dreams as omens of nine years to come, in which snowy winters (corresponding to the white oxen), then winters without snow (red), then the most severe winters of all (black) would interfere with the harvests. Such difficulties could be dealt with, however, by importing and storing grain. With this knowledge, she married Gorm and secured the country against disaster, thereby winning popular affection and the epithet "Denmark's Savior" (*Danmarkarbót*).[22] The title, but not necessarily the story, is historically attested in the inscription to the Little Jelling Stone.[23]

It is this quality of Thyri—her expertise in dream revelations and their interpretation—that Heimskringla transfered to "Thyrni," her (invented) sister, suggesting that such powers were common among women of this royal family. The point of all this, obviously enough, is the implication that Thyrni transmitted her mystic powers and learning to her daughter Ragnhild, who was fated to become the mother of Harald Fairhair.

III

Revelatory dreams figure prominently in the accounts of Harald's nativity. Three sources—Fagrskinna, Heimskringla, and the "Tale of Hálfdan the Black"—tell that King Hálfdan was a man who never dreamed. Seeking advice about this from Thorleif the Prophetically-Gifted (*þorleifr spaki*), he was advised to sleep in a pigsty as a means of dream incubation.[24] While some have understood this as a technique that permits one to commune with the deity Yngvi-Freyr (founder of the Yngling line, whose emblematic animal was the pig),[25] it is also possible to imagine some satiric intent. In any event, the method worked and Hálfdan obtained his dream (synoptic table 6.3):

It seemed to him that he was the best haired of all men, and his hair was all in locks, some long to the ground, some to the middle of his leg, some to his knee, some to his waist, some to the middle of his side, some to his throat, and some only sprouted out of his head like horns. His locks were of all different colors, but one lock vanquished all in fairness, radiance, and size.[26]

Incapable of interpreting his dream, the king recounted it to Thorleif, who took the many locks to signify the abundance of Hálfdan's descendants who would rule with distinction. Not all would be equal, however, for the big, beautiful, outstanding lock signaled the one king who would be greatest of all.[27] In the immediate context, one might infer that this was the newborn royal heir, but the text intervenes to set things straight. "People take it to be true," it reports, "that this lock betokens King Olaf the Saint."[28] Seemingly, a prediction originally associated with Harald—as witness the central trope of long, fair hair—was reinterpreted by subsequent generations, who preferred to privilege St. Olaf (r. 1015–28), the king who converted Norway to Christianity. At issue in this postconversion reinterpretation of prophecy is something akin to a Nietzschean revaluation of values, with religion displacing warfare as the sphere where human excellence is best realized.

While the two other sources that tell this story (Fagrskinna and the "Tale of Hálfdan the Black") go on to sing St. Olaf's praises, Heimskringla remains silent.[29] It also reorganizes the narrative and makes some important additions. Thus, where the other variants place Hálfdan's dream immediately after Harald's birth, Heimskringla follows this sequence:

1   Marriage of Hálfdan and Ragnhild.
2   Additional genealogical information (unattested elsewhere), connecting Ragnhild to Thyri Denmark's-Savior.
3   Additional information about Ragnhild's abilities (unattested elsewhere): "Queen Ragnhild dreamed great dreams. She was prophetically gifted in her intellect."[30]
4   Ragnhild gives birth to Harald.

Having thus established that the women of Ragnhild's family were particularly gifted at prophesy, dreams, and mystic learning (in contrast to Hálfdan, who never dreamed and had to be coached by Thorleif), Heimskringla takes the step for which it has laid such careful groundwork. Before introducing Hálfdan's dream, it gives Ragnhild a portentous dream of her own.

Queen Ragnhild dreamed great dreams. She was prophetically gifted in her wisdom. One of her dreams was that she seemed to be standing in her garden and taking a thorn out of her shirt. And as she held it, it grew so much that it became a large twig, so that one end of it went down to the earth and quickly took root. Then the other end of the tree quickly went high up in the air. Then the tree seemed so large to her that she could hardly see over it, and it was wonderfully thick. The lowest part of the tree was red as blood, but up the stem it was bright green, and up in the branches it was snow white. There were a great many large branches of the tree, some high and some low. The branches of the tree were so great that it seemed to her they spread over all Norway and even further.[31]

While Hálfdan's dream is immediately interpreted, Ragnhild's goes without commentary for a very long while. Only after narrating the entirety of Harald's career from birth to death does Heimskringla return to the dream that presaged these events. By way of closure, we are then told what "wise men" (*fróðir menn*) understood, that is, that the tree was red at the bottom in token of the battles the king waged as a young man, green in the middle for the flowering of his reign, and white at the top for the hoary old age he achieved. Finally, the tree's limbs and branches "proclaim his descendants, who spread over all the land and ever since the kings of Norway have been of his lineage."[32]

Ragnhild's dream generally mirrors that of her husband, which it is meant to complement and confirm. One vision is the product of a master of prophetic dreams, the other of a relative novice. One needs expert interpretation, the other initially speaks for itself. One employs the imagery of hair, the other that of vegetation, homologous substances in Old Norse cosmology, where hair is the microcosmic counterpart of plants.[33] There is, in fact, only one main point on which the two dreams diverge, for Ragnhild's tree contains no supremely privileged branch to parallel the outstanding lock in Hálfdan's head of hair. Similarly, when her dream is interpreted, there is no mention of St. Olaf (synoptic table 6.4).

What is one to make of this? It may simply be that the text, having identified two preeminent members of the royal line, effects a division of dynastic labor, assigning concern for the religious hero of the distant future to Hálfdan, while making Ragnhild responsible for the state-founding hero whose birth is imminent. We should note, however, that such a distribution inevitably makes reference to the gendered identity of the two dreamers and does so in ways that points subtly toward the dynamics of the royal family and potential stresses therein. For however close the relation of husband and wife might be, and however well the efforts of mother and father may complement and support each other, we come to understand that their interests still diverge somewhat, and this divergence has its significance. Thus, the father's attention is focused on the *longue durée* of the dynasty he is founding and on a descendant whose appearance lies a full century and a half in the future. Of his own son, Hálfdan's dream says nothing at all: a silence that may signal certain problems, reservations, or evasions. For if the king is to imagine his child's ascent and glory, implicit in this is acknowledgment of his own demise and eclipse. In contrast, Ragnhild's dream focuses on the child she carries in her womb, anticipating the incomparable feats he will soon accomplish. While she shows a generalized interest in the dynasty as a whole, no other individuals are singled out, for the queen's expectations are entirely centered on Harald.[34]

Following its presentation of these two subtly differing perspectives, Heimskringla narrates the birth of the child who has been ignored in his father's dream and lionized in his mother's. The language is spare, but all the more effective for its brevity.

> Queen Ragnhild gave birth to a son. He was sprinkled with water and named Harald. He was soon large and most handsome. He grew up there and quickly made himself a very accomplished man, having been born wise. His mother loved him greatly, but his father less.[35]

IV

The hint of difficulties between father and son is a theme that deserves fuller attention, and we will pursue it in the next chapter. Before doing so, however, we need to consider one last variant of the story in which a revelatory dream anticipates Harald's birth. This is found in Barð's Saga, a fabulous tale written in Iceland sometime between the end of the thirteenth and the middle of the fourteenth century. The story begins with a certain King Dumb, born of giants who aspired to rule the far north. Seeking to protect his ten-year-old son from the conflicts his ambitions unleashed, he took Barð to the cave of a giant named Dofri, located in the Dovrefjell mountains, which form the natural barrier between northwest and southeast Norway. At Dumb's request, Dofri agreed to serve as Barð's foster father, and in that capacity he taught him "all kinds of art, including genealogy and feats of arms . . . spells and heathen lore, so that he was both very wise and possessed of prophetic powers."[36] Having absorbed this learning, Barð had a dream.

> One night, Barð lay in his bed and he dreamed that a great tree rose up in the hearth of his foster father, Dofri. It had a great many branches all through its limbs and it grew so fast that it curled up the rock cave and then out through the rock. It was so big that this bud seemed to him to take over all Norway

and on one branch there was the fairest flower, although all were blooming greatly. One branch was the color of gold.[37]

Clearly, this passage synthesizes the dreams Heimskringla attributes to Ragnhild and Hálfdan, for its central image is a multibranched tree (as in Ragnhild's dream) that possesses one outstanding branch (like the favored lock of hair in Hálfdan's). Particularly noteworthy, however, is the way it departs from both of the others. Thus, they have the future dynasty originate with the dreamer, Hálfdan deriving the royal lineage from his own body (i.e., his head and hair), while Ragnhild traces it from the thorn she found in her shirt.[38] In contrast, Barð's dream disrupts any idea of biological continuity, for the tree-cum-dynasty grows out of Dofri's hearth and Dofri is neither a king nor a father and ancestor of kings. Rather, his hearth is the affective center of his cave, the place where guests are received, fed, and entertained. Seemingly, it is Dofri's hospitality—and above all, the very specialized hospitality he shows to those he fosters—that replaces the king's seed and queen's fertile womb as *fons et origo* for the wondrously blessed royal line whose appearance is prophesied.

Given that he was at that moment being fostered by Dofri, Barð might well be expected to imagine that this mystic vision revealed his own future, fate, and descendance. Such, however, was not the case. Having been well tutored by the giant in the magical arts, Barð was able to understand the import of his dream, which brought him no satisfaction.

> Barð interpreted this dream to mean that some royal-born man might come to Dofri's cave and would be raised there, and this same man would become sole king over Norway. And the fair branch would signify that king who descended from the ancestor who grew up there, and that king would proclaim a new religion. To him, this dream was not very pleasant.[39] People take it to be true that the bright flower designated King Olaf Haraldsson.[40]

Here, Barð's dream is closer to Hálfdan's than to Ragnhild's, as it dwells on St. Olaf, while ignoring Harald. Convinced that he will gain nothing from the events presaged in his dream, Barð leaves Dofri's cave, taking the giant's daughter with him. Shortly thereafter, Harald arrives and is welcomed by Dofri, who then "raised him to be king over Norway, as is told in the Saga of King Harald, Dofri's Foster Son."[41]

Apparently a text with this title once circulated, although no manuscript of it survives. The "Tale of Hálfdan the Black" and the "Tale of Harald Fairhair" both speak of the young Harald with the epithet "Dofri's Foster Son," and there the giant figures in a complex story of how Harald came to the throne.[42]

That narrative will concern us in the next chapter. For now, we need only note what realization of these mystic visions looked like from Barð's perspective. Thus, shortly after Barð left Dofri's care, he learned that his father had been killed by his enemies, against whom Barð then waged a campaign of vengeance. Before this could be completed, however—and before Barð could regain his father's throne—Harald had conquered Norway and was forcing everyone to pay him tribute. Bitter and unwilling to submit, Barð made his way to Iceland.[43] For him, the dream foretold not the divinely ordained coming of proper kingship, but the advent of tyranny.

As in the differing stories of Guthorm, the variant accounts of premonitory dreams fall into three clear categories. Norwegian sources (here, Fagrskinna) tell the story in such a way as to be fully supportive of Hálfdan, Harald, the royal line, the institution of kingship, and that of the state. At the other extreme, the Icelandic sagas (here, Barð's Saga) offer fairly sharp criticism, equating the process of state formation with violence, injustice, the imposition of oppressive taxes, and a new regime the protagonist defines as intolerable. The hero of the story as told by these sources is not the state-founding king, but the people who fled and created a freer, more egalitarian society on Icelandic soil, consistent with the traditional order that preceded Harald's labors of state creation. Finally, Heimskringla—a text written by Icelanders about, and at least in part for, the Norwegian king—once again occupies a middle position, telling a version of the story that mostly celebrates kingship and the state Harald inaugurated, while introducing a few choice details that disrupt the happy picture and hint at potentially serious problems. These hints are subtle, however, and easily overlooked. To find other incidents that shed light on the strained relations of Hálfdan and Harald, one must look to the lost *Saga of King Harald, Dofri's Foster Son and the curious figure of Dofri.

7

Dofri the Giant

I

As we saw in the last chapter, Barð's Saga cites a now-lost *Saga of King Harald, Dofri's Foster Son as one of its sources.[1] From the surviving work, one can infer that the earlier text described the cave-dwelling giant as a foster father of princes and something of an initiatory master, who instructed his charges in martial and mystic arts. Other late sagas show Dofri in a similar role,[2] and several recent studies have noted that giants, who are closely associated with the land, the powers of nature, autochthony, magic and learning, as well as brute force, make vital contributions to future kings, these gifts being theorized as an essential component of kingship. Dofri is regularly identified as a prime example of this pattern.[3]

This scholarly trend provides a useful corrective to stereotypes of Old Norse giants as doltish brutes fit only for conquest and plunder. Like all revisionisms, however, it runs the risk of reproducing an older paradigm in inverted image, rather than developing a higher synthesis and more nuanced reading.[4] Thus, for instance, one needs to distinguish among the giant race on the basis of gender. While giantesses do show affection, erotic attraction, and real generosity to gods and heroes in many stories, male giants are seldom so straightforwardly benevolent, for their attitude is always informed by a long string of conflicts, deeply resented wrongs, and demands for revenge, all of which date to the events of creation.[5]

Thus, according to Eddic poems and prose, the first living creature was a giant named Ymir who was subsequently murdered by Óðinn and his brothers: gods who were his younger kinsmen.[6] After butchering his corpse, these deities used Ymir's bodily matter to create the world, of which they made themselves master, transforming his flesh into earth, bones into stones, and blood into the sea.[7] His blood flowed so copiously, moreover, that all giants drowned, save one family.[8] To survive, they moved to the world's periphery and made their home by the edge of the sea.[9] There, they repopulated the giant race, and the sight of the waters—which were, in effect, their ancestor's blood—presumably served to remind them of the need for vengeance against Óðinn and his kin.[10] The latter included not only gods, but also those kings—Ynglings, Scyldings, Völsungs, and others—who claim descent from All-Father Óðinn.[11]

In short, giants nursed a grudge and had ancient scores to settle. When they tried to do so via open combat, they consistently met with defeat, prompting further resentment and need for revenge, which will ultimately be accomplished in the cataclysm of Ragnarök.[12] On occasion, however, the giants were shrewd enough to win a round by strategy and guile, as in the episode of Útgarða-Loki.[13] The Dofri narrative should be interpreted in similar fashion.

II

The fullest surviving version of the Dofri story is found in the "Tale of Hálfdan the Black," as preserved in Flateyjarbók. It begins when money mysteriously disappears from the treasury of King Hálfdan, who sets a trap to catch the thief. Once captured, the culprit—"an enormous giant, a fiend both fat and tall"[14]—was taken to the king for questioning.

> King Hálfdan asked his name. He declared himself to be called Dofri and he had his home in the mountain that is named for him [i.e., the Dovrefjell]. The king asked if he had stolen his gold. He answered that was true. Then he asked for mercy and offered to pay threefold for the gold. But the king said he would never have mercy. Bound there, he would await the Assembly, where he would be condemned to the most disgraceful death. And the king told Dofri he would grant him no means of subsistence, and should anyone provide help for him or give him food, he would make that person cede his life and would execute all others.[15]

Pitying the giant, the king's five-year-old son Harald cut his fetters, as depicted in one of the finest illustrations in the Flateyjarbók manuscript (fig. 7.1). Once free, Dofri thanked the boy for saving his life and quickly made his escape.[16]

Learning what happened, Hálfdan raged at his son, renounced him, and sent him out to help capture the giant.[17] After five days in the wilderness, exhausted and hungry, Harald came across Dofri, who offered to take him

FIGURE 7.1: Young Harald freeing the giant Dofri from his bonds. Illumination from the Flateyjarbók, manuscript 1.565 (late fourteenth century). Photograph © The Árni Magnússon Institute, Reykjavík.
Photograph by Jóhanna Ólafsdóttir.

to safety. Harald agreed and as they passed the threshhold to the giant's cave,
the boy hailed him as his foster father (*fostri minn*).[18] Five years then passed,
during which Dofri instructed the boy in various forms of knowledge (magic
is hinted, but not specified), as Harald grew rapidly in size and strength.[19]

Here, it is important to note how sharply this fosterage differs from the
norm of such relations. Ordinarily, fosterage is a triangular relation, established at the behest of the biological father, which helps cement whatever
bonds (kinship, friendship, alliance, e.g.) exist between the men who now
share responsibility for the son of the man who made the request. Here,
however, there is no such request and no triadic system of cooperation. Not
only is this fosterage established without involving the biological father; it
takes place in flight from, fear of, and opposition to him. Both foster father
and foster son have escaped from Hálfdan's imposition of justice, and this

shared experience unites them, although there are important differences in their situations.

Thus, Dofri was hostile to Hálfdan from the start and initiated their conflict by stealing from him. However extreme Hálfdan's actions may be, they respond to acts of illegality and aggression. In contrast, although prior relations between Hálfdan and Harald may have been less than ideal,[20] there was no history of conflict, nor does conflict begin with an indefensible transgression of one against the other. Rather, it is the Dofri episode that makes the son react to his father and the king to his son in ways that are increasingly antagonistic, producing a rupture that permits the giant to act more aggressively still by taking Harald as his own.

Here, one should note three different aspects to the disjuncture between Hálfdan and Harald. First, there is the level most obvious to readers nurtured on Freud, but which the text barely mentions: the Oedipal family drama. Second, the father and son have very different ideas about morality, justice, and compassion. Two models of kingship—the harsh and the merciful ruler—are here in conflict, as is often the case in Kings' Sagas.[21] Thus, when the son's sympathetic (perhaps also gullible) nature interferes with his father's implacable demand that thieves be punished, the father construes his boy as one who has thwarted justice and the boy construes him as a tyrant. The drama takes the form of what Gregory Bateson termed "schismogenesis," that is, a process in which two initially dissimilar parties expand and exaggerate their points of divergence in reaction to one another until they become irreconcilable.[22]

Third, and most important, there is the structural tension endemic to all royal dynasties. Thus, although the dynastic principle is meant to help consolidate and stabilize state power by making kingship pass seamlessly from fathers to sons, it regularly has the effect of exacerbating tensions between the monarch and his heir apparent. The younger man experiences his father as a check on his ascent and an obstacle to his ambition, while the older man comes to recognize his son's impatience and resentment as a potentially lethal threat.

All of this is at issue when the story reaches its culmination.

> It is told that one day Dofri came to speak with Harald and said this: "Now I think I have repaid you for having saved my life, because I have now brought to you the kingdom, as your father is dead and I was not far from there. Now you shall go home and take up your realm. I proclaim this to you that you will not let anyone cut your hair or your nails, until you become sole king over all Norway. I shall be in your service and in battles with you. I will be of assistance to you because I will be able to inflict wounds because I will not

be visible. Go now, be hale and well, and go all the way to glory and times of honor, and may you have no less good fortune than if you had been next to me."

Harald felt much for Dofri when they parted. And when Harald came home, he was made king over all the districts his father had previously ruled. He told his men where he had been these past five years, and he was then called Harald Dofri's Foster Son.[23]

This passage is stunning in its implications. In the first place, Dofri claims to have repaid Harald by delivering the kingship to him. The verb used (*launa*) is quite precise, suggesting not just payment or even repayment, but reward, that is, an extraordinary counterprestation through which an extraordinary accomplishment or service is compensated.[24] But what can this mean? Clearly, it is not just *news* of Hálfdan's death that the giant conveys, for in that case simple information, however welcome, could hardly balance what Dofri earlier received from Harald: his life and freedom. The subtext is as sure as it is disquieting: Dofri did not just learn of the old king's demise, but caused it. Although he dares not openly claim the deed, he hints so, telling Harald "your father is dead *and I was not far from there*,"[25] while also announcing his ability to inflict lethal blows while remaining invisible.[26]

Having made Harald king, the old giant keeps the boy under his wing. In this variant of the story, it is he—and not Gyða or Guthorm—who instills the ambition to conquer all rivals and unite the nation, suggesting the terms of the vow to be sworn, and providing the assistance, both military and magical, that insures the new ruler's triumphs.[27]

III

Writing in 1900, Sophus Bugge was the first to recognize that the Dofri story reworked themes and motifs from older mythology, as attested in the prologue and epilogue to Grímnismál, a poem of the elder Edda.[28] The story told there begins with a quarrel between Óðinn and Frigg. Tired of her husband's boasts concerning his foster son Geirroð, Frigg ridicules this king, of whom she says: "He is so stingy of food that he tortures his guests if it seems to him that too many come."[29] Óðinn dismisses this as baseless slander, and the two wager on the question, which Óðinn will test by paying Geirroð a visit in disguise. Not wishing to lose, Frigg sends word to the king, warning him against the sneak attack of an evil magician, who can be recognized by the way dogs fear him.

The text says that Frigg's charges were groundless, but the message she sent did its work. When Óðinn arrives at court disguised as a traveler, the dogs shy away from him, whereupon Geirroð has the stranger seized, tortured, and interrogated, thereby validating Frigg's accusations.[30] Hung between two fires for eight days without food or drink, Óðinn finally receives a horn of beer from the king's young son Agnar, who proclaims "the king did ill when he had an innocent man tortured."[31] At this, the god reveals himself, informs Geirrøð he has lost the divine favor that made him king, and predicts his time will be short.[32]

The denouement is handled carefully. Hoping to save himself, Geirrøð unsheathes his sword and hurries to cut Óðinn down from his place of torment, but the king stumbles, falls on the sword, and dies. By way of closure, the text simply states, "Then Óðinn disappeared. And Agnar was king there for a long time thereafter."[33] Nowhere is it directly stated that Óðinn caused Geirrøð's death and Agnar's ascension, but not even the densest reader can miss the implication.

The similarity between Grímnismál and the Dofri episode is too close to be coincidental, both for the general shape of the narratives and many of their details (see synoptic table 7.1). Bugge argued that the later text represented a Christian recoding of the pagan myth, with the giant Dofri assuming the role of the now-rejected deity. Others have generally accepted this line of interpretation, and the two stories are surely related, but their points of divergence are as instructive as their similarities.[34] One can begin by observing that to replace a god with a giant is not a neutral substitution that leaves all else unchanged; rather, it has strong effects on other aspects of the story, especially its moral dimensions.

Consider, for instance, the initial incident that sets the plot in motion. On the one hand, Geirrøð's treatment of the disguised Óðinn violates all considerations of decency, above all the cardinal virtues of hospitality and generosity.[35] Young Agnar is thus right to denounce his father, and Geirrøð's death is fully deserved. The story gives confidence in the justice of a cosmos where gods test the morality of kings and depose those who prove wicked. That Frigg has deceived Geirrøð only serves to underscore this point. While the gods themselves may not be perfectly moral, the narrative suggests there can be no excuse for Geirrøð's failure to entertain a guest hospitably. Regardless of the suspicions Frigg has provoked and regardless of whether they be justified, he still must give his visitor food and drink or he proves himself unworthy of royal office.

In contrast, Hálfdan's treatment of Dofri is much more open to debate, for Dofri comes not as a divine guest seeking a civilized reception, but as a thief who preys on the king and his court.[36] Hálfdan's response may be harsh, but it does not violate the demands of hospitality or justice. He captures the thief, holds him, announces his intention to have the culprit tried for his crime, and refuses requests for mercy. That he denies food to his prisoner and threatens anyone who might feed him is, however, surely vindictive and excessive.

Harald's intervention thus has some basis, but it is more ambiguous than Agnar's. Conceivably, his moral judgment is better than his father's, but it is also possible that he is a naive child whose pity blinds him to the stern requirements of justice. The text also suggests that Dofri manipulates and exploits Harald's tenderheartedness, for it says that when Harald first beheld Dofri bound in fetters, the giant "*made himself* look bad and all full of grief."[37] Apparently the gambit worked, as Harald immediately set Dofri free, unsuspecting that the liberated giant would compound his theft with kidnapping, murder, and usurpation. Hardly so reassuring as Grímnismál, this variant opens the possibility of an unjust, opportunistic world, where the prize of kingship can be won by the most ruthless and cunning of actors, and where a nice boy like Harald is not God's chosen, but a pawn in the machinations of a conniving giant.

At its highest level of abstraction, the Grímnismál narrative strives to reconcile dynastic and charismatic models of kingship by asserting that every king should be son and heir of his predecessor, but that he must also be chosen by Óðinn. Once on the throne, moreover, a king must meet certain expectations if he is to retain his divine patron's favor. Among these are demands for generosity and hospitality, which virtues are occasionally tested by visits of the god in disguise. Should the king fail such tests, Óðinn will shift his support to a more deserving successor. Ideologically, this set of ideas serves to check the ruthless exercise of royal power and provides assurance that if kings are to be successful, blessed, and long lived, they will also have to be moral.

The Dofri story is a good deal less comforting, for there is no god at its center to guarantee the moral order. Rather, there are three flawed and dubious actors: a vengeful, cunning, and thievish giant; a hot-headed king capable of excess and cruelty, even against his own son; and a tender-hearted youth with very little experience of the world, whose judgment is open to question. The narrative, moreover, undermines both the charismatic and dynastic principles. In the first instance, there is no charisma in the strict sense, for the favor Harald enjoys is not divine, but quite literally monstrous. In the second, dynastic succession has been subverted by the machinations of a foster father who disrupts the royal line by stealing the son and killing the father (fig. 7.2). Where the argument of the Grímnismál gave one confidence in the sacred and moral foundations of kingship, the *Saga of King Harald, Dofri's Foster Son seems designed for the opposite effect.

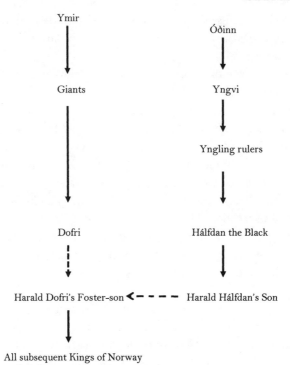

FIGURE 7.2: Effect of Dofri's aggressive fostering of Harald on dynastic succession. Harald's epithet and identity are changed, such that the royal line descends from the giants, rather than from the gods.

IV

There is one more text that makes use of the Dofri material, although it declines to use Dofri's name. This is Heimskringla, which modifies the tradition in other ways, many of which soften the story's critical edge (synoptic table 7.2).[38] The account runs as follows:

> King Hálfdan was on a Yule visit in Haðaland. Something wondrous happened on Yule eve. When men had come to table and there were a great many people, all of the food and all the ale disappeared from the table. The king remained in his seat, bitterly afflicted, and everyone else went home. In order that he might know what happened and what had caused this event, the king had his men seize a Finn who was wise about many things. He wished to compel him to tell the truth and he tortured him, but got nothing from him. The Finn cried out mightily for help, turning to Harald, his son. Harald begged mercy for him but got nothing. Harald let him escape, against the king's will, and he accompanied the man himself. Traveling, they came to a place where a chief held a great feast, and they were apparently well received there. They

remained there until spring. Then, one day the chief said to Harald: "Your father suffered a wondrously great loss when I took some food from him this winter, but I must repay you for that with joyful news. Your father is now dead and you shall go home now. You shall take all the kingdom he had and in addition you shall possess all Norway."[39]

Among many modifications introduced by Heimskringla, the actions assigned to Dofri in the "Tale of Hálfdan the Black" are here distributed to two different characters: an unnamed "Finnish" magician (presumably a Saami) and an equally anonymous chieftain, presumably also a Finn, but not explicitly named as such.[40] While Old Norse literature typically treats Finns as treacherous characters, they are nowhere so ominous as giants.[41] Thus, the Finn of this story, in contrast to Dofri, is not caught stealing, nor does he confess to any misdeeds. Rather, Hálfdan seizes him without evidence and has him tortured, but to no avail. Protesting his innocence, the Finn appeals to young Harald, who begs his father to show mercy. Only when this is refused does Harald take direct action, liberating the Finn and fleeing with him to the chief's court (seemingly a palace, and not a cave).

Ultimately, the chief takes responsibility for the theft, which has a role in Hálfdan's undoing, but nothing implicates the chief or the Finn in murder, regicide, or usurpation, once again in contrast to Dofri. Rather, the details of the story connect more closely to the ideology of Grímnismál. Thus, the theft that sets the Heimskringla plot in motion is not a theft of gold from the royal treasury, but a theft of food and drink from the table King Hálfdan prepared for the Yule celebration.[42] The loss of these supplies turns him into a miserly host, forcing cancellation of the banquet, and all of the guests are sent home. This is not just a spoiled party, as a secular view might have it. Rather, it is a failure of hospitality and a ritual affront to gods and humans alike. Like Geirroð, he has shown himself unworthy of kingship, and accordingly his days are numbered. Meanwhile, the chief hosts a proper Yule banquet, presumably with the stolen victuals. He receives Harald as his guest, and the young man passes a few months (December until spring), in contrast to the five years he spent with Dofri. There is, moreover, no talk of fosterage or esoteric and martial instruction, nor is there any promise of subsequent support or coaching in how to conquer Norway. To be sure, the chief is a somewhat unsavory character, but much less so than Dofri, and Harald's relation to him is less close, also less enduring.

Here, as in the Guthorm and Ragnhild episodes, Heimskringla appears to seek a middle path by advancing a guarded critique of Harald's accession, of certain problems in dynastic and charismatic models of kingship, and of kingship itself. In all of this, it goes further than the Norwegian sources, which contain no characters or incidents even vaguely reminiscent of Dofri. It is, however, considerably less aggressive than the Icelandic "Tale of Hálfdan the Black" and *Saga of King Harald, Dofri's Foster Son. Clearly, it knows some version of the Dofri story but reshapes it in fairly drastic fashion to tamp down harsher aspects of its message that depend on its representation of Dofri as a shrewd and unscrupulous giant who avenges himself on Hálfdan by causing his death, stealing his son, and making Harald the instrument through which giants gain hold of—or at a bare minimum, gain influence over—the royal office, line, and power (see table 7.1). Presumably, Heimskringla is hedging its bets, leaving some hints of critique for those who have ears to hear them, but not advancing these so forcefully as to be audible by all.

TABLE 7.1. Variants of the story of King Hálfdan and the thief

Variant 1: From the *Saga of King Harald Dofri's Foster Son	Variant 2: From Heimskringla
Dofri₁	*The Finn*
Steals money,	Accused of stealing food,
is captured,	is tortured,
confesses his crime,	insists on his innocence,
manipulates young Harald's sympathy,	gains Harald's sympathy,
escapes, causes breach between Harald and his father,	escapes,
takes Harald to his cave.	takes Harald to the chief's palace.
Dofri₂	*The Chief*
Adopts Harald in fosterage,	Receives Harald hospitably,
keeps him for five years,	keeps him for a few months,
teaches him martial and mystic arts,	
kills Hálfdan,	informs him of his father's death,
makes Harald king,	
teaches him oath,	
urges him to conquer all Norway,	prophesies his conquest of all Norway.
promises occult support that will render him invincible.	
Hálfdan	*Hálfdan*
Angry at theft of money,	Despondent at spoiled feast,
sets trap for the giant,	accuses the Finn,
threatens him with trial and execution,	

TABLE 7.1. (*continued*)

Variant 1: From the *Saga of King Harald Dofri's Foster Son*	Variant 2: From Heimskringla
Hálfdan	*Hálfdan*
denies him food,	tortures him,
quarrels with Harald,	refuses Harald's request for mercy,
renounces his son,	
deprives him of food,	
is murdered by Dofri.	dies.
Harald	*Harald*
Hears what happened,	Finn asks him for help,
feels sorry,	unsuccessfully asks father to show mercy,
approaches Dofri, who makes himself look miserable,	
sets the giant free,	sets the Finn free,
tells Hálfdan what he has done,	
is renounced by father,	
is denied food, but his life is spared,	
runs off,	runs off with the Finn,
meets Dofri,	
is taken to giant's cave,	is taken to the chief's Yule feast,
accepts Dofri as foster father,	
learns martial and mystic arts,	
stays five years,	stays a few months,
grows to young manhood,	
learns of his father's death (murder),	learns of his father's death,
accepts kingship from Dofri,	
takes instruction from Dofri regarding oath to be sworn and wars to be waged,	hears prophecy of his conquests from the chief.
anticipates mystic aid from Dofri,	
upon accession to throne is hailed as "Dofri's foster son."	

Note: To the extent that variant 1 constitutes Harald as dependent on Dofri and the instrument through which Dofri achieves his ambitions, it represents a much harsher critique of kingship than does variant 2.

8

Hálfdan the Black

I

None of the Norwegian sources mention Dofri, the chief, or the Finnish magician. All agree, however, that Hálfdan the Black died after a banquet held in Haðaland, the same place where Heimskringla locates the Yule feast where all his food was stolen (synoptic table 8.1).[1] The most succinct account is that of Ágrip:

> This is the manner of Hálfdan's death day. He feasted at Haðaland, and when he traveled from there in a sledge, he drowned in [Lake] Rönd in Rykinvík, where there was a well for watering cattle.[2]

The presence of the sledge sets the scene in winter or sufficiently early in spring that a Norwegian could still expect safe travel across deeply frozen lakes. Historia Norwegiæ gives more details of the accident:

> While he was making his way by night over the ice of a certain lake named Rönd, coming back from a feast with carts and a large body of horsemen, Hálfdan was unexpectedly carried into a certain fissure, where herdsmen were accustomed to water their herds, and he died under the ice.[3]

Neither of the Fagrskinna variants add much to this picture, although the longer and later version from the A-Text adds a touching vignette in which loyal—if drunken—members of Hálfdan's retinue rush to save their king, with the result that their added weight makes the ice break faster, engulfing them in the disaster.[4] "These tidings seemed bad," that text concludes, "to all men who heard of them."[5]

All variants treat this as a freakish and horrible turn of events, but they disagree on when, how, and why it happened. The time of year is a crucial piece of the history, thin ice being more common in May than in December.

Thus, Ágrip puts these events at Yule, which makes them quite preternatural.[6] In reaction, perhaps, two of the later variants place them in early spring,[7] making the broken ice unusual, but possible. The other three variants let Hálfdan take his last ride in an icy winter, without calendric precision.

The Fagrskinna Appendix treats it all as an "unfortunate accident,"[8] and this attitude is typical of the Norwegian variants (Historia Norwegiæ, Ágrip, Fagrskinna, and Fagrskinna Appendix). Construing Hálfdan's death as a regrettable but entirely natural event, they see no need to inquire after motives, sinister forces, or hidden conspiracies behind the sad occurence. In contrast, Icelandic variants prepared their readers to understand the king's death as having been set in motion by resentful and cunning enemies: the giant Dofri according to the "Tale of Hálfdan the Black" or the Finnish sorcerer and his chief according to Heimskringla. Behind an otherwise inexplicable catastrophe, they perceive magical assault and the working out of revenge.

On the question of how the accident occurred, Norwegians and Icelanders generally agreed, although not with perfect unanimity. Quite appropriately, discussion focused on a single point: Why did the ice crack at a time when it should have been solid? Consistent with its naturalistic approach, the appendix to Fagrskinna—one of the last of these texts to be written—blames the season and the weather. "It was in the spring," it explains, "the time when the ice begins to break up on the lakes."[9] All others fix responsibility on an item of culture: a "well for watering cattle" (Old Norse *nautabrunnr*, Latin *scissuram . . . ubi pastores gregem suum adaquare solebant*) cut into the lake to serve the livestock's needs in winter.[10] Presumably, this man-made rupture weakened the surface of the ice, with fatal results for poor Hálfdan.

Straddling the issue of nature, supernature, and culture, Heimskringla cites both cattle hole and weather as causal factors, while noting that the sun of that particular spring was unusually hot.[11] Still not satisfied, it added a third cause where all other variants were content with one:[12] a pile of cattle dung (Old Norse *mykr*) atop the ice of the water hole.[13]

> Hálfdan the Black drove off from the feast at Haðaland and went on his way, such that he drove over Lake Rönd. It was spring, when there was an exceptionally sudden thaw. And when they drove by Rykinsvík, there had been wells for watering cattle there over the winter, and where the dung had fallen on the ice, a hole opened up because of the sudden thaw. When the king drove by there, the ice crashed down and King Hálfdan perished there, and a great host with him.[14]

The logic is clear, if belabored. In early spring, an unseasonably hot sun began thawing the dung pile on the ice near a water hole that served cattle over the long Nordic winter. The dark color of the dung attracted the sun's rays, the energy of which stimulated heat-generating catabolic reactions associated with the dung's decomposition, and this accelerated the ice's melting. Enter Hálfdan by night, a bit worse for drink. Accidents will happen.

II

Heimskringla thus offered a meticulously detailed explanation of the broken ice, sufficiently rational to quell the doubts of anyone who might think the king's death suspicious. Yet this same account could also stimulate and nurture suspicions via a set of subtextual allusions connecting these events to Old Norse myths of creation. To appreciate this, we must consider Gylfaginning's account of the cosmogony, which Heimskringla assumes and transforms when narrating Hálfdan's demise.

In that text, creation begins with the same binary oppositions we have just encountered: a set so perfect they might have been scripted by Claude Lévi-Strauss.[15] Thus, originally there was nothing, save ice to the north and fire to the south. Gradually an ice floe from the north and a warm breeze from the south moved toward the center of cosmic space—a yawning void known as Ginnungagap—where they met and modified each other. From their contact, life-quickening drops of liquid (*kvikudropum*)[16] appeared that were warm like the breeze and moist like the ice, but more vital than either in isolation.[17] From these drops, life first took shape in the form of the giant Ymir, followed by two other beings of a different sort, named Auðhumla and Buri.

> Then Gangleri said: "Where did Ymir dwell, and what did he live on?"
>
> "It was thereafter, when the ice dripped, that from it there was a cow, who was called Auðhumla, and four streams of milk ran from her teats, and she fed Ymir."
>
> Then Gangleri said: "On what did the cow feed?"
>
> High One said: "She licked the frost stones, which were salty. The first day on which she licked the stones, by evening there came from the stones a man's hair, the second day a man's head, and on the third day all of the man was there: he was named Buri. He was fair in appearance, big and strong. He begat that son who was called Bor. That one took himself a wife, who was called Bestla, the daughter of the giant Bölthorn, and they had three sons. One was called Óðinn, the next Vili, and the third Vé, and it is my belief that this Óðinn and his brothers must be the rulers of heaven and earth."[18]

At the dawn of time, radiant warmth and frozen moisture thus combined to generate life. Conversely, the interaction of these same elements produced death for Hálfdan, and the image of the king sinking beneath the surface of Lake Rönd neatly inverts the episode when Buri, first of the gods, rose up from the rime under the coaxing of Auðhumla's tongue. If divine history began in the moment of Buri's emergence, a major era of it ends when Hálfdan slips back into the icy depths.

III

Gylfaginning continues the story, telling how Buri's grandsons—Óðinn and two other gods—made themselves lords of creation by killing Ymir, dismembering his corpse, and using its pieces as the raw material with which they built the cosmos. To that end, they refashioned the giant's bodily matter to produce a habitable space for the world's living creatures, turning Ymir's flesh into soil, his bones into mountains, his hair into vegetation, and his blood into the sea.[19] Beyond the labor of physical transformation, their work also had a geopolitical aspect, as the gods claimed the central territory for themselves and their human protégés, while relegating giants to peripheral areas beside the earth-encircling sea. Resenting the murder of their ancestor Ymir, giants remained ever hostile to the gods and periodically they threatened to attack. Anticipating this, the gods erected a defensive perimeter within which they could be safe, taking their raw material once again from Ymir's corpse.

> On the shore of the sea they gave lands for dwelling to the races of giants, and on the inner side of the earth they built a stronghold all around the world because of the hostility of the giants. For this stronghold, they used the [very bushy] eyebrows of the giant Ymir, and they called that stronghold Miðgarð.[20]

Paralleling this narrative, Heimskringla introduced the idea that once it was retrieved from the ice, Hálfdan's corpse was dismembered and creatively redistributed, much in the manner of Ymir. The account is highly innovative, for the oldest Norwegian texts (Theodricus Monachus, Historia Norwegiæ) show no interest in the fate of Hálfdan's body, while Ágrip and Fagrskinna tell that the corpse was buried in a funerary mound in Hringariki, consistent with standard practice. In contrast, Heimskringla describes events without precedent, at least at the level of humans (synoptic table 8.2):

> So highly did men value him that when they heard he was dead and his body was brought to Hringariki with the intention of being buried there, powerful men from Raumariki, Vestfold, and Heiðmark came and all requested to have

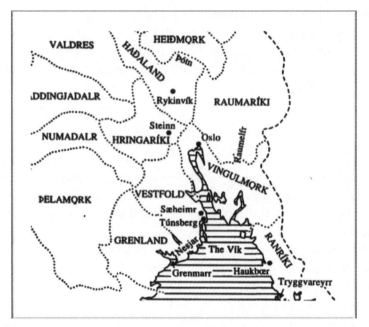

FIGURE 8.1: Districts of southern Norway included in the realm of Hálfdan the Black. From *Fagrskinna, a Catalogue of the Kings of Norway*, a translation with introduction and notes by Alison Finlay (Leiden: Brill 2004). © Copyright 2004 by Koninklijke Brill NV, Leiden, The Netherlands.

the body for themselves and to bury it in a mound in their district. And they thought there would be good harvests for those who got it. But they settled it so the body was divided into four parts. The head was buried in a mound at Steinn in Hringariki and each group took home their portion and buried it in a mound, and all these are called Hálfdan's Mounds.[21]

Heimskringla begins where Ágrip and Fagrskinna leave off, that is, at the attempt to bury Hálfdan in Hringariki's town of Steinn, which was located near the geographic center of his realm (fig. 8.1). Where the Norwegian texts see this as a proper and unproblematic final resting place for the king, Heimskringla introduces competing claims by other districts, all eager to share his relics and the life-sustaining powers they bear. Accordingly, Hálfdan's body is divided into four pieces and distributed in ways that integrate time and space, for the four provinces involved map neatly onto the cardinal points (Hringariki to the west, Raumariki to the east, Vestfold to the south, and Heiðmark to the north), while they also mark phases in the expansion of Hálf-dan's kingdom (Vestfold having been inherited from his father, Raumariki and Heiðmark being among his first conquests, and Hringariki being his last acquisition, gained via his marriage).[22] These portions are not equal, however, for Hringariki received Hálfdan's head in token of its primacy.

Two later texts adopt this story from Heimskringla and quibble about its details. Thus, the "Tale of Hálfdan the Black" introduces Vingulmark in place of Heiðmark, making for a more compact little kingdom.[23] The appendix to Fagrskinna revises more radically still, listing three burial sites on a north-south axis and placing Hálfdan's entrails at Haðaland in the north, his head at Vestfold to the south, which was also his father's original realm, and the rest of his body at Hringariki, the space in between. These differences notwithstanding, all three texts describe a similar process whereby the realm is reconstituted and its parts redefined in relation to the dead king's body. Districts that receive Hálfdan's bodily members are thereby enriched, for these contained his capacity to produce abundant harvests and prosperous years.[24] A hierarchy was also established among the districts, insofar as the one receiving the head (Hringariki in two variants, Vestfold in the other) thereby outranked the others. More important, however, was the distinction between the districts inside the realm and those construed as peripheries outside the life-sustaining, protective, blessed areas destined to remain in intimate contact with King Hálfdan, which had become, in a certain sense, consubstantial with his body. The border of his territories thus played much the same role as the barricade made from Ymir's eyebrows, separating inside from out, gods from giants, Miðgarð from Útgarð, good from evil, us from them, and civilization from chaos. In ways, this repeats the events of creation, Hálfdan's corpse having suffered the same fate as Ymir's. A new world, with new conditions of existence, took shape as a result of these two deaths and more particularly as a result of the way these two bodies were treated, including a radical division between a central territory associated with all that is good and peripheries associated with hostile others.[25]

There is, however, one way in which Hálfdan's death does not parallel Ymir's, but actually inverts it. For Gylfaginning passes harsh moral judgment on Ymir: "He was evil, as are all his kinsmen."[26] From the perspective of this text, Ymir's death was a good thing, and it ensured that good beings rule the world and occupy its center, although they remain embattled by Ymir's descendants, representing evil and the periphery. Heimskringla, in contrast, treats Hálfdan as an extremely good king.[27] And here one must ask: If this sign is reversed, how does that affect the rest of the story? Does Hálfdan's death represent the triumph of evil? Have those responsible for his death—the Finnish magician and chief, or the giant Dofri—now gained control of the center? Are Hálfdan's heirs now embattled and obliged to avenge him? If so, do they attack from the periphery, or do they hold and defend the center?

IV

Among those who appear in the cosmogonic drama, Auðhumla is unique in several ways. The sole animal and the sole female (save the giantess Bestla, who is mentioned only in passing), the primordial bovine plays a role of foundational importance, nourishing Ymir with her abundant milk and licking Buri into existence out of the ice as she seeks salt for own sustenance. All gods and all giants thus depend on Auðhumla for their very being.

Notwithstanding her significance to the story, Auðhumla, her milk, and her creative lick are unattested in any surviving text antecedent to the composition of Gylfaginning, whether Icelandic, Scandinavian, Anglo-Saxon, or more broadly Germanic.[28] She seems to have been Snorri's invention: the one new detail he introduced into a bricolage of preexisting constituent pieces.[29] One is thus tempted to compare it with the lone innovative detail Heimskringla introduced to its account of Hálfdan's death, that is, the cattle dung. Indeed, the two details introduced by Snorri are construed as having had a certain affinity, for just as Hálfdan is the descendant of Buri, so the cattle responsible for the dung had Auðhumla as their ancestor.[30]

If Buri was licked from the ice by a cow who gave milk at that very spot, so conversely Hálfdan fell beneath the ice at a place where cattle took water but gave no milk. Rather, according to Heimskringla, what they produced was the dung that accumulated atop the ice of the watering hole: the dark, foul end of the nutritional process, rather than its radiant, life-sustaining beginning. One reads here an implicit homology of extraordinary length, complexity, and importance.

Milk : Dung
:: Light/Day : Dark/Night
:: Nourishment : Refuse
:: Sweet-tasting liquid : Foul-smelling solid
:: Promising beginnings : Wretched, humiliating end
:: Infancy and growth : Death and decay
:: Creation : Cataclysm

In its treatment of the cow dung—a detail that it alone introduces—Heimskringla thus seems to invert the account of Auðhumla's milk introduced in Gylfaginning.[31] Other variants perform similar operations, however, inverting the myth of Buri's birth in their accounts of Hálfdan's icy death, while performing a less radical inversion of Ymir's death in the treatment of Hálfdan's body.

In all these ways, the later Kings' Sagas, led by Heimskringla, are making much the same point. The world that took shape with Ymir, Buri, and Auðhumla comes to its end with Hálfdan, whose death deconstructs everything they created. The question is: What kind of a world will follow?

Shaggy Harald

I

As we have seen, the question of what kind of world came into being after Hálfdan's death was construed as complex and momentous. Among the texts that had most bearing on this issue were those that introduced Hálfdan's successor upon his ascent to the throne. All present Harald as Hálfdan's son, and all save one treat him in positive terms, but some go much farther than others (synoptic table 9.1). The earliest Norwegian sources are quite terse, but each iteration builds on its predecessor. Thus, Theodricus Monachus tells only that Harald was the first to overcome all district kings, making himself the first sole king over Norway.[1] Historia Norwegiæ adds mention of his physical beauty, explaining that he had his epithet Fairhair (*Haraldus comatus*) "because of his elegant locks."[2]

Ágrip expands its account at two points. First, having acknowledged Harald's youth, it insists this is no problem, for "he was soon a brave man and imposing in stature."[3] Second, having summarized his conquests, it characterizes them as beneficial to all. "It was ten years that he fought," the text explains, "until he became all-powerful king over the land of Norway, *and he greatly improved his land and pacified it*."[4]

It is Fagrskinna, however, that goes furthest in extolling the new king's virtues, taking pains to mention his maturity, graciousness, beauty, size, strength, wisdom, prescience, administrative abilities, generosity, valor, and more. It also introduces the idea of his *hamingja*, a term that some scholars identify with divine favor and charisma, while others insist it denotes nothing more than good luck.[5] Debates over interpretation of this word have figured prominently in still-larger debates over the existence of "sacred kingship" in pagan Scandinavia and among ancient Germanic peoples more broadly.[6] For my part, I am inclined to think the importance of this question has been overemphasized. Most basically, *hamingja* is the term through which success—particularly consistent, extreme, or unexpected success—was mystified ex post facto and attributed to some uncanny quality possessed by the person who enjoyed it. *Hamingja* was a discursive construct that actively constituted that of which it spoke, for once *hamingja* had been attributed to a man, others hesitated to oppose him, as his reputation for success prompted discouragement and intimidation. Interacting with whatever other advantages the fellow enjoyed, *hamingja* became a self-fulfilling prophecy. Whether theorized with reference to the deity or not, the results were very much the same.

Hamingja, then, is but one part of the idealized portrait Fagrskinna gives of Harald, celebrating his manifold excellence and obviating whatever doubts might exist regarding the era he inaugurated.

> His son Harald took the kingship after his father, Hálfdan the Black. He was then a youth to reckon by his age, but full grown in all the manly accomplishments that it beseemed a gracious king to have. His growth of hair was great with a wonderful color, in appearance most like fine silk. Of all men he was the most handsome and the strongest and one can see how big he was from his burial stone, which is in Haugasund. He was a great man of wisdom, farsighted and ambitious. Here, *hamingja* and Providence strengthened him, that he should be lord over the realm of Northmen and that the land that up to now his lineage had made glorious might continue to be so. Old men attached themselves to him with wise counsels and help for his plans. Young worthies and men of valor desired to be with him for the sake of fine gifts of money and royal pomp. . . . And it was ten years that he fought until he became all-powerful king over the land of Norway, and he greatly improved his land and pacified it.[7]

Icelandic sources were more reserved in their praise, with considerable variation among them. Thus, the "Tale of Harald Fairhair" largely follows Fagrskinna, but redirects some of its passages so they apply to Guthorm, rather than Harald,[8] and it introduces a detail—to which we will return—that reframes the entire description. Heimskringla is praising, but much less so than Fagrskinna, and one senses reserve in its diction.[9] Quite different is the way Egil's Saga introduces Harald.

> Harald, son of Hálfdan the Black, had taken his inheritance from his father in Vik, to the east. He had sworn this vow not to have his hair cut or combed until he was sole king over Norway. He was called "Shaggy Harald." After that he fought with those kings who were nearest, and he conquered them. There are long narratives of that.[10]

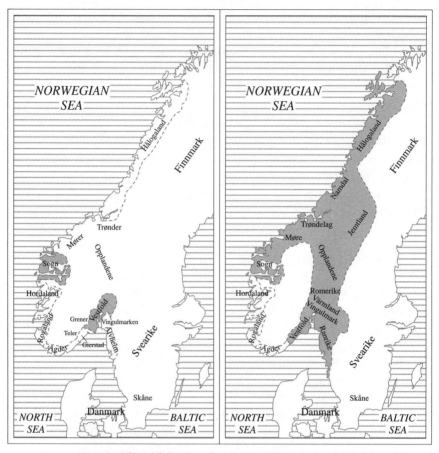

FIGURE 9.1: Expansion of Harald's kingdom, from the time of his accession, ca. 858 (Sogn and Vest-fold on the coasts), until the end of his military campaigning, ca. 868 (to the far north and inland). Map courtesy of Dick Gilbreath, Gyula Pauer Center for Cartography and GIS, University of Kentucky.

Three of the other variants introduce the topic of King Harald's hair in order to comment on its beauty,[11] but this is the only one that mentions his vow and his epithet "Shaggy" (*lúfa*), with reference to the long, unkempt tangle that the vow produced. Having made these points part of its nega-tive portrait, the saga goes on to describe Harald's conquests to the north and west, where he expanded his father's kingdom and ultimately made the whole country his own (fig. 9.1).

Rather than celebrating Harald's victories, the saga lets us see how things looked to the vanquished. Particularly poignant is the speech of Sölvi Klofi, a prince of Northern Mæri, who pleaded with district kings elsewhere to unite in opposition to the man he refers to simply—and curtly—as Harald.

"Although this trouble now afflicts us, it will not be long until the same trouble will come to you, for I think Harald will come here quickly, when he has subjected all the men in North Mæri and Raumsdale to slavery and oppression, as he wishes. You will have the same choice before you as we had: to defend your property and freedom and to risk all those men whose support you can hope for. I will offer myself and my troops against this arrogance and injustice. On the other hand, you may wish to follow the same counsel as the Naumdalers did: to go of your own volition into bondage and become Harald's thralls. To my father it seems praiseworthy to die in his kingdom with honor, rather than become the subordinate of another king in his old age. I think it will seem the same to you and to those others who have some pride and wish to be men of courage."[12]

The vocabulary of this passage provides a catalogue of the way Harald's new order appeared to those who stood in its way: trouble (*vandræði*), slavery (*þrælkan*), oppression (*áþján*), arrogance (*ofsi*), injustice/inequity (*ójafnaðr*), bondage (*ánauð*), subordination (*gøra undirmaðr*). Its most immediate consequence was loss of one's property and freedom (*fé . . . ok frelsi*), an unbearable prospect for courageous men (*kappsmenn*), whose sense of dignity depended on their independence. Yet however ideologically effective or emotionally moving Sölvi Klofi's appeal might be, it was not enough to turn the tide. By this point in the action, Harald had assembled too many troops and gained too much momentum. No district king could muster enough force to oppose him, and the old order, with its multitude of rivalrous petty states, made it difficult to forge a solid alliance.

Kveld-Ulf, the saga's protagonist at this moment, delivers a crushing response to Sölvi Klofi's call. Like the latter, he has no illusions about young Harald's magnanimity or virtue, but he does understand that the process of violent state formation the upstart has set in motion is now virtually unstoppable. Before too many chapters pass, Kveld-Ulf's firstborn son will be a victim of that process, after which he and his surviving son will be on their way to Iceland. For the moment, he answers Sölvi Klofi's call in blunt and realistic fashion. Where the latter spoke of the enemy as Harald, refusing to grant him the title of king, Kveld-Ulf goes him one better and names him "Shaggy Harald," the saga's only character who dares to do so.[13] His usage is complicated, however, for this epithet grudgingly acknowledges the man's extraordinary power, while denying him respect—let alone legitimacy—on any other grounds.[14]

"I understand myself unobliged to go north to Mæri and defend their land. . . . Kveld-Ulf will sit at home during this call to arms and he will not raise troops

and will not journey from home to fight against Shaggy Harald, for I think
that man has a big box full of *hamingja* and our king hasn't a handful."[15]

Whether *hamingja* here denotes good luck or god's favor matters relatively little—except, perhaps, to theorists of sacred kingship—for the results
are the same in either case. In this passage, Kveld-Ulf uses the word to signal
neither admiration, nor affection, nor awe and dread, although it may have
conveyed some tinge of envy. Most of all, it captures his realistic assessment
that "Shaggy Harald" has proven himself an irresistible force that only fools
would openly challenge.

II

Earlier, we observed that the "Tale of Harald Fairhair" largely follows Fagrskinna when introducing Harald but frames its description in a way that mit-
igates the praise it offers. This is accomplished in its first sentence: "When he
was ten years old, Harald Hálfdan's son, **who was called Dofri's foster son,**
took the kingship over Hringariki, Vestfold, Vingulmark, and Raumariki."[16]

Although Harald acquires his father's realm (the districts named being
those where Hálfdan's body was buried),[17] the text leaves doubt as to whether
he assumes the throne as "Hálfdan's son" or as "Dofri's foster son." As we
have seen, much hinges on this question. In the former case, he is represented as a rightful heir to the dynasty, descended from gods through a line of
kings; in the latter, as a quasi usurper and near parricide, who has been refashioned by the giant who slew his father and who taught him magic and
martial arts, perhaps also conveying giants' moral disposition. To see Hálfdan succeeded by "Hálfdan's son" stresses continuity and provides reas-
surance of a world restored. To see him followed by "Dofri's foster son" is to
accentuate rupture and heighten anxiety about the era now beginning. The
"Tale of Harald Fairhair" straddles this issue by using both epithets, and for
the most part it follows Fagrskinna in its glowing portrait of the new king. It
does introduce one novel detail, however, that arouses trepidation, describing Harald as "obstinate and determined" (*þralyndr ok otalhlydinn*): dangerous qualities both, and typical of giants.[18]

Here we must note a curious fact. Harald is never given the epithet
Hálfdánarson in skaldic poetry contemporary with his reign, and this patronym is similarly absent in all the Kings' Sagas.[19] In later prose works, it
appears twice only, and both times its use is unstable and transitional, for
instead of establishing Harald as "Hálfdan's son," these texts indicate that
his birth identity yielded to one defined by his fosterage. One of these is the

TABLE 9.1. The stages of Harald's life and the epithets associated with them

Age and Stage of Life	Epithet	Attested in Skaldic Poetry	Attested in Norwegian Sources	Attested in Heimskringla	Attested in Other Icelandic Sources
Birth–5 years old: while living under his father's roof	Hálfdan's son (Hálfdánarson)	–	–	–	(+)
5–10 years old: from his flight to Dofri's cave until the moment he swears his oath	Dofri's Foster Son (Dofrafóstri)	–	–	–	+
10–20 years old: from the moment he swears his oath until he has conquered all rivals, created the state of Norway, and made himself the first sole king of this realm	Shaggy (Lúfa)	+	+	+	+
20–72 years old: from the moment his vow is accomplished until his death	Fairhair (Hárfagr)	+	+	+	+

Note: The plus sign in parentheses represents a small number of occurrences that tend to be self-deconstructing.

passage we have just considered; the other is Barð's Saga, which we discussed in chapters 6 and 7.

> A little while later, Harald Hálfdan's son came [to the cave], and he was reared there by Dofri the giant. Dofri raised him to be king over Norway, as is told in the Saga of Harald, Dofri's Foster Son.[20]

The two sentences of this brief passage are to be read as a sequence, a contrast, and an argument on the question of what qualifies this boy to be king. The first sentence points to Harald's dynastic claim by using his patronym. He arrives at the cave a refugee, however, estranged from his royal father. The second sentence then identifies other qualifications, emphasizing the way "Dofri raised him to be king over Norway" (*efldi Dofri hann síðan til konungs yfir Noregi*). A weak reading of the passage would conclude that both birth and training were necessary conditions for kingship, neither one being sufficient in itself. It is possible, however, to take the passage as suggesting that royal birth is neither necessary or sufficient, proper training alone being requisite. In either case, one thing is clear: Although Harald arrived at the cave as "Hálfdan's son," he left it as "Dofri's foster son" and ascended to the throne in the latter capacity.

The epithet *Dofrafostri* thus largely displaced Harald's patronym within certain Icelandic variants of his story attested no earlier than the last quarter of the thirteenth century.[21] One of these, Flóamanna Saga, presents Harald's epithets as forming a chronological sequence: "The son of Ragnhild and Hálfdan the Black was Harald, who was first called 'Dofri's Foster Son,' but then 'Shaggy Harald,' and finally 'Harald the Fairhaired.'"[22] If we restore the patronym, we can correlate the whole set with different stages of Harald's life, as shown in table 9.1.

It thus appears that the epithet "Dofri's Foster Son" was belatedly introduced in Iceland as a means to discredit King Harald and the regime he introduced. Where it appears, this term suggests not only dynastic discontinuity, but something more radical still: a world where a giant's fosterling assumed the throne and created a larger and far more ambitious, violent, and menacing form of kingship and state once poor Hálfdan sank beneath the ice and the old order was deconstructed.

III

The critique associated with the Dofri narrative was not part of the Norwegian tradition, which had relatively little to say about Harald in the time before he was king. Within Norwegian texts, only two epithets occur: "Shaggy" (*lúfa*) and "Fairhair" (*hárfagr*), both of which are attested in ninth-century poems of Harald's own skalds.[23] Together, these epithets frame an opposition between the Hideous and the Magnificent, Chaos and Cosmos, Nature and Culture, the Raw and the Cooked, while also distinguishing a Before from an After. The moment that establishes this temporal divide, however, is *not* the day of Harald's accession, since both epithets reference him in his royal office. What they differentiate most precisely is two sequential phases and aspects of his kingship: the shaggy conqueror and the fair-haired sovereign. Within this binary, Harald's oath assumes prime importance, being the ritual means through which he made himself into a radically new type of ruler, who, much like Shaka Zulu or Qin Shi Huangdi, was intent on creating a new kind of world by a new mode of action and a higher level of violence.

In swearing this oath, the young king deployed a particularly solemn speech act, effectively consecrating himself to a sacred mission while constituting his words as irrevocable and unforgettable. Heimskringla describes the oath as sworn by "the god . . . who created me and who rules over all."[24] With this phrase, it construes Harald as intuitively guided by religious truth even if not yet a Christian, and it represents his oath as a sacred vow that binds him to the deity. When he succeeds—and on this, there can be no doubt—he will do so not just by his own strength of arm, but as a result of the divine favor his devotion elicits from his creator.

However persuasive this theistic construction of Harald's oath may be, it is original to Heimskringla. Seven texts describe the oath, and only two make mention of the deity: Heimskringla and the Greater Saga of Olaf Tryggvason, which copies Heimskringla's wording (synoptic table 9.3). All seven agree, however, on what it is that Harald swore: "Never shall my hair be cut or combed until I have taken possession of all Norway,"[25] but none explains why this should be effective. A few minor variations appear, none of them terribly significant. Thus, Fagrskinna provided geographic detail, noting that Harald's ambitions extended "east to the Marches and north to the sea."[26] The "Tale of Hálfdan the Black" specified that nails, as well as hair, should go uncut.[27] And Heimskringla foregrounded political economy, specifying that Harald had designs not only on territory, but also on "tributes, taxes, and administration."[28] It further related that Harald swore to succeed or die trying, with the Greater Saga of Olaf Tryggvason following it once more.[29]

The two remaining sources (Egil's Saga and the "Tale of Harald Fairhair") underscore the importance of the gestures involved with the vow, as both announce that Harald received a new name, "Shaggy Harald" (*Haraldr lúfa*), referencing the new state—simultaneously physical, social, and religious—that he entered as a result of his pledge.[30] This name replaced his patronym

(*Haraldr Hálfdanarson*) and remained his until he completed his conquests, fulfilled his vow, cut his hair, and received from Earl Rögnvald the contrastive title by which he became known to history, "Harald Fairhair" (*Haraldr hárfagr*).[31] Until then, "shaggy" he surely was, since his locks grew unabated during ten full years of military campaigns.[32] By the end, he must have possessed a fairly spectacular set of dreadlocks. As Fagrskinna put it: "Harald's hair was long and matted, for which reason he was called 'Shaggy.'"[33]

Nothing in any of these sources offers any explanation of the role this precise gesture—this ritualized, superabundant growth of hair—was expected to play in obtaining the desired results, but several lines of interpretation seem possible.[34] In some measure, Harald's hair may serve as a trope for his realm, insofar as the unchecked growth of the one corresponds to the centrifugal expansion of the other. The connection between the two is not causal in any clear way, but neither is it arbitrary. Rather, there is a deep affinity between the two comparanda: both are processes of growth and change that disrupt an established order, producing considerable shock. That the conquest of a nation involves violence and is deeply disturbing comes as no surprise. As regards King Harald's coiffure, one can easily generate a large set of examples, ranging from antiquity to the present, in which long, wild, uncontrolled male hair is not just a sign, but also implicitly a source of volatile and explosive force, whether the power in question is creative or destructive, physical or mental, natural or supernatural. Such power is associated not only with hirsute kings and state founders (figs. 9.2–9.6), but also with rebels and outlaws (9.7–9.10), prophets and holy men (9.11–9.14), and artists, poets, and visionaries (9.15–9.18).

Under the normal conditions of virtually all societies, multiple interrelated systems of constraint—including considerations of aesthetics, etiquette, grooming, modesty, comfort, and health, with ethics participating in more limited fashion—conspire to enforce a regime of tonsorial control that is respected by those whom the group regards as its members in good standing.[35] In brief, people cut their hair because they have been raised to worry about how others will react to them if they fail (or worse yet, refuse) to make this a regular part of their corporeal practice.

By contrast, to stop cutting one's hair for any prolonged length of time is to defy such norms. More strongly, it is to announce one has no consideration for propriety, tradition, what anyone else thinks, or what anyone else construes as normal, civilized, and decent behavior. It is to abandon—better yet, to transcend—all conventional systems of control: to transform oneself into a wild, untamed and untamable force of nature, characterized by growth that knows and accepts no limits.

FIGURE 9.2: William Borde, *Harald Fairhair* (2007), founder of the Norwegian national state and royal line. Courtesy of the artist.

FIGURE 9.3: Alexander the Great, tetradrachm minted at Memphis (315 BCE). Courtesy of Shutterstock.

FIGURE 9.4: Attila the Hun, from Hartmann Schedel's *Nuremberg Chronicle* (1493).

FIGURE 9.5: King Mswati III of Swaziland. Photograph by Pam Gillespie.

FIGURE 9.6: François-Louis Dejuinne, *Clovis, King of the Francs* (1835), founder of the Merovingian dynasty (465–511). Musée National du Château et des Trianons, Versailles.

FIGURE 9.7: Martin M. Lawrence, *John Brown* (1859). From a pamphlet made shortly after the raid at Harper's Ferry from an original daguerreotype. Library of Congress, Prints and Photographs Division, Washington, DC.

FIGURE 9.8: Brandon Allen, *Jack* (2007). From the American Biker Project. Courtesy of the artist.

FIGURE 9.9: Samar Sesapzai, *Che Guevara* (2011). Courtesy of the artist.

FIGURE 9.10: Miles Teves, *Blackbeard the Pirate* (Edward Teach) (2011). Courtesy of the artist.

FIGURE 9.11: Brendan Kulp, *St. John the Baptist.* Courtesy of the artist.

FIGURE 9.12: Grigorij Rasputin (ca. 1900).

FIGURE 9.13: Rabbi Meyer Schneerson (1987). Photograph by Mordecai Bar-On.

FIGURE 9.14: Unidentified sadhu from Kathmandu. Courtesy of Shutterstock.

FIGURE 9.15: Albrecht Dürer, *Self-Portrait* (1500). Alte Pinakothek, Munich.

FIGURE 9.16: George C. Cox, *Walt Whitman* (1887). Library of Congress, Prints and Photographs Division, Washington, DC.

FIGURE 9.17: Oren Jack Turner, *Albert Einstein* (1947). Library of Congress, Prints and Photographs Division, Washington, DC.

FIGURE 9.18: David Corio, *Bob Marley* (n.d.). Collection: Redferns. Courtesy of Getty Images.

As "Shaggy Harald," the unprecedentedly ambitious monarch thus presented himself as an asocial creature without any sense of accountability, shame, or guilt, and therefore beyond any semblance of cultural, moral, or self-control. The topos of king as monster is, in fact, a familiar one that takes many forms. Most often, it is the ruler of an enemy group who is perceived and described as monstrous or bestial, justifying fear of the (savage) power he wields and legitimating desperate acts of resistance.[36] Alternatively, the power of one's own rulers may be perceived as so awesome, so threatening, so inhuman in its nature as to be utterly alien. This perspective finds expression in myths of the stranger-king: figures like Aeneas (or Óðinn) who brought the impressive but monstrous institution of the state and imposed it from outside, bequeathing it to hybrid descendants, who wield that power thereafter for better and worse.[37] Yet again, there are people who make their beast-kings a source of pride and confidence, as well as a cause for fear. Rather than experiencing the monstrosity of power as a threat (whether exogenous or not), they understand their survival depends upon it, for it is precisely the king's monstrous traits—his ferocity, cruelty, his capacity for implacable rage and appalling violence, his lack of moderation and (seeming?) irrationality—that permit him to repel invaders, intimidate enemies, conquer territory, punish lawbreakers, or discourage lawbreaking altogether. The crucial question here is not whether the king is monstrous (that much is given), but against whom and to what end he uses his awesome powers. Those powers, moreover, are ritually renewed, so they should be ready for use as needed.[38]

In his "Shaggy" aspect, King Harald becomes such a monster, whose unprecedented, unfathomable violence was theorized in two different fashions. Those who identified with and benefited from it construed Harald's monstrosity as the necessary instrument for conquest, subjugation of rivals, unification of the nation, and formation of the state, suggesting that although such violence might seem excessive, it was not limitless, for it ceased when these projects were accomplished, at which point their king was a monster no more and became "Harald Fairhair."

Viewed from the safety of the "Fairhair" era, the turbulence of the prior decade can be "put in perspective," that is, minimized and redefined ex post facto as a regrettable but necessary phase that made possible the creation of a new and better world. Those Norwegians who wrote Kings' Sagas generally construed things in this light, emplotting Harald's oath, his hair, and his violence as necessary parts of a historical process, but embedded in a moment that was quickly surpassed as the story moved to its resolution. When these texts mention "Shaggy Harald" at all, they do so in the manner of Fagrskinna, which makes the wild man responsible for a civilizing project that perfected himself, as well as his holdings.

> After he civilized the land, those who were close by paid taxes, as did those far away. Now he had become a man full grown in his strength, size, and skill in counsel. His hair was long and matted: for this reason was he called "Shaggy." Then Earl Rögnvald of Mæri cut his hair and gave him a name and called him "Harald the Fairhair." He was then more than twenty years in age. He had many children, and from his lineage have come all the kings of Norway. It was ten years that he fought for the land until he became sole king of Norway. He pacified his land well and improved it.[39]

"Pacified and improved"—the same could be said of Shaggy Harald himself, as he became Harald Fairhair. One could ask, however, whether this transformation was deep and thoroughgoing or superficial and cosmetic only. Where Norwegian advocates of the royal state theorized a brief but necessary stage of the monstrous, its Icelandic critics took the institution of kingship as ever involved in oppressive acts of coercion, oppression, and extraction, all made possible by the threat of armed force: the iron fist in the velvet glove or, to use the operative metaphor, the shaggy reality that always lurked beneath the fair-haired veneer. Some texts were more willing to voice that perspective openly, especially the sagas celebrating Iceland's founding fathers. Others—and Heimskringla, above all—were more ambivalent, guarded, and discreet, but also subtlest and most biting in the critiques they offered.

Recoding the profoundly disquieting events associated with state formation as "pacification and improvement" is an operation that takes place ex post facto, and gaining control of that process is, as many theorists have observed, among the sweetest spoils of victory.[40] The historical record is thus neither complete nor neutral, but employs such methods as euphemism, amnesia, embellishment, and erasure to normalize, stabilize, even sanctify the state, which is both protagonist and patron of the story.

Still, no state ever succeeds as fully as it would like in the projects of legitimation and naturalization through which it tries to consolidate what its monstrous founders won in more open battles. Never does it manage to persuade all those to whom it tells its tale that it is just, kind, and without contradiction, or that its origins are noble, heroic, or divine. Some refuse to believe the story. Others refuse to listen. And those who are not just resistant but downright subversive retell the tale with subtle changes of vocabulary, characterization, plot, or dramatis personae. In so doing, they continue the struggle, now waged on discursive terrain, where battles are not always won by monster-kings and their big battalions.

Ingjald the Wicked

I

Virtually all texts that report Harald's epochal words describe them as a vow or an oath (Old Norse *heit*), and his speech act as a *heit-strenging*, that is, the solemn pronouncement of a binding pledge.[1] *Heitstrenging*, in fact, was a fairly specialized practice that usually occurred in one of a very few ritual contexts, specifically weddings, the Yule festival, and ceremonies of royal accession.[2] Of these, the last is most relevant, suggesting that Harald's oath may have been understood as a part of the ritualized process through which he assumed the throne.

Such ceremonies were staged in the context of funeral feasts, a high point of which was the moment when the heir apparent drank a toast to his deceased father.[3] So important was this gesture that the ceremony took its name from it: *erfis-drykka* "the drink of the funeral feast" or *erfi-ǫl*, "the ale of the funeral feast" (cf. the cognate term in Middle English, *arval*).[4] The fullest description is found in an early chapter of Heimskringla.

That text—Ynglingasaga 36—actually describes the *erfiǫl* twice, and both descriptions have their interest. The first provides an ideal scenario for the ritual, while the second details its anomalous performance by Ingjald the Wicked (*Ingjaldr inn illráðr*), twenty-fourth king in the Yngling line, whose oath serves as typological precedent for the one later sworn by Harald. Heimskringla describes Ingjald as a district king, whose realm centered on Uppsala, the original Yngling capital. Although this dynasty once ruled all Sweden, under Agni—twelfth king in the line, and twelve generations before Ingjald—its monarchy fractured, and the Ynglings were reduced to the status of other district kings, with whom they intermarried, fought occasional wars, and made treaties of variable duration.[5] Within this context, the death of any ruler was potentially destabilizing, for it created a situation in which others were tempted to test the strength of his heir. In the face of this threat, rituals of succession were meant to assert the continuity of the new king with the old, both in his qualities and his possessions. Heimskringla describes the ritual procedures:

> At that time, it was the custom when a funeral feast would be made for a king or earl that he who made the feast and who would assume the inheritance should sit on the step in front of the high seat until the ceremonial cup was brought in. This was called the Bragafull ["Goblet of the best"]. He should then stand up facing toward the Bragafull and swear an oath, then drink from the cup. Thereafter he should be conducted to the high seat—that which his father had. He then came into all the inheritance from his father.[6]

Clearly, the purpose of this ceremonial performance was to effect the transformation of its central actor from the status of heir and pretender to that of legitimate king. To do so, it correlated his sociopolitical promotion with his spatial elevation from a step just beneath his father's throne to the "high seat" (*há-sæti*) itself. Access to this place of honor and power followed and depended on the heir's swearing an oath (*strengja heit*) while holding a ceremonial vessel: the Bragafull, whose contents he drank as his last act before becoming king.[7] In this moment, heirs often vowed to accomplish great deeds, including risky military ventures. The oaths they swore included a good deal of boasting, some of which could backfire.[8]

II

It is at this point that the story of King Ingjald acquires considerable interest. An intrinsically compelling narrative, it also has strong subtextual connections to the story of Harald Fairhair. For in all the earlier chapters of Heimskringla, only this one incident of *heitstrenging* appears. Anyone seeking precedents for Harald's oath would inevitably be led to Ingjald and the events of his reign, which the text skillfully embroidered for its own purposes.

To appreciate this, one must know a bit about the methods and sources used in Ynglingasaga, the opening portion of Heimskringla, which falls into two parts. The first (Ynglingasaga, chaps. 1–10) contains an attempt to euhemerize Óðinn, Njord, and Yngvi-Frey, whom the text treats as migrants from Asia: not gods, but men possessed of such great physical beauty, martial gifts, and magical powers that they were (mistakenly) hailed as deities when they reached northern Europe. There, they founded kingship and the Yngling line in Uppsala, which became their capital. The sources for this part of the narrative remain unclear, despite considerable research. The second section of the Ynglingasaga, however (chaps. 11–50), depends primarily on Ynglingatal, a poem by Thjoðólf of Hvin, composed shortly before the accession of Hálfdan the Black.[9] This poem traces the Yngling line through thirty generations, giving a brief description of these kings—whom Heimskringla construes as Hálfdan's predecessors—and the curious circumstances of their deaths.[10] Working from this material, Ynglingasaga produced a pseudohistorical account of each king's reign, toward which end it regularly went far beyond the scant information preserved in this poem.[11]

In no other case, however, does the saga expand upon the poem in such extreme fashion as it does when speaking of Ingjald. Thjoðólf's verses—which the saga cites—tell only that the king died in a fire at Rœning (an island in Lake Mälaren, south of Uppsala) and that his people were not displeased at his death. The text reads as follows:

> Fire [= the emitter-of-smoke] trod Ingjald
> lifeless at Rœning.
> When the house thief [= fire] with feet of flame
> strode through the man known to the gods [= the king].
> And this fate seemed most fitting[12]
> to all the people among the Swedes,
> that he himself should be first,
> to depart boldly from his life.[13]

Historia Norwegiæ adds that Ingjald suffered great fears (*ultra modum timens*) before dying at the hands of Ívar Widefathomer (*Ivarum cognomine withfadm* = *Ívarr inn víðfaðmi*) and Heimskringla has the same information.[14] From these scanty traditions, the latter text proceeded to fashion an elaborate life history, filling eight chapters. The story begins with Ingjald as a small and delicate child, who wept when bested in play by Alf Yngvarsson, the son of a rival district king. Taking pity on Ingjald's physical weakness and delicate spirit—which were also cause for concern in a royal heir—his foster father, Svipdag the Blind, resolved to rectify them. "The next day, Svipdag had the heart taken out of a wolf, and he cooked it on a spit and he gave Prince Ingjald that to eat. Thereafter, he was the cruelest and worst tempered of all men."[15]

Having thus indelibly established Ingjald's character, the text had no interest in further episodes of his youth. After describing the death of his father, it cuts to Ingjald's succession.

> When Ingjald took the realm and kingdom, there were many district kings, as has been written. King Ingjald had a great feast prepared at Uppsala, intending to honor King Önund, his father, with a funeral feast. He had a hall

prepared that was no smaller or less worthy than Uppsala was, which he called the "Hall of Seven Kings." High seats were put up there. King Ingjald sent men throughout all Sweden and invited kings and earls and other men of rank. To this funeral feast came King Algaut, Ingjald's father-in-law, King Yngvarr of Fjaðryndaland and his two sons, Agnar and Alf, King Sporsnjall of Næríki, and King Sigverk of Áttundaland. King Granmar of Suðrmannaland did not come. There were six kings given seats in the new hall. One high seat that King Ingjald had put up was unoccupied. All of the troops who came with the kings were assigned seats in the new hall. King Ingjald had placed his bodyguard and all his troops in Uppsala.[16]

Here, the text describes the standard oath-swearing rituals in the passage quoted above (p. 96) and contrasts Ingjald's performance to that ideal.

Now, in this case it was done thus. When it was time for the Bragafull, King Ingjald stood up and accepted a large drinking horn. Then he swore an oath [*strengði hann þá heit*] that he would increase his realm by half in each direction or else die. Then he drank down the horn. And when men were drinking that evening, King Ingjald said to Svipdag's sons Folkvið and Hulvið that they should arm themselves and their host, as had been planned. They went out and brought fire into the new hall, and next they set the hall aflame. There, they burned the six kings and all their troops and those who came out were quickly killed. After that, King Ingjald put under himself all those realms that the [six] kings had had, and he took tribute from them.[17]

Obviously, the wolf's heart had done its work. Ingjald's shocking actions can be understood as originating in the cruelty his foster father instilled in him as a boy. The text also hints that these crimes fulfilled his long-suppressed wish for revenge, since one of the six kings Ingjald burned was none other than Alf Yngvarsson, who had bested him in child's play and prompted his metamorphosis into a monster.

After seizing the land of the six kings he murdered in this gruesome parody of a feast, Ingjald then had to deal with King Granmar, the one rival who had escaped his trap. Initially, he tried to defeat him in battle, but after serious losses, the two concluded a treaty, secured with solemn pledges.[18] Predictably, Ingjald was not to be trusted. Consistent with his earlier acts—and once again, with his wolf's heart—he ambushed Granmar and his allies, burned them in their hall, then took their lands and possessions.[19]

This pattern was to continue. "Men say King Ingjald killed twelve kings, all by treacherous violation of truces. He was called 'Ingjald the Wicked.' He was king over most parts of Sweden."[20] One should be particularly attentive to the last part of this statement and how it connects to the entire story of which it is the culmination. On the one hand, the text makes clear that Ingjald more than fulfilled the oath he swore at his father's funeral, when he vowed to expand the size of his realm or die trying. On the other, it constructs a clear parallel between Ingjald and Harald Fairhair, two men who began their careers as district kings, but who, by virtue of vows and subsequent ruthless action, transformed themselves into full-fledged monarchs, conquering and uniting their nations.

III

This parallel makes all the more fascinating the way Ynglingasaga brings Ingjald's tale to a close. Trying to gain possession of Skåne, the northernmost province of Denmark, King Ingjald married his daughter Ása to Guðrøð, the district king there. Ása, whose ruthlessness equaled her father's, then despatched both her husband and his brother as part of a plan to secure the Danish throne for herself and Ingjald. Here, however, the chain of violence and betrayal finally rebounded, for the last Danish heir, Ívar Widefathomer, son of her husband's brother, rallied an army and proceeded against Ása and Ingjald, whom he surprised at Rœning. Surrounded and outnumbered, father and daughter concluded that resistance, escape, and surrender were all of them impossible. Accordingly, "They got the people dead drunk, after which they had fire set to the hall. The hall burnt up, as did all the people that were in it, including King Ingjald."[21]

Here, it is worth contemplating Ingjald's position in the Yngling line. As we saw, that dynasty began with a period of glory, when kings from Óðinn through Agni ruled all of Sweden. After Agni's death, however, Yngling power declined and devolved to an ever-growing number of petty district kings. The initial phase of Ingjald's reign reversed this process of entropy and fragmentation. Through his campaign of treacherous violence, he reconsolidated royal power and reunited the nation, but his triumph was short lived and ironic. For his death marked a second rupture, after which the realm passed to Ívar Widefathomer—a Scylding and not an Yngling—from whom descended all subsequent kings of Sweden and Denmark.[22] After the debacle at Rœning, Ingjald's son was forced to flee, "because all the common people of Sweden rose up with a single accord to reject the lineage of King Ingjald."[23] With a small group of followers, he first went southwest to Næríki, then left Sweden altogether, journeying across the marches to Vermaland, an interstitial territory between Sweden and Norway (fig. 10.1). Here, he cleared forests to create dwelling space, earning the epithet "Olaf Treecutter" (Óláfr trételgja) in the process, and establishing himself as a district king in this novel terrain (fig. 10.2).

FIGURE 10.1: Migration of the Ynglings from Uppsala, their traditional capital in Uppland, southwest to Vermaland on the border of Sweden and Norway. From *Fagrskinna, a Catalogue of the Kings of Norway*, a translation with introduction and notes by Alison Finlay (Leiden: Brill 2004). © Copyright 2004 by Koninklijke Brill NV, Leiden, The Netherlands.

Virtually all sources treat Olaf as the trailblazer who brought his people into new lands after the Danes drove them out of Sweden.[24] Heimskringla is unique, however, in treating Ingjald's monstrous villainy as the cause of these events. Most other texts that speak of Ingjald emphasize his weakness and fear and have nothing that associates him with ambition, ruthlessness, or unbridled aggression. Consider, for instance, the way he is depicted in Historia Norwegiæ.

> After that, [Önund's] son Ingjald was elevated to the kingship. He was fearful beyond measure of King Ívar Widefathomer, who at that time was terrifying to many. Ingjald burned himself to death, together with all his retinue, whom he enclosed in his banquet hall.[25]

Both Historia Norwegiæ and Heimskringla worked with the same account of Ingjald's immolation that they found in Ynglingatal, which they

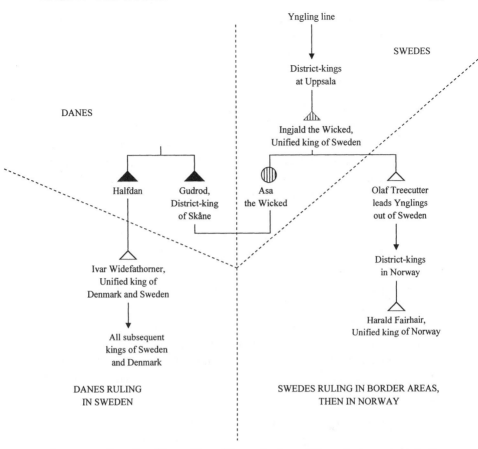

FIGURE 10.2: Formation of the royal lines of Norway, Sweden, and Denmark, as recounted in Ynglingasaga 39–42. Fully shaded areas indicate those killed by Ingjald and Ása. Lined areas indicate those who killed themselves, rather than submit to Ívar Widefathomer.

developed in very different ways. Heimskringla's portrait of Ingjald's vicious-ness and treachery, and also its description of the oath he swore at the start of his reign, seems to have been carefully crafted to resonate with later events: not only Harald Fairhair's state-founding conquests—that much is obvi-ous—but also Norway's designs on Iceland in the mid-thirteenth century. Thus, through the story of Ingjald, the text argued that national unification under a single monarch was a project that could be accomplished only by violence and treachery, and that a king capable of this project was a wolf-hearted miscreant, situated halfway between man and beast. Beyond this, it suggested that the violence of state formation and expansionist ambitions could be expected to prompt reactions. Those who establish their rule by killing their rivals, taking their lands, and imposing their will (along with

their taxes) will not prosper forever, but provoke resentment that will inevitably rebound on them and/or their progeny. Ingjald's suicidal self-
immolation is the image that clinches the argument: both in the short and
the long term, the wicked king is author of the violence of which he is also
the victim.

Finally, in its shift to Olaf Treecutter, the story suggested that state formation drives some hardy and desperate souls to abandon their homeland.
Here, it is important to notice that the final sections of Ynglingasaga and all
subsequent books of Heimskringla followed the Ynglings in their Norwegian
diaspora, rather than focusing on the new line of kings that Ívar founded in
Sweden. The text thus becomes the history of a lineage and an institution, not
that of a nation or a territory.

Beyond this, the text introduced a new and suggestive set of associations
to complement those it had already developed. In its emplotment and thematization of Ingjald's life and deeds, Ynglingasaga consistently, if implicitly, made them transparent to Harald Fairhair. Once Ingjald was dead, it
entertained a second, less thorough, line of comparison, with Ívar Widefathomer and Harald as its points of reference, insofar as both men succeeded—in contrast to Ingjald—in unifying a nation, founding a state, and
establishing a dynasty. The point of this comparison was not to recuperate
Harald by acknowledging his achievements, but to frame a complex analogy,
the terms of which are as follows:

> Ívar Widefathomer : Olaf Treecutter
> :: Dynasty-founder : Emigrant and innovator ::
> :: End of the past, : Beginning of the future,
> which has no further interest   which holds all importance
> :: Harald Fairhair : Icelandic *landnámsmenn.*

Neither Ingjald nor Ívar is the hero of Ynglingasaga, as the former is a
brute, and the latter, an outsider. Having denounced Ingjald and revealed his
failings, the saga has no interest in the Scylding who now sits on the throne in
Uppsala. The hero it follows is Olaf, who leads his people westward, through
difficult times and harsh terrain, so that they can rebuild on new soil the kind
of life they knew and valued.

In similar fashion, Heimskringla subtextually managed to suggest that
the real heroes of the state-founding story were not Harald, Gyða, Rögnvald,
Guthorm, Hálfdan, or any of the others who fought to unite Norway under
the power of one conquering king. Rather, these people were simultaneously
villains, accomplices, and victims, who put a terrible system in place and
set violent deeds in motion, usually to their own detriment as well as that

of others. The narrative's heroes are those who emigrated rather than accept Harald's rule and the consequences of their defeat. These were Iceland's founding fathers (*landnámsmenn*, lit. "the men who took the land"), who created a polity where law, rather than king, kingship, nation, or state, was the central institution.[26] While they figure less prominently in Heimskringla than does King Harald, they still manage to haunt his story.

Conclusions

I

There are further episodes we could consider, all of which would be instructive. The story of Hálfdan's parentage, birth, and accession, for instance, is sufficiently rich and fascinating to deserve a book to itself, for it appears he was a usurper whom skalds and historians skillfully sutured to the Yngling line.[1] Certain incidents in Harald's campaigns of conquest would also reward close study, like King Hrollaug of Naumdal's decision to demote himself in literal fashion, rolling down from his royal high seat to the lower seat of an earl, rather than face Shaggy Harald in battle.[2] At a certain point, however, it becomes apparent that there is no convenient point of closure. The characters keep multiplying, the plot keeps ramifying, and every incident connects to others. Although one surely would like to complete the job, that goal keeps receding, *and that is just the point.* It seems that narratives meant to stabilize state institutions and secure the political order are themselves profoundly unstable. Why should this be so? Do they suffer from some inevitable and inescapable contradiction? Have they been set an impossible task?

Few things are so unstable as the past, which survives and persists—to the extent that it does—at first through memory and then, after a relatively short time, through stories that are told and retold. Whatever importance an event may have had in its own proper moment interacts with and ultimately yields to the importance accorded it in subsequent retellings and to the importance those narratives acquire in their own moments and contexts.

The more important such a story is—or becomes—to any given group, the more often it will be retold, repetition being an index of its importance, as well as an instrument through which that importance is reasserted and renewed. Another index of importance is the degree of elaboration a narrative acquires over the course of its retellings, for when a story matters deeply, none of its details are trivial. Each piece, no matter how small, does work of some sort or another, establishing some point, influencing some judgment, or adding some nuance to an audience's impressions. Every narrator is thus obliged to treat these details with care, although "care" need not imply fidelity. Thus, some narrators will use their skill to modify certain details, innovating even—perhaps especially—in stories that represent themselves as traditional accounts of well-known historical events. What prompts such interventions is not some drive to explore a full range of logical permutations, still less a sense of narrative play and aesthetic pleasure, as certain theorists would have it. Rather, revision and modification reflect the fact that a great deal is at stake and one gains control over the narrative by controlling the way it is told.

Narrators never achieve total control, however, for stories do not belong exclusively to those who tell them. Rather, every retelling is suspended between narrator and audience, reflecting the interests of both. Variants thus reflect not only narrators' interests and situation of interest, but also their expectations and calculations considering the interests (and situation of interest) of the audience they hope to engage. Conversely, in reception the hearers selectively rework the story they have heard to make it better engage and reflect their actual—and not simply their presumed—interests and situation of interest, toward which end they ignore some details and focus on others, while creatively misapprehending others still. In doing so, they take possession of the story, making it more theirs and less the narrator's. And should they choose to retell it, they will put the same processes into play with those who become their audience.

Every retelling thus reflects not only the interests of the narrator, but also the strategic and tactical decisions s/he makes with the hope of (*a*) engaging a certain audience; (*b*) persuading it of certain things; (*c*) reshaping its attitudes and consciousness by so doing (even if this involves nothing more than reinforcing the views and dispositions it already holds); and (*d*) competing successfully against rival narrators, the rival interests those narrators represent, and the rival variants of the story through which rival narrators seek to advance their rival interests. Audiences, conversely, pay selective attention to stories in the degree that these actually engage their interests, and they reshape a narrative's content so that those interests are better served. Each detail thus is—or can become—a skirmish site in this field of battle.

Unless all narrators and all audiences come to share the same interests and the same identical perspective (a condition that can never be realized), so long as they regard a given set of events as important, they will recount them in different ways, and every moderately successful iteration of the story will prompt novel and rival retellings. Only when the story no longer engages strong interest can this process finally cease. Even then, the process of telling and retelling, hearing, rethinking, and retelling once more is one that never ceases, although it may move to other episodes or stories when old ones have seemingly been drained of interest.

The medieval Scandinavian data we have considered provide a good demonstration of such processes. There, establishment of the Norwegian monarchic state in the mid-ninth century by King Harald was among the events most often narrated. Early variants of the story took the form of skaldic poems, some of which have been preserved, and oral traditions that have been lost, although one perceives their influence in later retellings that were committed to writing. Over time, narrators of different statuses, nationalities, and interests repeated the story and introduced novel characters, episodes, subplots, intertextual allusions, and subtextual suggestions for one purpose or another. Once introduced, these details spread, as other variants sought to engage, advance, rebut, appropriate, and/or modify them.

Among the first details to make its appearance was the fact that early in his career, the state-founding king bore the epithet "Shaggy," in which form he became a terror to his neighbors. This is already attested in poems more or less contemporary with the events themselves, composed by Harald's own skalds, as in this stanza composed by Thorbjorn Hornklofi:

> The thick-necked prince
> Let an island serve as a shield for himself
> As he tired of holding
> His land against Shaggy.
> Those who were wounded
> Withdrew under bench planks,
> Let their rumps stick up,
> But thrust their heads into the hold.[3]

Prose versions of Harald's story began to be written only in the twelfth century, both in Norway and Iceland. The earliest variants are brief, and only one of them (Ágrip) gestures toward the tradition that contrasts a "Shaggy" king to his "Fair-Haired" successor. It does so, however, in extremely gentle and circumspect ways, avoiding any details that might suggest that the Harald who created the Norwegian state did so as a monster or beast.

> He was made sole king. He was then called "Shaggy Harald," because the man was not then fair haired. But thereafter, his name was changed and he was called Harald Fairhair, because he was the most handsome and best haired of men.[4]

What Ágrip reports is the process of euphemization that sought to clean up potentially embarassing details. In so doing, it acknowledges that Harald was once known as "Shaggy," but its primary interest is to insist that his name and his appearance changed in the course of his reign. One senses a suggestion that his nature and behavior also changed and became more "fair," but that is never openly articulated. To make the point effectively, one would have to acknowledge that in his earlier years, the monarch was rougher and his conduct more repulsive, but on these topics the text prefers to remain silent. That which the text reports—the discursive consolidation of power, which involves renaming some things while erasing others—is also that which it does.

Only in one of the Norwegian Kings' Sagas—Fagrskinna, written some decades after the others—is Harald's oath explicitly mentioned, and there it is treated in two different ways. One manuscript (the older, so-called B-Text) describes the king's pledge not to cut his hair until he conquers and unites the nation. This variant contains a hint of what the oath entails, for it acknowledges Harald's intention to extract tax and tribute from the territories he will conquer and concludes, "After that, there were many battles for a long while."[5] The other Fagrskinna variant (that of the later, so-called A-Text) ignores such things altogether. Instead, it has Harald pledge he will have no other wife than the one who suggested he conquer all Norway and that he will accomplish that task for her sake.[6] Clearly, this constituted an attempt to rebut variants of the story produced by Icelandic authors for antimonarchic audiences, in which Harald took inspiration for his state-building project from Gyða, a brilliant and beautiful woman whom he later betrayed. At the same time, Fagrskinna A is concerned to rebut the charge that Harald sought to enslave his opponents (literally, to make them his thralls, Old Norse þræll).[7] In contrast, in this text's version of the oath, he swears to make all Norwegians his *subjects*, pointedly using a term that signals their free and dignified status (Old Norse þegn).[8]

In general, the Icelandic sources were considerably longer and more elaborate than their Norwegian counterparts. They were also more aggressive and critical in their treatment of Harald's story, making particularly effective use of the oath and the contrast of "Shaggy" and "Fairhair" that it introduced. Delighting in the possibilities this *topos* opened up, they introduced characters and episodes—Gyða and her father, Rögnvald and his sons, Guthorm and Ragnhild, Dofri and his cave, Hálfdan's aborted banquet and his last ride—that let them call attention to problematic aspects of the king's state-building project. In contrast, the Norwegian sources either omitted these episodes and details or engaged them in defensive fashion.

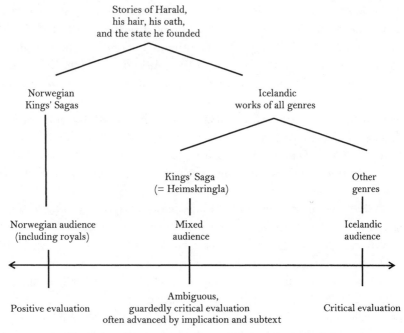

Norwegian
Kings' Sagas

Icelandic
works of all genres

Stories of Harald,
his hair, his oath,
and the state he founded

Kings' Saga
(= Heimskringla)

Other
genres

Norwegian audience
(including royals)

Mixed
audience

Icelandic
audience

Positive evaluation

Ambiguous,
guardedly critical evaluation
often advanced by implication and subtext

Critical evaluation

FIGURE 11.1: Distribution of texts, authors, audiences, attitudes, and styles in relation to one another.

Although an author's nationality helped determine the interests of a given text, it was not the sole causal factor. Also important were two considerations that interacted with each other: the national identity of the text's anticipated audience and the genre in which it was written. Thus, Kings' Sagas, whether written by a Norwegian or an Icelander, a cleric or a layman, would be read with interest by Norwegians, including the king and his court. Works in other genres—Sagas of Icelanders (*Íslendingasǫgur*), Fabulous Stories of Ancient Times (*Fornaldarsǫgur*), and Short Tales (*þættir*) had no such expectations. Written by and primarily for Icelanders, these could be more open in their sallies against kings, kingship, and the state-founding hero who introduced them. Works like Egil's Saga or the *Saga of King Harald, Dofri's Foster Son could engage in blunt denunciations and satiric play. In contrast, Heimskringla, a comprehensive Kings' Saga written by an Icelander, had to be more discreet, which meant it also became more ambiguous, intricate, allusive, and indirect, more subject to internal contradiction, and much more shrewd in advancing its line of critique.

The field of relations—and field of struggle—among these texts is as represented in figure 11.1.

II

Just what kind of texts have we been considering? What tasks do these texts undertake and make their own? Why is it they tell these stories? What assumptions, methods, and ethics guide them in the way they make use of their sources? What claims to truth (accuracy, completeness, fairness, e.g.) do they customarily make? Are they best regarded as history or myth? Or is this distinction exogenous, anachronistic, and irrelevant?

Two of the texts—the earliest ones, which were written in Latin and produced by clerical authors—title themselves histories (*historia*), and both contain serious prologues that address some of the questions we are raising. Theodricus Monachus thus begins his History of the Antiquity of Norwegian Kings (Historia de Antiquitate Regum Norwagiensium) by addressing his patron, Eysteinn Erlendsson, chief prelate of the Norwegian Church from 1161 to 1188.

> To his lord and father, the most reverend man Eysteinn, Archbishop of Niðaros, the humble sinner Theodricus (offers) the submission owed by a servant and the tribute of his prayers. I considered it worthy labor, most illustrious sir, briefly to record these few things concerning the antiquity of Norwegian kings, as we have been able to learn most accurately from those among whom memory is believed to thrive especially well, that is, those whom we call Icelanders, who recall these much-repeated things in their ancient songs. And because almost no nation is so wild and uncivilized that it did not transmit some monuments of its predecessors to its descendants, I deemed it proper to hand down these remembrances of our ancestors for posterity, granting that they are few. But because it is certain that no sure succession of the royal line existed in this land before the time of Harald Fairhair, we take our beginning from him.[9]

Several things are noteworthy in this remarkable passage. First, the author expresses profound humility—whether sincere or formulaic and conventional—about the extent of his knowledge and the magnitude of his accomplishment. Twice he characterizes the things he has to recount as regrettably few (*pauca*). As he defines his task, it is one of collection, preservation, and transmission, and he understands this as a minimal mark and instrument of civilization, for only the rudest savages fail to do so (those who belong to a *natio . . . rudis et inculta*).

That which is to be transmitted plays a crucial role in the construction of a people's collective identity and its reproduction over time. All peoples convey "some monuments of their predecessors to their descendants" (*aliqua monumenta suorum antecessorum ad posteros*). Similarly, Theodricus understands his work as a service to the nation, as indicated by his use of the first person plural when he speaks of his desire to hand down "remembrances of *our* ancestors for posterity" (*majorum **nostrorum** memoriæ posteritatis tradere*). To gain dependable knowledge, however, Theodricus has been forced to go outside of Norway, for the Norwegian people apparently have not preserved these traditions (whence the need for his researches). Accordingly, he has consulted the wise men of Iceland, commonly understood as the north's foremost specialists in memory,[10] who preserve knowledge of the past by constant repetition of well-known events (*percelebrata*) in their traditional poems (*suis antiquis carminibus*), and the verb Theodricus employs (*recolunt*) has a wide semantic range including acts of recollection, renewal, revisitation, and—most literally—recultivation, in both botanic and cultural senses.[11] By constant repetition of their poems, Icelandic skalds and sages thus cultivate and recultivate the field of collective memory so that knowledge of the same historical events keeps sprouting in each generation. It is exposure to these poems, then, that makes Icelanders *cultured* and *cultivated* (both derived from *colō*) in the most literal sense.

On the face of it, Theodricus would seem to be a scrupulous historian, concerned to recover knowledge of the past from the most reliable sources through a process of rigorous inquiry (*sagaciter perquirere*); to transmit that knowledge so that future generations will remember and appreciate their ancestors' deeds; and to record the few things that can be known with certainty (*pauca . . . breviter annotare*), while introducing nothing new. There are, however, three places where the monk undercuts his historical principles and practice. First, he mistakes the history of kings for that of the nation (is it really "our" history or only the history of "our kings"?). Second, in his search for knowledge of the deeper past, he depends on Icelanders, who were not only outsiders (is it still "our" history if we get it from "them"?), but of all outsiders, the ones most hostile to kings, kingship, and Harald Fairhair above all. Third, their reputation for historical knowledge so impresses Theodricus that he takes Icelanders to be supremely reliable in their transmission of the past, severely underestimating the extent to which Icelandic discourse could also be supple, innovative, strategic, and tendentious.

Caught in a situation where he was forced to depend on sources who may not be dependable, Theodricus adopted two defensive strategies. First, he said very little. The totality of his report on King Harald consists of two sentences.

> In the year 858 from the incarnation of our Lord, Harald Fairhair, son of Hálf-
> dan the Black, began his reign. He first drove out all petty kings and gained
> sole rule over all Norway for seventy years, and [then] he died.[12]

Having advanced a relatively small number of factual propositions (a
name, a date, parentage, military and political success, length of reign), Theodricus immediately backtracks on one of them and airs his epistemological concerns about the pastness—and thus the ultimate unknowability—of
the past, while also fretting about the reliability of Icelanders, who may be
the best available experts, but who still cannot know all that they claim. The
short passage just cited continues as follows:

> The number of years of our Lord was researched as diligently as we were
> able among those whom we call in our language by the name Icelanders. It
> is known beyond any doubt that they have always been the most curious and
> best trained of all the northern people in such things. But it is exceedingly
> difficult in such things to comprehend the elusive truth, especially where the
> authority of writings offers no help.[13]

III

Because he is, in fact, such a responsible historian, Theodricus tells very little
and warns against fully trusting the little he tells. He is also the only author we
have considered who took full responsibility for his text by placing his name
on it alongside that of his patron. And since the monk Theodore wrote for
an archbishop, the milieu is clearly that of the Norwegian Church, connected
but not identical to the milieu of the court and the king.[14] Historia Norwegiæ
and Ágrip are similar in this, and they share the general character of Theodricus's text, although they each expand a bit on the spare narrative he offers.
For its part, Historia Norwegiæ maintains an entirely favorable portrait of
King Harald, and Ágrip begins in similar fashion but includes a long excursus, describing Harald's dubious affair with Snæfrið, following folklore of the
Trondheim area and a poem on the topic attributed to Harald himself.[15]

This story seems to have circulated widely, and in some variants it reflected badly not only on Harald, but on all Norwegian kings after 1045. For
from that date onward, they all traced their line of descent to Harald via his
marriage to Snæfrið, the "Finnish" (i.e., Saami) sorceress who so bewitched
him (literally and figuratively) that he abandoned his kingly duties for her.
Even after she died, Snæfrið's uncanny hold persisted, and the king continued to adore her corpse, until others helped break the spell.[16] Ágrip seemingly

included the story in order to control its damage, not through denial, but by guiding the tale to a happy ending.

Toward that end, the text introduces a character we have met elsewhere: Thorleif the Prophetically-Gifted, the man who taught Hálfdan the Black how to dream (above, chap. 6), who is here enlisted to rescue poor Harald. Once relieved of his magically induced obsession, the king is then depicted as having drawn important lessons that made him a model ruler for the rest of his long, happy reign.

> Snæfrið sank into ash, but the king rose to wisdom and abandoned his folly. Thereafter, he governed his realm and strengthened it. He took pleasure from his subjects, his subjects from him, and the realm from them both. He ruled over Norway as sole king for sixty years thereafter.[17]

Fagrskinna, the last of the comprehensive Kings' Sagas to be written in Norway, goes further still. Its praise for the ruler's virtues is copious and varied. Not only his conquests and physical beauty, but also his kindness and generosity (*mildi*), wisdom (*speki*), eloquence (*fagrmæli*), royal majesty (*konunglig tign*), even his sense of humor,[18] are all singled out for admiring comment, and long passages of skaldic poetry are quoted to confirm the text's construction of him as an ideal ruler. Additions to a later redaction (the A-Text) fend off criticism embedded in the Gyða narrative, as we saw in chapter 2, and go on to construe Harald as a champion of law, a respectful lover, a pioneer of women's rights, and a religious visionary who renounced sacrifice to all deities, save the Creator.[19]

Fagrskinna goes far beyond its predecessors in the variety and the extent of its advocacy for King Harald, and it is not hard to understand why. Whereas Theodricus Monachus, Historia Norwegiæ, and Ágrip all were written within clerical milieux, Fagrskinna was apparently written for King Hákon Hákonarson (r. 1217–63).[20] In all likelihood, this was the very text Hákon had read to him as he lay on his deathbed[21] and inferential evidence suggests he played a strong hand in the way it was written.[22] The master narrative it offered was meant to serve the interests of the crown, and that narrative began with the epoch-ending death of Hálfdan the Black and the ascent of Harald Fairhair, blameless founder of an ideal state.

Fagrskinna thus constitutes an official history in a way that its predecessors do not. It is written at the behest of the same institution it describes, and its project is one of celebration, advocacy, and apologetics (in the theological sense). While the early histories, written within an ecclesiastical context, normally treat the king and kingship with high respect, they do not offer the same high level of praise, nor do they engage in the kind of elaboration, invention, and defensive maneuvering that Fagrskinna does in the service of King Harald's reputation. The ideal of the earlier historians' practice is succinctly summarized in the prologue to Historia Norwegiæ, where the author tells his (ecclesiastical) patron:[23] "I have added nothing new or unheard-of from the oldest chain of transmission, but in all things have followed the statements of elders."[24] This claim may have been disingenuous, and his practice may well have fallen short of the ideal, but it is still surely the case that clerical authors writing for clerical patrons told the story of state origins in much more restrained and disciplined fashion than did Fagrskinna, a product of state patronage and thus written by, for, and about the state.

Clearly, Fagrskinna sought to advance state interests, projecting the state's ideal image of itself, its origins, essential purpose and nature. The text also responded to those who told versions of "the same story" in ways that undercut the state's goals, threatened its control, and wounded its pride (which means it was not "the same story" at all). Such variants came from Iceland, where many of them circulated. Some such texts have survived ("Tale of Hálfdan the Black," "Tale of Harald Fairhair," Heimskringla, Egil's Saga, and chapters in several other sagas of the Icelanders), while some have not (*Saga of King Harald, Dofri's Foster Son, *Turf-Einar's Saga), and some oral traditions never assumed written form. Some of these were fairly open in their denunciation, while others were more circumspect. But all proceded in much the same manner, embedding their critique in details of the story they told. These are not works of political philosophy, moral exhortation, or abstract reflection. Rather, like the official histories against which they struggled, these are exercises in historical revisionism: attempts to sway opinion and shape consciousness by the way they narrate significant events of the past, accepting (*a*) that these events happened, (*b*) that one can know them, and (*c*) that their details have continuing importance in and for the present.

IV

As we saw, the earliest authors who committed Harald's story to writing did so in Latin and they titled their works *Historia*. Later authors wrote in the vernacular, however, and called their texts *Saga* (if they were long) or *þáttr* (if they were short). Neither of these terms is a precise equivalent of the Latin, or of its cognates in the later Scandinavian languages (Danish *historie*, Norwegian *historie*, Swedish *historia*, Icelandic *historia*). Most literally, *saga* means "that which is said," being derived from the verb "to say" (Old Norse *segja*), much as English *tale* comes from the verb "to tell."[25] The standard dictionary goes on about this at considerable length.

SAGA, **A story, tale, legend, history.** The very word owes its origin to the fact that the first historical writings were founded on tradition only; the written record was a "saga" or legend committed to writing; the story thus written was not even new, but had already taken shape and had been told to many generations under the same name; hence the written history and the story told were both alike called Saga, just as in Greek both were called λόγος (Herodotus 1.184, 2.161, 6.19).[26]

As a category and genre, saga thus hovers between orality and text, past and present, stability and flux, preservation and innovation. The term *þáttr* is more poetic but less rich in its core meaning, as it denotes a single strand, whether of yarn or narrative. In the latter case, it can stand on its own or serve as one of the elements from which a broader web of story is woven. *þáttr* thus denotes something like a short story or tale, but it can also be a chapter in a larger work. Nowhere, however, does the indigenous terminology correspond neatly to any of the lexemes we normally use to classify discourses that speak of (putative) events in the (putative) past that had some (putative) importance. Words like "myth," "legend," "testimonial," and "history" are our terms, and the distinctions among them reflect our values, habits, ethics of research and narration, and principles of reception. Ultimately, the question of whether Harald Fairhair's Saga is history, myth, or something in between is *our* question, but that does not make it an idle or foolish question, or one with a simple answer. Better still is the question of what we can learn about the contrast we are accustomed to draw between "history" and "myth" from the story—no, from the variant tellings of "the story"—of Harald, his oath, and his founding of the Norwegian state.

This question holds interest for me because of a flippant sentence I wrote in a moment of weakness. It stands as the culminating argument in my book on myth and it probably has been cited more often than anything else I have written: "If myth is ideology in narrative form, then scholarship is myth with footnotes."[27] This is not quite Napoleon's dictum "History is an agreed-upon fable,"[28] or John Ford's "When the legend becomes fact, print the legend,"[29] but like these bons mots it was meant to point up the fluidity, porosity, and arbitrary nature of the categories under discussion, while problematizing the privilege accorded the one, by virtue of its contrast to the other. My study of the materials presented in this book was prompted by a resolve to do better, and it has permitted me to draw some more nuanced—if less epigrammatic—conclusions.

Within the broad category of narrative, I would suggest that a fundamental distinction separates those that purport to represent significant pieces of the past with seriousness, responsibility, and fidelity from those that acknowledge themselves as primarily exercises of the imagination: fiction ≠ nonfiction. Within the latter category, one can further distinguish two ideal types, one of which—the one we tend to call "myth"—tends to reach deeper into the past, concerning itself with the time of origins, foundations, creation. It also frequently (but not always) admits nonhuman actors and agency, including gods, spirits, animals, and other exotics, including ancestors of humanity who are not yet subject to all the limitations of our species. Again, this category usually claims for itself more than simple truth, constituting itself as a paradigmatic model for proper existence, always valid, always authoritative, always demanding of deep respect. Further, this category permits itself more imaginative flights of fancy than does its counterpart, acknowledging—at least in some variants—that the truths it conveys may be of a metaphoric, poetic, structural-logical, or theo-logical sort, not being willing to limit itself to truths of a literal nature. Finally, stories in this category frequently make strong claims for their own origin, authority, and status, constituting themselves as timeless ancestral tradition, wisdom of the ages, or the product of revelation, for example. Stories of this subcategory can devolve toward the fictive, even while maintaining their self-conscious posture of conveying deep truths about the most significant and consequential events of the past.

Analysis ought not to stop at this point, however, and one can make further distinctions within the other subcategory of nonfictive accounts, which we normally dub "history." First, I would distinguish official history from other, more critical forms. Diagnostic of the official form of "true story" is a knot of relations that bind the narrator to a patron and to a set of events in the past that must be narrated in a particular way in order to best serve the patron's present interests. All of this influences the details that are included or excluded and the way the former are treated. Insofar as their patrons include society's wealthiest and most powerful institutions (state, church, noble families, grant-making foundations, e.g.), official histories often bear impressive authorizing imprimaturs and find it relatively easy to find their way into prestigious venues and influential genres, thereby establishing themselves as the orthodoxy against which any alternative has to struggle. The authors of official history tell their story with great confidence, and the stories they tell are often larger than life, filled with noble characters, heroic actions, and messages of lasting value, all read out of—or into—their accounts of "our founding fathers" (to cite a familiar example). In all these ways, official history tends to devolve toward myth.

Regrettably, so too do many of the attempts at critical history, which set themselves in opposition to the ideological hegemony of official history, with all of its pretentions, manipulations, exaggeration, obfuscation, sanitizing, euphemizing, and sanctimonious, self-interested preaching. Thus, one form of critical history—the one I would characterize as revisionist—seeks to beat the official version at its own game by retelling a familiar story in novel ways that change its details to foster interpretations and advance interests that are different from those of the standard account. There is much to like and admire about revisionist retellings, which can be exceptionally inventive and audacious, while also showing shrewd tactical acumen. Insisting on the false teeth of a man famed for never lying, for instance, complicates and destabilizes his story, making it difficult—if not impossible—to perpetuate the unspoken assumption that the country he founded maintains his absolute and unwavering commitment to truth. History as told by revisionists thus differs from that of official historians, in substance as in style. The one tends to be preachy, smug and sanctimonious; the other can also feel self-righteous, but it also frequently involves some measure of malicious fun. Above all, the two differ in the specific interests they serve. Official history tends to legitimate, stabilize, and naturalize things as they are, thereby helping the advantaged consolidate and preserve their advantage. Revisionist history tries to destabilize, afflicting the comfortable and comforting the afflicted. The two modes resemble each other, however, in their understanding that stories about the past have such profound implications for the world of the present that one handles the details of such stories in ways that will help create—or preserve—the kind of world one desires. This is a crucial point of historical ethics and teleology, and on both counts revisionist histories, like their official counterparts, frequently devolve toward myth.

There is, however, a second form of critical history that maintains a principled distance not only from fiction, myth, and official history, but from revisionism as well. This is the kind of storytelling that self-consciously emphasizes the gap separating the present from the past, taking note of how much has been irretrievably lost, and stressing the unsatisfactory, lacunary, and potentially misleading nature of the slender and always tendentious sources on which we rely when attempting to conjure up some vision of "what actually happened." Critique founded on epistemological doubt, evidentiary inadequacy, and scholarly humility, it seems to me, is that form of narrative least inclined to stray toward the mythic (fig. 11.2).

As sagas and *þættir*, the stories we have been discussing fit imperfectly into the ideal-type categories just sketched, which are grounded in considerations of our own culture and historical moment. It is thus interesting to note that they fit much more easily into the middle categories than to those at the extremes of the system. Thus, although texts like Barð's Saga, the *Saga of King Harald, Dofri's Foster Son, or Heimskringla's variant of Hálfdan's death may

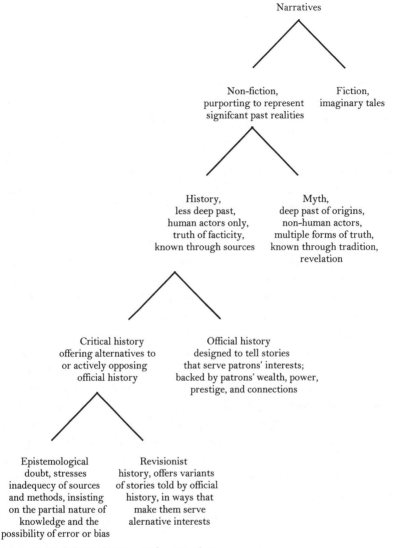

FIGURE 11.2: Ideal-typical taxonomy of narrative forms.

contain strong elements of myth (supernatural actors, uncanny occurences, moments when new eras come into being), they are all more concerned to defeat and deflate other variants and the interests those serve than to establish strong claims for themselves as essential truths and paradigms for present existence. Thus, they are more accurately described as devolving toward the mythic than as themselves constituting myths in any strict sense.

Similarly, a text like Theodricus Monachus has certain clear affinities with critical histories grounded in epistemological doubt, including its caution, reserve, and such aspects of its humility that are honest and principled, not just conventional and affected. These manifest themselves, however, chiefly in the text's relative modesty, its unwillingness to tell things of which it does not feel sure, and its moments of open self-doubt. Admirable though these might be, the critical impulse that animates Theodricus is directed exclusively inward, constraining his ability to tell much of a story and never polemically mobilized against other, less scrupulous authors and variants that have no qualms about guesswork, exaggeration, and embellishment but are willing to exploit whatever pieces of the narrative can be made to serve their purpose, while projecting absolute confidence in the veracity of their version. Although his text devolves toward critical history of epistemological doubt, it really is better characterized as official history that is crippled in some measure by its author's self-consciousness, integrity, and sincere humility.

Virtually all the variants we have studied are thus best regarded as either official or revisionist histories, with the understanding that some of them involve official revisions of a story that are designed to disarm revisionist sallies or, alternatively, revisionist responses to official counterrevisions. Once their conflict is joined, the two types are locked in ongoing competition for the attention and credence of audiences.

The way variants fall out along the categorical divide between official and revisionist histories in our data set is as clear as it is instructive. Without exception, those variants produced in Norway are best understood as official histories: Fagrskinna most fully so and Theodricus Monachus least, with Historia Norwegiæ and Ágrip falling somewhere in between. Conversely, the Icelandic variants are all revisionist in varying degrees. They range from the open, fierce, and confrontational style of Egil's Saga to the subtleties and complex veiling of Heimskringla, and the difference seems to correlate with the extent to which they addressed an exclusively Icelandic and nationalist audience or that to which they also directed themselves to Norwegian readers.

Over the course of the time these texts were written—from 1180 (Theodricus Monachus, Historia Norwegiæ) or thereabouts to about 1240 (Text A of Fagrskinna)—the debate heats up between official and critical variants, and narrators strive not only to tell versions of the story that will serve their interests (or those of their patrons), but also to make these versions more engaging, more appealing, more popular than those told by their rivals. The stories become richer, fuller, more dramatic, and more gripping. Their characters become grander (in the case of official histories), more outsized and obvious in their flaws (in revisionist versions); episodes multiply and become more impressive or more scurrilous, but in either case more inventive and more riveting. In all these ways, there is a Darwinian coevolution toward narratives that are livelier, more audacious, more engaging, and more successful in their manipulation of their audiences' sympathies, beliefs, and consciousness in general. The stories become better and better, culminating in the extraordinary accomplishments of Heimskringla. And in the course of this progress toward ever-better stories, both official and revisionist histories devolve ever further toward myth.

Victory in the competition does not always go to the variant that best serves powerful interests, or to that which adopts any particular voice or genre. Sometimes it is comedy, sometimes tragedy, sometimes epic, farce, fairy tale, or picaresque that prevails, sometimes even a moral fable. Few generalizations are possible, save, perhaps, that the more scrupulous a variant is, the less likely its triumph. No one finds much interest or pleasure in Theodricus Monachus's spare remarks or in his self-conscious hand-wringing about the reliability of dates. No one, perhaps, save other historians, who may take him as a model of integrity. Most of the other variants we have considered are also largely forgotten to all save specialists and antiquarians. In contrast, Heimskringla—the version that is most muddled, complex, contradictory in its politics and moral judgment, but richest in its storytelling—not only endures, but has achieved classic status and eclipsed all others.

There is a logic to this and lessons to be learned, even if those lessons offend one's sense of ideal justice. Thus, the more honestly a historical account talks about the process of its own formation, acknowledging the difficulties it faced and the gaps in its knowledge, the less effectively it can engage and move an audience or (re-)shape collective memory. The sole utility of such an account is to act as a brake or check on less responsible variants of "the same story," but that is hardly a negligible contribution.

Conversely, the more a variant is willing to embroider, to invent lively episodes and outsized characters, to emplot its action in dramatic fashion and to guide it toward a denouement the audience will find gratifying, the more memorable—and therefore more effective—it becomes.

This is not as it should be. In an ideal world, at least the world I would like to imagine, official histories ought to be vanquished by revisionisms, and revisionisms ought to yield to epistemological doubt. The past would then become an object occasioning curiosity and respect, but also frustration, doubt, and reserve, and as a corollary, stories about the past would serve less well as instruments of power and fields of contestation. In the world we inhabit, however—a world that did not originate with Hollywood, talk radio, high school textbooks, and Fox News—this is not the case. The more a variant veers toward myth, the better become its chances.

A Reader Reflects

I

Conventional views of Heimskringla and the other comprehensive Kings'
Sagas normally identify their master narrative as that of Norway's progress
toward a medieval model of perfection in which the unified monarchic state
was established by Harald Fairhair, then the Christian religion by St. Olaf.
Such a reading is accurate and true enough, but it is also partial, focusing on
certain aspects of a larger, more complicated whole.

Toward the beginning of our inquiry, I suggested that reading the sagas of
the long-haired state founder and his father, Hálfdan the Black, could modify
that picture, provided the readings were close and critical enough. Subsequent chapters of this book pursued that project, giving particular attention
to two incidents at the heart of the narrative: Hálfdan's death and Harald's
oath. Collectively, these inquiries uncovered a pattern whereby certain variants worked a distinctly critical perspective into their tellings of the story,
portraying the state-founding Noble Heathen as dependent on women he
exploited and betrayed; a destroyer of prestate institutions, including marriage, family, aristocracy, property, and law; an unscrupulous, violent, and
vengeful man; and a willful child who flirted with giants, criminals, and ma-
gicians to cause his father's ignominious death. That death, moreover, is portrayed as having thrown existence into chaos, after which a new world and a
whole set of new institutions came into being. These institutions, moreover,
bear the same ambiguity as their founder, for one can read kingship, kingdom, nation, and state as noble and glorious, or as sinister, cunning, violent,
unscrupulous, and oppressive. In this, they are much like Harald.

The implicit foil to the Norwegian kingdom in these critical retellings was
usually Iceland, the place of refuge for those who refused to accept the new

order of Harald's making. There, settlers created the antithesis of his Norway: an acephalous society, united by a law the Icelanders made, shared, and enforced together, in which neither king nor state was established or welcome.[1] It is from that antimonarchic refuge that critique emerged, including that woven into Heimskringla: a text with a mixed audience, mixed tone, and mixed purpose. Written with extraordinary skill, subtlety, and shrewdness, it is by design a multivalent text, open to multiple, indeed to antithetical readings. When read at and by the Norwegian court, it could seem a proper celebration of kings, consistent with the same conventions—and conventional expectations—that shaped Historia Norwegiæ, Fagrskinna, and other Norwegian works in the genre of Kings' Sagas. Icelandic audiences could read between the lines, however, where they perceived something different from what Norwegians saw, albeit something equally delicious to them: blame, and not praise; royal villains, and not heroes; a mixture of tense melodrama and low farce, rather than an inspiring epic. Readers of all persuasions, however, took the text as an accurate account of past rulers' doings and, simultaneously, as a paradigmatic description conveying the eternal essence of kingship and state. Temporal and atemporal, universal and contingent, myth and history alike.

II

Much of my analysis follows from a set of fairly obvious and, I hope, noncontroversial assumptions. First, that no reading of any text is ever perfect and complete. Second, that all readers are disposed to see certain things and to remain somewhat blind to others. Third, that this selectivity is a product, a reflection, and a means for the reproduction of their preexisting situation of interest. Fourth, that this situation of interest is itself shaped by many factors, including—but not limited to—social and geographic locus, material and socioeconomic interests, formal and informal education, sedimented habit, personal and familial history, the latter stretching over many generations. Norwegian nobles read these stories as they did because they were who they were and because of everything—personal, social, historical—that had made them so. The same goes for the Icelanders. All saw what they were prepared, and also that which they desired, to see. A study of the text leads one to its readings, and a study of its readings leads one to its readers.

III

So the question inevitably arises: How did I come to read these texts in the way that I did? Up to now, I have stressed certain points of method: close reading, comparison of Heimskringla's words to those of other variants, tracing narrative threads and ramifications, sensitivity to ambiguities, implications, and innuendo. I also could have invoked certain theoretical works that have influenced me, along with others: Mikhail Bakhtin's notion of laughter from below,[2] Antonio Gramsci on counterhegemony,[3] Walter Benjamin's injunction to read history "against the grain,"[4] Jim Scott's understanding of the dialectic relation between states and what states are not.[5] All these and others played their part.

And yet, as I reflect on it, I realize—rather unexpectedly and surprisingly late—that there is more.

IV

Some time in the 1880s, the most distant ancestor whose name I know, Leopold Mazel, my father's father's father, left his home in Russia (Kiev, I believe, or perhaps it was Minsk). He was not yet twenty, and it was neither *Wanderlust* nor the desire to make his fortune that motivated his journey. Rather, he was facing conscription into the Imperial Russian army, and as a committed anarchist, he was implacably opposed to military service for any state. Over the next decade, he made his way to Dublin, where he learned English, then to New York, where people remarked on his brogue, to Providence, Rhode Island, and finally to Philadelphia, making this final journey by streetcar.

Throughout his life, he retained his anarchist convictions. Although there were many things he appreciated about his adoptive country (its movies, music, and public transportation, for instance), its government was not among them, for a state is always a state, just as an army is always an army. Having fled one state and its military, he was not about to embrace another.

At a certain point, he decided to change his name, although family legends differ on his immediate motives and circumstances. More important than the details of why he stopped being Mazel is the question of why he chose to become Lincoln. Surely, it was part of some Americanization process, but for an anarchist to take a president's name is more than a little curious, and it gives some insight into the way he read American history, for he honored and emulated Lincoln not as head of state or commander in chief, but as the Great Emancipator who freed slaves and struggled to advance human equality. Not the incarnation of the state and its oppressive power, but the very antithesis of same.

V

I wasn't fortunate enough to have known my great-grandfather, but learned what I did of this ancestor from stories retold in my family over the years, all variants of which are uniformly admiring, affectionate, and official devolving toward mythic. Initially I heard them from my grandparents, parents, aunts and uncles. Now my cousins and occasionally our children recount how it was he who brought us to this country, gave us our name, and transmitted his values. I never had an adequate word to describe his role in family lore until I studied Old Norse and realized he was our *landnámsmaðr*, the man who first claimed the land where we live and established the way we live there. It is through him, moreover, that I have come to understand and admire the Icelandic *landnámsmenn*. Like Leo Mazel, they left a land where a violent king held power. And while they could not defeat him, their pride, independence, and integrity made it impossible for them to submit and enter his service. So they voyaged overseas to create a new home in strange territory, bringing relatively little with them, save memories of the world they resented, resisted, and fled. When creating a new life for themselves, they labored to make it different from—and better than—the one they abandoned, doing their best to construct a more egalitarian, less militaristic order: a society against the king.

Had my great-grandfather stumbled across Heimskringla and the other Icelandic accounts of Hálfdan and Harald, I think he would have read these texts with considerable interest and pleasure. Like all readings, his would have been partial and tendentious, but also accurate and insightful, for he— like his great-grandson—would have recognized them as clever anarchists' Books of Kings.

Acknowledgments

This book evolved over many years, beginning as an ill-advised attempt to recover the lost myths, rituals, and religious ideology of pre-Christian Europe, but slowly discovering its current focus, methods, and raison d'être, which—I hope—are not only more intellectually defensible, but also more challenging, innovative, consequential, and lively. Collegial input was crucial to that metamorphosis at all stages, and there are many people to thank. Several colleagues invited me to present individual chapters at various stages of their development, and the critical feedback I received on these occasions helped me refine my thinking. Along these lines, I'm grateful to Anders Andrén, Tamara Chin, Magnus Fiskesjø, Joseph Harris, Anders Hultgård, Kristina Jennbert, John Lindow, Robin McNeal, Rory McTurk, Catarina Raudvere, Rick Rosengarten, and Terence Turner. Equal if more diffuse collegial gratitude is due to Clifford Ando, Maurizio Bettini, Claude Calame, Wendy Doniger, Chris Faraone, Carlo Ginzburg, Cristiano Grottanelli, Richard Leppert, Bernard McGinn, Michael Murrin, Martin Riesebrodt, Marshall Sahlins, Stefanie von Schnurbein, James C. Scott, Kathleen Self, Hugh Urban, Kevin Wanner, Morten Warmind, Christian Wedemeyer, and others with whom I've had the occasion to discuss some of the materials and issues treated in the preceding pages. Particular thanks are owed to Nicolas Meylan and Margaret Clunies Ross, who read and commented on an earlier draft of the full manuscript. Professor Ross gave particularly close attention to details and nuances of the Old Norse and pointed out many shortcomings of my earlier translations. I have benefited greatly from her criticisms and such errors as remain are in spite of her good efforts. I'm also grateful to the University of Chicago and to Dean Margaret Mitchell of its Divinity School for funds that helped support publication of this book. Deepest thanks, as ever, go to Louise Lincoln, for support and encouragement of more sorts than one can imagine or articulate.

An earlier version of chapter 8 was published as "Kings, Cowpies, and Creation: Intertextual Traffic between 'History' and 'Myth' in the Writings of Snorri Sturluson," in *Old Norse Religion in Long-Term Perspectives: Origins, Changes, and Interactions*, ed. Anders Andrén, Kristina Jennbert, and Catharina Raudvere (Lund: Nordic Academic Press, 2006), 381–88.

Appendix: Synoptic Tables

SYNOPTIC TABLE 2.1 Gyða's response to Harald

A. Harald Fairhair's Saga 3	B. Greater Saga of Olaf Tryggvason 2 (Flateyjarbók 1.39–40)	C. Tale of Harald Fairhair 3 (Flateyjarbók 1.569)
1 King Harald sent his men after a maiden *Haraldr konungr sendi menn sína eptir meyju einni,*	Next he sent his men after a maiden *þui næst sende hann menn sina eftir mey einne*	Then King Harald took [= married?] *Da fek Haralldr konungr*
2 who was named Gyða, the daughter of King Eirik of Hörðaland *er Gyða er nefnd, dóttir Eiríks konungs af Hǫrðalandi*	called Gyða, the daughter of King Eirik of Hörðaland, *er Gyða het. dottir Æireks konungs af Hǫrdalande.*	Gyða, the daugher of King Eirik of Hörðaland. *Gydu dottur Æreks konungs af Hörðalande.*
3 — she was in fosterage at Valdres with a powerful landowner. *—hon var at fóstri á Valdresi með ríkum bóanda—*(Cf. B6)		
4 whom he wanted to take as his concubine, *er hann vildi taka til frillu sér,*	whom he wanted to take as his concubine, *er hann villde taka til fridlu ser*	
5 because she was an extremely beautiful woman and rather proud. *þvíat hon var allfríð mær ok heldr stórlát;*	because she was an extremely beautiful woman and extremely proud. *þuiat hon var allfrid mær ok allstorlát.*	
6	She was in fosterage at Valdres with a powerful landowner. *hon var a fostri a Valldrese med rikum bonda.* (Cf. A3)	
7 But when the messengers came there and presented his message to the maiden, she answered in this manner. *en er sendimenn kómu þar, þá báru þeir upp erendi sín fyrir meyna; hon svaraði á þessa lund,*	But when the messengers came there and presented their message to the maiden, she answered: *En er sendimenn kuomu þar ok baru fram eyrende sin vid meyna. hon svarar.*	
8	"Much less do I want to be his concubine *þui sidr uil ek vera fridla hans*	

(continued)

A. Harald Fairhair's Saga 3	B. Greater Saga of Olaf Tryggvason 2 (Flateyjarbók 1.39–40)	C. Tale of Harald Fairhair 3 (Flateyjarbók 1.569)
9 She was not going to waste her maidenhood in order to take a man who, as king, has no more realms than a few districts to manage. *at eigi vill hon spilla meydómi sínum, til þess at taka til mannz þann konung, er eigi hefir meira ríki, en nǫkkur fylki, til forráða,*	and I will not waste my maidenhood in order to have a king who has no more than one district to manage. *at ek vil æigi spilla meydomi minu(m) til þess at eiga þann konungr er æigi hefir mæirr en eitt fylki til forrada.*	
10 "And it seems extraordinary to me," she said, "that there is no king who wants to take possession of Norway and to be sole ruler over it, as have King Gorm in Denmark and Eirik in Uppsala." *"en þat þykki mér undarligt, segir hon, er engi er sá konungr, er svá vill eignask Nóreg ok vera einvaldi yfir, sem hefir Gormr konungr at Danmǫrku eða Eiríkr at Upsǫlum."*	And it seems extraordinary to me," she said, "that there is no king who wants to take possession of all Norway for himself and to be sole ruler over it, like King Gorm in Denmark or Eirik in Uppsala." *en þat þiki mer undarligt sagde hon at einge er sa konungr er ser vile æignna Noreg allan ok vera æinualldr yfir sem Gormr konungr yfir Danmǫrk ok Eirekr konungr at Uppsolum.*	
11 Her answer seemed extremely proud to the messengers, and they asked of her speech: what reply should come to this? They said that Harald was so powerful a king that he was a fitting match for her. *Sendimǫnnum þykkir hon svara furðustórliga ok spyrja hana máls um, hvar til svǫr þessi skulu koma, segja, at Haraldr er konungr svá ríkr, at henni er fullræði í,*	Her answer seemed extremely proud to the messengers, and they asked of her speech: what reply should come to this? They said that King Harald was so powerful a king that he was a fitting match for her. *Sendemonnum þotte hon helldr storliga suara ok spyria hana mals vm huar til þesse suor skulu koma. segia at Haralldr er sua rikr konungr at henni uæri fullkosta.*	
12 Although her answer led their mission in a way other than they might wish, they saw they had no choice, for they could not take her against her will, and they prepared to depart. And when they were ready, she led the men out. *en þó at hon svari á annan veg þeira erendum, en þeir mundu vilja, þá sjá þeir engan sinn kost til þess at sinni, at þeir mundu hana í brot hafa, nema hennar vili væri til þess, ok búask þeir þá ferðar sinnar. En er þeir eru búnir, leiða menn þá út.*	Although her answer led their mission in a way other than they might wish, they saw they had no choice, for they could not take her against her will, so after that they prepared to depart. And when they were ready, she led the men out. *En þoat hon suaradi annan ueg þeirra eyrendum en þeir munde vilia. þa sa þeir ǫnguan sinn kost til þess at sinne at hafa hana burtu nema hennar uile se til buazst þeir sidan til ferdar. Ok sem þeir eru bunir, leida menn þa vt.*	

	A. Harald Fairhair's Saga 3	B. Greater Saga of Olaf Tryggvason 2 (Flateyjarbók 1.39–40)	C. Tale of Harald Fairhair 3 (Flateyjarbók 1.569)
13	Then Gyða spoke with the messengers and bade them to take these words of hers to King Harald. *þá mælti Gyða við sendimenn, bað þá bera þau orð sín Haraldi konungi,*	Then Gyða said to the messengers: "Bear these words of mine to King Harald *þa mællti Gyða til sendemanna. berit þau min ord Haralldi konungi*	But she said this to the king *en hon mællti þat til vid konung*
14	She would consent to become his proper wife if he will first do this for her sake: *at hon mun því at einu játa at gerask eigin kona hans, ef hann vill þat gera fyrir hennar sakir áðr,*	that I will consent to become his proper wife if he will first do this for my sake: *at ek mun þui at eins iata at georaz hans eiginkona. ef hann uill þat adr geora firir mina skylld*	
15	place all of Norway under him and rule that realm just as independently as King Eirik rules Sweden and King Gorm, Denmark. *at leggja undir sik allan Nóreg ok ráða því ríki jafnfrjálsliga, sem Eiríkr konungr Svía-veldi eða Gormr konungr Danmǫrku,*	place all of Norway under him and rule that realm just as independently as King Eirik rules Sweden and King Gorm, Denmark. *at leggja undir sig allan Noreg ok rada þij riki jafnfrialsliga sem Æirekr konungr Suiauellde edr Gormr konungr Danmork.*	that he should conquer all Norway and bring it under him, *at hann skyllde vinna allan Noreg undir sig*
16	"Because then, it seems to me," she said, "he might really be called a sovereign king." *"þvíat þá þykki mér, segir hon, hann mega heita þjóðkonungr."*	Because then, it seems to me he might really be called a sovereign king." *þuiat þa þiki mer hann þiodkonungr mega heita.*	
17			as it says in another chapter of the Saga of Olaf Tryggvason. *eptir þui sem segir j odrum kapitula j Olafs sogu Trygguasonar.*

	A. Harald Fairhair's Saga 20	B. Greater Saga of Olaf Tryggvason 2 (Flateyjarbók 1.40)	C. Tale of Harald Fairhair 3 (Flateyjarbók 1.569)
1	King Harald had now become sole ruler over all Norway.	Now, as he had become sole king over all the land	
	Haraldr konungr var nú einvaldi orðinn allz Nóregs.	*Nu sem hann er ordinn einualldzkonungr yfir ollu lande*	
2	Then he recalled that which the maiden, the one who was very proud, had said to him.	Then he recalled that which the maiden, the one who was very proud, had said to him.	
	þá mintisk hann þess, er mærin sú in mikilláta hafði mælt til hans;	*þa minntizst hann þess er mærin su hin mikilata hafde mælit til hans.*	
3	Then he sent men to her	He sent his men after her	
	hann sendi þá menn til hennar	*sendi hann menn sina eftir henni*	
4	and had them bring her to him	and had them convey her to him	Then King Harald took [=married?] Gyða, the daughter of King Eirik of Hörðaland. . . .
	ok lét hana hafa til sín	*ok let hana til sin fara*	
			Da fek Haralldr konungr Gydu dottur Æreks konungs af Hörðalande. . . .
5	and he laid her beside him.	and he laid her in bed beside him.	
	ok lagði hana hjá sér;	*ok lagde hana j sæng hia ser.*	
6	These were their children: Álof was the oldest, then was Hrœrek, then Sigtrygg, Fróði, and Thorgils.		He had these sons with Gyða: Guthorm, Harek, and Guðrøð.
	þessi váru bǫrn þeira: Álof var ellzt, þá var Hrœrekr, þá Sigtryggr, Fróði ok þorgils.		*hann atti vid Gydu þessa sonu Guthorm Harek Gudrǫd.*

SYNOPTIC TABLE 2.3 Negative and positive accounts of Harald's courtship

A. Harald Fairhair's Saga 3	B. Fagrskinna Appendix 3 (from the A-Text)
1	King Harald sent his men after a maiden who was named Gyða . . . *Haraldr konungr sendi menn sína eptir meyju einni, er Gyða er nefnd . . .*	Harald fell greatly in love with Ragna. *En Haraldr lagði elsku mikla á Rǫgnu.*
2	whom he wanted to take as his concubine . . . *er hann vildi taka til frillu sér,* (Cf. B6)	
3	But when the messengers came there and presented his message to the maiden, *en er sendimenn kómu þar, þá báru þeir upp erendi sín fyrir meyna;*	But when Harald let his words of love to Ragna be known, *En þá er Haraldr lét ástaryrði sín í ljós við Rǫgnu,*
4	she answered in this manner. *hon svaraði á þessa lund,*	she answered in this manner: *svaraði hón á þessa lund:*
5		"I say this surely in truth, that I could have no better sweetheart than you. This is because of both your kingly birth and all the kingly rank and beauty that are yours. But before I give my full love to you, I would like to know this: Who shall be the heir of your kinsman Nerið the Wise in Counsel—you, lord King, or Gandalf's sons?" *"þat mæli ek víst með sannyndum, at eigi em ek betra unnusta verð en þér eruð. Veldr því hvárttveggja konunglig byrð yður ok svá ǫll konunglig tign ok fegrð, er á yðr er. En þó áðr en ek fella fulla ást til yðar, þá vil ek þess verða vǫr, hvárt heldr skulu verða arfar Neriðs ens ráðspaka, frænda yðvars, herra konungr, þér eða synir Gandálfs."*
6		Then Harald answered angrily and said: "I thought, Ragna, that you would be led to my bed with great honor for the sake of love, but because you have upbraided me with these reproaches, it is now the case that you should be led to my bed as a poor concubine." *þá svaraði Haraldr reiðr ok mælti svá: "þat ætlaða ek, Ragna, at þú skyldir fyrir ástar sakar með ágætri sæmð vera leidd til minnar sængr, en fyrir því at þú hefir brugðit mér þessum brizlum, þá er nú þess vert, at þú sér svá leidd til minnar sængr sem ein fátœk frilla."* (Cf. A2)

(continued)

A. Harald Fairhair's Saga 3	B. Fagrskinna Appendix 3 (from the A-Text)
7	Ragna said this to the king: "Do not be angry, lord King, although we speak playfully and it does not exalt your kingship to contend with women, still less with little girls like me. Better it is, lord King, to contest with other kings, who now take up all the land within.
	þat mælti Ragna við konunginn: "Eigi skulu þér, herra konungr, reiðask við, þó at vér mælim oss gaman ok hæfir þat ekki konungdómi yðrum at brjóta kapp við kvenmenn ok þó allra sízt við meybǫrn smá, sem ek em, heldr er yðvar sæmð þat, herra konungr, at deila kappi við konunga aðra, er nú skipaðir um allt land innan.
8 She was not going to waste her maidenhood in order to take a man who, as king, has no more realms than a few districts to manage.	And I want to tell you this, if I have my own way, I will become neither your concubine, nor that of any other man.
at eigi vill hon spilla meydómi sínum, til þess at taka til mannz þann konung, er eigi hefir meira ríki, en nǫkkur fylki, til forráða,	*þat vil ek ok segja yðr, ef ek ræð mér sjálf, þá verð ek hvártki yðvar frillu né einskis manns annars,*
9 "But it seems extraordinary to me," she said, "that there is no king who wants to take possession of Norway and to be sole ruler over it, as have King Gorm in Denmark and Eirik in Uppsala."	I shall have for my own man that one who will make all Norway's men his subjects or I shall have no one."
"en þat þykki mér undarligt, segir hon, er engi er sá konungr, er svá vill eignask Nóreg ok vera einvaldi yfir, sem hefir Gormr konungr at Danmǫrku eða Eiríkr at Upsǫlum."	*ok annat hvárt skal ek hafa þann at eignum manni, er alla Nóregs menn gǫrir sér at þegnum eða skal ek engan hafa."*
10 . . . The messengers now went back to King Harald and told him the maiden's words . . .	
. . . Sendimenn fara nú aptr til Haraldz konungs ok segja honum þessi orð meyjarinnar ok telja . . .	
11 And then he said: "This vow I swear and I call on God to witness it, he who created me and rules over all.	When King Harald heard these words, he straightaway swore an oath, swearing on his head
ok enn mælti hann: "þess strengi ek heit, ok því skýt ek til guðs, þess er mik skóp ok ǫllu ræðr,	*þá er Haraldr konungr heyrði þessi orð, þá strengði hann þegar heit ok sór við hǫfuð sitt,*
12	that he would have no proper wife in Norway, save Ragna and with this measure as well
	at hann skyldi enga eigna konu eiga í Nóregi nema Rǫgnu ok þó með þeim hætti,

SYNOPTIC TABLE 2.3 (continued)

A. Harald Fairhair's Saga 3	B. Fagrskinna Appendix 3 (from the A-Text)
13 Never shall I cut or comb my hair,	
at aldri skal skera hár mitt né kemba,	
14 until I have taken possession of all Norway, with its tributes, taxes, and administration, or otherwise to die."	—that he would make all men in Norway his subjects.
fyrr en ek hefi eignazk allan Nóreg með skǫttum ok skyldum ok forráði, en deyja at ǫðrum kosti."	*at hann gørði alla menn at þegnum sér í Nóregi.*
15	He also let that follow, that a woman who has so manly a speech in her mouth as Ragna deserved to have a noble king rather than some district ruler.
	þat lét hann auk fylgja, at sú kona var verðari at eiga ágætan konung heldr en einhvern heraðs hǫlð, er svá skǫrulig orð hefir í munni sér sem Ragna.

SYNOPTIC TABLE 3.1 Harald's haircut

A. Fagrskinna 3	B. Harald Fairhair's Saga 23	C. Tale of Harald Fairhair 7 (Flateyjarbók 1.575)
1	King Harald was at a feast given by Earl Rögnvald in Mæri.	
	Haraldr konungr var á veizlu á Mæri at Rǫgnvaldz jarls;	
2 Here, after he civilized the land, those who were close by paid taxes, as did those far away.	By then, he had taken possession of all the land.	
Hér eptir siðaðisk landit, guldusk skattar et øfra sem et ýtrsa.	*hafði hann þá eignazk land alt;*	
3 Now he had become a man full grown in his strength, size, and skill in counsel.		Now King Harald had become a surpassing man in his power and size.
Nú er hann orðinn fullgǫrr maðr um afl, vǫxt ok ráðagerð.		*Nu er Haralldr konungr uordinn frageordu madr vm afl ok uoxst,*
4	The king took a bath there, and King Harald let his hair be dressed	
	þá tók konungr þar laugar ok þá lét Haraldr konungr greiða hár sitt,	

(continued)

SYNOPTIC TABLE 3.1 (continued)

A. Fagrskinna 3	B. Harald Fairhair's Saga 23	C. Tale of Harald Fairhair 7 (Flateyjarbók 1.575)
5	His hair was long and matted: *Hár hans var sítt ok flókit;* (Cf. B8)		His hair was now long and matted: *hans har var nu sitt ok flokit* (Cf. B8)
6	for this reason he was called "Shaggy." *fyrir þá sǫk var hann lúfa kallaðr.* (Cf. B9)		for this reason, he was called "Shaggy." *firir þa sok uar hann kalladr lufa.* (Cf. B9)
7	Then Earl Rögnvald of Mæri cut his hair *þá skar Rǫgnvaldr jarl á Møri hár hans*	and then Earl Rögnvald cut his hair, *ok þá skar Rǫgnvaldr jarl hár hans,*	Then Earl Rögnvald of Mæri cut his hair *þa skar Rognualldr jall af Mære hár hans*
8		which previously had been uncut and uncombed for ten years. *en áðr hafði verit óskorit ok ókembt x. vetr.* (Cf. A5, C5)	
9		At that time, they called him "Shaggy Harald," *þá kǫlluðu þeir hann Harald lúfu,* (Cf. A6 and C6)	
10	and gave him a name and called him "Harald the Fairhair." *ok gaf hónum nafn ok kallaði Harald enn hárfagra.*	but thereafter Rögnvald gave a nickname to him and called him "Harald the Fairhair." *en síðan gaf Rǫgnvaldr honum kenningarnafn ok kallaði hann Harald inn hárfagra,*	and gave him a name and called him "Harald the Fairhair." *ok gaf honum nafnn ok kallade hann Haralld hinn hárfagra.*
11	He was then more than twenty years in age. *þá var hann meirr en tvítøgr at aldri.*		He was then more than twenty. *þa uar hann mæirr en .xx.*
12		And all who saw him said that that was the truest of names, *ok sǫgðu allir, er sá, at þat var it mesta sannnefni,*	
13		because he had hair that was both abundant and fair. *þvíat hann hafði hár bæði mikit ok fagrt.*	

SYNOPTIC TABLE 3.1 (continued)

A. Fagrskinna 3	B. Harald Fairhair's Saga 23	C. Tale of Harald Fairhair 7 (Flateyjarbók 1.575)
14	He had many children *Hann átti margt barna,*		
15	and from his lineage have come all the kings of Norway. *ok af hans ætt eru komnir allir Nóregskonungar.*		From his lineage have come all the kings of Norway. *Af hans ætt eru komnir aller Noregs konungar.*

SYNOPTIC TABLE 3.2 Rögnvald enters Harald's service

	A. Harald Fairhair's Saga 10	B. Tale of Harald Fairhair 6 (Flateyjarbók 1.572–73)
1	Then King Harald put these two districts under himself *lagði Haraldr konungr þá undir sik þessi tvau fylki*	After this battle, King Harald took possession of North Mæri and Raumsdal. *Haraldr konungr æignadizst eftir þessa orrostu Nordmære ok Raumsdale.*
2	and tarried there for the summer, arranging the laws for the people. Around harvest time, he prepared to go north to Trondheim. *Ok dvalðisk þar lengi um sumarit ok skipaði þar réttum með mǫnnum, en um haustit bjósk hann at fara norðr til þrándheims.*	
3	During that summer, Rögnvald, Earl of Mæri, son of Eystein Glumra, had made himself King Harald's man. *Rǫgnvaldr Mæra-jarl, sonr Eysteins glumru, hafði þá of sumarit gǫrzk maðr Haraldz konungs.*	then Earl Rögnvald, son of Eystein Glumra, came to him and made himself his man *þa kom til hans Rognualldr jall, son Eysteins glumro ok gerdizst hans maðr*
4		and for a long time thereafter, he was a great friend of King Harald. *ok var leinge sidan mikill vinr Haralldz konungs.*
5	Harald made him ruling noble over these two districts, North Mæri and Raumsdal, and provided him with support for both from the nobility and landholders, as well as a naval force to defend the land against attack. *Haraldr setti hann hǫfðingja yfir þessi .ii. fylki, Norð-Mæri ok Raumsdal, ok fekk honum þar styrk til bæði af ríkismǫnnum ok bóndum, svá ok skipakost at verja landit fyrir ófriði.*	... Then King Harald put Earl Rögnvald over both parts of Mæri and Raumsdal, and he had with him a great many men. *... þa setti Haraldr konungr Rognualld jall yfir Mære huoratueggiu ok Raumsdal ok hafde hann vm sig fiolmenni mikit.*

(continued)

SYNOPTIC TABLE 3.2 (continued)

A. Harald Fairhair's Saga 10	B. Tale of Harald Fairhair 6 (Flateyjarbók 1.572–73)
6 He was called Rögnvald the Powerful or the Wise in Counsel, and men say that both were true names. *Hann var kallaðr Rǫgnvaldr inn ríki eða inn ráðsvinni, ok segja menn, at hvártveggja væri sannefni.*	
7 King Harald spent the next winter in Trondheim. *Haraldr konungr var um vetrinn eptir í þrándheimi.*	Then King Harald returned north to Trondheim. *Haraldr konungr sneri þa nordr aftr til þrandheims.*

SYNOPTIC TABLE 3.3 Rögnvald's death

A. Orkneyinga Saga 8	B. Harald Fairhair's Saga 30	C. Greater Saga of Olaf Tryggvason 183 (Flateyjarbók 1.223)
1	King Harald was then forty years old. *þá er Haraldr konungr var xl. at aldri,*	
2 When the sons of Harald the Fairhair were full grown in age, they became extremely overbearing and unruly at home.* *þá er synir Haralds ins hárfagra váru fulltíða at aldri, gerðusk þeir ofstopamenn miklir ok óhœgir innan lands,*	There were many sons of his who were quite grown up. They were all precocious in their accomplishments. *þá váru margir synir hans vel á legg komnir; þeir váru allir bráðgǫrvir.*	When the sons of Harald Fairhair were grown up, they became extremely overbearing and unruly at home, as has been told before. *þá er synir Haraldz hárfagra voru rosknir georduzst þeir ofstopamenn myklir ok vhœgir innanlandz sem fyr segir.*
3	It came about that they were ill pleased with the fact that the king gave them no realms, but set an earl in each district, and it seemed to them that the earls were lower born than they were. *Kom þá svá, at þeir urðu illa við, er konungr gaf þeim ekki ríki, en setti jarl í hverju fylki, ok þótti þeim jarlar vera smábornari, en þeir váru.*	

SYNOPTIC TABLE 3.3 (continued)

A. Orkneyinga Saga 8	B. Harald Fairhair's Saga 30	C. Greater Saga of Olaf Tryggvason 183 (Flateyjarbók 1.223)
4	They attacked the king's earls, killed some, and drove some off their property.† *fóru á hendr jǫrlum konungs, drápu suma, suma ráku þeir af eignum sinum.*		
5	Snæfrið's sons, Hálfdan High-Leg and Guðrøð the Radiant attacked Rögnvald, earl of Mæri, killed him, and took over his realm. *Snæfriðarsynir, Hálfdan háleggr ok Guðrøðr ljómi fóru at Rǫgnvaldi Mœrajarli ok drápu hann, en tóku undir sik ríkit.*	One spring, it happened that Hálfdan High-Leg and Guðrøð the Radiant, with a great company of men, surprised Rögnvald, earl of Mæri, surrounded his house, and burned him in it, with sixty men. *þá fóru til á einu vári Hálfdan háleggr ok Guðrøðr ljómi með mikla sveit manna ok kómu á óvart Rǫgnvaldi Mœra-jarli ok tóku hús á honum ok brendu hann inni við lx. manna.*	Snæfrið's sons, Hálfdan High-Leg and Guðrøð the Radiant, killed Rögnvald, earl of Mæri. *Snæfriðar synir Halfdan haleggr ok Gudrǫdr liome drapu Rǫgnvalld Mœra jall.*
6	But when King Harald learned that, he was very angry and attacked his sons. *En er Haraldr konungr spurði þat, varð hann reiðr mjǫk, ok fór at sonum sinum.*		For that, Harald was very angry. *þui uard Haralldr ræiðr miog.*

* Cf. Harald Fairhair's Saga 34: "They became extremely overbearing within the land, and there were disagreements among themselves." *þeir gerðusk margir ofstopamenn miklir innan landz ok váru sjálfir ósáttir.*

† Cf. Harald Fairhair's Saga 34: "They drove the kings' earls off their property and even killed some." *þeir ráku af eignum jarla konungs, en suma drápu þeir.*

SYNOPTIC TABLE 3.4 Harald's response to Rögnvald's death

A. Orkneyinga Saga 8	B. Harald Fairhair's Saga 30	C. Greater Saga of Olaf Tryggvason183 (Flateyjarbók 1.223)
1	Snæfrið's sons, Hálfdan High-Leg and Guðrøð the Radiant, attacked Rögnvald, earl of Mæri, killed him, and took over his realm. *Snæfriðarsynir, Hálfdan háleggr ok Guðrøðr ljómi fóru at Rǫgnvaldi Mærajarli ok drápu hann, en tóku undir sik ríkit.*	One spring, it happened that Hálfdan High-Leg and Guðrøð the Radiant, with a great company of men, surprised Rögnvald, earl of Mæri, surrounded his house, and burned him in it, with sixty men. *þá fóru til á einu vári Hálfdan háleggr ok Guðrøðr ljómi með mikla sveit manna ok kómu á óvart Rǫgnvaldi Mæra-jarli ok tóku hús á honum ok brendu hann inni við lx. manna.*	Snæfrið's sons, Hálfdan High-Leg and Guðrøð the Radiant, killed Rögnvald, earl of Mæri. *Snæfriðar synir Halfdan haleggr ok Gudrǫdr liome drapu Rǫgnvalld Mæra jall.*
2	But when King Harald learned that, he was very angry and attacked his sons. *En er Haraldr konungr spurði þat, varð hann reiðr mjǫk, ok fór at sonum sinum.*		For that, Harald was very angry *þui uard Haralldr ræiðr miog*
3	Hálfdan leaped on a ship and sailed west by sea, *Hálfdan hljóp á skip ok sigldi vestr um haf,*	Then Hálfdan took three longships and set sail west across the sea, *þá tók Hálfdan langskip iii. ok skipaði ok siglir síðan vestr á haf,*	and Hálfdan fled the land, going west by sea, *ok uard Halfdan landflotti uestr um haf,*
4		but Guðrøð settled on the land that previously Earl Rögnvald had had. *en Guðrøðr settisk þar at lǫndum, sem áðr hafði haft Rǫgnvaldr jarl.*	but Guðrøð settled *en Guðrøðr settisk*
5		And when King Harald learned this, he went thence with a great army against Guðrøð. *En er Haraldr konungr spurði þetta, þá fór hann þegar með liði miklu á hendr Guðrøði,*	
6	but Guðrøð surrendered to his father. *en Guðrøðr gaf sik upp í vald fǫður sins.*	Guðrøð had no other choice and surrendered to King Harald, *sá Guðrøðr engan annan sinn kost, en gefask upp í vald Haraldz konungs,*	with his father *vid fǫdur sinn*

SYNOPTIC TABLE 3.4 (continued)

A. Orkneyinga Saga 8	B. Harald Fairhair's Saga 30	C. Greater Saga of Olaf Tryggvason 183 (Flateyjarbók 1.223)
7	and the king sent him east to Agðir. *ok sendi konungr hann austr á Agðir.*	
8	King Harald then set Thorir, Earl Rögnvald's son, over Mæri, *En Haraldr konungr setti þá yfir Mæri þóri, son Rǫgnvaldz jarls,*	
9	As compensation for his father, King Harald gave Thorir his own daughter, Alof Who-Makes-the-Harvest-Better *Haraldr konungr gaf þóri í fǫðurbœtr Álofu árbót, dóttur sína,*	and gave to him his daughter, Alof, who was called "She Who Makes the Harvest Better." *ok gipti honum Álofu, dóttur sína, er kǫlluð var árbót.*	
10	and an earl's title and his father's inheritance. *ok jarlsnafn ok fǫðurleifð sína.*	Earl Thorir the Silent then had the same realm as his father, Earl Rögnvald, had had. *þórir jarl þegjandi hafði þá ríki þvílíkt, sem haft hafði Rǫgnvaldr jarl, faðir hans.*	

SYNOPTIC TABLE 3.5 Rögnvald's sons

	A. Fagrskinna 74	B. Orkneyinga Saga 4	C. Harald Fairhair's Saga 24	D. Landnamabók (Hauksbók = Sturlubók 309)	E. Greater Saga of Olaf Tryggvason 179 (Flateyjarbók 1.221)
1		He married Ragnhild, daughter of Hrolf Nefja. *Hann átti Ragnhildi, dóttur Hrólfs nefju;*	Rögnvald married Hild, daughter of Hrolf Nefja. *Rognvaldr átti Hildi, dóttur Hrólfs nefju;*	Rögnvald married Ragnhild, daughter of Hrolf Nefja. *Rognvalldr átti Ragnilldi dóttur Rolfs Nefiu.*	He married Ragnhild, daughter of Hrolf Nefja. *hann átti Ragnnhilldi dóttur Hrolfs nefiu.*
2				Their son was Ívar, who died in the Hebrides when with King Harald the Fairhair. *þeira s(vn) var Ivar er fell i Sudreyium med Haralldi konungi hinum Harfagra.* (Cf. B7 and E7)	
3	Earl Walking-Hrolf was the son of Rögnvald, earl of Mæri, *Gongu-Hrólfr jarl var sonr Rognvalds Mærajarls,*	Their son was Hrolf, *þeira sonr var Hrólfr,*	Their sons were Hrolf *synir þeira váru þeir Hrólfr*	The second was Walking-Hrolf, *Annarr var Gongu-Rolfr*	Their son was Hrolf, *þeira son var Hrolfr*
4		who conquered Normandy. *er vann Norðmandi.*		who conquered Normandy. *er vann Nordmandi.*	who conquered Normandy. *er uann Normandi.*
5		He was so big that a horse could not carry him. Therefore, he was called Walking-Hrolf. *Hann var svá mikill, at hann báru eigi hestar; þvi hét hann Gongu-Hrólfr;* (Cf. C17)			He was so big that no horse could carry him. He was called Walking-Hrolf. *hann var sua mikill at hann baru ongir hestar hann uar kalladr Ganuguhrolfr.* (Cf. C17)

6		The earls of Rouen and kings of England have descended from him. *fra honum eru kommir Rudujarlar ok Englakonungar.*		The earls of Rouen and kings of England have descended from him. *frá hanum er(u) Rvdu iarlar kommir ok Engla konungar.*	The earls of Rouen and kings of England have descended from him. *fra honum eru kommir Rudu jallar ok Æingla konungar.*
7		Their sons were also Ívar *þeira sonr var ok Ívarr (Cf. D2)*			These were (also) their sons: Ívar *þeirra synir voru þeir Ívarr (Cf. D2)*
8	brother of Earl Thorir the Silent, *bróðir þóris jarls þegianda*	and Thorir the Silent. *ok þórir þegiandi.*	and Thorir. *ok þórir.*	The third was Earl Thorir the Silent, *þridi var þórir iarl þegiandi*	and Thorir the Silent. *ok þorir þegiande.*
9				who married Alof Who-Makes-the-Harvest-Better, daughter of King Harald Fairhair. Their daughter was Bergljot, mother of Earl Hakon the Powerful. *er atti Alofu Arbót dottur Haralds konungs Hárfagra. ok var þeira dottir Bergliót modir Hakonar iarls hins rika.*	
10		Rögnvald also had sons by concubines *Rognvaldr átti ok frillusonu,*	Earl Rögnvald also had sons by concubines. *Rognvaldr jarl átti ok frillusonu*	Rögnvald also had three sons by concubines. *Rognvalldr atti frillu s(vnv) iij.*	Rögnvald also had sons by concubines. *Raugnualldr atti ok fridlusonu.*

(continued)

SYNOPTIC TABLE 3.5 (continued)

	A. Fagrskinna 74	B. Orkneyinga Saga 4	C. Harald Fairhair's Saga 24	D. Landnámabók (Hauksbók = Sturlubók 309)	E. Greater Saga of Olaf Tryggvason 179 (Flateyjarbók 1.221)
11		named Hallað *hét Hallaðr* (Cf. D13)	One was called Hallað, *hét einn Hallaðr,* (Cf. D13)	The first was called Hrollaug, *het einn Rollaugr* (Cf. A13, B12, C13, and E12)	named Hallað *het Hallaðr* (Cf. D13)
12	Turf-Einar of the Orkneys, *ok Torf-Einars í Orkneyjum,* (Cf. D13 and E13)	and Hrollaug, *ok Hrollaugr* (Cf. A13, C13, and D11)	another Einar, *annarr Einarr,* (Cf. B13 and E13)	the second Einar, *ij Einarr,* (Cf. B13 and E13)	and Hrollaug, *ok Hrollaugr* (Cf. A13, B12 and C13)
13	and one who was called Hrollaug. *ok Hrollaugr hét einn,* (Cf. B12, D11 and E12)	and Einar—he was the youngest. *ok Einarr, hann var yngstr.* (Cf. A12, C12, and D12)	the third Hrollaug. *inn iii. Hrollaugr;* (Cf. B12, D11 and E12)	the third Hallað, who gave up the earldom of the Orkneys. *iij. Hallaðr sa er veltist or iarldominum í Orkneyiu(m)* (Cf. B11, C11, and E11)	and Einar—he was the youngest. *ok Æinar hann uar yngzstr.* (Cf. A12, C12 and D12)
14	So Einar said, when he had killed Hálfdan High-Leg, son of Harald the Fairhair, *svá sem Einarr segir, þá er hann hafði drepit Hálfdan hálegg, son Haralds ens hárfagra,*				

15	when the latter had killed his father.
	er áðr hafði drepit foður hans:
16	They were full grown when their legitimate brothers were born.
	þeir váru rosknir, þá er inir skírbornu bræðr þeira váru born.
17	Hrolf was a great Viking. He grew into so great a man that no horse could carry him and he walked wherever he went. He was called Walking-Hrolf.
	Hrólfr var víkingr mikill; hann var svá mikill maðr vexti, at engi hestr mátti bera hann, ok gekk hann, hvargi sem hann fór; hann var kallaðr Gongu-Hrólfr.
	(Cf. B5, E5)

SYNOPTIC TABLE 3.6 Rögnvald discusses the Orkney earldom with his sons

	A. Orkneyinga Saga 6	B. Harald Fairhair's Saga 27	C. Landnámabók (Hauksbók 270 = Sturlubók 309)	D. Greater Saga of Olaf Tryggvason 181 (Flateyjarbók 1.222–23)	E. Tale of Thidrandi and Thorhall 1 (Flateyjarbók 1.418)
1	And when Earl Rögnvald learned that [sc.: Hallað had returned from the Orkneys and renounced his title as earl], it pleased him very ill.	But when Earl Rögnvald heard that, he was ill pleased with Hallað's conduct.	And when Earl Rögnvald heard that, it pleased him very ill.	But when Earl Rögnvald heard that, it pleased him very ill.	
	Ok er Rognvaldr jarl spurði þetta, hugnaði honum stórilla,	*En er Rognvaldr jarl spurði þetta, lét hann illa yfir ferð Hallaðar,*	*Ok er Rognvaldr jarl spurði þetta, hugnaði honum stórilla,*	*en er Rognuallдr jall spyrr þetta likar honum stórilla*	
2		He said that his sons were becoming unlike his ancestors.			
		sagði, at synir hans myndi verða ólikir forellri sinu.			
3	He called his sons to him, Thorir and Hrollaug. Hrolf was then out raiding.		He called together his sons and asked which of them wanted to go to the Orkneys.	He called his sons to him, Thorir and Hrollaug. Hrolf was then out raiding.	But when the earl spoke with his sons, Hrolf and Hrollaug, about them both going to the Orkneys,
	ok heimti til sin sonu sina, þóri ok Hrollaug; Hrólfr var þá i hernaði.		*þa kalladi hann saman s(vnv) sina ok spurdi hverr þeira þa vildi til Orkneyia.*	*ok heimtir til sin sonu sina, þóri ok Hrollaug. Hrólfr var þá enn j hermnade.*	*En er jall talade uit sonu sina budu þeir honum Hrolfr ok Hrollaugr at fara til Orkmneyia.*
4	Rögnvald asked, which of them wanted the islands.			Rögnvald asked which of them wanted to go west to the islands.	The earl was not in favor of that.
	Rognvaldr spurði, hvárr þeira vildi eyjarnar.			*Rognualldr spurde huorr þeirra uillde uestr j eyjarnar.*	*en jalli var ekki um þat.*

(continued)

5	Thorir asked him if he should make the voyage. "I am of the opinion," said the earl, "that your advancement will be greatest here, and that your path does not lead elsewhere." *Þórir bað hann fyrir sjá um sína ferð. "Svá segir mér hugr um," segir jarl, "at hér mun þinn þroski mestr, ok liggja vegir þínir eigi heðan."*	Thorir asked him if he should make the voyage. The earl said he should take the realm there after his father. *enn þorir bad hann sia fyri sinni ferd. iarl kvad hann þar skylldi riki taka epter fodur sinn.*	Thorir asked him if he should make the voyage. The earl responded: "I am of the opinion that your advancement will be greatest here, and that your path does not lead elsewhere." *þorir bad hann fyrir sea vm sina ferd. Jall suarar. suo segir mer hugr um at her mune þinn þroski mestr vera ok liggia uegar þinir ekki hedan.*
6		Then Hrolf came forward and asked if he should go. *þa geck Rolfr framm ok baud sik til farar.*	
7		Rögnvald said he was well suited by way of strength and prowess. But he said that he thought he was so overbearing in his temper that he might immediately rule over the realm. *Rognvalldr qvat hanum vel hent fyri saker afls ok reysti. enn qvedzt ætla at meiri ofsi væri i skapi hans enn hann mætti þegar fyri riki ráda.*	

SYNOPTIC TABLE 3.6 (continued)

	A. Orkneyinga Saga 6	B. Harald Fairhair's Saga 27	C. Landnámabók (Hauksbók 270 = Sturlubók 309)	D. Greater Saga of Olaf Tryggvason 181 (Flateyjarbók 1.222–23)	E. Tale of Thidrandi and Thorhall 1 (Flateyjarbók 1.418)
8	Then Hrollaug asked: "Do you want me to go?" *þá spurði Hrollaugr: "Villtu, at ek fara?"*	Then Hrollaug came forward and asked if he wanted him to go. *þa geck Hrollaugr framm ok spurdi ef hann vildi at hann færi.*	Then Hrollaug came forward and asked if he wanted him to go. *þa geck Hrollaugr framm ok spurdi ef hann vildi at hann færi.*	"Father, do you want me to go?" said Hrollaug. *Uilltu fadir segir Hrollaugr at ek fara.*	
9	The earl said: "An earldom may not fall to your lot. Your fate leads to Iceland. There your lineage may be prolonged and you may become high-ranking in that land." *Jarl segir: "Eigi mun þér jarldóms auðit, ok liggja fylgjur þínar til Íslands, þar muntu auka ætt þína ok mun gøfug verða í því landi."*		Rögnvald told him: "You will not become an earl. You don't have a warlike temperament. Your way lies to Iceland and you may become high-ranking and family-fortunate in that land." *Rognvalldr qvad hann ecki iarl mvndu verda. hefir þu ecki styrialldar skaplyndi. mvnv vegar þinir ligia til Islands ok mvntu þar verda gøfugr ok kynsæll á þui landi.* But there is no provision for your living here." *en engi eru her forlog þin.*	The earl answered: "An earldom may not fall to your lot. Your way leads out to Iceland. There your lineage may be prolonged and you may become high-ranking." *Jall suarar. ekki mun þer jalldoms audit verda. vt vilea uegar þinir til Jslandz. þar muntu auka þina ætt ok mun gøfug uerda.*	He said to Hrollaug: "You may not be an earl, because you don't have a warlike disposition and I think that your way lies out to Iceland." *þui sagde hann Hrollaugi suo. ekki mattu iall vera þuiat þu hefir ekki styrialldar skaplynde ok þat hygg ek at uegar þinir liggi vt til Islanz.*
10					

11	Then Einar came forth, his youngest son, and said: *þá gekk Einarr fram, inn yngsti sonr hans, ok mælti:*	Then Einar answered: *þá svaraði Einarr:*	Then Einar came forward and said *þá geck Einarr framm ok mællti.*	Then Einar came forth, his youngest son, and said: *þa gek fram Æinarr hinn yngzsti son hans, ok mællti.*
12		"I have little respect from you, and I've had little love to share. *"ek hefi lítinn metnað af þér, á ek við lítla ást at skiljask.* (Cf. A15 and D15)		
13	"Do you want me to go to the islands? *"Villtu at ek fara til eyjanna?*	I will go west to the islands, if you will give me some help. *Mun ek fara vestr til Eyja, ef þú vill fá mér styrk nǫkkurn.*	"Let me go to the Orkneys *Lattu mik fara til Orkneyia*	"Do you want me to go to the islands? *uilltu at ek fara til eyianna*
14	I will promise this, which will seem most welcome to you: I will never come back to your sight. *Ek mun því heita, er þér mun mest veitt í þykkja, at ek mun aldrigi aptr koma þér i augsýn;*	I will promise you this, which should be extremely welcome: I will never come back to Norway." *Mun ek því heita þér, er þér mun allmikill fagnaðr á vera, at ek mun eigi aptr koma til Nóregs."*	and I will promise this, which will seem best: I will never come back to your sight." *ok mvn ek þer þvi heita er þer man best þickia at ek man alldri koma aptr ne þer i augsyn.*	And I will promise you this, which will seem most wonderful to you: I will never thereafter come into your sight. *ok mun ek þui hæita þer sem þer mun mest vndir þikia at ek mun alldri koma þer j augsyn sidan*

(continued)

SYNOPTIC TABLE 3.6 (continued)

	A. Orkneyinga Saga 6	B. Harald Fairhair's Saga 27	C. Landnámabók (Hauksbók 270 = Sturlubók 309)	D. Greater Saga of Olaf Tryggvason 181 (Flateyjarbók 1.222–23)	E. Tale of Thidrandi and Thorhall 1 (Flateyjarbók 1.418)
15	I receive little honor here, and it is not likely that my advancement will be less in another place than it is here." *á ek ok við lítit gott hér at skiljask, ok ørvænt um, at minn þroski verði annars staðar minni en hér."* (Cf. B12)			I enjoy little honor here, and it is not likely that my advancement will be less in another place than it is here." *ok a ek vid litit gott her at stydiazst, ok óruent vm at minn þroski uerde annarstadar minne en her.* (Cf. B12)	
16	The earl said: *Jarl segir:*	Rögnvald said *Rognvalds segir,*	The earl said *iarlinn mællti*	The earl answered: *Jall suarar:*	
17		it pleased him well that he would not return, *at þat líkaði honum vel, at hann kvæmi eigi aptr—*	"It seems good to me *vel þicki mer*		
18	"You are unlikely to become a chieftain by virtue of your mother. *"Ólíkligr ertu til hǫfðingja fyrir sakir móður þinnar.*	"because I have little hope that your kinsmen will be honored in you, *"þvíat mér er lítil ván, at frændum þínum sé sœmð at þér,*	that you go abroad, as there is little for me from you, *at þv farir brott enn lítils er mer von at þer,*	"You are unlikely to become a chieftain by virtue of your mother, *oliklighr ertu til hofdingia firir sakir modur þinnar*	

19	Since she is thrall-born in all her lineage. *því at hon er í allar ættir þrælborin;*	since your mother's lineage is all thrall-born.” *þvíat móðurætt þín ǫll er þrælborin.”*	since your mother's lineage is all thrall-born.” *því at þín moðor ætt er oll þrælborinn.”*	since she is thrall-born in all her lineage. *þuiat hon er þrælborin j allar ættir.*
20		Rögnvald gave Einar one longship and equipped it for him. *Rögnvaldr fekk Einari eitt langskip ok skipaði þat til handa honum.*	After that, Einar went west and placed the Orkneys under him, as is told in his saga. *Eptir þat fór Einarr vestr ok lagdi vnder sik Orkneyiar sem seger i sogu hans.*	
21	But true it is that it seems better to me that you go abroad and are slow to come back.” *en satt er þat, at því betr þætti mér er þú ferr fyrr á braut ok kemr seinna aptr.”*			But true it is that it seems better to me if you go abroad and are slow to come back.” *en satt er þat at þui betr þikir mer sem þu ferr fyrr j brott en kemr seinna aftr.”*
22	Earl Rögnvald gave Einar a fully manned twenty-oar ship, *Rögnvaldr fekk Einari tvítøgsessu alskipaða,*			Earl Rögnvald gave Einar a fully manned twenty-oar ship, *Rognualldr jall fek Æinari tuitøgsessu alskipada*
23	but King Harald gave him an earl's title. *en Haraldr konungr gaf honum jarlsnafn.*			but King Harald gave him an earl's title. *en Haralldr konungr gaf honum jalls nafn.*

SYNOPTIC TABLE 5.1 Harald and Guthorm

B. Harald Fairhair's Saga 1	C. Greater Saga of Olaf Tryggvason 2 (Flateyjarbók 1.39)	D. Tale of Harald Fairhair 1 (Flateyjarbók 1.567)
1	Harald took the kingship after his father. He was then ten years old.	Harald took the kingship after his father when he was ten years old.	When he was ten years old, Harald Hálfdan's son, who was called Dofri's Foster Son, took the kingship over Hringariki, Vestfold, Vingulmark, and Raumarike.
	Haraldr tók konungdóm eptir fǫður sinn; þá var hann x. Vetra gamall;	*Haralldr tok konungdom aftir fodur sinn þa [er hann] var .x. uetra gamall.*	*At lidnum tiu uetrum alldrs Haralldz Halfdanarsonar er kalladr uar Dofrafostri tok hann konungdom yfir Hringariki Uestfolld Uingulmork ok Raumarike.*
2			At that time Guthorm, his mother's brother, was sixteen years old.
			þa uar Guthormr modurbrodir hans .xvj. uetra gamall
3	He was the greatest, strongest, and most handsome of all men, a wise man and a great leader.	He was the greatest, strongest, and most handsome of all men, a wise man and a great leader.	He was the most promising and strongest of all men, handsome, a wise man and a great leader.
	hann var allra manna mestr ok sterkastr ok fríðastr sýnum, vitr maðr ok skǫrungr mikill.	*Hann var allra manna mestr ok sterkazstr ok fridazstr synum vitr madr ok skorungr mikill.*	*hann var allra manna uænstr ok sterkaszstr fridr synum uitr madr ok skorungr mikill.*
4	Guthorm, his mother's brother, became leader of the royal retinue and all the land's government.	Guthorm, his mother's brother, the son of Sigurð Hart, became leader of the royal retinue and all the land's government.	He became leader of the royal retinue and all the land's government.
	Guthormr, móðurbróðir hans, gerðisk forstjóri fyrir hirðinni ok fyrir ǫllum landráðum;	*Guthormr son Sigurdar hiartar modur brǫdir hans giordizst forstiore firir hirdinne ok firir aullum landradum.*	*Hann gerdizst forstiore firer hirdinne ok firir ollum landradum.*
5	He was commander of the troops.	He was commander.	King Harald made his kinsman Guthorm commander of all his troops.
	hann var hertogi fyrir liðinu.	*Hann var hertoge.*	*Haralldr konungr setti Guthorm frænda sinn hertoga yfir ollu lide sinu.*

SYNOPTIC TABLE 5.2 Guthorm's response to Harald's oath

A. Harald Fairhair's Saga 4	B. Greater Saga of Olaf Tryggvason 2 (Flateyjarbók 1.40)	C. Fagrskinna Appendix 3 (from the A-Text)
1	For this speech, Commander Guthorm thanked him greatly *þessi orð þakkaði honum mjǫk Guthormr hertogi*	For this vow, Commander Guthorm thanked him *þessa heitstreingin(g) þakkade honum Guthormr hertoge*	And when Guthorm, King Harald's kinsman, heard this speech, then Guthorm stood up and spoke softly before all King Harald's retinue, many landowners, and a great many other men, and this meeting was at Haðaland on the eighth day of Yule and Guthorm began to speak: *En þá er Guðþormr, frændi Haralds konungs, heyrdi þessi orð, þá stóð Guðþormr upp ok mælti í hljóði fyrir allri hirð Haralds konungs ok mǫrgum bóndum ok miklum fjǫlda annarra manna, ok var þessi fundr á Haðalandi enn átta dag jóla, ok tók Guðþormr svá til orðs:*
2			"I hardly think men have previously heard so wise a speech from the mouths of two children no older than twelve years of age as we have just heard from the mouths of King Harald and Ragna, Aðil's daughter. And it may be true that no man, either young or old, has heard in our day words equally becoming as King Harald has spoken today. *"Varla ætla <ek> menn hafa heyrt fyrr jafnsnotrlig orð ór munni tveggja barna, þeira sem eigi eru ellri en tólf vetra gǫmul, sem nú hǫfum vér heyrt ór munni Haralds konungs ok Rǫgnu Aðilsdóttur. En þat má vist mæla með sǫnnu, at engi maðr hefir heyrt um vára daga, hvártki ungs manns né gamals, þau sem jafnviðrkœmilig má þykkja, sem þau sem Haraldr konungr hefir mælt í dag,*
3			He has said some things which will greatly increase the work of these men who want to accompany him in doing what none of his lineage has accomplished before him, although they have all been mighty warriors. *ok hefir hann þau sum mælt, er mikit má auka starf þeira manna, er hónum vilja fylgja, um þat fram, er engi hans frænda hefir haft fyrir hónum, ok hafa þeir þó allir ýrit óróamenn verit,*

(continued)

	A. Harald Fairhair's Saga 4	B. Greater Saga of Olaf Tryggvason 2 (Flateyjarbók 1.40)	C. Fagrskinna Appendix 3 (from the A-Text)
4	and made it his royal task to fulfill his speech.	and called it royal to fulfill his speech well.	And because the speech proclaimed by King Harald is so chiefly, there is now no parting from his service, so long as life continues, for any followers who have previously served him, and for his kinsmen, until it is tested whether the things that King Harald has said may, with good fortune, be fully accomplished."
	ok lét þat vera konungligt verk at efna orð sín.	*ok kallade þat konungligt at efnna uel ord sin.*	*en fyrir því at svá hǫfðingjasamlig er orðin rœða Haralds konungs, þá er nú engum manni viðskiljandi, æ meðan líf má endask til fylgðar við hann, þeir sem áðr hafa þjónat hónum eða hans frændum, fyrr en þetta er reynt, hvárt þetta má með auðnu endask til fulls, er Haraldr konungr hefir mælt."*
5			In the same place, Guthorm swore by his head that he would never forsake King Harald so long as he had life, and he would worship no other god than the one who rules all.
			Á þeim sama stað sverr Guðþormr við hǫfuð sitt, at hann skyldi aldri skiljask við Harald konung æ meðan hann hefði líf, ok engan annan guð gǫfga nema þann, er ǫllu rœðr.

SYNOPTIC TABLE 6.1 Ragnhild's ancestry

	A. Fagrskinna 1	B. Skjöldunga Saga (as preserved in Ágrip af Sögu Danakonunga, p. 325)	C. Hálfdan the Black's Saga 5	D. Tale of Hálfdan the Black 1–2 (Flateyjarbók 1.562–63)
1	The king took another wife. *fekk konungr anarrar konu.*	Harald Fairhair's mother was *Móðir Haralds hárfagra var*		That same year Hálfdan took *þann sama uetr fek Halfdan*
2	She was also called Ragnhild. *Sú hét ok Ragnhildr; (Cf. C11)*	Ragnhild, *Ragnhildr; (Cf. C11)*		Ragnhild, *Ragnhilldar (Cf. C11)*
3	Her father was Sigurð Snake-in-the-Eye, the son of Ragnar Shaggy-Breeches. *faðir hennar var Sigurðr ormr í auga, sonr Ragnars loðbrókar.*	the daughter of Sigurð Hart. *dóttir Sigurdar hjartar.*	Sigurð Hart *Sigurðr hjortr*	the daughter of Sigurð Hart, *dottur Sigurdar hiartar*
4			was named king in Hringaríki. *er nefndr konungr á Hringaríki,*	and then he took possession of Raumaríki and Haðaland. *ok þa eignadizst hann Raumariki ok Hadaland.*
5			He was bigger and stronger than any other man. He was also the most handsome of all men. *meiri ok sterkari, en hverr maðr annarra; allra manna var hann ok friðastr sýnum;*	
6			His father was Helgi the Keen *faðir hans var Helgi inn hvassi,*	

(continued)

SYNOPTIC TABLE 6.1 (continued)

	A. Fagrskinna 1	B. Skjöldunga Saga (as preserved in Ágrip af Sögu Danakonunga, p. 325)	C. Hálfdan the Black's Saga 5	D. Tale of Hálfdan the Black 1–2 (Flateyjarbok 1.562–63)
7		Sigurð Hart's mother was Aslaug, the daughter of Sigurð Serpent-in-the-Eye. *Móðir hans var Áslaug, dóttir Sigurðar orms-í-auga.*	and his mother was Aslaug, the daughter of Sigurð Snake-in-the-Eye, *en móðir hans Áslaug, dóttir Sigurðar orms-í-auga*	
8		King Redbeard of Holmgard married Unn, the daughter of Ívar Widefathomer. Their son was Randver, the brother of Harald Wartooth. His son was Sigurð Hring, *Ráðbarðr konungr í Hólmgarði fekk Unnar, dóttur Ívars ins viðfaðma. þeira son var Randvér, bróðir Haralds hilditannar. Hans son var Sigurðr hringr;*		
9		his son Ragnar Shaggy-Breeches,his son was Sigurð Serpent-in-the-Eye; his son was Horda-Knut; his son was Gorm . . . *hans son Ragnarr loðbrók; hans son var Sigurðr ormr-í-auga; hans son Hǫrða-Knútr; hans son var Gormr . . .*	the son of Ragnar Shaggy-Breeches. *Ragnars sonar loðbrókar.*	

10 It is said of him [i.e., Sigurð Hart] that when he was twelve years old, he killed Hildibrand the berserk in single combat and the twelve men who were with him. He performed many heroic deeds, and there is a long saga about him. He had two children.

11 *Svá er sagt, at þá var hann xii. vetra, er hann drap Hildibrand berserk í einvígi ok þá xii. saman; mǫrg vann hann þrekvirki, ok er lǫng saga frá honum. Hann átti ii. bǫrn:*

His daughter was called Ragnhild.

Ragnhildr hét dóttir hans. (Cf. A2, B2, and D2)

SYNOPTIC TABLE 6.2 Klakk-Harald and Ragnhild

	A. Jomsviking Saga 2	B. Greater Saga of Olaf Tryggvason 63	C. Saxo Grammaticus, Gesta Danorum 9.266	D. Tale of the Jomsvikings 3 (Flateyjarbók 1.99)
1		When Gorm was a mature man in age, he took a wife, who was called Thyri. *þá er Gormr var roskinn maðr at aldri, fekk hann konu þeirar, er þyri hét.* (Cf. A4, A6, D4 and D6)	Having achieved majority, Gorm was admonished to celebrate the holy rites of marriage, and he pursued with zeal Thyra, *Hic a majoribus conjugalia sacra celebrare permonitus, Anglorum regis Edelradi filiam, Thyram, nuptiali studio insecutus est.* (Cf. A4, A6, D4 and D6)	
2	Harald was the name of the earl who ruled over Holstein. He was called Klakk-Harald. *Haraldr hét jarl er réð fyrir Holtsetalandi; hann var kallaðr Klakk-Haraldr.*	She was the daughter of Earl Harald of Jutland, who was called Klakk-Harald. *Hon var dóttir Haralds jarls af Jótlandi, er kallaðr var Klakk-Haraldr.*	the daughter of Ethelred, king of the English. *[Anglorum regis Edelradi filiam]*	Harald was the name of an earl who ruled over Holstein. He was called Klakk-Harald. *Haralldr er nefmdr jarll æinn er red firir Hollsetulande hann var kalladr Klakharalldr.*
3	He was a wise man. *Hann var vitr maðr.* (Cf. B8)			He was a wise man. *Hann var vitr madr.* (Cf. B8)
4	The earl had a daughter who was named Thyri. *Jarl átti dóttur er þyri hét.* (Cf. B1 and C1)			He had one daughter, who was named Thyri. *Hann atti ser dottur æina er þyry er nefmd* (Cf. B1 and C1)

5	She was prophetically gifted in her wisdom, the most beautiful of women to see, and she interpreted dreams better than did other people … *Hon var spọk at viti, kvenna fríðust at sjá, ok réð betr drauma en aðrir menn. . . .**	Thyri was the most beautiful and the wisest of women. And it is said that she was the most outstanding of the women in the northern lands. She was called Thyri Denmark's Savior. *Þyri var kvenna fríðust ok vitrust. Ok þat er mælt, at hon hafi verit mestr skọrungr af konum á Norðlọndum. Hon var kọlluð þyri Danmarkarbót.*	Inasmuch as she exceeded all others in seriousness and diligence, *Illa, ut erat gravitate atque industria ante alias præstans,* (Cf. B8)	Of all women she was the wisest, and she interpreted dreams better than did other people *ok var allra kuenna vitruzst ok red drauma betr en aðrir menn*
6	And when Gorm had placed his suit before the earl, *Ok er hann hefir upp borit ørendi sín fyrir jarl,* (Cf. B1 and C1)			Thereafter, Gorm placed his suit before the earl. *sidan berr hann upp sín eyrende fyrir jalli.* (Cf. B1 and C1)
7	then the earl gave the answer that she herself would decide, "because she is much wiser than I." *þá veitir jarl þau svọr at hon skal sjálf ráða "því at hon er miklu vitrari en ek."*			And the earl gave the answer that she herself would decide, because he said that she is much wiser than I. *en hann uæitir þau suọr at hon skyllde sealf firir rada, firir þui segir hann at hon er myklu uitrari en ek.*
8	Earl Klakk-Harald was called the wisest of the men who were then in Denmark. *Klakk-Haraldr jarl var kallaðr vitrastr þeira manna, er þá váru í Danmọrk.* (Cf. A3 and D3)			
9		she established a condition for her suitor. *conditionem proco attulit.*		

* Cf. Hálfdan the Black's Saga 6: "Queen Ragnhild dreamed great dreams. She was prophetically gifted in her wisdom." *Ragnhildr drótning dreymði drauma stóra; hon var spọk at viti.*

SYNOPTIC TABLE 6.3 Hálfdan the Black's portentous dream

	A. Fagrskinna 1	B. Hálfdan the Black's Saga 7	C. Tale of Hálfdan the Black 2–3 (Flateyjarbók 1.563)
1	There was one strange thing about Hálfdan: he never dreamed. *Með Hálfdani var kynligr einn hlutr; hann dreymði aldrigi.*	King Hálfdan never dreamed. That seemed extraordinary to him, *Hálfdan konungr dreymði aldri; honum þótti þat undarligt*	There was one strange thing about Hálfdan: he never dreamed. *Með Halfdani er kynligr hlutr æinn. hann dreymde aldrigi.*
2	That thing he presented to the man called Thorleif the Prophetically-Gifted .and he sought his counsel on what he could do. *En þann hlut bar hann upp fyrir þann mann, er hét þorleifr spaki, ok leitaði ráða, hvat at því mætti gøra.*	and he went to the man named Thorleif the Prophetically-Gifted and sought his counsel on what he might be able to do. *ok bar þat fyrir þann mann, er nefndr er þorleifr inn spaki, ok leitaði ráða, hvat at því myndi mega gera.*	That thing he presented to the man called Thorleif the Prophetically-Gifted, and he sought his counsel on what he could do. *en þann hlut bar hann fyrir þann mann er þorleifr spaki het, ok leitade rada, huat at þui matti gera.*
3	And he described what he did when he sought to know something: he went in a pigsty to sleep and then a dream never failed to come to him. *Ok hann sagði, hvat hann gørði, at þá er hann forvitnaði nǫkkurn hlut at vita, at hann fór í svinaból at sofa, ok brásk <honum þá eigi> draumr.*	Thorleif described what he did when he sought to know something: he went in a pigsty to sleep and a dream never failed to come to him. *þorleifr sagði, hvat hann gerði, ef hann forvitnaði at vita nǫkkura hlut, at hann fœri í svinabœli at sofa, ok brásk honum eigi draumr,*	And he described what he did when he wanted to know something: he went in a pigsty to sleep and a dream never failed to come to him. *ok hann sagde, huat hann gerde, at þa er hann uilde foruitnazst nokkura hluti at hann fór j suinaboæli at sofa ok brazst honum alldri draumr.*
4	The king did that and this dream came to him. *Ok konungr gørði þat ok birtisk hónum draumr þessi:*	The king did that and this dream came to him. *—ok konungr gerði þat ok birtisk honum draumr þessi,*	King Hálfdan now did thus: he went in a pigsty and sleeping, this remarkable dream quickly came to him. *Halfdan konungr gerde nu suo fór j suinabæle ok sofnnade bratt birtizst honum draumr æinn merkiligr.*
5	It seemed to him that he was naked and his hair was all in locks. *Hónum sýndisk, at hann væri maðr berr ok hár hans allt í lokkum.*	It seemed to him that he was the best haired of all men and his hair was all in locks, *honum sýndisk, at hann væri allra manna bezt hærðr ok var hár hans alt í lokkum,*	It seemed to him that he was the best haired of men and his hair was in locks. *honum syndizt at hann væri manna bezst hærdr ok væri har hans j lokkum*

A. Fagrskinna 1	B. Hálfdan the Black's Saga 7	C. Tale of Hálfdan the Black 2–3 (Flateyjarbok 1.563)
6 Some were long to the ground, but some to the middle of his leg or to the middle of his calf at his knee, or the middle of his side, some no longer than to his throat, and some only sprouted out of his head like horns. *Váru sumir síðir til jarðar, en sumir í miðjan legg eða í miðjan kálfa <á> kne, eða miðja síðu, en sumir eigi lengra en á háls, en sumir ekki meir en sprottnir ór hausi sem knýflar,*	some long to the ground, some to the middle of his leg, some to his knee, some to his waist, some to the middle of his side, some to his throat, and some only sprouted out of his head like horns. *sumir síðir til jarðar, sumir í miðjan legg, sumir á kné, sumir í mjǫðum, sumir miðja síðu, sumir á háls, en sumir ekki meir en sprotnir upp ór hausi sem knýflar,*	Some were long to the ground, some to the middle of his leg or to his knee, or the middle of his side, some no longer than to his throat, and some only sprouted out of his head like horns. *ok suo sider at sumir tæki til jarðar. sumir j midian legg edr a kne edr a midea sidu. sumir ægi leingri en a háls en sumir ægi meirr en sprottnir ór hause sem knyflar.*
7 His locks were of all different colors, but one lock vanquished all others in fairness, beauty, and radiance. *en á lokkum hans var hverskyns litr, en einn lokkr sigraði alla aðra með fegrð ok með fríðleik ok ljósleik.*	His locks were of all different colors, but one lock vanquished all in fairness, radiance, and size. *en á lokkum hans var hvers kyns litr, en einn lokkr sigraði alla með fegrð ok ljósleik ok mikilleik.*	
8 He told the dream to Thorleif, and Thorleif interpreted the dream thus: *En þorleifi sagði hann þann draum, ok þýddi þorleifr svá drauminn,*	He told Thorleif the dream, and he interpreted it thus: *þorleifi sagði hann þann draum, en hann þýddi svá,*	He told the dream to Thorleif the Prophetically-Gifted, and Thorleif interpreted it thus: *en þorleifui spaka sagde hann þann draum en þorleifr þydde suo*
9 Many offspring would come from him, and his offspring would rule the lands with great distinction, but not all with equal distinction. *at mikill afspringr myndi koma af honum, ok myndi hans afspringr lǫndum ráða með miklum veg, ok þó eigi allir með jǫfnum veg.*	Many offspring would come from him and they would rule the lands with great distinction, but not all equally great. *at mikill afspringr myndi af honum koma ok myndi sá lǫndum ráða með miklum veg ok þó eigi allir með jammiklum,*	Many offspring would come from him, and his offspring would rule the lands with great distinction, but not all with equal distinction. *at mikill afspringr munde koma af honum ok munde hans afspringr londum rada med myklum ueg ok þo ægi aller med iofnum ueg*
10 One would come from his lineage who would be better than all, *En einn mundi sá af hans ætt koma, er ǫllum myndi vera betri,*	And one would come from his lineage that would be greater and higher than all, *en einn mundi sá af hans ætt koma, at ǫllum myndi meiri ok œðri,*	One would come from his lineage who would be more worthy and more glorious than all, *en æinn munde sa af hans ætt koma, er ollum munde vera mæire mætri ok agætare*

(continued)

SYNOPTIC TABLE 6.3 (continued)

	A. Fagrskinna 1	B. Hálfdan the Black's Saga 7	C. Tale of Hálfdan the Black 2–3 (Flateyjarbok 1.563)
11	and people take it to be true that this lock betokens Saint Olaf, *ok hafa menn þat fyrir satt, at sá lokkr jartegnði enn helga Óláf,*	and people take it to be true that this lock betokens King Olaf the Saint. *ok hafa menn þat fyrir satt, at sá lokkr jartegnði Óláf konung inn helga.*	and people take it to be true that this lock designated Olaf Haraldsson, *ok hafa menn þat firir satt, at sa lokkr merkte Olaf Haralldzson*
12	who among all Norway's kings is holier and more illustrious in heaven and on earth, as all men know. *er ǫllum Nóregs konungum er helgari ok bjartari í himnum ok á jǫrðu, svá at allir menn viti.*		who among all Norway's kings is more with the holy company and more illustrious in heaven and on earth, as all know. *er ollum Noregs konungum er meire med helgi sinne ok biartari a himne ok a jordu suo at aller uite.*

SYNOPTIC TABLE 6.4 Variant dreams: Hálfdan and Ragnhild

	A. Hálfdan the Black's Saga 7	B. Hálfdan the Black's Saga 6 and Harald Fairhair's Saga 43
1	King Hálfdan never dreamed. That seemed extraordinary to him, and he went to the man named Thorleif the Prophetically-Gifted and sought his counsel on what he might be able to do. *Hálfdan konungr dreymði aldri; honum þótti þat undarligt ok bar þat fyrir þann mann, er nefndr er þorleifr inn spaki, ok leitaði ráða, hvat at því myndi mega gera.*	Queen Ragnhild dreamed great dreams. *Ragnhildr drótning dreymði drauma stóra;*
2	Thorleif described what he did when he sought to know something: he went in a pigsty to sleep, and a dream never failed to come to him. *þorleifr sagði, hvat hann gerði, ef hann forvitnaði at vita nǫkkura hlut, at hann færi í svinabœli at sofa, ok brásk honum eigi draumr,*	She was prophetically gifted in her wisdom. *hon var spǫk at viti;*
3	The king did that, and this dream came to him. *—ok konungr gerði þat ok birtisk honum draumr þessi,*	One of her dreams was that *sá var einn draumr hennar, at*

SYNOPTIC TABLE 6.4 (continued)

	A. Hálfdan the Black's Saga 7	B. Hálfdan the Black's Saga 6 and Harald Fairhair's Saga 43
4	It seemed to him that he was the best haired of all men and his hair was all in locks, *honum sýndisk, at hann væri allra manna bezt hærðr ok var hár hans alt í lokkum,*	she seemed to be standing in her garden and taking a thorn out of her shirt. And as she held it, it grew so much that it became a large twig, so that one end of it went down to the earth and quickly took root. Then the other end of the tree quickly went high up in the air. *hon þóttisk vera stǫdd í grasgarði sínum ok taka þorn einn ór serk sér, ok er hon helt á, þá óx hann svá, at þat varð teinn einn mikill, svá at annarr endir tók jǫrð niðr ok varð brátt rótfastr, ok því næst var brátt annarr endir trésins hátt í loptit upp;*
5	some long to the ground, some to the middle of his leg, some to his knee, some to his hip, some to the middle of his side, some to his throat, and some only sprouted out of his head like horns. *sumir síðir til jarðar, sumir í miðjan legg, sumir á kné, sumir í mjǫðum, sumir miðja síðu, sumir á háls, en sumir ekki meir en sprotnir upp ór hausi sem knýflar,*	Then the tree seemed so large to her that she could hardly see over it, and it was wonderfully thick. *því næst sýndisk henni treit svá mikit, at hon fekk varla sét yfir upp; þat var furðu digrt;*
6	His locks were of all different colors, *en á lokkum hans var hvers kyns litr,*	The lowest part of the tree was red as blood, but up the stem it was bright green and up in the branches it was snow white. *inn nezti hlutr trésins var rauðr sem blóð, en þá leggrinn upp fagrgrænn, en upp til limanna snjóhvítt;*
7	but one lock vanquished all in fairness, radiance, and size. *en einn lokkr sigraði alla með fegrð ok ljósleik ok mikilleik.*	
8		There were a great many large branches of the tree, some high and some low. The branches of the tree were so great that it seemed to her they spread over all Norway and even further. *þar váru kvistir af trénu margir stórir, sumir ofarr, en sumir neðarr; limar trésins váru svá miklar, at henni þóttu dreifask um allan Nóreg ok enn víðara.*
9	He told Thorleif the dream, and he interpreted it thus: *þorleifi sagði hann þann draum, en hann þýddi svá,*	. . . Wise men say that *. . . Svá segja fróðir menn, at*

(continued)

SYNOPTIC TABLE 6.4 (continued)

A. Hálfdan the Black's Saga 7	B. Hálfdan the Black's Saga 6 and Harald Fairhair's Saga 43
10	Harald the Fairhair became the most handsome of all men, also the strongest and greatest, the most openhanded with his wealth, and gifted with great popularity among his men. He was a great warrior at the beginning of his life, and men interpreted this with reference to the great tree his mother had seen in her dream before his birth, *Haraldr inn hárfagri hafi verit allra manna fríðastr sýnum ok sterkastr ok mestr, inn ǫrvasti af fé ok allvinsæll við sína menn; hann var hermaðr mikill ǫndverða æfi, ok þýða menn þat nú, at vitat hafi um tré þat it mikla, er móður hans sýndisk í draumi fyrir burð hans,*
11	where the lowest part of the tree was red as blood. The trunk above was fair and green, which betokened the flowering of his realm. And the tree was white at the top. That signified that he would achieve an old and hoary age. *er inn neðsti hlutr trésins var rauðr sem blóð, en þá var leggrinn upp frá fagr ok grœnn, at þat jartegnði blóma ríkis hans, en at ofanverðu var hvítt tréit; þar sýndisk þat, at hann mundi fá elli ok hæru;*
12 Many offspring would come from him and would rule the lands with great distinction, *at mikill afspringr myndi af honum koma ok myndi sá lǫndum ráða með miklum veg*	The limbs and branches of the tree proclaim his descendants, who spread over all the land, and ever since the kings of Norway have been of his lineage. *kvistir ok limar trésins boðaði afkvæmi hans, er um alt land dreifðisk, ok af hans ætt hafa verit jafnan síðan konungar í Nóregi.*
13 but not all equally great. *ok þó eigi allir með jammiklum,*	
14 And one would come from his lineage that would be greater and higher than all, *en einn myndi sá af hans ætt koma, at ǫllum myndi meiri ok œðri,*	
15 and people believe it to be true that this lock betokens King Olaf the Saint. *ok hafa menn þat fyrir satt, at sá lokkr jartegnði Óláf konung inn helga.*	

SYNOPTIC TABLE 6.5 Variant dreams: Hálfdan, Ragnhild, and Barð

	A. Hálfdan the Black's Saga 7	B. Hálfdan the Black's Saga 6 and Harald Fairhair's Saga 43	C. Barð's Saga 1
1	King Hálfdan never dreamed. That seemed extraordinary to him, and he went to the man named Thorleif the Prophetically-Gifted and sought his counsel on what he might be able to do. *Hálfdan konungr dreymði aldri; honum þótti þat undarligt ok bar þat fyrir þann mann, er nefndr er þorleifr inn spaki, ok leitaði ráða, hvat at því myndi mega gera.*	Queen Ragnhild dreamed great dreams. *Ragnhildr drótning dreymði drauma stóra;*	. . . Dofri trained Barð in all kinds of art, including genealogy and feats of arms, *. . . vandi Dofri hann á alls kyns íþróttir ok ættvísi ok vígfimi,*
2	Thorleif described what he did when he sought to know something: he went in a pigsty to sleep and a dream never failed to come to him. *þorleifr sagði, hvat hann gerði, ef hann forvitnaði at vita nǫkkura hlut, at hann fœri í svinabœli at sofa, ok brásk honum eigi draumr,*	She was prophetically gifted in her wisdom. *hon var spǫk at viti;*	and it was not clear that he did not acquire spells and heathen lore, so that he was both very wise and possessed of prophetic powers, for Dofri was endowed with these. . . . *ok eigi var traust at hann næmi ekki galdra ok forneskju, svá at bæði var hann forspár ok margvís, því at Dofri var við þetta slunginn.* . . .
3	The king did that, and this dream came to him. *—ok konungr gerði þat ok birtisk honum draumr þessi,*	One of her dreams was that *sá var einn draumr hennar, at*	One night, Barð lay in his bed, and he dreamed that *þá var þat á einni nótt, at Bárðr lá í sæng sinni, at hann dreymdi at*
4	It seemed to him that he was the best haired of all men and his hair was all in locks, *honum sýndisk, at hann væri allra manna bezt hærðr ok var hár hans alt í lokkum,*	she seemed to be standing in her garden and taking a thorn out of her shirt. And as she held it, it grew so much that it became a large twig, so that one end of it went down to the earth and quickly took root. Then the other end of the tree quickly went high up in the air. *hon þóttisk vera stǫdd í grasgarði sínum ok taka þorn einn ór serk sér, ok er hon helt á, þá óx hann svá, at þat varð teinn einn mikill, svá at annarr endir tók jǫrð niðr ok varð brátt rótfastr, ok því næst var brátt annarr endir trésins hátt í loptit upp;*	it seemed to him a great tree rose up in the hearth of his foster father, Dofri. *honum þótti tré eitt mikit koma upp í eldstó fóstra síns, Dofra.*

(continued)

SYNOPTIC TABLE 6.5 (continued)

	A. Hálfdan the Black's Saga 7	B. Hálfdan the Black's Saga 6 and Harald Fairhair's Saga 43	C. Barð's Saga 1
5	some long to the ground, some to the middle of his leg, some to his knee, some to his hip, some to the middle of his side, some to his throat, and some only sprouted out of his head like horns. *sumir síðir til jarðar, sumir í miðjan legg, sumir á kné, sumir í mjǫðum, sumir miðja síðu, sumir á háls, en sumir ekki meir en sprotnir upp ór hausi sem knýflar,*	Then the tree seemed so large to her that she could hardly see over it, and it was wonderfully thick. *því næst sýndisk henni treit svá mikit, at hon fekk varla sét yfir upp; þat var furðu digrt;*	It had a great many branches all through its limbs, and it grew so fast that it curled up the rock cave and then out through the rock. It was so big that this bud seemed to him to take over all Norway, *þat var harla margkvistótt upp til limanna. þat óx svá skjótt, at þat hrökk upp í helisbjargit ok því næst út í gegnum hellisbjargit. þar næst var þat svá mikit, at brum þess þótti honum taka um allan Noreg,*
6	His locks were of all different colors, *en á lokkum hans var hvers kyns litr,*	The lowest part of the tree was red as blood, but up the stem it was bright green and up in the branches it was snow white. *inn nezti hlutr trésins var rauðr sem blóð, en þá leggrinn upp fagrgrœnn, en upp til limanna snjóhvítt;*	
7	but one lock vanquished all in fairness, radiance, and size. *en einn lokkr sigraði alla með fegrð ok ljósleik ok mikilleik.*		and on one branch there was the fairest flower, although all were blooming greatly. One branch was the color of gold. *ok þó var á einum kvistinum fegrsta blóm, ok voru þó allir blómamiklir. Á einum kvistinum var gulls litr.*
8		There were a great many large branches of the tree, some high and some low. The branches of the tree were so great that it seemed to her they spread over all Norway and even further. *þar váru kvistir af trénu margir stórir, sumir ofarr, en sumir neðarr; limar trésins váru svá miklar, at henni þóttu dreifask um allan Nóreg ok enn víðara.*	
9	He told Thorleif the dream, and he interpreted it thus: *þorleifi sagði hann þann draum, en hann þýddi svá,*	. . . Wise men say that . . . *Svá segja fróðir menn, at*	Barð interpreted this dream to mean that *þann draum réð Bárðr svá, at*

SYNOPTIC TABLE 6.5 (continued)

A. Hálfdan the Black's Saga 7	B. Hálfdan the Black's Saga 6 and Harald Fairhair's Saga 43	C. Barð's Saga 1
10	Harald the Fairhair became the most handsome of all men, also the strongest and greatest, the most openhanded with his wealth, and gifted with great popularity among his men. He was a great warrior at the beginning of his life, and men interpreted this with reference to the great tree his mother had seen in her dream before his birth,	some royal-born man might come to Dofri's cave and would be raised there, and this same man would become sole king over Norway.
		í hellinn til Dofra mundi koma nokkr konungborinn maðr ok fæðast þar upp, ok sjá sami maðr mundi verða einvaldskonungr yfir Noregi.
	Haraldr inn hárfagri hafi verit allra manna fríðastr sýnum ok sterkastr ok mestr, inn ǫrvasti af fé ok allvinsæll við sína menn; hann var hermaðr mikill ǫndverða æfi, ok þýða menn þat nú, at vitat hafi um tré þat it mikla, er móður hans sýndisk í draumi fyrir burð hans,	
11	where the lowest part of the tree was red as blood. The trunk above was fair and green, which betokened the flowering of his realm. And the tree was white at the top. That signified that he would achieve an old and hoary age.	
	er inn neðsti hlutr trésins var rauðr sem blóð, en þá var leggrinn upp frá fagr ok grœnn, at þat jartegnði blóma ríkis hans, en at ofanverðu var hvítt tréit; þar sýndisk þat, at hann myndi fá elli ok hæru;	
12 Many offspring would come from him and would rule the lands with great distinction,	The limbs and branches of the tree proclaim his descendants, who spread over all the land, and ever since the kings of Norway have been of his lineage.	
at mikill afspringr myndi af honum koma ok myndi sá lǫndum ráða með miklum veg	*kvistir ok limar trésins boðaði afkvæmi hans, er um alt land dreifðisk, ok af hans ætt hafa verit jafnan síðan konungar í Nóregi.*	

(continued)

SYNOPTIC TABLE 6.5 (continued)

	A. Hálfdan the Black's Saga 7	B. Hálfdan the Black's Saga 6 and Harald Fairhair's Saga 43	C. Barð's Saga 1
13	but not all equally great. And one would come from his lineage that would be greater and higher than all, *ok þó eigi allir með jammiklum, en einn myndi sá af hans ætt koma, at ǫllum myndi meiri ok œðri,*		And the fair branch would signify the king who descended from the ancestor who grew up there and that king would proclaim a new religion. *En kvistr sá inn fagri mundi merkja þann konung er af þess ættmanni væri kominn er þar yxi upp, ok mundi sá konungr boða annan sið en þá gengi.*
14			To him, this dream was not very pleasant. *Var honum draumr sá ekki mjök skapfelldr.*
15	and people take it to be true that this lock betokens King Olaf the Saint. *ok hafa menn þat fyrir satt, at sá lokkr jartegnði Óláf konung inn helga.*		People take it to be true that the bright flower designates King Olaf Haraldsson. *Hafa menn þat fyrir satt, at þat it bjarta blóm merkti Ólaf konung Haraldsson.*
16			After this dream, Barð and Flaumgerð went away from Dofri. *ok eptir draum þennan fóru þau Bárðr ok Flaumgerðr í burt frá Dofra.*
17			And a little while later, Harald Hálfdan's son came there, and he was reared there by Dofri the giant. *En litlu síðar kom þar Haraldr Hálfdánarson ok fæddist þar upp með Dofra jötun.*
18			Dofri raised him to be king thereafter over Norway, as is told in the Saga of Harald, Dofri's Foster Son. *Efldi Dofri hann síðan til konungs yfir Noregi eptir því sem segir í sögu Haralds konungs Dofrafostra.*

SYNOPTIC TABLE 7.1 Myths of the unwelcome guest

A. Tale of Hálfdan the Black 5–6 (Flateyjarbók 1.564–66)	B. Grímnismál Prologue and Epilogue
1 Now, it is told of King Hálfdan that he stayed quietly at home in Uppland. *Nu er at segia fra Halfdani konungi er hann sat um kyrt heima a Upplondum.*	
2 Then, something novel occurred. *þat bar til nylundu at*	
3 Much money and valuable goods vanished from the king's treasury, and they knew not who caused this. *fee mikit ok gripir godir hurfu ór gullhuse konungs ok vissu þeir æigi huerr uallda munde.*	Frigg said: "[King Geirrøð] is so stingy of food that he tortures his guests if it seems to him that too many come." Oðinn said that was a big lie. They laid a wager on that question. Frigg sent her maid, Fulla, to Geirrøð. She told the king to beware, lest a magician attack him, one who had come into the land, and she said that he had a sign: that no dog was so fierce as to leap at him. . . . *Frigg segir: "Hann er matníðingr sá, at hann qvelr gesti sína, ef hánom þiccia ofmargir koma." Óðinn segir, at þat er in mesta lygi. þau veðia um þetta mál. Frigg sendi escismey sína, Fullo, til Geirroðar. Hon bað konung varaz, at eigi fyrgerði hanóm fiǫlkunnigr maðr, sá er þar var kominn í land, oc sagði þat marc á, at engi hundr var svá ólmr, at á hann myndi hlaupa . . . .*
4 It gave the king great anxiety because it seemed to him this might recur. *fek konungi þat mikillar ahyggiu þui at hann þottizst uita at sea munde uitea oftar.*	
5 He had preparations made with cunning devices and strong spells so that any man who might enter the house to take the money would remain there until the king's men came. *Lætr hann nu umbud uæita mede klokligum brǫgdum ok sterkum atkuædum suo at huerr sa madr er j husit færi ok fet uillde taka uard þar at vera ok þess at bida at menn kæmi.*	
6 It seemed to the king that the culprit might be both big and strong, so he had his men produce exceptionally large fetters of the strongest steel and had them twist the most powerful lead bands. *þat þottizst konungr vita at sa munde take báde mikill ok sterkr er a þessum oknyttum la þui let hann smida ser fiotur fragerda mikinn af hinu sterkazsta stale ok snua hinu ramligazstu blybond.*	

(continued)

SYNOPTIC TABLE 7.1 (continued)

A. Tale of Hálfdan the Black 5–6 (Flateyjarbók 1.564–66)	B. Grímnismál Prologue and Epilogue
7	Thereafter, there is this to tell: Early one morning, when his men came to the treasury, they saw there	[Geirrøð] had that man seized whom no dog wanted to attack.
	Sidan er þat at segia æinn morgin snemma er menn koma til gullhussins sa þeir þar	*lætr hann handtaca þann mann, er eigi vildo hundar á ráða.*
8	an enormous giant. This fiend was both fat and tall.	He was in a blue cloak and was named Grímnir.
	allmykinn jǫtun. þessi dolgr uar bade digr ok hárr.	*Sá var í feldi blám oc nefndiz Grímnir,*
9	Many men thronged around him and put the fetters on him, though he had much greater strength than they. Sixty men overpowered him and placed the fetters on him. They bound his hands firmly behind him with the lead bands. Then he bore himself rather poorly.	
	þeir hloduzst a hann margir ok baru at honum fioturinn ok uard hann þeim helldr handstyrkr .lx. manna foru til adr hann uard j fioturinn færdr. bundu þeir nu hendr hans ramliga a bak aptr med blybǫndunum. barzt hann þa raunlitt af.	
10	King Hálfdan asked his name. He declared himself to be called Dofri, and he had his home in the mountain that is named for him.	
	Halfdan konungr spurde hann at nafnni en hann letzst Dofri hæita ok æiga hæima j fialle þui er uit hann er kent.	
11	The king asked if he had stolen his gold. He answered that was true. Then he asked for mercy and offered to pay threefold for the gold. But the king said he would never have mercy. Bound there, he would await the Assembly, where he would be condemned to the most disgraceful death. And the king told Dofri he would grant him no means of subsistence, and should anyone provide help for him or give him food, he would make that person cede his life and would execute all others. Then the king went home and Dofri sat there, all bound up.	He said nothing more about himself, although he was asked. The king had him tortured to make him speak and set him between two fires. He stayed there eight nights.
	Konungr spurde huort hann hefde stolit gulle hans. hann quad þat satt vera ok beiddizst þa grida ok baud at þrigillda honum aftr gullit. en konungr sagde at hann skyllde alldri gridum na ok þar bundinn bida þess er þing væri kuatt ok honum skyllde dæma þar hinn haduligazsta dauda. sagde hann ok at honum skyllde æinge biargir ueita ne mat gefa nema huerr at gerde skyllde lifit lata ok ongu odru firirkoma. for konungr þa heim en Dofri sat þar bundinn eftir.	*oc sagði ecci fleira frá sér, þótt hann væri at spurðr. Konungr lét hann pína til sagna oc setia milli elda tveggia, oc sat hann þar átta nætr.*

A. Tale of Hálfdan the Black 5–6 (Flateyjarbók 1.564–66)	B. Grímnismál Prologue and Epilogue
12	A little later, Harald came home. He heard the news and also the words of his father. *Litlu sidar kom Haralldr heim. hann frettir þessi tidende ok suo vmmæli fǫdur sins.*	King Geirroð had a son, ten years old, and he was called Agnar. . . . *Geirroðr konungr átti son, tío vetra gamlan, oc hét Agnarr . . .*
13	He felt sorry for Dofri and wanted to plead for him. *þottizst hann þa uita at honum munde ekki gera at bidia firir honum.*	Agnar went to Grímnir and gave him a full horn to drink. *Agnarr gecc at Grímni oc gaf hánom horn fult at drecca,*
14	Harald was then five years old. He went over where Dofri sat. Dofri made himself look bad and all full of grief. *Haralldr uar þa .v. ara gamall. honum verdr þangat gengit er Dofri sat. hann gerdizst þa helldr hardlæitr ok miog harmþrunginn.*	
15	Then Harald said: "You are doing poorly. Would you like to receive your life from me?" *Haralldr mællti þa. litt ertu staddr edr uilltu þiggia lif ath mer.*	He said that the king did ill when he had an innocent man tortured. *sagði, at konungr gorði illa, er hann lét pína hann saclausan.*
16	"I don't know about that," said Dofri, "I would place you in great danger because of your father's words." *Ek uæit þat æigi suo uist segir Dofri sakir ummæla fǫdur þins huort ek uil koma þer j suo mykla hættu.*	Grímnir drank it down. *Grímnir dracc af.*
17	"Why do you need to consider that?" said Harald. *Huat muntu þurfa at sia firir þui segir Haralldr.*	
18	Then he drew the sword that he had with him that the Finn had given him, which was of very choice iron. He cut the fetters and lead bands from Dofri. *Hann bra þa saxi þui er hann hafde vid sig ok Finnrinn hafde gefit honum þat uar afburdar jarnn kosti. hann snidr fioturinn ok blybondin af Dofra.*	
19	When he was free, Dofri thanked Harald for having saved his life and thereafter he went off. He tied his shoes and laid his tail on his back and set off so that of him there was no trace. *en er hann uar laus uordinn þakkade hann Haralldi lifgiofina ok hafde sig sidan af stad. batt hann ekki læinge sko sina ok lagde halann a bak ser ok setti j burtu suo at huorke sa af honum uedr ne reyk.*	

(continued)

A. Tale of Hálfdan the Black 5–6 (Flateyjarbók 1.564–66)	B. Grímnismál Prologue and Epilogue
20 Not long thereafter, Hálfdan's men searched for Dofri. The king asked what was the truth of this business, and Harald said he had freed Dofri. *eigi myklu sidarr soknudu menn Dofra. spurde konungr huerr þessa uerks munde sannr en Haralldr sagdizst Dofra leyst hafa.*	
21 The king was furious at that, so enraged that he pushed his son Harald away, but he said he could not bear to have him killed. He added with severity that no one should give sustenance to him and he told him he needed to help catch Dofri the troll. *konungr vard uit þetta akafa ræidr suo at hann rak Haralld son sinn j burtu en kuezst eigi nenna at lata drepa hann. lagde hann þar suo rigt vid at honum skyllde einge biorg uæita bad hann þar nu hialp taka sem Dofri troll væri.*	
22 Harald now went off to the marches and woods. He lay out there by night. And when the troops had been there five nights, Harald remained in a clearing. He was quite exhausted by both hunger and thirst. Then he saw a huge monster walking by, and he recognized him as Dofri the troll. *gek Haralldr nu j brott a merker ok skoga la hann þa vti suo at nattum skifti. en er lidnar vǫru .v. nætr þa uar Haralldr staddr j einu riodri gerdizst hann þa þrekadr miog bade af hungri ok þosta. ser hann þa huar gengr greppur mikill þikizst hann þa kenna Dofra troll.*	
23 Dofri spoke: "Aren't you the king's son? Do you suffer on my account, and will you go with me to my household?" *hann mællti þa. æigi ertu nu ok vel staddr konungsson at suo er. ma þat kalla at þu hliotir þetta mest af mer edr uilltu nu fara med mer til heimkynna minna.*	
24 Harald agreed to that. *Haralldr iattade þui.*	

A. Tale of Hálfdan the Black 5–6 (Flateyjarbók 1.564–66)	B. Grímnismál Prologue and Epilogue
25 Dofri took Harald up in his arms and went with him very swiftly until he came to a large cave, carrying the lad on his forearm. But when he entered the cave, he bowed less low than he intended and he struck the boy on the cavern rock so hard that that he was knocked unconscious. *tok hann Haralld þa upp j fang ser ok gek med hann helldr snudigt allt þar til er hann kom at helli æinum storum hann bar þa pilltinn a handlegg ser. en er hann gengr inn j hellinn lytr hann minnr en hann ætlade ok keyrir upp sueininn undir hellisbergit ok suo hart at hann uar þegar j ouite.*	
26 Then it seemed to Dofri that there would be great talk of his mishap if he had killed the lad and he wept greatly over him. But as he screwed up his face and shook his head, Harald recovered his senses and looked up at Dofri the churl, who seemed even more huge when he began crying and puffed his cheeks and stretched his eyes that way. *Dofra þotti þa mikit ordit slys sitt ef hann hefde drepit pilltinn. fek honum þa suo mikit at hann gret þa uppi yfir honum. en er hann gerir skelpurnar ok skerr hofudit þa raknar Haralldr vid ok litr þa upp j mote Dofra karlle ok syndizst hann þa helldr storskorinn er hann beygde skaflinn ok belgde huoptana ok vtbitade þannueg augunum.*	
27 Then Harald spoke. "It is true to tell my foster father that foul is fair if he weeps, since it seems to me that you are now very ugly in appearance and you should be cheerful, since no harm has come to me." *þa mællti Haralldr. þat er þo satt at segia fostri minn at fárr er fagr ef grætr þuiat mer synizst þu nu helldr bragdillr ok yfirlita mikill ok vertu katr þuiat mig sakar ekki.*	
28 Dofri rejoiced then and laid Harald down in his cave. *Gladdizst Dofri þa ok let Haralld nidr j helli sinum.*	
29 Harald was there for five years and lacked nothing that he needed. Dofri waited on him so much that he would not let him do anything in return. *þar var Haralldr .v. uetr ok skorti ekki þat er hafa þurfti. Dofri unni honum suo mikit at hann matti ekki j mot honum lata.*	

(continued)

A. Tale of Hálfdan the Black 5–6 (Flateyjarbók 1.564–66)	B. Grímnismál Prologue and Epilogue
30	Dofri taught him much knowledge and trained him in the arts. Harald gained much in both strength and growth.	
	mart kende Dofri honum j frodum. suo uande Dofri hann uit jþrottir. mikit gekzst Haralldr vid bæde vm uoxst ok afl.	
31	It is told that one day Dofri came to speak with Harald and said this:	
	þat er sagt at æinn dag kom Dofri at male vid Haralld ok talade suo.	
32	"Now I think I have repaid you for having saved my life, because I have now brought to you the kingdom, as your father is dead and I was not far from there.	King Geirroð sat and held a sword on his knee and drew it halfway. But when he heard that it was Oðinn who had come, he stood up and wanted to remove Oðinn from the fires. The sword slipped from his hand, with its hilt down. The king struck his foot and stumbled forward. The sword went through him and killed him.
	nu þikiumzst ek hafa launat þer lifgiofina þuiat nu hefui ek komit þer til konungdomsins þuiat fadir þinn er daudr ok var ek þar ekki fiarre.	*Geirroðr konungr sat oc hafði sverð um kné sér, oc brugðit til miðs. Enn er hann heyrði, at Óðinn var þar kominn, stóð hann up oc vildi taca Óðin frá eldinom. Sverðit slap ór hendi hánom, visso hioltin niðr. Konungr drap fœti oc steyptiz áfram, enn sverðit stóð í gognom hann, oc fecc hann bana.*
33		Oðinn disappeared then.
		Óðinn hvarf þá.
34	Now you shall go home and take up your realm.	And Agnar was king there for a long time thereafter.
	nu skaltu fara heim ok taka vid riki þinu.	*Enn Agnarr var þar konungr lengi síðan.*
35	I proclaim this to you that you will not have your hair cut at all, or your nails until you become sole king over all Norway.	
	legg ek þat til med þer at þu latir huorke skera hár þitt ne negl fyrr en þu verdr æinualldzkonungr yfir ollum Noregi.	
36	I shall be in your service and in battles with you. I will be of assistance to you because I will be able to inflict wounds because I will not be visible.	
	skal ek ok þer j lidsinne vera ok j bardogum med þer. mun þer þat at gagnni verda þuiat ek mun skęinuhættr uera saker þess at ek mun ekki audsærr vera.	

SYNOPTIC TABLE 7.1 (continued)

A. Tale of Hálfdan the Black 5–6 (Flateyjarbók 1.564–66)	B. Grímnismál Prologue and Epilogue
37	Go now, be hale and well, and go all the way to glory and times of honor, and may you have no less good fortune than if you had been next to me." *far þu nu heill ok uel ok gangi þer allt til tirs ok tima heidrs ok hamingiu æigi at sidr þott þu hafir hea mer verit.*	
38	Harald felt much for Dofri when they parted. *Fann þa miog a Dofra er þeir skildu.*	
39	And when Harald came home, he was made king over all the districts his father had previously ruled. *En er Haralldr kom heim var hann til konungs tekinn yfir oll þau fylke er fadir hans hafde firir radit.*	
40	He told his men where he had been these past five years, and he was then called Harald Dofri's Foster Son. *sagde hann monnum sinum huar er hann hafde uerit þessa .v. uetr uar hann þa kalladr Haralldr Dofrafostri.*	

SYNOPTIC TABLE 7.2 Further variants on the theme of the unwelcome guest

	A. Tale of Hálfdan the Black 5–6 (Flateyjarbók 1.564–66)	B. Grímnismál Prologue and Epilogue	C. Hálfdan the Black's Saga 8
1	Now, it is told of King Hálfdan that he stayed quietly at home in Uppland. *Nu er at segia fra Halfdani konungi er hann sat um kyrt heima a Upplondum.*		King Hálfdan was on a Yule visit in Haðaland. *Hálfdán konungr var á jólavist á Haðalandi.*
2	Then, something novel occurred. *Þat bar til nylundu at*		Something wondrous happened on Yule eve. *þar varð undarligr hlutr jólaaptan,*
3	Much money and valuable goods vanished from the king's treasury, and they knew not who caused this. *fee mikit ok gripir godir hurfu ór gullhuse konungs ok vissu þeir æigi huerr uallda munde.*	Frigg said: "[King Geirroð] is so stingy of food that he tortures his guests if it seems to him that too many come." Oðinn said that was a big lie. They laid a wager on that question. Frigg sent her maid, Fulla, to Geirroð. She told the king to beware, lest a magician attack him, one who had come into the land, and she said that he had a sign: that no dog was so fierce as to leap at him. . . . *Frigg segir: "Hann er matníðingr sá, at hann qvelr gesti sína, ef hánom þiccia ofmargir koma." Óðinn segir, at þat er in mesta lygi. þau veðia um þetta mál. Frigg sendi escismey sína, Fullo, til Geirroðar. Hon bað konung varaz, at eigi fyrgerði hanóm fiolkunnigr maðr, sá er þar var kominn í land, oc sagði þat marc á, at engi hundr var svá ólmr, at á hann myndi hlaupa. . . .*	When men had come to table and there were a great many people, all of the food and all the ale disappeared from the table. *þá er menn váru til borða gengnir, ok var þat allmikit fjǫlmenni, at þar hvarf vist ǫll af borðum ok alt mungát;*
4	It gave the king great anxiety, because it seemed to him this might recur. *fek konungi þat mikillar ahyggiu þui at hann þottizst uita at sea munde uitea oftar.*		The king remained in his seat, bitterly afflicted, and everyone else went home. *sat konungr hryggr eptir, en hverr annarra sótti sitt heimili,*

	A. Tale of Hálfdan the Black 5–6 (Flateyjarbók 1.564–66)	B. Grímnismál Prologue and Epilogue	C. Hálfdan the Black's Saga 8
5	He had preparations made with cunning devices and strong spells so that any man who might enter the house to take the money would remain there until the king's men came.		
	Lætr hann nu umbud uæita mede klokligum brǫgdum ok sterkum atkuædum suo at huerr sa madr er j husit færi ok fet uillde taka uard þar at vera ok þess at bida at menn kæmi.		
6	It seemed to the king that the culprit might be both big and strong, so he had his men produce exceptionally large fetters of the strongest steel and had them twist the most powerful lead bands.		
	Þat þottizst konungr vita at sa munde take bade mikill ok sterkr er a þessum oknyttum la þui let hann smida ser fiotur fragerda mikinn af hinu sterkazsta stale ok snua hinu ramligazstu blybond.		
7	Thereafter, there is this to tell: Early one morning, when his men came to the treasury, they saw there	[Geirroð] had that man seized whom no dog wanted to attack.	In order that he might know what happened and what had caused this event, the king had his men seize
	Sidan er þat at segia æinn morgin snemma er menn koma til gullhussins sa þeir þar	*lætr hann handtaca þann mann, er eigi vildo hundar á ráða.*	*en til þess at konungr mætti viss verða, hvat þessum atburð olli, þá lét hann taka*
8	an enormous giant. This fiend was both fat and tall.	He was in a blue cloak and was named Grímnir.	a Finn who was wise about many things.
	allmykinn jǫtun. Þessi dolgr uar bade digr ok hárr.	*Sá var í feldi blám oc nefndiz Grímnir,*	*Finn einn, er margfróðr var,*
9	Many men thronged around him and put the fetters on him, though he had much greater strength than they. Sixty men overpowered him and placed the fetters on him. They bound his hands firmly behind him with the lead bands. Then he bore himself rather poorly.		
	Þeir hloduzst a hann margir ok baru at honum fioturinn ok uard hann þeim helldr handstyrkr .lx. manna foru til adr hann uard j fioturinn færdr. bundu þeir nu hendr hans ramliga a bak aptr med blybǫndunum. barzt hann þa raunlitt af.		

(continued)

SYNOPTIC TABLE 7.2 (continued)

	A. Tale of Hálfdan the Black 5–6 (Flateyjarbók 1.564–66)	B. Grímnismál Prologue and Epilogue	C. Hálfdan the Black's Saga 8
10	King Hálfdan asked his name. He allowed he was called Dofri and had his home in the mountain that is named for him. *Halfdan konungr spurde hann at nafnni en hann letzst Dofri hæita ok æiga hæima j fialle þui er uit hann er kent.*		
11	The king asked if he had stolen his gold. He answered it was true. He asked for mercy and offered to pay threefold for the gold. But the king said he would never have mercy. Bound there, he would await the Assembly, where he would be condemned to the most disgraceful death. And the king told Dofri he would grant him no means of subsistence and anyone who gave him food would cede his life. Then the king went home and Dofri sat there, all bound up. *Konungr spurde huort hann hefde stolit gulle hans. hann quad þat satt vera ok beiddizst þa grida ok baud at þrigillda honum aftr gullit. en konungr sagde at hann skyllde alldri gridum na ok þar bundinn bida þess er þing væri kuatt ok honum skyllde dęma þar hinn haduligazsta dauda. sagde hann ok at honum skyllde æinge biargir ueita ne mat gefa nema huerr at gerde skyllde lifit lata ok ongu odru firirkoma. for konungr þa heim en Dofri sat þar bundinn eftir.*	He said nothing more about himself, although he was asked. The king had him tortured to make him speak and set him between two fires. He stayed there eight nights. *oc sagði ecci fleira frá sér, þótt hann væri at spurðr. Konungr lét hann pína til sagna oc setia milli elda tveggia, oc sat hann þar átta nætr.*	He wished to compel him to tell the truth, and he tortured him but got nothing from him. *ok vildi neyða hann til saðrar sǫgu ok píndi hann ok fekk þó eigi af honum.*
12	A little later, Harald came home. He heard the news and also the words of his father. *Litlu sidar kom Haralldr heim. hann frettir þessi tidende ok suo vmmæli fǫdur sins.*	King Geirröð had a son, ten years old, and he was called Agnar. . . . *Geirroðr konungr átti son, tío vetra gamlan, oc hét Agnarr . . .*	The Finn cried out mightily for help, turning to Harald, his son. *Finnrinn hét þannug mjǫk til hjálpar, er Haraldr var, sonr hans,*
13	He felt sorry for Dofri and wanted to plead for him. *þottizst hann þa uita at honum munde ekki gera at bidia firir honum.*	Agnar went to Grímnir and gave him a full horn to drink. *Agnarr gecc at Grímni oc gaf hánom horn fult at drecca,*	Harald begged mercy for him but got nothing. *ok Haraldr bað honum eirðar ok fekk eigi,*

SYNOPTIC TABLE 7.2 (continued)

	A. Tale of Hálfdan the Black 5–6 (Flateyjarbók 1.564–66)	B. Grímnismál Prologue and Epilogue	C. Hálfdan the Black's Saga 8
14	Harald was then five years old. He went over where Dofri sat. Dofri made himself look bad and all full of grief. *Haralldr uar þa .v. ara gamall. honum verdr þangat gengit er Dofri sat. hann gerdizst þa helldr hardlæeitr ok miog harmþrunginn.*		
15	Then Harald said: "You are doing poorly. Would you like to receive your life from me?" *Haralldr mællti þa. litt ertu staddr edr uilltu þiggia lif ath mer.*	He said that the king did ill when he had an innocent man tortured. *sagði, at konungr gorði illa, er hann lét pína hann saclausan.*	
16	"I don't know about that," said Dofri, "I would place you in great danger because of your father's words." *Ek uæit þat æigi suo uist segir Dofri sakir ummæla fodur þins huort ek uil koma þer j suo mykla hættu.*	Grímnir drank it down. *Grímnir dracc af.*	
17	"Why do you need to consider that?" said Harald. *Huat muntu þurfa at sia firir þui segir Haralldr.*		
18	Then he drew the sword that he had with him that the Finn had given him, which was of very choice iron. He cut the fetters and lead bands from Dofri. *Hann bra þa saxi þui er hann hafde vid sig ok Finnrinn hafde gefit honum þat uar afburdar jarnn kosti. hann snidr fioturinn ok blybondin af Dofra.*		Harald let him escape, against the king's will, *ok hleypði Haraldr honum þó í brot at óvilja konungs*
19	When he was free, Dofri thanked Harald for having saved his life, and thereafter he went off. He tied his shoes and laid his tail on his back and set off so that of him there was no trace. *en er hann uar laus uordinn þakkade hann Haralldi lifgiofina ok hafde sig sidan af stad. batt hann ekki læinge sko sina ok lagde halann a bak ser ok setti j burtu suo at huorke sa af honum uedr ne reyk.*		and he accompanied the man himself. *ok fylgði honum sjálfr.*

(continued)

SYNOPTIC TABLE 7.2 (continued)

A. Tale of Hálfdan the Black 5–6 (Flateyjarbók 1.564–66)	B. Grímnismál Prologue and Epilogue	C. Hálfdan the Black's Saga 8
20 Not long thereafter, Hálfdan's men searched for Dofri. The king asked what was the truth of this business, and Harald said he had freed Dofri. *eigi myklu sidarr soknudu menn Dofra. spurde konungr huerr þessa uerks munde sannr en Haralldr sagdizst Dofra leyst hafa.*		
21 The king was furious at that, so enraged that he pushed his son Harald away, but he said he could not bear to have him killed. He added with severity that no one should give sustenance to him, and he told him he needed to help catch Dofri the troll. *konungr vard uit þetta akafa ræidr suo at hann rak Haralld son sinn j burtu en kuezst eigi nenna at lata drepa hann. lagde hann þar suo rigt vid at honum skyllde einge biorg uæita bad hann þar nu hialp taka sem Dofri troll væri.*		
22 Harald now went off to the marches and woods. He lay out there by night. And when the troops had been there five nights, Harald remained in a clearing. He was quite exhausted by both hunger and thirst. Then he saw a huge monster walking by and he recognized him as Dofri the troll. *gek Haralldr nu j brott a merker ok skoga la hann þa vti suo at nattum skifti. en er lidnar vǫru .v. nætr þa uar Haralldr staddr j einu riodri gerdizst hann þa þrekadr miog bade af hungri ok þosta. ser hann þa huar gengr greppur mikill þikizst hann þa kenna Dofra troll.*		
23 Dofri spoke: "Aren't you the king's son? Do you suffer on my account, and will you go with me to my household?" *hann mællti þa. æigi ertu nu ok vel staddr konungsson at suo er. ma þat kalla at þu hliotir þetta mest af mer edr uilltu nu fara med mer til heimkynna minna.*		

SYNOPTIC TABLE 7.2 (continued)

	A. Tale of Hálfdan the Black 5–6 (Flateyjarbók 1.564–66)	B. Grímnismál Prologue and Epilogue	C. Hálfdan the Black's Saga 8
24	Harald agreed to that.		
	Haralldr iattade þui.		
25	Dofri took Harald up in his arms and went with him very swiftly until he came to a large cave, carrying the lad on his forearm. But when he entered the cave, he bowed less low than he intended and he struck the boy on the cavern rock so hard that he was knocked unconscious.		
	tok hann Haralld þa upp j fang ser ok gek med hann helldr snudigt allt þar til er hann kom at helli æinum storum hann bar þa pilltinn a handlegg ser. en er hann gengr inn j hellinn lytr hann minnr en hann ætlade ok keyrir upp sueininn undir hellisbergit ok suo hart at hann uar þegar j ouite.		
26	Then it seemed to Dofri that there would be great talk of his mishap if he had killed the lad and he wept greatly over him. But as he screwed up his face and shook his head, Harald recovered his senses and looked up at Dofri the churl, who seemed even more huge when he began crying and puffed his cheeks and stretched his eyes that way.		
	Dofra þotti þa mikit ordit slys sitt ef hann hefde drepit pilltinn. fek honum þa suo mikit at hann gret þa uppi yfir honum. en er hann gerir skelpurnar ok skerr hofudit þa raknar Haralldr vid ok litr þa upp j mote Dofra karlle ok syndizst hann þa helldr storskorinn er hann beygde skaflinn ok belgde huoptana ok vtbitade þannueg augunum.		
27	Then Harald spoke. "It is true to tell my foster father that foul is fair if he weeps, since it seems to me that you are now very ugly in appearance and you should be cheerful, since no harm has come to me."		
	þa mællti Haralldr. þat er þo satt at segia fostri minn at fárr er fagr ef grætr þuiat mer synizst þu nu helldr bragdillr ok yfirlita mikill ok vertu katr þuiat mig sakar ekki.		

(continued)

A. Tale of Hálfdan the Black 5–6 (Flateyjarbók 1.564–66)	B. Grímnismál Prologue and Epilogue	C. Hálfdan the Black's Saga 8
28	Dofri rejoiced then and laid Harald down in his cave.		
	Gladdizst Dofri þa ok let Haralld nidr j helli sinum.		
29	Harald was there for five years and lacked nothing that he needed. Dofri waited on him so much that he would not let him do anything in return.		
	þar var Haralldr .v. uetr ok skorti ekki þat er hafa þurfti. Dofri unni honum suo mikit at hann matti ekki j mot honum lata.		
30	Dofri taught him much knowledge and trained him in the arts. Harald gained much in strength and growth.		
	mart kende Dofri honum j frǫdum. suo uande Dofri hann uit jþrottir. mikit gekzst Haralldr vid bæde vm uoxst ok afl.		
31			Traveling, they came to a place where a chief held a great feast, and they were apparently well received there. They remained there until spring.
			þeir kómu þar farandi, er hǫfðingi einn helt veizlu mikla, ok var þeim at sýn þar vel fagnat, ok er þeir hǫfðu þar verit til várs,
32	It is told that one day Dofri came to speak with Harald and said this:		Then, one day the chief said to Harald:
	þat er sagt at æinn dag kom Dofri at male vid Haralld ok talade suo.		*þá var þat einn dag, at hǫfðinginn mælti til Haraldz:*

SYNOPTIC TABLE 7.2 (continued)

A. Tale of Hálfdan the Black 5–6 (Flateyjarbók 1.564–66)	B. Grímnismál Prologue and Epilogue	C. Hálfdan the Black's Saga 8
33	"Now I think I have repaid you for having saved my life, because I have now brought you the kingdom, as your father is dead and I was there not long ago. *nu þikiumzst ek hafa launat þer lifgiofina þuiat nu hefui ek komit þer til konungdomsins þuiat fadir þinn er daudr ok var ek þar ekki fiarre.*	King Geirröð sat and held a sword on his knee and drew it halfway. But when he heard that it was Oðinn who had come, he stood up and wanted to remove Oðinn from the fires. The sword slipped from his hand, with its hilt down. The king struck his foot and stumbled forward. The sword went through him and killed him. *Geirroðr konungr sat oc hafði sverð um kné sér, oc brugðit til miðs. Enn er hann heyrði, at Óðinn var þar kominn, stóð hann up oc vildi taca Óðin frá eldinom. Sverðit slap ór hendi hánom, visso hiǫltin niðr. Konungr drap fœti oc steyptiz áfram, enn sverðit stóð í gognom hann, oc fecc hann bana.*	"Your father suffered a wondrously great loss when I took some food from him this winter, but I must repay you with joyful news. Your father is now dead *"furðu mikit torrek lætr faðir þinn sér at, er ek tók vist nǫkkura frá honum í vetr; en ek mun þér launa með feginsǫgu. Faðir þinn er nú dauðr*
34		Oðinn disappeared then. *Óðinn hvarf þá.*	
35	Now you shall go home and take up your realm. *nu skaltu fara heim ok taka vid riki þinu.*	And Agnar was king there for a long time thereafter. *Enn Agnarr var þar konungr lengi síðan.*	and you shall go home now. You shall take all the kingdom he had *ok skaltu nú heim fara, muntu fá ríki þat alt, er hann hefir átt,*
36	I proclaim this to you that you will not have your hair cut at all, or your nails until *legg ek þat til med þer at þu latir huorke skera hár þitt ne negl fyrr en*		
37	you become sole king over all Norway. *þu verdr æinualldzkonungr yfir ollum Noregi.*		and in addition you shall possess all Norway." *ok þar með skaltu eignask allan Nóreg."*

(continued)

A. Tale of Hálfdan the Black 5–6 (Flateyjarbók 1.564–66)	B. Grímnismál Prologue and Epilogue	C. Hálfdan the Black's Saga 8
38	I shall be in your service and in battles with you. I will be of assistance to you because I will be able to inflict wounds because I will not be visible. *skal ek ok þer j lidsinne vera ok j bardogum med þer. mun þer þat at gagnni verda þuiat ek mun skeinuhættr uera saker þess at ek mun ekki audsærr vera.*		
39	Go now, be hale and well, and go all the way to glory and times of honor, and may you have no less good fortune than if you had been next to me." *far þu nu heill ok uel ok gangi þer allt til tirs ok tima heidrs ok hamingiu æigi at sidr þott þu hafir hea mer verit.*		
40	Harald felt much for Dofri when they parted. *Fann þa miog a Dofra er þeir skildu.*		
41	And when Harald came home, he was made king over all the folk whom his father had ruled. *En er Haralldr kom heim var hann til konungs tekinn yfir oll þau fylke er fadir hans hafde firir radit.*		
42	He told his men where he had been these past five years, and he was then called Harald Dofri's Foster Son. *sagde hann monnum sinum huar er hann hafde uerit þessa .v. uetr uar hann þa kalladr Haralldr Dofrafostri.*		

SYNOPTIC TABLE 8.1 Hálfdan the Black's death

	A. Historia Norwegiae 10	B. Ágrip 1	C. Fagrskinna 1	D. Fagrskinna Appendix 2	E. Hálfdan the Black's Saga 9	F. Tale of Hálfdan the Black 7 (Flateyjarbók 1.566–67)
1		This is the manner of Hálfdan's death day. *En sjá er háttr á dauðdaga Hálfdanar.*	In this manner was Hálfdan's death: *En með þeima hætti var dauði Hálfdanar,*	One time an unfortunate accident happened thus: *Sva gerðiz eitthvert sinn til ugævo atburðr*		King Hálfdan went to his death in this manner: *Hálfdan konungr fék bana með þeim hætti at*
2				It was in the spring, the time when the ice begins to break up on the lakes. *þat var um varit þann tíma er ísa tekr at læysa a votnum.* (Cf. E7)		
3		He feasted at Haðaland, *Hann þá veizlu á Haðalandi;*	he feasted at Haðaland, *at hann þá veizlu á Haðalandi;*	Then the king had gone to a feast in the settlement that is called Brandabu in Haðaland. *þá hafði konongrinn farit til veizlu í bygð þa er Brandabu heitir a Haðalande.*	Hálfdan the Black drove off from the feast at Haðaland *Hálfdan svarti ók frá veizlu á Haðalandi;*	he was traveling in a cart from a feast in Haðaland, *honum var ekit frá ueitzlu af Hadalande* (Cf. A6)
4		and when he traveled from there in a sledge, *en þá er hann fór þaðan í sleða,*	and he traveled from there in a sledge. *en hann fór þaðan í sleða,*	And he traveled from the feast with a great host. *enn hann fór fra veizlunne með mikit tíð.* (Cf. A6, F6)	and went on his way, *ok bar svá til leið hans,*	

(continued)

SYNOPTIC TABLE 8.1 (continued)

	A. Historia Norwegiae 10	B. Ágrip 1	C. Fagrskinna 1	D. Fagrskinna Appendix 2	E. Hálfdan the Black's Saga 9	F. Tale of Hálfdan the Black 7 (Flateyjarbók 1.566–67)
5	While he was making his way by night over the ice of a certain lake named Rönd, *qui dum noctu per cujusdam stagni glaciem, quod Rönd nominatur, iter ageret,* (Cf. D4, F3)	he drowned in [Lake] Rönd in Rykinsvík, *[þá drukk]naði hann í Rönd [í R]ykinvík,* (Cf. E7)	Then he drowned in [Lake] Rönd in Rykinsvík, [which is] shamed for that, *þá drukknaði hann í Rönd í Rykinsvík, skammt frá því* (Cf. E7)	Then they drove over the ice on the lakes. On the lake known as Rönd, they came to the place known as Rykinsvík. There the ice broke under him and under his horse. *þa oco þeir at vaz isinum. a vatni því er Rönd heitir. enn þeir komo þar sem Rœkens vic heitir. þa brast isinn vndir honom oc vndir hesti hans.* (Cf. E7)	such that he drove over Lake Rönd. *at hann ók um vatnit Rönd;*	over the lake that is called Rönd. And when he came to Rinkilsvík, the ice broke under him and he perished there *um uatnn þat er Rond heitir ok þa er hann kom a Rinkkilsuik brast niidr issinn ok tyndizt hann þar* (Cf. A12, E7, E12)
6	coming back from a feast with carts and a large body of horsemen, *cum curribus et equitatu magno a cena rediens* (Cf. D4, F3)			Right away, the others saw that. Then all wanted to rescue the king and a great number of drunken men assembled. The ice broke more and more widely and there was no help for the king from the drunken men. *enn þegar er þeir sa þat. þa vildu allir biargha kononge. oc þyrftiz þingat mykill foldi druckinna manna. isinn brotnaðe því meir oc viðare. oc varð konongenom eighi meiri hiolp at drucknom monnom.*		with a large part of his host, *(ok) mikill hlute lids hans* (Cf. D4, E13)

(continued)

7				It was spring, when there was an exceptionally sudden thaw. And when they drove by Rykinsvík, *þat var um vár; þá váru sólbráð mikil; en er þeir óku um Rykinsvík—* (Cf. B5, C5, D2, D5, F5)	near the place where there had been wells for watering cattle. *því nærr sem verit hofðu nautabrunnar.*
8	he was unexpectedly carried into a certain fissure, where herdsmen were accustomed to water their herds, *in quandam scissuram . . . improvide advectus ubi pastores gregem suum adaquare solebant,*	where there was a well for watering cattle. *þar er nautabrunnr var,*	where there was a well for watering cattle. *er nautabrunnr var,*	there had been wells for watering cattle there over the winter, *þar hofðu verit um vetrinn nautabrunnar,*	
9					
10				and where the dung had fallen on the ice, *en er mykrin hafði fallit á ísinn,*	

SYNOPTIC TABLE 8.1 (continued)

	A. Historia Norwegiae 10	B. Ágrip 1	C. Fagrskinna 1	D. Fagrskinna Appendix 2	E. Hálfdan the Black's Saga 9	F. Tale of Hálfdan the Black 7 (Flateyjarbók 1.566–67)
11					a hole opened up because of the sudden thaw. *þá hafði þar grafit um í sólbráðinu—,*	
12	and he died under the ice. *sub glacie deperiit.* (Cf. F5)			So the king perished there, *enn sva at konongr tyndizk þar* (Cf. F5)	And when the king drove by there, the ice broke under him and King Hálfdan perished there, *en er konungr ók þar um, þá brast niðr íssinn, ok týndisk þar Hálfdan konungr* (Cf. D5, F5)	
13				along with Dagr the Wise, his father-in-law, and some twenty men with them. *oc Daghr hinn froðe maghr hans. oc nocorir tyttughu menn með þeim.*	and a great host with him. *ok lið mikit með honum;* (Cf. A6, F6)	
14				These tidings seemed bad to all men who heard of them, because he was a popular and prosperous man. *þesse tiðendi þotto ollum monnum ill vera er til spurðu, fyrir því at hann var maðr ársæll ok vinsæll.*		

SYNOPTIC TABLE 8.2 Hálfdan's burial

	A. Ágrip 1	B. Fagrskinna 1	C. Hálfdan the Black's Saga 9	D. Tale of Hálfdan the Black 7 (Flateyjarbók 1.566–67)	E. Fagrskinna Appendix 2 (from the A-Text)
1			Of all kings, he had been the one most gifted in the power of prosperity.	Of all kings, Hálfdan was most gifted in the power of prosperity.	He was a popular and prosperous man.
			hann hafði verit allra konunga ársælstr.	*Halfdan uar allra konunga ársælzstr*	*hann var maðr ársæll ok vinsæll.*
2			So highly did men value him that when they heard he was dead	So highly did men value him that when they heard that he was dead	So great was the king's ability to ensure prosperity that as soon as they found his body,
			Svá mikit gerðu menn sér um hann, at þá er þat spurðisk, at hann var dauðr,	*ok suo mikit gerdu menn ser vm þat at þa er þat spurdizst at hann uar daudr*	*En svá var mikil ársæli konungs, at þegar er þeir fundu lík hans,*
3			and his body was brought to Hringariki with the intention of being buried there,	and his body was brought to Hringariki with the intention of being buried there,	
			ok lík hans var flutt á Hringaríki ok var þar til graptar ætlat,	*ok lík hans var flutt af Hringariki ok ætlat til graftrar*	
4			powerful men from Raumariki, Vestfold, and Heiðmark came,	powerful men from Vestfold, Vingulmark, and Raumariki came up thither	
			þá fóru ríkismenn af Raumaríki ok af Vestfold ok Heiðmǫrk	*þa foru rikismenn af Uestfolld ok Vingulmork (ok) Raumariki upp þangat*	

(continued)

SYNOPTIC TABLE 8.2 (continued)

	A. Ágrip 1	B. Fagrskinna 1	C. Hálfdan the Black's Saga 9	D. Tale of Hálfdan the Black 7 (Flateyjarbók 1.566–67)	E. Fagrskinna Appendix 2 (from the A-Text)
5			and all requested to have the body for themselves and to bury it in a mound in their district. And they thought there would be good harvests for those who got it. *ok beiddusk allir at hafa líkit með sér ok heygja í sínu fylki, ok þótti þat vera árvænt, þeir er næði.*	and all requested to have the body for themselves and to bury it in a mound in their district, and it seemed to them that there would then be good harvests. *ok beidduzst aller at hafa likit með ser ok heygja j sínu fylke ok þotti sem þat munde þeim til árs verda.*	
6			But they settled it so the body was divided into four parts. *En þeir sættusk svá, at líkinu var skipt í fiora staði,*	But they settled among themselves that the body was divided in pieces into four parts. *En þeir sættuzst með þui at likamanum var skift j sundr j fiora stade.*	they divided his body in pieces, *þá skiptu þeir líkam hans í sundr,*
7					and his entrails were buried at Thengilsstaðir in Haðaland, *ok váru innyfli hans jörðuð á þengilsstoðum á Haðalandi,*
8	He was brought to Steinn in Hringaríki thereafter and was buried there in a mound. *var fœrðr til Steins síðan á Hringaríki ok var þar heygðr.*	Thereafter, he was brought to Steinn in Ringaríki and there buried in a mound. *en síðan var hann fœrðr til Steins á Hringaríki ok þar heygðr.*	The head was buried in a mound at Steinn in Hringaríki, *ok var hofuðit lagit í haug at Steini á Hringaríki,*	The head was buried in a mound at Steine in Hringaríki. *Uar hofuðit lagt j haug at Steine a Hringariki.*	his corpse was buried at Steinn in Hringaríki, *en líkamr hans var jarðaðr á Steini á Hringaríki,*

9		and his head was carried to Skírnssal in Vestfold and was buried there.
		en hǫfuð hans var flutt í Skírnssal á Vestfold ok var þar jarðat.
10	and each group took home their portion and buried it in a mound, and all these are called Hálfdan's Mounds.	and each chieftain took his portion home with him and had a mound thrown up in each district, and these are called Hálfdan's Mounds.
	en hverir fluttu heim sinn hluta ok heygðu, ok eru þat alt kallaðir Hálfdanar-haugar.	*En huerr hofdinge hafde sinn hluta heim med ser ok letu uerpa haug j hueriu þui fylke ok eru þeir kalladir Halfdanarhaugar,*
11		They had blood poured on them, following the belief of many men in the past, but that was forbidden to his kinsmen.
		ok hellt vid blot ok atrunat af morgum monnum adr en þat var bannat af frændum hans.
12		And they divided his body because they believed that his ability to ensure prosperity would be the same, whether he were alive or dead.
		En fyrir þvi skiptu þeir likam hans, at þeir triðu þvi, at ársæli hans myndi jafnan með hónum vera, hvárt sem hann væri lifs eða dauðr.

SYNOPTIC TABLE 9.1　Descriptions of Harald upon his accession

	A. Theodricus Monachus 1	B. Historia Norwegie 11	C. Ágrip 2	D. Fagrskinna 2	E. Harald Fairhair's Saga 1	F. Tale of Harald Fairhair 1 (Flateyjarbók 1.567)	G. Egil's Saga 3
1	In the year 858 from the incarnation of our Lord, Harald Fairhair, son of Hálfdan the Black, began his reign. *Anno ab incarnatione Domini octigentesimo quinquagesimo octavo regnavit Haraldus pulchre-comatus, filius Halfdan nigri.*	After [Hálfdan] came his son, Harald Fairhair, *Post istum filius suus Haraldus comatus,*	After Hálfdan, Harald took the realm that his father had had *Haraldr tók efptir Hálfdan ríki þat er faðir hans hafði haft,*	His son Harald took the kingship after his father, Hálfdan the Black. *Haraldr sonr hans tók konungdóm eptir foður sinn Hálfdan svarta.*	Harald took the kingship after his father. *Haraldr tók konungdóm eptir foður sinn;*	When he was ten years old, Harald Hálfdan's son, who was called Dofri's Foster Son, took the kingship over Hringaríki, Vestfold, Vingulmark, and Raumaríke. *At liðnum tiu uetrum alldrs Haralldz Halfdanarsonar er kalladr uar Dofrafostri tok hann konungdom yfir Hringariki Uestfolld Uingulmork ok Raumarike.* (Cf. E5)	Harald, son of Hálfdan the Black, had taken his inheritance from his father to the east, in Vík. *Haraldr, sonr Hálfdanar svarta, hafði tekit arf eptir foður sinn í Vík austr;*
2		who had this epithet because of his elegant locks. *ob decoram cesariem sic cognominatus,* (Cf. D6, F11)					
3						At that time Guthorm, his mother's brother, was sixteen years old. *þa uar Guthormr modurbrodir hans .xvj. uetra gamall*	

(continued)

4	He was first to obtain royal power over the entire maritime zone. *totius maritimæ zonæ regnum nactus est primus;*			
5		and gained for himself more realms than Hálfdan had. *ok aflaði sér meira ríkis með þeim hætti—*	He was then a youth to reckon by his age, but full grown in all the manly accomplishments that it beseems a gracious king to have. *Hann var þá æskumaðr at vetra tali, en fullkominn til mannanar allrar, þeirar er kurteisum konungi byrjaði at hafa.* (Cf. F10)	He was then ten years old. *þá var hann x. vetra gamall;* (Cf. F1)
6			His growth of hair was great with a wonderful color, in appearance as fair as silk. *Hans hárvoxtr var mikill með undarligum lit, því líkastr at sjá sem fagrt silki.* (Cf. B2, F11)	

SYNOPTIC TABLE 9.1 (continued)

	A. Theodricus Monachus 1	B. Historia Norwegiæ 11	C. Ágrip 2	D. Fagrskinna 2	E. Harald Fairhair's Saga 1	F. Tale of Harald Fairhair 1 (Flateyjarbók 1.567)	G. Egil's Saga 3
7			He grew quickly into a brave and imposing man, *er maðrinn var snemma rǫskr ok risuligr vexti—*	Of all men he was the most handsome and the strongest, and one can see how big he was from his burial stone, which is in Haugasund. *Hann var allra manna friðastr ok sterkastr ok svá mikill sem sjá má á legsteini hans, þeim er í Haugasundum er.*	He was clearly the greatest, strongest, and most handsome of all men, *hann var allra manna mestr ok sterkastr ok friðastr sýnum,*	He was the most promising and strongest of all men, handsome, *hann var allra manna uænstr ok sterkaszstr friðr synum*	
8				He was a great man of wisdom, farsighted and ambitious. *Hann var spekimaðr mikill ok langsýnn ok ágjarn,*	a wise man and a great leader. *vitr maðr ok skǫrungr mikill.*	a wise man and a great leader. *uitr maðr ok skorungr mikill.*	

(continued)

9

He made himself leader of the royal retinue and all the land's government. King Harald made his kinsman Guthorm commander of all his troops.	
Hann gerdizst forstiore firer hirdinne ok firir ollum landradum. Haralldr konungr setti Guthorm frænda sinn hertoga yfir ollu lide sinu.	
Harald was then a youth to reckon by his age, but full grown in the development of his strength and size.	
Haralldr var þa æskumadr at uetratale en fullgerr at þroska afls ok mikilæiks ok þroadizst langra hrid her eftir sem edli ok alldr uisar til. (Cf. D5)	

10

SYNOPTIC TABLE 9.1 (continued)

	A. Theodricus Monachus 1	B. Historia Norwegiæ 11	C. Ágrip 2	D. Fagrskinna 2	E. Harald Fairhair's Saga 1	F. Tale of Harald Fairhair 1 (Flateyjarbók 1.567)	G. Egil's Saga 3
11						His growth of hair was just like silk in beauty, and the hair of no one known in the northern lands at that time, man or woman, was equal to his in strength, length, or thickness. *Hans haruoxstr ma iafrnazst við silke at fegurd en þar við matti ekki iafrnazst at hæd ne þyklæik nokkurs mannz hár kallmannz ne konu suo at kunnikt væri j þann tima a Nordrlondum.* (Cf. B2, D6)	He had sworn this vow not to have his hair cut or combed until he was sole king over Norway. He was called "Shaggy Harald." *hann hafði þess heit strengt, at láta eigi skera hár sitt né kemba fyrr en hann væri einvaldskonungr yfir Nóregi; hann var kallaðr Haraldr lúfa.*
12						Thereafter, his beauty, bodily growth and strength, mind and prowess, determination and courage, all these were fully developed in him. *Her eftir uar fegurd likamans uoxstr ok afl hugr ok hreysti orleikr ok areede. Uar þetta allt með honum fullgert.*	

(continued)

#					
13					He was obstinate and determined. *þralyndr ok otalhlydinn.*
14	For the first time he drove out all petty kings and gained sole rule over all Norway for seventy years, and (then) he died. *Hic primum expulit omnes regulos et solus obtinuit regnum totius Norwagie annis septuaginta et defunctus est.*	Heretofore, petty kings presided over the inland zones, although virtually under his domination. *mediterraneae quidem zonae adhuc reguli praesidebant, sic tamen quasi sub ejus dominio.*	so that he made battle against neighboring kings and conquered them all. At twenty years old, he was the first single king to take possession of Norway. … *at hann helt orrostu við næsta konunga ok sigraði alla, ok eignaðisk hann fyrstr konunga einn Nóreg á tvítogs aldri …*	Here, *hamingja* and Providence strengthened him so that he should be lord over the realm of Northmen and so that the land that up to now his lineage had made glorious might continue to be so. *hér með styrkði hann hamingja ok fyrirætlan, at hann skyldi vera yfirmaðr Norðmanna rikis, er af hans ætt hefir tignazk þat land hér til ok svá mun vera jafnan.*	He was so strong in good fortune (*hamingja*) that it was allotted to him to become lord over the realm of Northmen and so that all that up to now his lineage had made glorious might continue to be so. *Her med var hann suo styrkr at hamingiunne at honum var ætlat at verda yfirmaðr Norðmanna rikis er af hans ætt hefir tignazst allt her til ok suo mun vera hedan af …*
15					Harald was popular with his men. *Haralldr var vinsæll af sinum monnum*

SYNOPTIC TABLE 9.1 (continued)

	A. Theodricus Monachus 1	B. Historia Norwegiæ 11	C. Ágrip 2	D. Fagrskinna 2	E. Harald Fairhair's Saga 1	F. Tale of Harald Fairhair 1 (Flateyjarbók 1.567)	G. Egil's Saga 3
16				Old men attached themselves to him with wise counsels and help for his plans. *Hónum þýddusk gamlir menn með spekiráðum ok ásjá fyrirætlanar.*		Old men attached themselves to him with wise counsels and help for his plans. *honum þýdduzst gamler menn með spekiradum ok asia frirætlunar.*	
17				Young men, bold and valiant, desired to be with him for the sake of fine gifts of money and royal pomp, as the skald Hornklofi says. . . . *Ungir drengir ok hreystimenn girndusk til hans fyrir sakar virðiligra fégjafa ok hirðþrýði, svá sem segir Hornklofi skáld . . .*		Many bold and valiant men desired to be with him for the sake of good positions, gifts of money, and royal pomp, as says Thjóðolf of Hvinn. *Margir dreingir ok hreystimenn girnntuzst til hans sakir uelsetningar fegiafa ok hirdpryde sua sem segir þiodulfr hinn huinuerske.*	

| 18 | It was ten years that he became all-powerful king over the land of Norway, and he greatly improved his land and pacified it.

En þat var .x. vetr er hann barðisk áðr til lands en hann yrði allvaldskonungr at Nóregi, ok siðaði vel land sitt ok friðaði | It was ten years that he fought until he became all-powerful king over the land of Norway, and he greatly improved his land and pacified it.

En þat var tíu vetr, er hann barðisk áðr til lands en hann yrði allvaldskonungr at Nóregi ok siðaði vel land sitt ok friðaði. | After that he fought with those kings who were closest and he conquered them. There are long narratives of that.

Siðan barðisk hann við þá konunga, er næstr váru, ok sigraði þá, ok eru þar langar frásagnir |

	A. Egil's Saga 3	B. Harald Fairhair's Saga 11
1	Although this trouble now afflicts us, it will not be long until the same trouble will come to you,	To us all, the choice is now clear,
	þótt þetta vandræði hafi nú borit oss at hendi, þá mun eigi langt til, at sama vandræði mun til yðvar koma,	*Ǫllum er oss sjá kostr nú auðsær,*
2	for I think Harald will come here quickly, when he has subjected all the men in North Mæri and Raumsdale to slavery and oppression, as he wishes.	
	því at Haraldr ætla ek at skjótt mun hér koma, þá er hann hefir alla menn þrælkat ok áþját, sem hann vill, á Norðmæri ok í Raumsdal.	
3	You will have the same choice before you as we had: to defend your property and freedom and to risk all these men whose support you can hope for.	that we all rise up against King Harald.
	Munu þér inn sama kost fyrir hǫndum eiga, sem vér áttum, at verja fé yðvart ok frelsi ok kosta þar til allra þeira manna, er yðr er liðs at ván,	*at vér rísim allir upp móti Haraldi konungi;*
4		May we then have enough strength, and fate will then award the victory,
		munu vér þá hafa gnógan styrk, ok mun þá auðna ráða sigri,
5	I will offer myself and my troops against this arrogance and injustice.	
	ok vil ek bjóðask til með mínu liði móti þessum ofsa ok ójafnaði;	
6	On the other hand, you may wish to follow the same counsel as the Naumdalers did: to go of your own volition into bondage and become Harald's thralls.	but otherwise there is no choice for men who are not less noble than Harald than to become his thralls.
	en at ǫðrum kosti munu þér vilja taka upp þat ráð, sem Naumdælir gerðu, at ganga með sjálfvilja í ánauð ok gerask þrælar Haralds.	*en hitt er ella, ok er þat engi kostr þeim mǫnnum, er eigi eru ótignari at nafni, en Haraldr, at gerask þrælar hans.*
7	To my father it seems praiseworthy to die in his kingdom with honor, rather than become the subordinate of another king in his old age.	To my father it seems the better choice to fall in battle in his kingdom, than to become a subordinate of King Harald.
	þat þótti fǫður mínum vegr, at deyja í konungdómi með sœmð, heldr en gerask undirmaðr annars konungs á gamals aldri;	*þótti fǫður mínum betri sá kostr, at falla í bardaga í konungdómi sínum, en gerask undirmaþr Haraldz konungs.*
8	I think it will seem the same to you and to those others who have some pride and wish to be men of courage.	
	hygg ek, at þér muni ok svá þykkja ok ǫðrum þeim, er nǫkkurir eru borði ok kappsmenn vilja vera.	

SYNOPTIC TABLE 9.3 Harald's oath

	A. Fagrskinna 3	B. Fagrskinna Appendix 3 (from the A-Text)	C. Harald Fairhair's Saga 4	D. Egil's Saga 3	E. Greater Saga of Olaf Tryggvason 2 (Flateyjarbók 1.40)	F. Tale of Halfdan the Black (Flateyjarbók 1.566)	G. Tale of Harald Fairhair 3 (Flateyjarbók 1.569)
1	Then King Harald swore a vow *þá strengir Haraldr konungr heit,*	When King Harald heard this speech, he straightaway swore a vow, *þá er Haraldr konungr heyrði þessi orð, þá strengði hann þegar heit*	And then he said: "This vow I swear, *ok enn mælti hann: "þess strengi ek heit,*	He had sworn this vow: *hann hafði þess heit strengt,*	Now this vow I swear, *Nu stræingi ek þess heit*	[The giant Dofri said]: "I proclaim this to you: *legg ek þat til med þer*	Then King Harald swore this vow: *ok þa streingde Haralldr konungr þess hæith*
2		swearing on his head, *ok sör við hǫfuð sitt,*	and therefore I appeal to God, who created me and who rules over all: *ok því skýt ek til guðs, þess er mik skóp ok ǫllu ræðr,*		and therefore I appeal to God, he who created me and who rules over all: *ok þui skyt ek til guds þess er mig skóp ok ǫllu rædr*		
3	that he would not cut his hair *at eigi skal skera hár hans*		Never shall my hair be cut or combed *at aldri skal skera hár mitt né kemba,*	not to have his hair cut or combed *at láta eigi skera hár sitt né kemba,*	Never shall my hair be cut or combed *at alldri skal skera har mitt ne kemba*	that you will not let anyone cut your hair or your nails, *at þu latir huorke skera hár þitt ne negl*	not to let anyone comb his hair or cut it *at lata huorke kemba har sitt ne skera*

(continued)

SYNOPTIC TABLE 9.3 (continued)

	A. Fagrskinna 3	B. Fagrskinna Appendix 3 (from the A-Text)	C. Harald Fairhair's Saga 4	D. Egil's Saga 3	E. Greater Saga of Olaf Tryggvason 2 (Flateyjarbók 1.40)	F. Tale of Hálfdan the Black (Flateyjarbók 1.566)	G. Tale of Harald Fairhair 3 (Flateyjarbók 1.569)
4		that he would have no wife in Norway save Ragna, and also with this stake— *at hann skyldi enga eigna konu eiga í Nóregi nema Rǫgnu ok þó með þeim hætti,*					
5	until he had subdued all the inland valleys of the outlying areas as far as Norway goes *áðr en hann hefir skatt af hverjum uppdal sem af útnesi, svá vítt sem Nóregr*	that he would make all men in Norway his subjects. *at hann gærði alla menn at þegnum sér í Nóregi.*	until I have taken possession of all Norway, *fyrr en ek hefi eignazk allan Nóreg*	until he was sole king over Norway. *fyrr en hann væri einvaldskonungr yfir Nóregi.*	until I have won all Norway, *fyrr en ek hefir vnnit Noreg allan*	until you become sole king over all Norway." *fyrr en þu verdr æinualldzkonungr yfir ollum Noregi.*	until he became sole king over Norway. *fyrr en hann yrde einualldzkonungr yfir Noregi.*

6	east to the Marches and north to the sea. *er austr til marka ok norðr til hafs*		
7		with its tributes, taxes, and administration, *með skǫttum ok skyldum ok forráði;*	with its tributes, taxes, and administration. *með skauttum ok skylldum ok forræde.*
8		or otherwise to die." *en deyja at ǫðrum kosti."*	Or I shall die." *ella skal ek deyia.*
9		He was called "Shaggy Harald." *Hann var kallaðr Haraldr lúfa.*	For that reason, he was then called "Shaggy Harald." *því uar hann þa kalladr Haralldr lufa.*

Notes

Chapter One

1. See, inter alia, Cristiano Grottanelli, *Kings and Prophets: Monarchic Power, Inspired Leadership, and Sacred Text in Biblical Narrative* (New York: Oxford University Press, 1999); Sylvie Coirault-Neuberger, *Le roi juif: Justice et raison d'état dans la Bible et le Talmud* (Paris: L'Harmattan, 2007); Reinhard Müller, *Königtum und Gottesherrschaft: Untersuchungen zur alttestamentlichen Monarchiekritik* (Tübingen: Mohr Siebeck, 2004); James Richard Linville, *Israel in the Book of Kings: The Past As a Project of Social Identity* (Sheffield: Sheffield Academic Press, 1998); Tomoro Ishida, *The Royal Dynasties in Ancient Israel: A Study on the Formation and Development of Royal-Dynastic Ideology* (Berlin: W. de Gruyter, 1977).

2. Inter alia, Eve Adler, *Vergil's Empire: Political Thought in the Aeneid* (Oxford: Rowman and Littlefield, 2003); Jean-Luc Pomathios, *Le pouvoir politique et sa représentation dans l'Éneide de Virgile* (Brussels: Collection Latomus, 1987); Philip Hardie, *Virgil's Aeneid: Cosmos and Imperium* (Oxford: Clarendon Press, 1986).

3. M. L. Weems, *A History of the Life, Death, Virtues, and Exploits of General George Washington: Faithfully taken from authentic documents* (Philadelphia: Bioren, 1800), and frequently reprinted thereafter. For a discussion of this text and its influence, see Marcus Cunliffe, "Parson Weems and George Washington's Cherry Tree," *Bulletin of the John Rylands Library* 45 (1962): 58–96.

4. In recent years it is actually the foundation myths of nations, and not those of states, that have received most attention. The constantly growing literature includes Patrick Geary, *The Myth of Nations: The Medieval Origins of Europe* (Oxford: Oxford University Press, 2003); Anthony D. Smith, *Chosen Peoples: Sacred Sources of National Identity* (Oxford: Oxford University Press, 2003); Smith, *Myths and Memories of the Nation* (Oxford: Oxford University Press, 1999); Geoffrey Hosking and George Schöpflin, eds., *Myths and Nationhood* (New York: Routledge, 1997).

5. On the concrete processes of state formation in Norway, see Aron Gurevich, "The Early State in Norway," in *The Early State*, ed. Henri J. M. Claessen and Peter Skalník (The Hague: Mouton, 1978), 403–23; Kåre Lunden, "Was There a Norwegian National Identity in the Middle Ages?," *Scandinavian Journal of History* 20 (1995): 19–33; Claus Krag, "The Early Unification of Norway," in *The Cambridge History of Scandinavia*, vol. 1, *Prehistory to 1520*, ed. Knut Helle

(Cambridge: Cambridge University Press, 2003), 411–20; Sverre Bagge, "Division and Unity in Medieval Norway," in *Franks, Northmen, and Slavs: Identities and State Formation in Early Medieval Europe*, ed. Ildar Garipzanov, Patrick Geary, and Przemyslaw Urbanczyk (Turnhout, Belgium: Brepols, 2008), 145–66; Bagge, *From Viking Stronghold to Christian Kingdom: State Formation in Norway, c. 900–1350* (Copenhagen: Museum Tusculanum Press, 2010).

6. For convenient discussions of the genre, see Theodore Andersson, "Kings' Sagas (*Konungasögur*)," in *Old Norse-Icelandic Literature: A Critical Guide*, ed. Carol J. Clover and John Lindow (Ithaca, NY: Cornell University Press, 1985), 197–238; and Stefán Einarsson, *A History of Icelandic Literature* (Baltimore: Johns Hopkins University Press, 1957), 110–21. Fuller treatment of the different Kings' Sagas and the relation among them is available in Gudrun Lange, *Die Anfänge der isländisch-norwegischen Geschichtsschreibung* (Reykjavík: Bókaútgáfa Menningarsjóðs, 1989); Svend Ellehøj, *Studier over den Ældste Norrøne Historieskrivning* (Copenhagen: Einar Munksgaard, 1965); Siegfried Beyschlag, *Konungasögur: Untersuchungen zur Königssaga bis Snorri* (Copenhagen: Einar Munksgaard, 1950); and Bjarni Aðalbjarnarson, *Om de Norske Kongers Sagaer* (Oslo: Det Norske Videnskaps Akademi, 1937). On the ideology of kingship as articulated in this genre, see Ármann Jakobsson, *Í Leit að Konungi: Konungmynd Íslenskra Konungasagna* (Reykjavík: Háskólaútgáfan, 1997).

7. An incident from the saga of Hákon Hákonarson (chap. 329) suggests that Norwegian history was conventionally understood to have begun with Hálfdan the Black.

> In his illness, King Hákon first had Latin books read to him. But then it seemed much trouble to him to ponder over how to interpret that [language]. Then he had Norse books read to him night and day, first the sagas of holy men. And when these were finished, he had the Konungatal [Account of kings] read to him **from Hálfdan the Black, and thereafter all the Kings of Norway, one after the other.**

> *Í sóttinni lét hann fyrst lesa sér Látinu-bækr. En þá þótti hónum sér mikil mæða í, at hugsa þar eptir hversu þat þýddi. Lét hann þá lesa fyrir sér Norænu-bækr, nætr ok daga; fyrst Heilagra-manna-sögur; ok er þær þraut, lét hann lesa sér Konungatal* **frá Hálfdani Svarta, ok síðan frá öllum Noregs-konungum, hverjum eptir annan.** (Emphasis added)

8. Egil's Saga 8 reports:

> Of all his retainers, [King Harald] valued his skalds most. They occupied the seat of second highest honor. Among them, Auðun the poetaster had the inmost position. He was the oldest of them and he had been the skald of Hálfdan the Black, King Harald's father. Next there sat Thorbjorn Hornklofi, next there sat Ölvir Hnúfa, and the place next to him was occupied by Barð. There he was called Barð the White or Barð the Strong. He was well liked by each of the men. There was a close fellowship between him and Ölvir Hnúfa.

> *Af öllum hirðmönnum virði konungr mest skáld sín; þeir skípuðu annat öndvegi. þeira sat innast Auðun illskælda; hann var elztr þeira, ok hann hafði verit skáld Hálfdanar svarta, föður Haralds konungs. þar næst sat þorbjörn hornklofi, en þar næst sat ölvir hnúfa, en honum it næsta var skipat Bárði; hann var þar kallaðr Bárðr hvíti eða Bárðr sterki; hann var þar vel hverjum manni; með þeim ölvi hnúfu var félagskapr mikill.*

9. Historia Norwegiæ 11: *De hoc memorantur multa et mirabilia, quæ nunc longum est narrare per singula.*

10. On the transition from orality to literacy, the literature has grown rapidly and includes Judy Quinn, "From Orality to Literacy in Medieval Iceland," in *Old Icelandic Literature and Society*, ed. Margaret Clunies Ross (Cambridge: Cambridge University Press, 2000), 30–60; Arnved Nedkvitne, *The Social Consequences of Literacy in Medieval Scandinavia* (Turnhout, Belgium: Brepols, 2004); Gisli Sigurðsson, *The Medieval Icelandic Saga and Oral Tradition* (Cambridge, MA: Harvard University Press, 2004); Heather O'Donaghue, *Skaldic Verse and the Poetics of Saga Narrative* (Oxford: Oxford University Press, 2005); Stefan Brink, "*Verba Volant, scripta manent?* Aspects of Early Scandinavian Oral Society," in *Literacy in Medieval and Early Modern Scandinavian Culture*, ed. Pernille Hermann (Odense: University Press of Southern Denmark, 2005), 77–135; Theodore M. Andersson, "From Tradition to Literature in the Sagas," in *Oral Art Forms and Their Passage into Writing*, ed. Else Mundal and Jonas Wellendorf (Copenhagen: Museum Tusculanum Press, 2008), 7–17.

11. The Saints' Sagas have been collected by C. R. Unger, ed., *Heilagra manna sögur: Fortællinger og legender om hellige mænd og kvinder; Efter gamle hanskrifter*, 2 vols. (Christiana: B. M. Bentzen, 1877).

12. This general pattern—from lives of saints to those of sainted kings to those of kings in sequence—recurs elsewhere and plays a similar role in the development of national literatures, identities, and historical sensibilities, as has been shown by Lars Boje Mortensen, "Sanctified Beginnings and Mythopoietic Moments: The First Wave of Writing on the Past in Norway, Denmark, and Hungary," in *The Making of Christian Myths in the Periphery of Latin Christendom (c. 1000–1300)*, ed. Lars Boje Mortensen (Copenhagen: Museum Tusculanum Press, 2006), 247–73.

13. The text most commonly known as Heimskringla takes this name from its opening words (*Kringla heimsins*, "the circle of the world"), but it also bears the more descriptive title "Sagas of Norway's Kings" (*Noregs konunga sögur*). For the best general discussion, see Diana Whaley, *Heimskringla: An Introduction* (London: Viking Society for Northern Research, 1991). Regarding the establishment of Snorri's authorship, see Whaley, 13–17; Jakob Benediktsson, "Hvar var Snorri nefndur höfundur Heimskringlu?," *Skírnir* 129 (1955): 118–27; and Jonna Louis-Jensen, "Heimskringla: Et værk af Snorri Sturluson?," *Nordica Bergensia* 14 (1997): 230–45.

14. Sverrir Jakobsson, "Myter om Harald Hårfagre," in *Sagas and the Norwegian Experience: Preprints for the 10th International Saga Conference* (Trondheim: Senter for Middelalderstudier, 1997), 597–610, offers a thorough and thoughtful review of historians' attempts to extract historical actuality from the testimony of the Kings' Sagas, along with a critical discussion of the limited utility of the skaldic poetry that both medieval and modern historians consider the best available evidence. In a subsequent publication, "'Erindringen om en mægtig Personlighed': Den norsk-islandske historiske tradisjon om Harald Hårfagre i et kildekritisk perspective," *Historisk tidsskrift* 81 (2002): 213–30, Jakobsson went further still, arguing that the sources are so far removed from the (putative) events and are so intrinsically insecure that one should understand Harald "as a mythic or legendary person, not a historic figure" (*Harald Hårfagre skal skjønes som en mytisk eller legendarisk person, ikke en historisk skikkelse*, 213; English summary at 230).

15. For summary discussions of this material, see Jan de Vries, "Harald Schönhaar in Sage und Geschichte," *Beiträge zur Geschichte der deutschen Sprache* 66 (1942): 55–116; and Gert Kreutzer, "Das Bild Harald Schönhaars in der altisländischen Literatur," in *Studien zum Altgermanischen: Festschrift für Heinrich Beck*, ed. Heiko Uecker (Berlin: Walter de Gruyter, 1994), 443–61.

16. Heimskringla describes its use of sources in two different passages of its prologue. The

first shows reliance on written documents (esp. genealogies) and oral testimony (poems and the testimony of "wise men," *fróðir menn*).

> In this book, I had the old accounts written down concerning those rulers who have held power in the northern lands and spoke in the Norse tongue, such as I have heard wise men tell, as well as some of their genealogies, according to that which was known to me. Some of this is found in pedigrees in which kings and other men of great lineages have collected their kin, and some is written according to ancient songs or historical poems that men have used for their entertainments. Although we do not know the truth on this, we know that, as precedents for this, that ancient wise men have held it for true.

> *Í bok þessi lét ek rita forna frásagnir um hofðinga þá, er riki hafa haft á Norðrlondum ok á danska tungu hafa mælt, svá sem ek hefi heyrt fróða menn segja, svá ok nokkurar kynkvíslir þeira, eptir því, sem mér hefir kent verit, sumt þat er finnsk í langfeðgatali, því er konungar hafa rakit kyn sitt eða aðrir stórættaðir menn, en sumt er ritit eptir fornum kvæðum eða soguljóðum, er menn hafa haft til skemtanar sér, en þó at vér vitim eigi sannyndi á því, þá vitum vér dæmi til þess, at gamlir fræðimenn hafa slíkt fyrir satt haft.*

The second passage is quite specifically concerned with the sources that treat Harald Fairhair. Particular privilege here is accorded to skaldic poems, but the statement that "we take *most* of the account from what was said in those poems" clearly implies that there were also other sources.

> And when Harald Fairhair was king in Norway, then Iceland was settled. With Harald were skalds, and men still know their poems and the poems of all the kings there have been in Norway since then. We take most things from what is said in the poems that were recited before the rulers themselves or their sons. We take all to be true that is found in these poems about their journeys or battles. It is the habit of skalds to praise the most him whom they serve, but no one would dare to recount a king's deeds in his presence when all those who heard would know the story to be stuff and nonsense, as would he himself. That would be mockery, and not praise.

> *En er Haraldr inn hárfagri var konungr í Nóregi, þá byggðisk Ísland. Með Haraldi váru skald ok kunna menn enn kvæði þeira ok allra konunga kvæði, þeira er síðan hafa verit at Nóregi, ok tokum vér þar mest dæmi af því, er sagt er í þeim kvæðum, er kveðin váru fyrir sjálfum hofðingjunum eða sonum þeira; tokum vér þat alt fyrir satt, er í þeim kvæðum finnsk um ferðir þeira eða orrostur; en þat er háttr skálda, at lofa þann mest, er þá eru þeir fyrir, en engi myndi þat þora, at segja sjálfum honum þau verk hans, er allir þeir, er heyrði, vissi, at hégómi væri ok skrok, ok svá sjálfr hann; þat væri þá háð, en eigi lof.*

Similar discussions of sources are found in the prologues to Theodricus Monachus and to Saxo Grammaticus's Gesta Danorum. The former privileges poems and discussions with Icelandic informants; the latter, poems, rock-cut inscriptions, and Icelandic narrative traditions.

17. For a good discussion of this literary and ideological structure, see Gerd Wolfgang Weber, "*Intellegere historiam*: Typological Perspectives of Nordic Prehistory (in Snorri, Saxo, Widukind and Others)," in *Tradition og historieskrivning: Kilderne til Nordens ældste historie*, ed. Kirsten Hastrup and Preben Meulengracht Sørensen (Århus: Aarhus Universitetsforlag, 1987), 95–141, esp. 109–10. On the interaction of monarchy and church in the process of state formation, see Gurevich, "The Early State in Norway," 403–23; Kåre Lunden, "Overcoming Re-

ligious and Political Pluralism: Interactions between Conversion, State Formation and Change in Social Infrastructure in Norway, c. AD 950–1260," *Scandinavian Journal of History* 22 (1997): 83–97; and Sverre Bagge, "Christianization and State Formation in Early Medieval Norway," *Scandinavian Journal of History* 30 (2005): 107–34.

18. Theodricus Monachus, Historia de Antiquitate Regum Norwagiensium 1: "In the year 858 from the incarnation of our Lord, Harald Fairhair, son of Hálfdan the Black, began his reign" (*Anno ab incarnatione Domini octigentesimo quinquagesimo octavo regnavit Haraldus pulchre-comatus, filius Halfdan nigri*). The manuscripts vary on the date itself, some having 852 and some 858. Gustav Storm, ed., *Monumenta Historica Norvegiæ: Latinske Kildeskrifter til Norges Historie i Middelalderen* (Christiania [Oslo]: A. W. Brøgger, 1880), 6, accepted the latter; while Vegard Skånland, "The Year of King Harald Fairhair's Access to the Throne according to Theodoricus Monachus," *Symbolae Osloenses* 41 (1966): 125–28, argued for the former; and others, including Paul Lehman, *Skandinavens Anteil an der lateinischen Literatur und Wissenschaft des Mittelalters: Sitzungsberichte der Bayerischen Akademie der Wissenschaften, Philosophisch-historisch Abteilung* (1936–37), 121, have suggesteed that the proper date ought to be 862.

19. Historia de Antiquitate Regum Norwagiensium 19: "Saint Olaf fell on the fourth of August, which was then a Wednesday, in the year 1029 from the incarnation of our Lord, as far as we have been able to investigate with certainty" (*Occubuit autem beatus Olavus quarto Kal. Augusti, quot tunc erat quarta feria, anno ab incarnatione Domini millesimo vicesimo nono, ut nos certius indagare potuimus*). This sentence ends chap. 19 of the text, and chap. 20 opens with a disclaimer on the unreliability of dating.

20. Royal power is thus understood as so radical and terrifying a transformation of society that it is utterly alien in its origins, following the mythic pattern of the "stranger king," as discussed by Marshall Sahlins, *Islands of History* (Chicago: University of Chicago Press, 1985). Ynglingasaga 2 theorizes kingship as a mix of overpowering military leadership and ambiguous religiosity. The ambiguity in the latter case is established first by the (pagan) sacrifices central to the worship performed by Óðinn and his countrymen, and second by the mitigating fact that their military success is secured by a quasi-Christian "blessing" that he grants his followers. The term used for this blessing, Old Norse *bjának* (or: *bjannak*), occurs nowhere other than this passage and is a loanword with strong connotations of a Christianity brought from foreign lands, by virtue of its derivation from Irish *beannacht* and Latin *benedictio*. In this fashion, Óðinn himself is portrayed as both a stranger-king and a Christian *avant la lettre*. The faith others have in him is misplaced, but this is an error that later history can and will correct.

> In Asia, east of the fork in the Don it was called Ásaland or Ásaheim, and they called the capital city that was in that land Ásgarð. In the city was a chief, who was called Óðinn. It was a great place for sacrifice. . . . Óðinn was a great man of war, very wide-faring, and he took possession of many realms. He was so blessed with victory that in every battle he prevailed. And so it came about that his men believed that he was entitled to victory in every battle. It was his habit that if he sent his men into battle or on other missions that he laid his hand on their head and gave them a blessing [*bjának*]. They believed that then things would go well. And when his men stood in need, on land or sea, they called on his name and it seemed they always got comfort from that. They thought they had every protection wherever he was.

> *Fyrir austan Tanakvísl í Ásía var kallat Ásaland eða Ásaheimr, en hǫfuðborgin, er var í landinu, kǫlluðu þeir Ásgarð. En í borginni var hǫfðingi sá, er Óðinn var kallaðr; þar var blótstaðr mikill. . . . Óðinn var hermaðr mikill ok mjǫk viðfǫrull ok eignaðisk mǫrg ríki;*

hann var svá sigrsæll, at í hverri orrostu fekk hann gagn; ok svá kom, at hans menn trúðu því, at hann átti heimilan sigr í hverri orrostu. þat var háttr hans, ef hann sendi menn sina til orrostu eða aðrar sendifarar, at hann lagði áðr hendr í hǫfuð þeim ok gaf þeim bjának; trúðu þeir, at þá myndi vel farask. Svá var ok um hans menn, hvar sem þeir urðu í nauðum staddir á sjá eða á landi, þá kǫlluðu þeir á nafn hans, ok þótti jafnan fá af því fró; þar þóttusk þeir eiga alt traust, er hann var.

21. Harald Fairhair's Saga 4: "*þess strengi ek heit, ok því skýt ek til guðs, þess er mik skóp ok ǫllu ræðr.*" The same wording recurs in the Greater Saga of Olaf Tryggvason 2 (Flateyjarbók 1.40) but is lacking in other versions of Harald's oath (Fagrskinna 3; Fagrskinna Appendix 3; Egil's Saga 3; "Tale of Hálfdan the Black" 6 [Flateyjarbók 1.566], and the "Tale of Harald Fairhair" 3 [Flateyjarbók 1.569]).

22. Fagrskinna Appendix 3 (from the so-called A-Text), in *Ágrip af Nóregskonunga Sögum [ok] Fagrskinna—Nóregs Konunga Tal*, ed. Bjarni Einarsson [Reykjavík: Íslenzka Fornritafélag, 1984], 366–69).

> *því heit ek ok, at engum guþi skal ek blót fœra, þeim er nú gǫfga menn, nema þeim einum, er sólina gørði ok heiminum hagaði ok hann gørði. Ok með því at ek berumk þat fyrir, at ek vil vera einvaldskonungr at Nóregi ok leggja undir mik alla aþra konunga, þá er áðr eru bæði ríkir ok máttugir, þá skal ek í þess trausti alla hluti gøra, er máttugastr er ok ǫllu ræðr. Engi skal ok sá mér allkærr vera at vináttu, er annan guð gǫfgar en þann, því at ek þykkjumk þat sjá til sanns, at sá guð má ekki mér hjálpa ok engum ǫðrum, er hann hefir ekki meira ríki en einn stein eða einn skóg. Ek em maðr einn, ok veit ek at ek skal deyja sem aðrir menn, ok kenni ek yfirgjarnligan hug með mér. En ef ek vissa, at ek skylda jafnan lifa sem ek veit, at guð lifir, þá mynda ek ekki una fyrr en ek hefða allan heiminn undir mér ok mínu forræði. Fyrir því er þat markandi um þessa guða, ef þeir hefði guðdóm nǫkkurn eða afl með sér, þá ynði þeir ekki svá litlu ríki at ráða einum steini eða litlum lund. Fyrir því skal hverr maðr viuandi láta sér þat skiljask,*" ^{‹segir›} *konungr,* "*sá er nǫkkut vit hefir fengit, at sá einn er sannr guð, er alla hluti hefir skapat, þá má hann einn fulla hjálp veita manninum, því at hann hefir manninn gǫrvan sem allt annat. Fyrir því mun ek á þat stunda meðan er ek lifi, at svá sem hugr minn stundar til þess, er ǫllum er máttugari, svá væntir mik ok, at af hans trausti skal ek enn verða máttkari ǫllum smákonungum, þeim sem nú eru í Nóregi.*"

23. Lars Lönnroth, "The Noble Heathen: A Theme in the Sagas," *Scandinavian Studies* 41 (1969): 1–29.

24. Thus, for instance, Kreutzer, "Das Bild Harald Schönhaars," 453–55, takes Heimskringla's portrayal of Harald to be "entirely positive" (*rein positiven, grundsätzlich positive*). Even such astute readers as Lars Lönnroth, "Ideology and Structure in Heimskringla," *Parergon* 15 (1976): 16–29; and Ármann Jakobsson, *Í Leit að Konungi*, have taken this text's attitude toward the Norwegian monarchy in general to be similarly supportive (on Harald in specific, see Jakobsson, 202–3). A more nuanced position is that of Theodore M. Andersson, "The Politics of Snorri Sturluson," *Journal of English and Germanic Philology* 93 (1994): 55–78, and "The King of Iceland," *Speculum* 74 (1999): 923–34, who sees Heimskringla as backing away from the antimonarchic position of texts like Morkinskinna and Egil's Saga, which were written at earlier and tenser moments in the conflict of Iceland and Norway. In contrast to Andersson's view that Heimskringla "softens" and "neutralizes" the polemic, I see it as developing a more intricate,

subtle, deeply coded, and deliberately ambiguous critique of kingship that invites superficial (mis)readings from readers sympathetic to the Norwegian throne.

Chapter Two

1. Much has been written on the formation of the Icelandic commonwealth in conscious opposition to the nature of the Norwegian royal state. Among others, see Ármann Jakobsson, *Í Leit að Konungi*; Jesse Byock, *Medieval Iceland* (Berkeley: University of California Press, 1988), 51–76; Kirsten Hastrup, *Culture and History in Medieval Iceland* (Oxford: Clarendon Press, 1985), 7–13, 105–37; and Richard Tomasson, *Iceland: The First New Society* (Minneapolis: University of Minnesota Press, 1980).

2. Most extensively on this text, see Alan Berger, "The Sagas of Harald Fairhair," *Scripta Islandica* 31 (1980): 14–29, and the earlier literature cited therein. Berger's closing suggestion attributing the lost saga to Snorri Sturluson is ill supported and gratuitous, but the analysis of relations among the surviving texts that made use of the lost saga is disciplined, detailed, and useful.

3. On this text and its relation to the versions of Ólafs saga Tryggvasonar by Oddr Snorrason and Gunnlaugr Leifsson, see Andersson, "Kings' Sagas," 216–19; and Jónas Kristjánsson, *Eddas and Sagas*, trans. Peter Foote (Reykjavík: Hið íslenska bókmenntafélag, 1988), 157–159. On its relation to Heimskringla, Jürg Glauser, "Vom Autor zum Kompilator: Snorri Sturlusons *Heimskringla* und die nachklassischen Sagas von Olav Tryggvason," in *Snorri Sturluson: Beiträge zu Werk und Rezeption*, ed. Hans Fix (Berlin: de Gruyter, 1998), 34–43.

4. The patronym occurs in "Tale of Harald Fairhair" (*þáttr Haralds hárfagra*), chap. 1 (Flateyjarbók 1.567). The epithet "Shaggy" is well attested from skaldic poetry contemporary to Harald's reign, such as Thjóðólf of Hvín's account of the Battle of Hafrsfjörð, quoted at Harald Fairhair's Saga 18 and Flateyjarbók 1.574 (cf. also Ágrip 1). "Fairhair" is the way he is usually known, and the Latin sources refer to him as Haraldus comatus (Historia Norwegiæ, chap. 11) or Haraldus pulchre-comatus (Theodricus Monachus, Historia de Antiquitate Regum Norwagiensium, chap. 1).

5. Although Norwegian and Icelandic legal texts are quite precise in specifying the three steps that constitute a proper marriage (negotiations between a suitor and a woman's male kin leading to betrothal [*festar*], payment of bridewealth [*mundr*], and a wedding ceremony [*gipt, brúðkaup*, or *brullaup*] culminating in the groom's taking his bride to bed, with at least six witnesses present), there is no fixed terminology that denotes the making of such a union. When the verb *fá* (more broadly "to fetch, catch, seize; get, gain, win, procure") has a woman as its object (in the genitive), it often means "to marry," but it can also signal more violent and less licit unions, as is apparent from Íslendinga Saga 2.191, where the same verb describes two sharply contrasted practices: "It's better that you choose my sister and marry [*fáir*] her than that the Vikings seize [*fái*] her" (*betr er þá séð fyrir kosti systur minnar at þú fáir hennar en vikingar fái hennar*). Cognate verbs in the other Germanic languages are not used of marriage, only more and less aggressive forms of taking and capture. Thus, e.g., Gothic *fāhan*, "to seize, capture, arrest" (used to translate Greek πιάζειν at John 7.44 and 8.20), and Anglo-Saxon *fōn*, "to grasp, catch, seize" (e.g., when Grendel's mother clutches wildly at the hero, *heó him to-geánes féng*, Beowulf 1542). Rather than marriage proper, *fá* plus a female object denotes an act of couple formation through the assertive and acquisitive action of a male subject, which can be conducted with

varying legality, aggressivity, etiquette, and affect. Context determines the nature of the act and of the union it establishes. Less ambiguous terminology was readily available, including the verbs *gipta* ("to give a woman in marriage"), *giptask* (reflexive, "to marry, give one's self," used of both sexes), *kvánga* and *kvángask* ("to take a wife"); the nouns *kván* ("wife" [and never simply "woman"]), *gipt* ("wedding"), *giptarmál* ("marriage"), *giptarorð* ("word or pledge of marriage"), *brúðkaup* ("wedding feast," lit. "bride's purchase"), *brullaup* ("wedding feast," lit. "bride's leap"), *hjún* ("married couple"); and the adjective *skilfengin* ("lawfully wedded"). Neither in this passage nor in any variant of the Gyða episode is any of this terminology deployed. One is free to infer a legal marriage, but the text leaves the point ambiguous. As we will see, other versions take pains to deny that a marriage occured. For the fullest discussion of marriage practices, terminology, etiquette, and law in medieval Scandinavia, see Jenny Jochens, *Women in Old Norse Society* (Ithaca, NY: Cornell University Press, 1995), 17–64. Also relevant is her article "The Politics of Reproduction: Medieval Norwegian Kingship," *American History Review* 92 (1987): 327–49.

6. "Tale of Harald Fairhair" 3 (Flateyjarbók 1.569): *Da fek Haralldr konungr Gydu dottur Æreks konungs af Hörðalande. en hon mællti þat til vid konung at hann skyllde vinna allan Noreg undir sig eptir þui sem segir j odrum kapitula j Olafs sogu Tryggguasonar ok þa streingde Haralldr konungr þess hæith at lata huorke kemba har sitt ne skera fyrr en hann yrde einualldzkonungr yfir Noregi. þui uar hann þa kalladr Haralldr lufa. hann atti vid Gydu þessa sonu Guthorm Harek Gudrod.*

7. On the dating of this battle, see Halvdan Koht, *Harald Hærfagre og Rikssamlinga* (Oslo: H. Aschehoug, 1955), 45–49.

8. Chap. 3 of Harald Fairhair's Saga contains Gyða's suggestion; chap. 4, Harald's oath; chaps. 5–18, the military campaigns culminating in the great battle of Hafrsfjörð; and chap. 20, the wedding.

9. Jenny Jochens, "The Female Inciter in the Kings' Sagas," *Arkiv för Norsk Filologi* 102 (1987): 100–119.

10. On institutions of vengeance, see Jesse Byock, *Feud in the Icelandic Saga* (Berkeley: University of California Press, 1982); William Ian Miller, *Bloodtaking and Peacemaking: Feud, Law, and Society in Saga Iceland* (Chicago: University of Chicago Press, 1990).

11. As Koht, *Harald Hærfagre og*, puts it, p. 31, the social, cultural, and economic preconditions for Norwegian unity were present in the early ninth century, but long-standing political divisions obstructed the realization of that unity.

12. Tacitus, Germania 8, Histories 4.61 and 65. The first of these passages reads as follows:

> They consider women to have some holy and prophetic quality. They neither fail to consult them nor ignore their responses. We saw under Vespasian how Veleda was long held by many in the place of a divine power. Earlier, Albruna and numerous others were venerated, not with obsequious flattery or in a way to make them out as goddesses.

> *inesse quin etiam sanctum aliquid et providum putant, nec aut consilia earum aspernantur aut responsa neglegunt. vidimus sub divo Vespasiano Veledam diu apud plerosque numinis loco habitam; sed et olim Albrunam et compluris alias venerati sunt, non adulatione nec tamquam facerent deas.*

13. In addition to the central figure of the Völuspá, other *völur* appear at Völuspá 22, Hávamál 87–88, Landnamabók 173, Thorfinns Saga Karlsefnis 3, Örvar-Odds Saga 3, and elsewhere.

The term is often equated with *spákona*, "prophetic woman." For occurrences, see Richard Cleasby and Gudbrand Vigfusson, *An Icelandic-English Dictionary*, 2d ed. (Oxford: Clarendon Press, 1957), 722. On the importance of seeress figures within Germanic myth and religion, see Jan de Vries, *Altgermanische Religionsgeschichte* (Berlin: Walter de Gruyter, 1970), 319–21, 324–26, 404–5; Hans Naumann, "Der König und die Seherin," *Zeitschrift für deutsche Philologie* 63 (1938): 347–58; Hans Volkmann, *Germanische Seherinnen in römischen Diensten* (Krefeld: Scharpe Verlag, 1964); and Ursula Dronke, ed. and trans., *The Poetic Edda*, vol. 2, *Mythological Poems* (Oxford: Clarendon Press, 1997), 105–6; pace Reinhold Bruder, *Die germanische Frau im Lichte der Runeninschriften und der antiken Historiographie* (Berlin: de Gruyter, 1974), 151–62. Regarding the possibility of Sibylline influence on the figure of the Völva, see Ursula Dronke, "Völuspá and Sibylline Traditions," in *Latin Culture and Medieval Germanic Europe*, ed. Richard North and Tette Hofstra (Groningen: Egbert Forsten, 1992), 3–23.

14. For discussion of how the nonpast (present and future) was theorized as emergent from layered residues of the past, see Paul Bauschatz, *The Well and the Tree: World and Time in Early Germanic Culture* (Amherst: University of Massachusetts Press, 1982).

15. Tacitus, Histories 4.65. On her power and divinity, cf. 4.61. The male leader with whom she was most closely associated was Civilis, who—as reported in this same passage (4.61)— swore an oath strongly reminiscent of that sworn by Harald:

> After he had taken up arms against the Romans, Civilis, following a barbarian vow, reddened his hair and let it grow. Having finally concluded the massacre of the legions, he cut it off.

> *Civilis barbaro voto post coepta adversus Romanos arma propexum rutilatumque crinem patrata demum caede legionum deposuit.*

16. Harald Fairhair's Saga 3: *Haraldr konungr sendi menn sína eptir meyju einni, er Gyða er nefnd, dóttir Eiríks konungs af Hǫrðalandi—hon var at fóstri á Valdresi með ríkum bóanda—er hann vildi taka til frillu sér, þvíat hon var allfríð mær ok heldr stórlát; en er sendimenn kómu þar, þá báru þeir upp erendi sín fyrir meyna; hon svaraði á þessa lund, at eigi vill hon spilla meydómi sínum, til þess at taka til mannz þann konung, er eigi hefir meira ríki, en nǫkkur fylki, til forráða, "en þat þykki mér undarligt, segir hon, er engi er sá konungr, er svá vill eignask Nóreg ok vera einvaldi yfir, sem hefir Gormr konungr at Danmǫrku eða Eiríkr at Upsǫlum." Sendimǫnnum þykkir hon svara furðustórliga ok spyrja hana máls um, hvar til svǫr þessi skulu koma, segja, at Haraldr er konungr svá ríkr, at henni er fullræði í, en þó at hon svari á annan veg þeira erendum, en þeir mundu vilja, þá sjá þeir engan sinn kost til þess at sinni, at þeir mundu hana í brot hafa, nema hennar vili væri til þess, ok búask þeir þá ferðar sinnar. En er þeir eru búnir, leiða menn þá út. þá mælti Gyða við sendimenn, bað þá bera þau orð sín Haraldi konungi, at hon mun því at einu játa at gerask eigin kona hans, ef hann vill þat gera fyrir hennar sakir áðr, at leggja undir sik allan Nóreg ok ráða því ríki jafnfrjálsliga, sem Eiríkr konungr Svía-veldi eða Gormr konungr Danmǫrku, "þvíat þá þykki mér, segir hon, hann mega heita þjóðkonungr."*

17. On concubinage, see Jochens, *Women in Old Norse Society*, 20–21; Else Ebel, *Der Konkubinat nach altwestnordischen Quellen: Philologische Studien zur sogenannte "Friedelehe"* (Berlin: de Gruyter, 1993); and Ruth Karras, "Concubinage and Slavery in the Viking Age," *Scandinavian Studies* 62 (1990): 141–62. For the etymology of *frilla*, Jan de Vries, *Altnordisches etymologisches Wörterbuch* (Leiden: E. J. Brill, 1977), 142–43 (under *friðill* and *frjá*) and the discussion of Ebel, 150–55.

18. Greater Saga of Olaf Tryggvason 2 (Flateyjarbók 1.40): *þui sidr uil ek vera fridla hans.* On the way these categories figure in the negotiations between Harald and Gyða, see Ebel, *Der Konkubinat,* 65–67.

19. On the legal conditions for constructing a proper marriage, see Jochens, *Women in Old Norse Society,* 24–29; Hastrup, *Culture and History in Medieval Iceland,* 89–97.

20. Harald Fairhair's Saga 4: *þá svarar Haraldr konungr, at eigi hefði þessi mær illa mælt, eða gǫrt svá, at hefnda væri fyrir vert, bað hana hafa mikla þǫkk fyrir orð sin—"hon hefir mint mik þeira hluta, segir hann, er mér þykkir nú undarligt, er ek hefi eigi fyrr hugleitt", ok enn mælti hann: "þess strengi ek heit, ok því skýt ek til guðs, þess er mik skóp ok ǫllu ræðr, at aldri skal skera hár mitt né kemba, fyrr en ek hefi eignazk allan Nóreg með skǫttum ok skyldum ok forráði, en deyja at ǫðrum kosti."* Cf. Flateyjarbók 1.40.

21. Harald Fairhair's Saga 5: *ok þá er hann kom ofan í byggðina, þá lét hann drepa menn alla ok brenna byggðina; en er fólkit varð þessa vist, þá flýði hverr, er mátti, sumir ofan til Orkadals, sumir til Gaulardals, sumir á markir, sumir leituðu griða, ok þat fengu allir, þeir er á konungs fund kómu, ok gerðusk hans menn.*

Flateyjarbók 1.569 is almost identical to this passage, the sole significant departure being its reference to Harald as "King Shaggy Harald" (*Haralldr konungr lufa*). Either it is dependent on Heimskringla at this point or both follow the same common source, presumably the lost *Haralds saga hárfagra.* The Greater Saga of Olaf Trygvason much more discreetly minimizes all mention of violence, saying only, "Thereafter, King Harald conquered and laid all Norway under him, as it says in his saga" (*þadan af vann Haralldr konungr ok lagde undir sig allan Noreg sem segir j sǫgu hans*; Flateyjarbók 1.40).

22. Close examination of nonliterary evidence (laws, wills, etc.) has led most Norwegian historians to conclude that the account of the way Harald transformed property relations to expand state power is exaggerated and anachronistic. Recognizing the extent to which his narrative departs from the historical actualities helps one perceive the tendentiously critical nature of the former. See Gurevich, "The Early State in Norway," p. 411 and the literature cited there. Helgi Skúli Kjartansson, "English Models for King Harald Fairhair?," in *The Fantastic in Old Norse / Icelandic Literature: Sagas and the British Isles; Preprint Papers of the 13th International Saga Conference* (Durham: Centre for Medieval and Renaissance Studies, 2006), 359–364, has suggested that legislation King Canute introduced in 1017, after his conquest of England, provided a model that Heimskringla and other sagas projected back into their accounts of Harald's reign.

23. On the nature of *óðal* property, see Aaron Gurevich, *Historical Anthropology of the Middle Ages* (Chicago: University of Chicago Press, 1992), 204–9.

24. Harald Fairhair's Saga 6:

> Wherever King Harald had won power, he established the law that he possessed all the *óðal*-lands. He made all the landowners pay him rent on land, both the powerful ones and those without power. He put an earl over each district, who would pass judgments and administer the law of the land and extract [*heimta*] fines and rents on land. The earl would have a third of the taxes for the maintenance of his own table. Each earl should have under him four chiefs [*hersar*, sing. *hersir*] or more, and each of them should have twenty marks allowance. Each earl should contribute sixty soldiers to the king's army, and each hersir, twenty men. But King Harald so increased the fines and the rents on land that his earls had more wealth than the [district] kings had before. And when they learned this around Trondheim, many powerful men sought out King Harald and they became his men.

Haraldr konungr setti þann rétt alt þar, er hann vann ríki undir sik, at hann eignaðisk óðul öll ok lét alla bóendr gjalda sér landskyldir bæði ríka ok órika; hann setti jarl í hverju fylki, þann er dæma skyldi lóg ok landzrétt ok heimta sakeyri ok landskyldir, ok skyldi jarl hafa þriðjung skatta ok skylda til borðz sér ok kostnaðar. Jarl hverr skyldi hafa undir sér iiii. hersa eða fleiri, ok skyldi hverr þeira hafa xx. marka veizlu; jarl hverr skyldi fá konungi í her lx. hermanna, en hersir hverr xx. menn. En svá mikit hafði Haraldr konungr aukit álóg ok landzskyldir, at jarlar hans höfðu meira ríki, en konungar höfðu fyrrum. En er þetta spurðisk um þrándheim, þá sóttu til Haraldz konungs margir ríkismenn ok gerðusk hans menn.

Cf. Flateyjarbók 1.569–70. The verb *heimta*, which is used to describe the collection of taxes, more broadly is applied to acts of drawing, pulling, and the milking of cattle. See Cleasby and Vigfusson, *Icelandic-English Dictionary*, 251–52.

25. Harald Fairhair's Saga 7 and 9. Cf. Flateyjarbók 1.570–71 and 575.

26. The Heimskringla variant differs on this from all other sources, and even the Greater Saga of Olaf Tryggvason, which follows it closely on other points, has a different account of the order and names of Harald's wives and children. Cf. Harald Fairhair's Saga 21; Historia Norwegiæ 11; Ágrip 2; Fagrskinna 3; Greater Saga of Olaf Tryggvason 2 (Flateyjarbók 1.40–41); and "Tale of Harald Fairhair" 1, 3, and 8 (Flateyjarbók 1.567, 569, and 575).

27. See, for instance, Egil's Saga 4:

> In every district, King Harald took possession of all the *óðal* property and all the land, inhabited and uninhabited, also the sea and the lakes. All the landowners became his tenants, as did those who cultivated the marches, the salt burners, and all hunters and fishers: they all became his subjects. But many men fled from the land for abroad because of this oppression, and uncultivated marches came to be widely settled, both east in Jamtaland, Helsingjaland, and in western lands: the Hebrides, the Dublin region, Ireland, Normandy in France, Caithness in Scotland, the Orkneys, Shetland, and the Faroes, and at that time Iceland was discovered.

> *Haraldr konungr eignaðiz í hverju fylki óðul öll, ok alt land, byggt ok óbyggt, ok jafnvel sjóinn ok vótnin, ok skyldu allir búendr vera hans leiglendingar; svá þeir, er á mórkina ortu, ok saltkarlarnir ok allir veiðimenn, bæði á sjó ok landi, þá váru allir þeir honum lýðskyldir. En af þessi áþján flýðu margir menn af landi á brott, ok byggðuz þá margar auðnir víða, bæði austr í Jamtaland ok Helsingjaland, ok Vestrlönd: Suðreyjar, Dyflinnar skíði, Irland, Normandí á Vallandi, Katanes á Skotlandi, Orkneyjar ok Hjaltland, Færeyjar, ok í þann tíma fannz Ísland.*

The key term is *áþján*, "oppression," from the verb *þja*, "to constrain, enthral, enslave." Cf. Íslendingabók 1.4; Laxdæla Saga 2; Eyrbyggja Saga 1; Grettir's Saga 3; et al. The most important texts have been conveniently gathered in appendix 3 of Patricia Pires Boulhosa, *Icelanders and the Kings of Norway: Mediaeval Sagas and Legal Texts* (Leiden: E. J. Brill, 2005), 228–32.

28. Harald Fairhair's Saga 18: *Tíðendi þau spurðusk sunnan ór landi, at Hörðar ok Rygir, Egðir ok þilir sómnuðusk saman ok gerðu upreist bæði at skipum ok vápnum ok fjölmenni; váru þeir uphafsmenn Eiríkr, Hörðalandz-konungr, Súlki konungr af Rogalandi ok Sóti jarl, bróðir hans, Kjótvi inn auðgi, konungr af Ógðum, ok þórir haklangr, sonr hans; af þelamörk brœðr ii. Hróaldr hryggr ok Haddr inn harði.*

Cf. Flateyjarbók 1.573.

29. Of the seven leaders of resistance to Harald who are named in this passage, only one— Kjötvi the Wealthy—is mentioned in the skaldic account of the battle (Haraldskvæði 7–12).

Heimskringla seems to have added the others, with Eirik of Hörðaland in first place, either drawing on unidentified sources or innovating for reasons of its own. Regarding this and other important differences between the accounts of Hafrsfjörð in the ninth-century poem and the much more elaborate description in Heimskringla, see Klaus von See, "Studien zum Harald-skvæði," *Arkiv för Nordisk Filologi* 76 (1961): 105–11.

30. Ebel finds the passage unambiguous: "Hier ist nun ganz eindeutig nicht von einer Heirat die Rede, sondern von einem minderen 'Verhältnis' " (*Der Konkubinat*, 67).

31. Harald Fairhair's Saga 20: *Haraldr konungr var nú einvaldi orðinn allz Nóregs. þá mintisk hann þess, er mærin sú in mikilláta hafði mælt til hans; hann sendi þá menn til hennar ok lét hana hafa til sín ok lagði hana hjá sér; þessi váru bórn þeira: Álof var ellzt, þá var Hrœrekr, þá Sigtryggr, Fróði ok þorgils.*

32. Flateyjarbók 1.575: *þat segia menn at Haralldr konungr ætti .x. konur j senn ok .xx. frillur* ("Men say that King Harald had ten wives and twenty concubines"). On Harald's marriages and children, see Koht, *Harald Hærfagre*, 71–77. Ebel, p. 63, notes that Heimskringla uses the verbs that normally denote the establishment of a legitimate marriage (*eiga* and the expression *hann fekk*) only for Harald's unions with Svanhild Eysteinsdóttir, Áshild Hringsdóttir, Ása Hákonar-dóttir, Snæfríðr, and Ragnhild Eireksdóttir.

33. Harald Fairhair's Saga 21: *Svá segja menn, at þá er Haraldr konungr fekk Ragnhildar ríku, at hann léti þá af ix. konum sínum.* Cf. Flateyjarbók 1.42.

34. Flateyjarbók 1.576: *Æirekr konungr med rade dottur sinnar sende honum ord at hann munde gifta honum meyna ef hann leti af æiginkonum sinum ok fridlum. fara sendemenn aftr vid suo bvit. þa sendir konungr heim allar konur sinar til frænda þeirra. en eftir þat sende Haralldr konungr sudr til Danmerkr eftir Ragnhilldi ok var hon þa send honum. gerde hann sidan brudhlaup til hennar ok var hon hinn meste skorungr.*

35. Snorri attributes this poem, which is also sometimes called the Hrafnsmál, to Thorbjorn Hornklofi (Harald Fairhair's Saga 21). The "Tale of Harald Fairhair" credits Thjóðólf of Hvín (Flateyjarbók 1.576), but both quote the same text (cited here from Finnur Jónsson, ed., *Snorri Sturluson, Heimskringla: Nóregs Konumga Sögur* [Copenhagen: G. E. C. Gads Forlag, 1911], 54):

Hafnaði Holmrýgjum   ok Hólga ættar
ok Hǫrða meyjum   konungr enn kynstóri,
hverri enni heinversku   es tók konu danska.

The Greater Saga of Olaf Tryggvason credits Hornklofi but cites a different passage that gives rather less information (Flateyjarbók 1.42).

36. For discussion of this verse and Harald's marriage to Ragnhild, see Ebel, *Der Konkubinat*, 63–64.

37. Cf. Theodricus Monachus, Historia de Antiquitate Regum Norwagiensium, chap. 1; Historia Norwegiæ, 103–4; Ágrip 2; Fagrskinna 2–3.

38. On the manuscripts and their history, see Alison Finlay, trans., *Fagrskinna, a Catalogue of the Kings of Norway: A Translation with Introduction and Notes* (Leiden: E. J. Brill, 2004), 35–37.

39. Fagrskinna Appendix 3:

Here the property of Ragna is recounted: There was a maiden called Ragna the Mag-nificent, who then possessed nearly all the territory that is called Thotn and known as Land, also all the island that now is called the isle Byggða. It was also said of Ragna that she was the fairest of all maidens. Ragna was the daughter of Aðils the Rich. Aðils was the son of Ása, Thora's daughter. Thora was the daughter of King Eystein and Astrið, daughter of King Aðils, who was called Aðils the Black. But Aðils, Ragna's father, had just then died, and Ragna was his only child.

Hér segir frá eignum Rǫgnu. Ragna en ríkuláta hét mær ein, er átti byggð þá náliga alla, en þótn er kǫlluð ok Land heitir, ok ey þá alla, er nú er Eyn byggða kǫlluð. þat var ok mælt um Rǫgnu, at hón var allra meyja fegrst. Ragna var dóttir Aðils ens auðga. Aðils var Ásusonr þórudóttur. En þóra var dóttir þeira Eysteins konungs ok Ástríðar, dóttur Aðils konungs, er Aðils svarti var kallaðr. En Aðils, faðir Rǫgnu, var þá frá fallinn, en Ragna var einberni hans.

40. Ibid.: "Harald fell greatly in love with Ragna." *En Haraldr lagði elsku mikla á Rǫgnu.*
41. Ibid.:

But when Harald let his words of love to Ragna be known, she answered in this manner: "I say this surely in truth, that I am not worthy of a better lover than you are. This is because of both your kingly birth and all the kingly rank and beauty that are yours. But before I give my full love to you, I would like to know this: Who shall be the heir of your kinsman Nerið the Wise in Counsel—you, lord King, or Gandalf's sons?"

En þá er Haraldr lét ástaryrði sín í ljós við Rǫgnu, svaraði hón á þessa lund: "þat mæli ek víst með sannyndum, at eigi em ek betra unnusta verð en þér eruð. Veldr því hvárttveggja konunglig byrð yður ok svá ǫll konunglig tign ok fegrð, er á yðr er. En þó áðr en ek fella fulla ást til yðar, þá vil ek þess verða vǫr, hvárt heldr skulu verða arfar Neriðs ens ráðspaka, frænda yðvars, herra konungr, þér eða synir Gandálfs."

42. Ibid.: *þá svaraði Haraldr reiðr ok mælti svá: "þat ætlaða ek, Ragna, at þú skyldir fyrir ástar sakar með ágætri sœmð vera leidd til minnar sængr, en fyrir því at þú hefir brugðit mér þessum brigzlum, þá er nú þess vert, at þú sér svá leidd til minnar sængr sem ein fátœk frilla."*

43. Ibid.: *þat mælti Ragna við konunginn: "Eigi skulu þér, herra konungr, reiðask við, þó at vér mælim oss gaman ok hœfir þat ekki konungdómi yðrum at brjóta kapp við kvenmenn ok þó allra sízt við meybǫrn smá, sem ek em, heldr er yðr sœmð þat, herra konungr, at deila kappi við konunga aðra, er nú skipaðir um allt land innan. þat vil ek ok segja yðr, ef ek ræð mér sjálf, þá verð ek hvártki yðr frilla né einskis manns annars, ok annat hvárt skal ek hafa þann at eignum manni, er alla Nóregs menn gørir sér at þegnum eða skal ek engan hafa."*

44. Ibid.:

When King Harald heard these words, he straightaway swore a vow, swearing on his head, that he would have no wife in Norway, save Ragna, and with this measure as well—that he would make all men in Norway his subjects.

þá er Haraldr konungr heyrði þessi orð, þá strengði hann þegar heit ok sór við hǫfuð sitt, at hann skyldi enga eigna konu eiga í Nóregi nema Rǫgnu ok þó með þeim hætti, at hann gørði alla menn at þegnum sér í Nóregi.

Note that the first portion of this oath contains a loophole whereby the text makes it possible for King Harald to acquire other wives, provided they are not Norwegian.

45. Ibid.:

Concerning the new law: Then Harald made a new law concerning the rights of women: If a man takes a woman by force, a charge of outlawry shall be lodged against him and he shall purchase his freedom back with forty marks of six ells. And the woman who cohabits in secret, she shall go to the king's yard and lose her freedom until she is redeemed from there by three marks of six ells. "And I establish this law so that any woman who wants to be good, she will have liberty to preserve her chastity against any man. And any woman who wants to be bad, she will pay for her unchastity, as I have now proclaimed."

Um ný lǫg. Þá gørði Haraldr ný lǫg um kvenna rétt, at sá maðr, er tekr konu nauðga, þá skal hónum þat verða at útlegðar sǫk, ok skal hann kaupa sik með fjǫgurra tiga marka sex álna eyris í frið aptr. En sú kona, er hón legsk á laun, þá skal hón ganga í konungs garð ok týna frelsi sínu, þar til er hón er leyst þaðan með þrimr mǫrkum sex álna eyris. "En fyrir því set ek þessi lǫg, at hver sú kona, er hón vill góð vera, þá vill at hón hafi sjálfræði á sér at halda kvensku sinni fyrir hverjum manni. En sú kona, er hón vill ill vera, þá gjaldi hón ókvensku sinnar eptir því, sem nú hefi ek mælt."

The text goes on, quite anachronistically and at considerable length, to have Harald renounce worship of the old gods and to dedicate himself to the one true god who is creator of all.

Chapter Three

1. Fagrskinna 3; "Tale of Harald Fairhair" 7 (Flateyjarbók 1.573–75).

2. Harald Fairhair's Saga 22.

3. Harald Fairhair's Saga 23: *Haraldr konungr var á veizlu á Mæri at Rǫgnvaldz jarls; hafði hann þá eignazk land alt; þá tók konungr þar laugar ok þá lét Haraldr konungr greiða hár sitt, ok þá skar Rǫgnvaldr jarl hár hans, en áðr hafði verit óskorit ok ókembt x. vetr. þá kǫlluðu þeir hann Harald lúfu, en síðan gaf Rǫgnvaldr honum kenningarnafn ok kallaði hann Harald inn hárfagra, ok sǫgðu allir, er sá, at þat var it mesta sannnefni, þvíat hann hafði hár bædi mikit ok fagrt.*

4. Both Fagrskinna 3 and "Tale of Harald Fairhair" 7 (Flateyjarbók 1.575) specify: "His hair was long and matted." *Hár hans var sítt ok flókit.*

5. Harald Fairhair's Saga 12. Cf. Fagrskinna 3 and the verses from Eyvind Skáldaspillir's Háleygjatal quoted therein.

6. Harald Fairhair's Saga 24: *Rǫgnvaldr Mæra-jarl var inn mesti ástvin Haraldz konungs, ok konungr virði hann mikils.* Cf. "Tale of Harald Fairhair" 6 (Flateyjarbók 1.572): *Rognualldr jall . . . var leinge sidan mikill vinr Haralldz konungs.*

7. Harald Fairhair's Saga 12.

8. Harald Fairhair's Saga 10: *Hann var kallaðr Rǫgnvaldr inn ríki eða inn ráðsvinni, ok segja menn, at hvártveggja væri sannefni.*

9. Intimate bodily services to the monarch also became a prerogative of the highest nobility in royal courts on the continent. See the discussion of Norbert Elias, *The Court Society* (New York: Pantheon, 1983).

10. Marxist and non-Marxist historians have debated the extent to which monarchy and aristocracy ultimately achieved a community of interest in opposition to the population at large, but there has been general agreement on the tensions between noble and royal strata at least through the reign of St. Olaf. See further Halvdan Koht, "Sagaenes opfatning av vår gamle historie," in *Innhogg og utsyn i Norsk Histori* (Oslo: H. Aschehoug, 1921), 76–91; Gudmund Sandvik, *Hovding og Konge i Heimskringla* (Oslo: Akademisk Forlag, 1955); Knut Helle, "Norway in the High Middle Ages," *Scandinavian Journal of History* 6 (1981): 161–89; and Sverre Bagge, *Society and Politics in Snorri Sturluson's Heimskringla* (Berkeley: University of California Press, 1991), esp. 121–45.

11. Cf. Ágrip 2; Fagrskinna 3; Historia Norwegiæ, p. 104; Harald Fairhair's Saga 21 (with other sons mentioned in chaps. 17, 20, 25, and 37); Greater Saga of Olaf Tryggvason 3 (Flateyjarbók 1.41); and "Tale of Harald Fairhair" 8 (Flateyjarbók 1.575–76, with mention of other sons at chaps. 1 and 3 [Flateyjarbók 1.567 and 569]). The Norwegian sources do not specify the mothers for each of Harald's children, but the Icelandic sources list his sons according to the order of Harald's marriages, rather than the absolute order of their birth.

12. Fagrskinna 2 describes Snæfrið's father thus: "He was called a magician, that is, a seer. He dwelt in Haðaland and worked magic [seiðr]. He was called an evil sorcerer." *var hann kallaðr seiðmaðr, þat er spámaðr, ok var staðfastr á Haðalandi ok siddi þar ok var kallaðr skratti.*

13. Harald Fairhair's Saga 25–26. Cf. Fagrskinna 2, "Tale of Harald Fairhair" 1 (Flateyjarbók 1.567); and Greater Saga of Olaf Tryggvason 3 (Flateyjarbók 1.41).

14. Only two of Harald's sons ascended to the throne: Eirik Bloodaxe (ruled ca. 932–35), his firstborn son by the Danish princess Ragnhild, and Hákon the Good (ruled ca. 935–60), his last son, born to his servant Thora Morstrstong, but neither of them founded lines that endured. By Svanhild, daughter of Earl Eystein, he had sons three of whose descendants came to the throne: Olaf Tryggvason (r. 995–1000), St. Olaf (r. 1015–28), and Magnus the Good (r. 1035–47), but these lines also gave out after Magnus. In contrast, Sigurð Hrísi, one of the sons Snæfrið bore to Harald, founded a line that produced Harald Hard-Ruler (r. 1045–66), from whom descend all subsequent Norwegian kings. In that Snæfrið is the least auspicious of all Harald's wives and Hard-Ruler one of the harshest kings, this development is open to some highly critical readings.

15. Heimskringla cites Orkneyinga Saga 19 directly at St. Olaf's Saga 103, referring to it by its older name, The Earls' Sagas (*Jarla sǫgur*).

16. Regarding the relation of Orkneyinga Saga and Heimskringla to each other and to their sources, see Alexander Burt Taylor, ed. and trans., *The Orkneyinga Saga* (Edinburgh: Oliver and Boyd, 1938), 33–98. *Turf-Einar's Saga is mentioned in Landnámabók (Hauksbók 270, Sturlubók 309): "Einar went west and placed the Orkneys under him, *as is told in his saga*" (*fór Einarr vestr ok lagdi vnder sik Orkneyiar* **sem seger i sogu hans**; emphasis added.). Also useful is the discussion of Berger, "The Sagas of Harald Fairhair," 27–28.

17. Orkneyinga Saga 8: *þá er synir Haraldz hin hárfagra váru fulltíða at aldri, gerðusk þeir ofstopamenn miklir ok óhœgir innanlandz, fóru á hendr jǫrlum konungs, drápu suma, en suma ráku þeir af eignum sinum. Snæfriðar synir, Hálfdan háleggr ok Goðrøðr ljómi fóru at Rǫgnvaldi Mœrajarli ok drápu hann, en tóku undir sik rikit. En er Haraldr konungr spurði þat, varð hann reiðr mjǫk, ok fór at sonum sinum.* Text from Finnbogi Guðmundsson, ed., *Orkneyinga Saga*, Íslenzk Fornrit, vol. 34 (Reykjavík: Íslenzka Fornritafélag, 1965). Cf. Harald Fairhair's Saga 30; and Greater Saga of Olaf Tryggvason 183 (Flateyjarbók 1.223).

18. Harald Fairhair's Saga 30: *þeir váru allir bráðgǫrvir.*

19. Harald Fairhair's Saga 30: *Kom þá svá, at þeir unðu illa við, er konungr gaf þeim ekki ríki, en setti jarl í hverju fylki, ok þótti þeim jarlar vera smábornari, en þeir váru.*

20. Harald Fairhair's Saga 30: *þá er Haraldr konungr var xl. at aldri.*

21. Harald Fairhair's Saga 34: *Haraldr konungr var þá l. at aldri, er synir hans váru margir rosknir, en sumir dauðir.* **þeir gerðusk margir ofstopamenn miklir innan landz** ok váru sjálfir ósáttir; **þeir ráku af eignum jarla konungs, en suma drápu þeir** (emphasis added).

22. Harald Fairhair's Saga 34: "Then he gave his sons the title of king and established it in the laws that men of his lineage should each inherit a kingdom from their father, but the earldom that came from their maternal lineage." *þá gaf hann sonum sínum konunganǫfn ok setti þat í lǫgum, at hans ættmenn skyldi hverr konungdóm taka eptir sinn fǫður, en jarldóm sá, er kvensifr væri af hans ætt kominn.*

23. Harald Fairhair's Saga 34:

In each of these districts, he gave his sons half of the revenue and kept half for himself. In addition, they would sit on a high seat a step higher than the earls, but a step lower than his own. Each of his sons desired that seat after his death, but he himself desired it for Eirík. The Trondheimers desired it for Hálfdan the Black, those of Vík and Uppland wanted the best part of the realm for those who ruled over them. As a result of this, there was yet again much discord among the brothers.

Hann gaf sonum sínum í hverju þessu fylki hálfar tekjur við sik, ok þat með, at þeir skyldu sitja í hásæti, skǫr hæra en jarlar, en skǫr lægra, en hann sjálfr, en þat sæti eptir hans dag ætlaði sér hverr sona hans, en hann sjálfr ætlaði þat Eiriki, en þrœndir ætluðu þat Hálfdani svarta, en Vikverir ok Uplendinar unnu þeim bezt ríkis, er þar váru þeim undir hendi. Af þessu varð þar mikit sundrþykki enn af nýju milli þeira brœðra.

Violence among the half brothers comes in the immediately subsequent chapters, Harald Fairhair's Saga 35–36.

24. Orkneyinga Saga 8: "As compensation for his father, King Harald gave Thorir his own daughter, Álof Who-Makes-the-Harvest-Better, also an earl's title and his father's inheritance." *Haraldr konungr gaf þóri i fǫðurbœtr Álofu árbót, dóttur sína, ok jarlsnafn ok fǫðurleifð sina.*

25. See the classic discussion of Fritz Kern, "The Limitation of the Monarch by Law," in *Kingship and Law in the Middle Ages,* trans. S. B. Chrimes (Oxford: Basil Blackwell, 1956), 69–79. With specific reference to Norway, Sverre Bagge, *The Political Thought of the King's Mirror* (Odense: Odense University Press, 1987); and Erik Gunnes, "Rex iustus et iniustus," in *Kulturhistoriskt Lexikon för Nordisk Medeltid* (Malmö: Allhems förlag, 1974), 14: 154–56.

26. This epithet occurs at Harald Fairhair's Saga 30, near the story's conclusion. It also appears in Fagrskinna 74; Hauksbók 270; Sturlubók 309; Orkneyinga Saga 4; Greater Saga of Olaf Tryggvason 179 (Flateyjarbók 1.221); and the poem of Turf-Einar contemporary to these events (i.e., ca. 890), which is quoted in Fagrskinna 74; Orkneyinga Saga 8; Harald Fairhair's Saga 31; and Greater Saga of Olaf Tryggvason 183 (Flateyjarbók 1.223–24).

27. Turf-Einar, *Lausavísa* 1, quoted, inter alia, at Fagrskinna 74; and Harald Fairhair's Saga 31:

Sékat ek Hrólfs ór hendi	*en í kveld, meðan knýjum,*
né Hrollaugi fljúga	*of kerstraumi, rómu,*
dǫf á dolga mengi,	*þegjandi sitr þetta*
dugir oss fǫður hefna;	*þorir jarl á Mœri.*

Cf. Orkneyinga Saga 8; Harald Fairhair's Saga 31; and Greater Saga of Olaf Tryggvason 183 (Flateyjarbók 1.223). On the earl's poems, see Klaus von See, "Der Skalde Torf-Einar," *Beiträge zur Geschichte der deutschen Sprache und Literatur* 82 (1960): 31–43.

28. Orkneyinga Saga 4: "In one battle Ívar fell, the son of Earl Rögnvald. And when King Harald sailed from the west, he gave Shetland and the Orkneys to Earl Rögnvald in compensation-for-a-son." *Ok i einni orrostu fell Ívarr, son Rǫgnvaldz jarls. En er Haraldr konungr sigldi vestan, þá gaf hann Rǫgnvaldi jarli i sonarbœtr Hjaltland ok Orkneyjar.* Cf. Harald Fairhair's Saga 22; Greater Saga of Olaf Tryggvason 179 (Flateyjarbók 1.221).

29. Orkneyinga Saga 5: "[Hallað's] noble office became tiresome to him. He gave up his earldom and assumed the status of a *hǫldr* [i.e., the second of four social strata recognized in medieval Norway, that of nonnobles who possess allodial land], and he went back to Norway."

His conduct seemed most disgraceful" (*leiddisk honum tignin. Hann veltisk ór jarldóminum ok tók hǫldzrétt, ok fór aptr til Noregs; ok þótti hans ferð hin hæðiligsta*). Cf. Hauksbók 270; Sturlubók 309; Harald Fairhair's Saga 27; and Greater Saga of Olaf Tryggvason 180 (Flateyjarbók 1.222).

30. The story of Hrólf's banishment and later exploits is told at Harald Fairhair's Saga 24; St. Olaf's Saga 28 (Flateyjarbók 2.30); and elsewhere. Norwegian sources play up his foreign exploits, on the basis of which they advance halfhearted claims for Norwegian rights over Normandy and England. They are silent, however, regarding Hrólf's outlawry and his difficulties with King Harald. Thus, Fagrskinna 74; and Historia Norwegiæ 6. Orkneyinga Saga 4; Landnámabók (Hauksbók 270; Sturlubók 309); and Greater Saga of Olaf Tryggvason 179 (Flateyjarbók 1.221) follow much the same pattern. This character is often referred to as Gǫngu-Hrólfr, and in Latin and French sources, he bears the name Rollo. See further Gwyn Jones, *A History of the Vikings*, 2d ed. (Oxford: Oxford University Press, 1984), 229–32.

31. Orkneyinga Saga 6: *Jarl segir: "eigi mun þér jarldóms auðit, ok liggja fylgjur þinar til Íslandz; þar muntu auka ætt þína ok mun gǫfug verða í því landi."* Cf. Greater Saga of Olaf Tryggvason, chap. 181 (Flateyjarbók 1.222). The variant of this story found in Landnámabók (Hauksbók 270; Sturlubók 309) has Rögnvald describe why it is that Hrollaug will not become an earl, a piece of information rooted in views of Icelandic national character: "You don't have a warlike temperament" (*hefir þu ecki styrialldar skaplyndi*). Cf. *þáttr þiðranda ok þorhallz* 1 (Flateyjarbók 1.418).

32. Hauksbók 270; Sturlubók 309. The "Tale of Thidrandi and Thorhall" (*þáttr þiðranda ok þorhallz* 1 [Flateyjarbók 1.418]), another late text, also makes note of Hrollaug's good relations with Harald: "It came about as the Earl said, and Hrollaug traveled to Iceland. He was a great chief and he had a good friendship with King Harald, but he never traveled back to Norway." *þat kom fram sem jall sagde at Hrollaugr for til Islandz. hann uar hofdinge mikill ok hellt vel vingan vid Haralld konung en for alldri sidan til Noregs.*

33. Íslendingabók 2.1–4.

34. Harald Fairhair's Saga 27: *þá svaraði Einarr: "ek hefi lítinn metnað af þér, á ek við lítla ást at skiljask. Mun ek fara vestr til Eyja, ef þú vill fá mér styrk nǫkkurn. Mun ek því heita þér, er þér mun allmikill fagnaðr á vera, at ek mun eigi aptr koma til Nóregs." Rǫgnvaldr segir, at þat líkaði honum vel, at hann kvæmi eigi aptr—"þvíat mér er lítil ván, at frændum þínum sé sœmð at þér, þvíat móðurætt þín ǫll er þrælborin."* Cf. Orkneyinga Saga 6; Hauksbók 270; Sturlubók 309; and Greater Saga of Olaf Tryggvason 181 (Flateyjarbók 1.222–23).

35. This gesture, through which the victor debases his victim, is described as follows: "Einar had an eagle carved on his back with the sword and cut all the ribs from the spine and drew the lungs out from there and he gave him to Óðinn for his victory." *lét Einarr reista ǫrn á baki honum með sverði ok skera rifin ǫll frá hrygginum ok draga þar út lungun ok gaf hann Óðni til sigrs sér.* Orkneyinga Saga 8; cf. Harald Fairhair's Saga 31; and Olafs Saga Tryggvasonar 183 (Flateyjarbók 1.223). See further Roberta Frank, "Viking Atrocity and Scaldic Verse: The Rite of the Blood-Eagle," *English Historical Review* 99 (1984): 332–43.

36. Orkneyinga Saga 8. Cf. Harald Fairhair's Saga 31–32; Greater Saga of Olaf Tryggvason 183 (Flateyjarbók 1.223–24); and St. Olaf's Saga 96. Einar's poem is also cited in Fagrskinna 74.

37. Harald Fairhair's Saga 32: *festi þá jarl alt í konungs dóm; Haraldr konungr dœmði á hendr Einari jarli ok ǫllum Orkneyingum at gjalda lx. marka gullz; bóndum þótti gjald ofmikit; þá bauð jarl þeim, at hann myndi einn saman gjalda ok skyldi hann eignask þá óðul ǫll í eyjunum; þessu játuðu þeir mest fyrir þá sǫk, at inir snauðu áttu litlar jarðir, en inir auðgu hugðusk mundu leysa sin óðul, þegar er þeir vildu; leysti jarl alt gjaldit við konung; fór konungr þá austr eptir um haustit.*

Var þat lengi síðan í Orkneyjum, at jarlar áttu óðul ǫll . . . Cf. Orkneyinga Saga 8 and Greater Saga of Olaf Tryggvason 183 (Flateyjarbók 1.224).

38. St. Olaf's Saga 96: *Haraldr konungr lét Orkneyinga sverja sér ǫll óðul sín. Eptir þat sættusk þeir konungr ok jarl, ok gerðisk jarl hans maðr ok tók lǫnd í lén af konungi ok skyldi enga gjalda skatta af, þvíat þar var herskátt mjǫk. Jarl galt konungi lx. marka gullz.*

39. Historia Norwegiæ 6: *Interim socii ejus in Orchadibus suum regnum firmiter stabilierunt, revera enim usque hodie illorum posteritatis dominio subjacent,* **excepto quod jure tributario** *regibus Norwegiæ deserviunt* (emphasis added).

40. Only two traces of Hrollaug remain in the entire Heimskringla, both of them where its use of sources forced retention of a character well known to the audience, but inconvenient to the text's purposes. These are Hrollaug's appearance in the list of Rögnvald's sons (Harald Fairhair's Saga 24) and in Turf-Einar's poem (ibid., 31). In the first instance, Heimskringla follows Orkneyinga Saga 4; in the second, Orkneyinga Saga 8 and Fagrskinna 74.

41. Harald Fairhair's Saga 10.

42. The title *Jarla sǫgur* appears in St. Olaf's Saga 103; Fagrskinna 40; Flateyjarbók 2.347 and 3.270. Orkneyinga Saga, which has become its commonly accepted name, is not attested prior to the seventeenth century.

43. Orkneyinga Saga 1–3, which resembles *Hversu Noregr Bygðiz* (Flateyjarbók 1.21–24) in many of its details. It is also extremely close to "The Founding of Norway" (*Fundinn Noregr* = Flateyjarbók 1.219–21), which, interestingly enough, given its title, culminates in Rögnvald's genealogy, rather than Harald's. Regarding Heimskringla's knowledge of these materials, see Margaret Clunies Ross, "Snorri Sturluson's Use of the Norse Origin-Legend of the Sons of Fornjótr in His Edda," *Arkiv för Norsk Filologi* 98 (1983): 47–66; and on the significance of this alternate tradition, Preben Meulengracht Sørensen, "The Sea, The Flame, and the Wind: The Legendary Ancestors of the Earls of Orkney," in *At fortælle Historien/Telling History: Studier i den gamle nordiske litteratur/Studies in Norse Literature,* ed. Preben Meulengracht Sørensen (Trieste: Edizioni Parnaso, 2001), 221–30.

44. For the various etymological suggestions that have been advanced, see de Vries, *Altnordisches etymologisches Wörterbuch,* 138–39.

45. Orkneyinga Saga 1–2. Cf. "The Founding of Norway" (*Fundinn Noregr* = Flateyjarbók 1.219–20); and *Hversu Noregr Bygdiz* (Flateyjarbók 1.21–24).

46. Orkneyinga Saga 2: "From there, Nórr turned back north to this realm, which he had subjugated. He called it Nor-way. He ruled this realm while he lived and his sons after him, and they divided the land among themselves." *þadan sneri Nórr aptr norðr til ríkis þess, er hann hafði undir sik lagt; þat kallaði hann Nórveg. Réð hann því ríki meðan hann lifði, en synir hans eptir hann, ok skiptu þeir landi með sér.* The Latinized form *Northwagia* shows that the name of the country was derived from *Norð-vegr* ("Northway"), not *Nórs-vegr* ("Nor's way"). The hero of this story thus appears to be a back-formation based on a folk etymology.

47. Orkneyinga Saga 3: *þeir váru sækonungar ok ofstopamenn miklir. þeir gengu mjǫk á ríki sona Nórs, ok áttu þeir orrostur margar ok sigruðusk ýmsir.*

48. Ibid.: "Górr's son Heiti was the father of Sveið the Sea-King, the father of Hálfdan the Old, the father of Ívar, earl of the Upplanders, the father of Eystein Glumra, the father of Earl Rögnvald the Powerful and Wise-in-Counsel." *Heiti, sonr Górs, var faðir Sveiða sækonungs, fǫður Hálfdanar ins gamla, fǫður Ívars Upplendingajarls, fǫður Eysteins glumru, fǫður Rǫgnvalds jarls ins ríka ok ins ráðsvinna.* Cf. "The Founding of Norway" 3 (Flateyjarbók 1.221).

Chapter Four

1. Along these lines, see Beryl Smalley, *Historians in the Middle Ages* (London: Thames and Hudson, 1974); Neil Wright, *History and Literature in Late Antiquity and the Early Medieval West: Studies in Intertextuality* (Aldershot: Variorum, 1995); Gabrielle Spiegel, *The Past as Text: The Theory and Practice of Medieval Historiography* (Baltimore: Johns Hopkins University Press, 1997); Diana Whaley, "A Useful Past: Historical Writing in Medieval Iceland," in *Old Icelandic Literature*, ed. Margaret Clunies Ross (Cambridge: Cambridge University Press, 2000), 161–202; and Deborah Mauskopf Deliyannis, ed., *Historiography in the Middle Ages* (Leiden: E. J. Brill, 2003).

2. On the sources used by Heimskringla and the way these were processed, see Tatiana N. Jackson, "On Snorri Sturluson's Creative Activity: The Problem of Writer Intrusion into the Narrative," *Arkiv för Nordisk Filologi* 99 (1984): 107–25; Whaley, *Heimskringla: An Introduction*; Oskar Bandle, "Tradition und Fiktion in der Heimskringla," in *Snorri Sturluson: Kolloquium anläßlich der 750. Wiederkehr seines Todestages*, ed. Alois Wolf (Tübingen: Gunter Narr Verlag, 1993), 27–47; Alois Wolf, "Snorris Wege in die Vergangenheit und die Besonderheiten altisländischer Mündlichkeit und Schriftlichkeit," in Wolf, ed., *Snorri Sturluson*, 267–93; and Kolbrún Haraldsdóttir, "Der Historiker Snorri: Autor oder Kompilator?," in *Snorri Sturluson: Beiträge zu Werk und Rezeption*, ed. Hans Fix (Berlin: Walter de Gruyter, 1998), 97–108. The groundbreaking work of Gustav Storm, *Snorre Sturlassons Historieskrivning: En kritisk Undersögelse* (Copenhagen: B. Lunos bogtrykkeri, 1873), is still worth consulting.

3. This model of Snorri's authorial activity has been most fully explored by Lars Lönnroth, "Tesen om de två kulturerna: Kritiska studier i den isländska sagaskrivningens sociala forutsättningar," *Scripta Islandica* 15 (1964): 83–97. An English summary of his position is available in Lars Lönnroth, *European Sources of Icelandic Saga-Writing: An Essay Based on Previous Studies* (Stockholm: Akademisk Avhandling, 1965), 14. See also Haraldsdóttir, "Der Historiker Snorri: Autor oder Kompilator?"; and, more broadly, A. J. Minnis, *Medieval Theories of Authorship* (Aldershot: Wildwood House, 1988).

4. Most recently Boulhosa, *Icelanders and the Kings of Norway*, has reconsidered the relations of Iceland and Norway that culminated in Icelandic submission in 1262, arguing that these relations were closer, more complex, and more subject to ongoing negotiation than has usually been recognized.

5. Foreign authors acknowledged Icelanders' preeminent historical knowledge in the prologues to their own texts, most notably Saxo Grammaticus in Denmark and Theodricus Monachus in Norway.

6. Thus, one of the earliest Kings' Sagas is Sverris Saga, written in the 1180s for Sverrir Sigurðarson (r. 1177–1202). According to its prologue, it "was first written by Abbot Karl Jonsson, over whom sat King Sverrir himself and advised him what he should write." *er fyrst ritaði Karl ábóti Jónsson, en yfir sat sjálfr Sverrir konungr ok réð fyrir hvat rita skyldi.*

7. Regarding Icelanders' production of texts for local consumption, but also for export to Norway, see Stefan Karlsson, "Islandsk bogeksport til Norge i middelalderen," *Maal og minne*, 1979, 1–17.

8. For a summary of the arguments in favor of Snorri's authorship, see Whaley, *Heimskringla: An Introduction*, 13–17; for a critical view, Boulhosa, *Icelanders and the Kings of Norway*, 6–21. Others who have voiced doubts in recent years include Jon Gunnar Jørgensen, "Snorre

Sturlesons fortale paa sin chronicke: Om kildene til opplysningen om *Heimskringlas* forfatter," *Gripla* 9 (1995): 45–62; Louis-Jensen, "Heimskringla: Et værk af Snorri Sturluson?"; and Alan J. Berger, "Heimskringla and the Compilations," *Arkiv för Nordisk Filologi* 114 (1999): 5–15. Implicitly or explicitly, critics are working within postmodern paradigms shifting attention away from authors to texts, audiences, and contexts. In doing so, they are always provocative and refreshing, but the specific arguments they advance are not always terribly convincing or well founded, as, for instance, Berger's suggestion that Snorri may be the author of Fagrskinna, and not Heimskringla.

9. The standard biography in English remains Marlene Ciklamini, *Snorri Sturluson* (Boston: Twayne, 1978), but our understanding of Snorri's work, life, and political and literary activity has been dramatically deepened by Kevin Wanner, *Snorrri Sturluson and the Edda: The Conversion of Cultural Capital in Medieval Scandinavia* (Toronto: University of Toronto Press, 2008). See also Sigurður Nordal, *Snorri Sturluson* (Reykjavík: n.p., 1920); and Finnur Jónsson, "Snorri Sturluson i Norge," *Historisk Tidsskrift* 5 (1924): 116–22. Virtually all our information about Snorri's life comes from Íslendinga Saga.

10. Íslendinga Saga 34:

> With these cases, Snorri made his reputation with most people here in this land. He became a good skald and was skilled at all to which he turned his hand. He always had the best advice on all that one should do. He composed a poem for Hákon Galin, and the earl sent gifts in return: a sword, shield, and coat of mail. . . . The earl wrote to Snorri that he should go abroad, and he let it be known that great honors would be prepared for him. That appealed much to Snorri, but the earl died just then and therefore he put off his voyage for some years. Still, he had decided to make his journey as soon as the time was right.

> *Ok í þessum málum gekk virðing hans við mest hér á landi. Hann gerðist skáld gott ok var hagr á allt þat, er hann tók hǫndum til, ok hafði inar beztu forsagnir á ǫllu því, er gera skyldi. Hann orti kvæði um Hákon Galinn, ok sendi jarlinn gjafir út á mót, sverð ok skjǫld ok brynju. . . . Jarlinn ritaði til Snorra, at hann skyldi fara útan, ok lézt til hans gera mundu miklar sæmðir. Ok mjǫk var þat í skapi Snorra. En jarlinn andaðist í þann tíma, ok brá þat útanferð hans um nǫkkurra vetra sakir. En þó hafði hann ráðit fǫr sína, þegar tími væri til.*

11. Íslendinga Saga 35:

> But when Sæmund, his father, learned that, he was extremely angry and he pursued legal action, charging that Pál had died by the doings of the Bergen men. He gathered a large troop around him and went abroad to Eyr and brought these charges against the Bergen men. And there was no alternative but that the Norwegians had to pay him as much gold as he wanted to demand of them. There were many who had a part in pacifying Sæmund, and his brother Orm, the biggest of all. He behaved best of all the men from Oddi. But it availed nothing. Sæmund seized three hundred hundreds from the merchants there.

> *En er þetta spurði Sæmundr, faðir hans, varð hann reiðr mjǫk ok tók svá upp, at Páll hefði látizt af vǫldum Bjǫrgynjarmanna. Hann safnaði at sér liði miklu ok fór út á Eyrar ok bar þessar sakir á Bjǫrgynjarmenn. Ok var þar engi kostr annarr en Austmenn skyldi festa honum gjǫld svá mikil sem hann vildi á þá leggja. Áttu þar margir hlut at at svefja*

Sæmund—ok Ormr, bróðir hans, mestan. Ok honum fór bezt af ǫllum Oddaverjum. En ekki stoðaði. Tók Sæmundr þar upp þrjú hundruð hundraða fyrir kaupmǫnnum.

12. Ibid.

13. Ibid.: "That summer, when Orm was killed, Snorri Sturluson decided to voyage abroad. . . . Snorri didn't know about Orm's murder until he came to Norway." *Sumar þat, er Ormr var veginn, réðst Snorri Sturluson til útanferðar. . . . Snorri frétti eigi víg Orms, fyrr en hann kom í Norég.* The Saga of Hákon Hákonarson 56 confirms the fact of Snorri's voyage to the Norwegian court but provides no details.

14. Ibid.: *þá er Snorri kom til Nóregs, váru hǫfðingjar orðnir Hákon konungr ok Skúli jarl. Tók jarl forkunnar vel við Snorra, ok fór hann til jarls. En þeir menn, er útan fóru með Snorra, réðust til suðrferðar, Ingimundr Jónsson ok Árni, sonr Brands Gunnhvatssonar. Snorri var um vetrinn með jarli. En um sumarit eftir fór hann austr á Gautland á fund Áskels lǫgmanns ok frú Kristínar, er átt hafði áðr Hákon Galinn. Snorri hafði ort um hana kvæði þat, er Andvaka heitir, fyrir Hákon jarl at bæn hans. Ok tók hon sæmiliga við Snorra ok veitti honum margar gjafir sæmiligar. Hon gaf honum merki þat, er átt hafði Eiríkr Sviakonungr Knútsson. þat hafði hann, þá er hann felldi Sǫrkvi konung á Gestilsreini. Snorri fór um haustit aftr til Skúla jarls ok var þar annan vetr í allgóðu yfirlæti.*

15. Íslendinga Saga 38: "Snorri Sturluson was with [Earl] Skúli for two years, as was written before. King Hákon and Skúli made him their page." *Snorri Sturluson var tvá vetr með Skúla, sem fyrr var ritat. Gerðu þeir Hákon konungr ok Skúli hann skutilsvein sinn.*

16. Íslendinga Saga 38.

But in the spring, Snorri decided to go to Iceland. Still, the Norwegians were very un-friendly to the Icelanders, most of all the men of Oddi, due to the plundering that had taken place at Eyr. Therefore, it came about that they decided they would raid Iceland in the summer. There were ships and men who would go, following their decision. But most of the wisest men were very uneager for that voyage and said many things against it.

En um várit ætlaði Snorri til Íslands. En þó váru Nóregsmenn miklir óvinir Íslendinga ok mestir Oddaverja—af ránum þeim, er urðu á Eyrum. Kom því svá, at ráðit var, at herja skyldi til Íslands um sumarit. Váru til ráðin skip ok menn, hverir fara skyldi. En til þeirar ferðar váru flestir inir vitrari menn mjǫk ófúsir ok tǫlðu margar latar á.

17. Íslendinga Saga 38: *Snorri latti mjǫk ferðarinnar ok kallaði þat ráð at gera sér at vinum ina beztu menn á Íslandi ok kallaðist skjótt mega svá koma sínum orðum, at mǫnnum myndi sýnast at snúast til hlýðni við Nóregshǫfðingja. Hann sagði ok svá, at þá váru aðrir eigi meiri menn á Íslandi en bræðr hans, er Sæmund leið, en kallaði þá mundu mjǫk eftir sínum orðum víkja, þá er hann kæmi til. En við slíkar fortǫlur slævaðist heldr skap jarlsins, ok lagði hann þat ráð til, at Íslendingar skyldi biðja Hákon konung, at hann bæði fyrir þeim, at eigi yrði herferðin. Konungrinn var þá ungr, en Dagfinnr lǫgmaðr, er þá var ráðgjafi hans, var inn mesti vinr Íslendinga. Ok var þat af gert, at konungr réð, at eigi varð herfǫrin.*

18. Further possibilities exist that are even more destabilizing. Since all our knowledge of this episode probably derives from Snorri himself, one must wonder to what extent the narra-tive follows events, and to what extent it reshapes—or even invents—them for one strategic purpose or another.

19. Íslendinga Saga 38: *En þeir Hákon konungr ok Skúli jarl gerðu Snorra lendan mann sinn,*

var þat mest ráð þeira jarls ok Snorra. En Snorri skyldi leita við Íslendinga, at þeir snerist til hlýðni við Nóregs hǫfðingja. Snorri skyldi senda útan Jón, son sinn, ok skyldi hann vera í gíslingu með jarli, at þat endist, sem mælt var.

20. Ibid.:

Snorri was very late to sail and had a difficult passage. He lost his mast off the eastern fjörðs and landed at Vestmannaeyjar. The earl had given him the ship in which he traveled and fifteen impressive gifts. . . . When Snorri came to Vestmannaeyjar, his arrival was soon reported inland, and he was received with all honors. The men of the south quarter were very angry with him at that time, most of all the affinal relatives of Orm Jónsson. It seemed to them as if he might be aligned with the Norwegians to stand in opposition, so that they might take no legal action for Orm's slaying. Most upset about this was Björn Thorvaldsson [Orm's son-in-law], who then dwelt at Breiðabólstað and seemed likely to become a chieftain.

Snorri varð heldr síðbúinn ok fekk harða útivist, lét tré sitt fyrir Austfjǫrðum ok tók Vestmannaeyjar. Jarlinn hafði gefit honum skipit, þat er hann fór á, ok fimmtán stórgjafir. . . . En er Snorri kom í Vestmannaeyjar, þá spurðist brátt inn á land útkváma hans ok svá með hverjum sæmðum hann var út kominn. Ýfðust Sunnlendingar þá mjǫk við honum ok mest tengðamenn Orms Jónssonar. þótti þeim sem hann myndi vera settr til af Nóregsmǫnnum at standa á móti, svá at þeir mætti engu eftirmáli fram koma um víg Orms. Var mest fyrir því Bjǫrn þorvaldsson, er þá bjó á Breiðabólstað ok þótti vænn til hǫfðingja.

Note that Björn and the southerners make no mention of the invasion threat, and seemingly have no knowledge of it. Their sole concern is legal action against Orm's killers, and they fear Snorri's dealings with the Norwegians may have compromised their ability to pursue this case. Conceivably, Íslendinga Saga is contrasting their limited perspective with Snorri's fuller understanding of international politics and events. Alternatively, the invasion story may have been part of propaganda through which Snorri obscured his more petty and sordid dealings, which Björn and the others understood accurately.

21. Note, however, that under Icelandic law, slander against any of the Scandinavian monarchs was punishable by full outlawry, a situation that encouraged development of subtlety in the production and reception of antiroyal critique. The statute in question (Grágás II §238) is discussed by Boulhosa, *Icelanders and the Kings of Norway*, 67–68.

If a man inflicts shame on the Danish, Swedish, or Norwegian king, he is punished by outlawry, and the king's housecarls own the lawsuits. If they will not have them, then the suit falls to whoever wants it.

Ef maðr yrkir haðung um konung dana eða suia eða norð manna oc varðar scog gang oc eigo hus carlar þeirra sacarnar. Ef þeir vilia eigi. oc a sa söc er vill.

Chapter Five

1. This characterization of Guthorm recurs at Harald Fairhair's Saga 2; Egil's Saga 26; Fagrskinna Appendix 3 (from the A-Text); and the "Tale of Harald Fairhair" 1 and 2 (Flateyjarbók 1.567 and 1.569).

2. The classic discussion of relations between mother's brother and sister's son remains

A. R. Radcliffe-Brown, "The Mother's Brother in South Africa," in *Structure and Function in Primitive Society* (Glencoe, IL: Free Press, 1952), 15–31. The special importance of the mother's brother–sister's son relation among the Germanic peoples was noted already by Tacitus (*Germania* 20: *sororum filiis idem apud avunculum qui apud patrem honor*). Regarding its role in medieval Scandinavia, see Guðrún Nordal, *Ethics and Action in Thirteenth-Century Iceland* (Odense: Odense University Press, 1998), 86–89.

3. "Tale of Harald Fairhair" 1 (Flateyjarbók 1.567): "When he was ten years old, Harald Hálfdan's son, who was called Dofri's foster son, took the kingship over Hringariki, Vestfold, Vingulmark, and Raumarike. At that time Guthorm, his mother's brother, was sixteen years old." *At lidnum tiu uetrum alldrs Haralldz Halfdanarsonar er kalladr uar Dofrafostri tok hann konungdom yfir Hringariki Uestfolld Uingulmork ok Raumarike. þa uar Guthormr modurbrodir hans .xvj. uetra gamall.* Hálfdan the Black's Saga 5 is less specific but states that when Guthorm's sister was twenty years old, her brother was just a youth (*hon var þá á tvítøgsaldri, en Guthormr bróðir hennar á ungmennisaldri*). This was just before she married Hálfdan and gave birth to Harald, which would establish that uncle and nephew were relatively close in age. We will discuss the tradition that treats Harald as "Dofri's foster son" (*Dofrafostri*) in chap. 10.

4. Fagrskinna Appendix 1 (from the A-Text):

There was a man called Dag who dwelt at the farm in Haðaland that is called Thengilsstaðir and he was called Dag the Wise and was a powerful chief. Dag the Wise had two children, a son and a daughter. His son was called Guthorm the Wise in Council.

Dagr hét maðr, er bjó á bœ þeim á Haðalandi, er þengilsstaðir heita. En hann var kallaðr Dagr enn fróði ok var ríkr hersir. Dagr enn fróði átti tvau bǫrn, son ok dóttur. Sonr hans hét Guðþormr enn ráðspaki.

With regard to the status of *hersir*, Cleasby and Vigfusson, *Icelandic-English Dictionary*, 259, says this: "*A chief, lord*, the political name of the Norse chiefs of the earliest age, esp. before the time of Harald Fairhair and the settlement of Iceland; respecting the office and authority of the old *hersar* the records are scanty, as they chiefly belonged to the prehistorical time; they were probably not liegemen, but resembled the *goðar* of the Icelandic commonwealth, being a kind of patriarchal and hereditary chiefs.

5. Fagrskinna Appendix 1 (from the A-Text):

His daughter was called Helga the Well-Mannered and some called her Helga of the Magnificent Hair. It was also said of Helga that men knew no other woman who was better than Helga in her nobility and her appearance and all her conduct.

Helga hét dóttir hans en siðláta; sumir kǫlluðu Helgu ena hárprúðu. þat var ok mælt um Helgu, at enga vissu menn þá aðra konu, er betr væri um skǫruleik sinn ok um ásjá ok um alla meðferð en Helga.

6. Ibid.:

King Hálfdan fell in love with Helga and courted her and took her as wife and had a son by her. Many men have heard of that son, and he is called Harald Hairfair.

Hálfdani konungi fell hugr til Helgu ok bað hennar, ok svá fekk hann hennar ok gat með henni son þann, sem margir menn hafa heyrt getit, er Haraldr hét enn hárfagri.

7. Hálfdan the Black's Saga 5:

Sigurð Hart was the name of the king in Hringariki. He was bigger and stronger than any other man. He was also the most handsome of all men. His father was Helgi the Keen and his mother was Aslaug, the daughter of Sigurð Snake-in-the-Eye, who was the son of Ragnar Shaggy-Breeches. It is said of him that when he was twelve years old, he killed Hildibrand the berserk in single combat and the twelve men who were with him. He performed many heroic deeds, and there is a long saga about him. He had two children. His daughter was called Ragnhild. She was the most outstanding of all women. She was then twenty years old, and Guthorm her brother was a youth.

Sigurðr hjǫrtr er nefndr konungr á Hringaríki, meiri ok sterkari, en hverr maðr annarra; allra manna var hann ok fríðastr sýnum; faðir hans var Helgi inn hvassi, en móðir hans Áslaug, dóttir Sigurðar orms-í-auga Ragnars sonar loðbrókar. Svá er sagt, at þá var hann xii. vetra, er hann drap Hildibrand berserk í einvígi ok þá xii. saman; mǫrg vann hann þrekvirki, ok er lǫng saga frá honum. Hann átti ii. bǫrn: Ragnhildr hét dóttir hans; hon var allra kvenna skǫruligust; hon var þá á tvítǫgsaldri, en Guthormr bróðir hennar á ungmennisaldri.

Two other texts follow Heimskringla in naming Sigurð Hart as Guthorm's father: Egil's Saga 26 and the Greater Saga of Olaf Tryggvason 2 (Flateyjarbók 1.39).

8. Hálfdan the Black's Saga 5.

9. Harald Fairhair's Saga 1: *Haraldr tók konungdóm eptir fǫður sinn; þá var hann x. vetra gamall; hann var allra manna mestr ok sterkastr ok fríðastr sýnum, vitr maðr ok skǫrungr mikill. Guthormr, móðurbróðir hans, gerðisk forstjóri fyrir hirðinni ok fyrir ǫllum landráðum; hann var hertogi fyrir liðinu.* As shown in synoptic table 5.1, the "Tale of Harald Fairhair" 1 (Flateyjarbók 1.567) follows this passage closely but rearranges the order of its sentences so that the praise of Harald as greatest, strongest, etc., is there applied to Guthorm.

10. Cleasby and Vigfusson, *Icelandic-English Dictionary*, 225, define the reflexive forms of *gøra* as meaning "to become, grow, arise, and the like," but most of the examples cited are instances where the subject of the verb has succeeded in elevating himself to high status, e.g., "King Sigurð became/made himself an overbearing man . . . he became/made himself a great man and a strong one" (*Sigurðr konungr gerðisk ofstopa-maðr . . . görðisk mikill maðr ok sterkr*, Fornmanna Saga vii.238) or "He soon became/made himself a powerful man and fit to rule" (*hann görðisk brátt ríkr maðr ok stjórnsamr*; idem, xi 233).

11. "Tale of Harald Fairhair" 1 (Flateyjarbók 1.567): *Haralldr konungr setti Guthorm frænda sinn hertoga yfir ollu lide sinu.*

12. Thus, Harald Fairhair's Saga 2, 4, 17, 21, 28, and 29; Greater Saga of Olaf Tryggvason 2 (Flateyjarbók 1.40); Fagrskinna Appendix 3 (from the A-Text); "Tale of Harald Fairhair" 1 and 2 (Flateyjarbók 1.567 and 568–69).

13. Old Norse *hertogi* occurs first as a descriptive term, being derived from the masculine substantive *herr* ("host, crowd, army, troops") and the verb *teyja* ("to draw up"). Only in the thirteenth century, probably under the influence of Middle Low German *hertoge, hertoch* (German *Herzog*) does it become a ducal title, first bestowed on Earl Skúli in 1237. See further the discussion in Cleasby and Vigfusson, *Icelandic-English Dictionary*, 259; and de Vries, *Altnordische etymologisches Wörterbuch*, 225. Tacitus, *Germania* 7, makes a clear distinction between the roles of king (*rex*) and war leader (*dux*) among the Germanic peoples, but these seem to operate independent of each other, rather than forming a system in which the latter is clearly subordinated to the former.

14. Harald Fairhair's Saga 1:

After the death of Hálfdan the Black, many chiefs encroached on the realm that he had left. The first were King Gandalf, the brothers Högni and Fróði, sons of King Eystein of Heiðmark, and Högni Karuson, who ranged widely beyond Hringariki. Then Haki Gandalfsson ventured out of Vestfold with 300 men, traversed the high ground over a certain valley and meant to take King Harald by surprise. King Gandalf stayed in Londir with his army and thought he would cross over the fjörð at Vestfold.

Eptir líflát Hálfdanar svarta gengu margir hǫfðingjar á ríkit, þat er hann hafði leift; var inn fyrsti maðr Gandálfr konungr ok þeir brœðr, Hǫgni ok Fróði, synir Eysteins konungs af Heiðmǫrk, ok Hǫgni Káruson gekk viða yfir Hringaríki. þá byrjar ferð sína Haki Gandálfsson út á Vestfold með ccc. manna, ok fór it øfra um dali nǫkkura ok ætlaði at koma á óvart Haraldi konungi, en Gandálfr konungr sat i Lóndum með her sinn, ok þat ætlaði hann at flytjask yfir fjǫrðinn á Vestfold.

15. Harald Fairhair's Saga 1: *En er þat spyrr Guthormr hertogi, samnat hann her ok ferr með Haraldi konungi, ok vendir fyrst móti Haka uppa á land ok finnask þeir í dal nǫkkurum.*

16. Ibid.: *varð þar orrosta ok fekk Haraldr konungr sigr.*

17. Thus, in Harald Hairfair's Saga 2: "they advanced" (*fara*), "they turned" (*venda*), "they learned" (*þeir spyrja*), "they arrived" (*koma*), "they set fire" (*lǫgðu eld*). Twice, the men are named together, and Harald is given precedence on both occasions (*Haraldr konungr ok Guthormr hertogi*).

18. Harald Fairhair's Saga 2: *Eptir fall þessa iiii. hǫfðingja eignaðisk Haraldr konungr **með krapt ok framkvæmð Guthorms, frænda síns,** Hringaríki ok Heiðmǫrk, Guðbrandzdali ok Haðaland, þótn ok Raumaríki, Vingulmǫrk, allan inn nørðra* (emphasis added). Cf. "Tale of Harald Fairhair" 2 (Flateyjarbók 1.568–69).

19. See John Hines, "Kingship in Egil's Saga," in *Introductory Essays on Egil's Saga and Njals Saga*, ed. John Hines and Desmond Slay (London: Viking Society, 1992), 15–32. I have also discussed this aspect of Egil's Saga in *Authority: Construction and Corrosion* (Chicago: University of Chicago Press, 1994), 55–73.

20. Egil's Saga 26: *Guttormr hét maðr, sonr Sigurðar hjartar; hann var móðurbródir Haralds konungs; hann var fóstrfaðir konungs ok ráðamaðr fyrir landi hans, því at konungr var þá á barns aldri, fyrst er hann kom til ríkis. Guttormr var hertogi fyrir liði Haralds konungs, þá er hann vann land undir sik, ok var hann i ǫllum orrostum, þeim er konungr átti, þá er hann gekk til lands í Nóregi.*

21. Old Norse *barn*, from the verb *bera*, "to bear, give birth to," can be used to denote a child, an infant, or even a fetus in utero, as in the expression *vera með bjarni*, "to be with child." Had it been the text's intention to mitigate Harald's youth, alternative terminology was available, including *sveinn* ("lad"), *piltr* ("boy"), or *ungr maðr* ("youth").

22. See Hastrup, *Culture and History in Medieval Iceland*, 98–100; or Gurevich, *Historical Anthropology of the Middle Ages*, 187–88, regarding the institution of fosterage.

23. Thus, the early campaigns are recounted in Harald Fairhair's Saga 1–2. He sends his messengers to Gyða in chap. 3.

24. Harald Fairhair's Saga 4: *ok enn mælti hann: "þess strengi ek heit, ok því skýt ek til guðs, þess er mik skóp ok ǫllu ræðr, at aldri skal skera hár mitt né kemba, fyrr en ek hefi eignazk allan Nóreg með skǫttum ok skyldum ok forráði, en deyja at ǫðrum kosti." þessi orð þakkaði honum mjǫk Guthormr hertogi ok lét þat vera konungligt verk at efna orð sín.*

25. Only two other texts make mention of Guthorm's response to the oath. The Greater Saga of Olaf Tryggvason 2 (Flateyjarbók 1.40) follows Heimskringla almost exactly. Fagrskinna Appendix 3 (from the A-Text) offers a strikingly different variant, for all that it stresses Guthorm's loyalty. In contrast to Heimskringla's version, Guthorm speaks at some length, takes note of Harald's youth, recognizes the difficulty of the task he has set for himself, pledges his own absolute devotion to accomplishing that task, and suggests that others will feel similarly obliged. He does not, however, voice confidence in ultimate success. What is more, he goes on to swear an oath of his own that picks up on the religious, rather than the military-political side of what Harald has sworn (synoptic table 5.2).

26. Harald Fairhair's Saga 5: *Eptir þetta samna þeir frændr liði miklu ok búa ferð sina á Uplǫnd ok svá norðr um Dali ok þaðan norðr um Dofrafjall, ok þá er hann kom ofan í byggðina, þá lét hann drepa menn alla ok brenna byggðina; en er fólkit varð þessa vist, þá flýði hverr, er mátti, sumir ofan til Orkadals, sumir til Gaulardals, sumir á markir, sumir leituðu griða, ok þat fengu allir, þeir er á konungs fund kómu, ok gerðusk hans menn.*

27. The Greater Saga of Olaf Tryggvason 2 (Flateyjarbók 1.40) is even more economical in its handling of this transition:

> For this vow, Guthorm, his commander, thanked him and called it royal to fulfill his speech well. Thereafter, King Harald was victorious and laid all Norway under him, as it says in his saga.
>
> *þessa heitstreingin(g) þakkade honum Guthormr hertoge ok kallade þat konungligt at efnna uel ord sin. þadan af vann Haralldr konungr ok lagde undir sig allan Noreg sem segir j sǫgu hans.*

28. There is some confusion about which territories were given to Guthorm, as shown in the table below.

Text	Territories Assigned to Guthorm by King Harald	Guthorm's Responsibilities	Date and Circumstances of the Assignment
Harald Fairhair's Saga 17	North of the Gotha River, west of Lake Vænir, and all Vermaland	Guarding (*gæzla*) the territory	Immediately after Harald's conquest of this area
Harald Fairhair's Saga 21	Vík and Upland	All direction (*stjórn*) of the territories when the king was elsewhere	
Harald Fairhair's Saga 28	Vík	Defense of the land (*landvǫrn*)	
Fagrskinna Appendix 3	"The realm that Skjöld had previously ruled . . . east to Svinasund" (i.e., in Vingulmark)	To be commander (*hertogi*) over it	Immediately after Harald swore his oath and Guthorm swore loyalty to him
Egil's Saga 26	"Vestfold, East Agðir, Hringariki, and all the land that had belonged to Hálfdan the Black"		When Harald had become sole king over Norway

29. Harald Fairhair's Saga 17: "[King Harald] then began to have children. Ása had these sons: Guthorm was the oldest, Hálfdan the Black and Hálfdan the White—they were twins— Sigfröð was the fourth. They were all reared in Trondheim with many honors." *Hann tók þá at eiga bǫrn; þau Ása áttu sonu þessa: Guthormr var ellztr; Hálfdan svarti, Hálfdan hviti—þeir váru tvíburar, Sigfrøðr inn iiii.; þeir váru allir upp fœddir í þrándheimi með miklum sóma.* Other sources differ as regards the status of young Guthorm. Ágrip 2 and Fagrskinna 3 make him the fifth born of Harald's sons and do not specify his mother, while the "Tale of Harald Fairhair" 3 (Flateyjarbók 1.569) makes him the first son born to Harald by Gyða. There is also a contradiction internal to Heimskringla: whereas the passage just cited has Guthorm raised in Trondheim with his siblings, Harald Fairhair's Saga 21 has him fostered in Vík, as we shall see.

30. Harald Fairhair's Saga 21: *Bǫrn Haraldz konungs váru þar hver upp fœdd, sem móðerni áttu. Guthormr hertogi hafði vatni ausit inn ellzta son Haraldz konungs ok gaf nafn sitt; hann knésetti þann svein ok fóstraði ok hafði með sér í Vík austr; fœddisk hann þar upp með Guthormi hertoga. Guthormr hertogi hafði alla stjórn landzins um Vikina ok um Uplǫndin, þá er konungr var eigi nær.*

31. On the imaginary practice of water sprinkling (*ausa vatni*), see Walter Baetke, "Christliches Lehngut in der Sagareligion," in *Kleine Schriften: Geschichte, Recht und Religion in germanischem Schriftum* (Weimar: Hermann Böhlaus Nachfolger, 1973), 330–31.

32. Harald Fairhair's Saga 28:

> Most often, Commander Guthorm stayed in Tunsberg and he had control all around the Vik when the king was not near, and he was responsible for defense of the land. There was much exposure to Viking raids, and there was conflict up in Gautland as long as King Eirik Emundarson lived. He died when King Harald Hairfair had been king in Norway for ten years. [The last sentence refers to King Eirik, not Commander Guthorm, as is made clear in the following chapter.]

> *Guthormr hertogi sat optast í Túnsbergi ok hafði yfirsókn alt um Víkina, þá er konungr var eigi nær, ok hafði þar landvǫrn; var þar mjǫk herskátt af víkingum, en ófriðr var upp á Gautland, meðan Eiríkr konungr lifði Emundarson; hann andaðisk, þá er Haraldr konungr inn hárfagri hafði verit x. vetr konungr í Nóregi.*

33. Harald Fairhair's Saga 29: *Guthormr hertogi varð sóttdauðr í Túnsbergi. þá gaf Haraldr konungr yfirsókn ríkis þess allz Guthormi syni sínum ok setti hann þar hǫfðingja yfir.*

34. Egil's Saga 26: *Guttormr átti sonu tvá ok dœtr tvær; synir hans hétu Sigurðr ok Ragnarr, en dœtr hans Ragnhildr ok Áslaug. Guttormr tók sótt; en er at honum leið, þá sendi hann menn á fund Haralds konungs ok bað hann sjá fyrir bǫrnum sínum ok fyrir ríki sínu; litlu síðar andaðisk hann. En er konungr spurði andlát hans, þá lét hann kalla til sín Hallvarð harðfara ok þá brœðr, sagði, at þeir skyldu fara sendifǫr hans austr í Vík; konungr var þá staddr í þrándheimi. þeir brœðr bjuggusk til ferðar þeirar sem vegligast; vǫldu sér lið ok hǫfðu skip þat, er þeir fengu bezt; þeir hǫfðu þat skip, er átt hafði þórólfr Kveld-Ulfsson ok þeir hǫfðu tekit af þorgísli gjallanda. En er þeir váru búnir ferðar sinnar, þá sagði konungr þeim ørendi, at þeir skyldu fara austr til Túnsbergs; þar var þá kaupstaðr; þar hafði Guttormr haft atsetu. "Skulu þit," sagði konungr, "fœra mér sonu Guttorms, en dœtr hans skulu þar upp fœðask, til þess er ek gipti þær; skal ek fá menn til at varðveita ríkit ok veita meyjunum fóstr." En er þeir brœðr váru búnir, þá fara þeir leið sína ok byrjaði þeim vel; kómu þeir um várit í Vík austr til Túnsbergs ok báru þar fram ørendi sín; taka þeir Hallvarðr við sonum Guttorms ok miklu lausafé. Fara þeir, þá er þeir eru búnir, aptr á leið; byrjaði þeim þá nǫkkurum mun seinna, ok varð ekki til tíðenda í þeira ferð, fyrr en þeir sigla norðr um Sognsæ byr góðan ok bjart veðr ok váru þá allkátir.*

35. The story of Hallvarð and Sigtrygg's conflict with Thorolf Kveld-Ulfsson is recounted in chaps. 17–22 of Egil's Saga. It is ultimately King Harald himself who kills Thorolf, prompting his family to emigrate to Iceland, but the brothers have played important roles in the provocations leading to this finale.

36. The same noun—*aftak*—governs two objects in this sentence, *manna* and *fé*. Most literally, this word denotes an act of taking away, in which case the phrase *aftǫku manna eða fé* might describe the abduction of people and expropriation of their wealth. When applied to people, however, *aftak* usually refers to the act of taking away their life, i.e., their execution or assassination (Cleasby and Vigufsson, *Icelandic-English Dictionary*, 9). The ambiguity is probably intentional and heightens suspense about the fate of Guthorm's sons, the objects of a sinister and not an innocent "taking:" an abduction at the very least, and perhaps an abduction preparatory to a murder.

37. Egil's Saga 18: *Sigtryggr snarfari ok Hallvarðr harðfari hétu brœðr tveir; þeir váru með Haraldi konungi, víkverskir menn; var móðurætt þeira á Vestfold, ok váru þeir í frændsemistǫlu við Harald konung . . . þeir Sigtryggr ok Hallvarðr hǫfðu sendiferðir konungs allar, bæði innan lands ok útan lands, ok hǫfðu margar ferðir þær farit, er háskasamligar váru, bæði til aftǫku manna eða fé upp at taka fyrir þeim mǫnnum, er konungr lætr heimferðir veita. þeir hǫfðu sveit mikla um sík; ekki váru þeir vingaðir alþýpu manns, en konungr mat þá mikils, ok váru þeir allra manna bezt fœrir bæði á fœti ok á skíðum, svá ok í skipfǫrum váru þeir hvatfœrri en aðrir menn; hreystimenn váru þeir ok miklir ok forsjálir um flest.*

38. M. C. van den Toorn, *Zur Verfasserfrage der Egilssaga Skallagrímssonar* (Cologne: Böhlau Verlag, 1959); Peter Hallberg, *Snorri Sturluson och Egils saga Skallagrímssonar: Ett försök till språklig författarbestämning* (Reykjavík: Menningarsjöður, 1962); Vésteinn Ólason, "Er Snorri höfundur Egils sögu?," *Skirnir* 142 (1968): 48–67; Jónas Kristjánsson, "Egilssaga og Konungasögur," in *Sjötíu Ritgerðir: Helgaðar Jakobi Benediktssyni*, ed. Einar Pétursson and Jónas Kristjánsson (Reykjavík: Stofnun Árna magnússonar, 1977), 449–72; Ralph West, "Snorri Sturluson and Egils Saga: Statistics of Style," *Scandinavian Studies* 52 (1980): 163–93; Melissa Berman, "Egilssaga and Heimskringla," *Scandinavian Studies* 54 (1982): 21–50; Kolbrún Haraldsdóttir, "Hvenær var Egils saga rituð?," in *Yfir Íslandsála: Afmælisrit til heiðurs Magnúsi Stefánssyni sextugum*, ed. Gunnar Karlsson and Helgi þorláksson (Reykjavík: Sögufræðslusjóður, 1991), 131–45.

Chapter Six

1. Fagrskinna Appendix 1 (from the A-Text).

There was a man called Dag who dwelt at the farm in Haðaland that is called Thengilsstaðir, and he was called Dag the Wise and was a powerful chief. Dag the Wise had two children, a son and a daughter. . . . His daughter was called Helga the Well-Mannered, and some called her Helga of the Magnificent Hair. It was also said of Helga that men knew no other woman who was better than Helga in her nobility and her appearance and all her conduct. King Hálfdan fell in love with Helga and courted her and took her as wife and had a son by her. Many men have heard of that son, and he is called Harald the Hairfair.

Dagr hét maðr, er bjó á bæ þeim á Haðalandi, er þengilsstaðir heita. En hann var kallaðr Dagr enn fróði ok var ríkr hersir. Dagr enn fróði átti tvau bǫrn, son ok dóttur. . . . Helga hét dóttir hans en siðláta; sumir kǫlluðu Helgu ena hárprúðu. þat var ok mælt um Helgu, at enga vissu menn þá aðra konu, er betr væri um skǫruleik sinn ok um ásjá ok um alla meðferð en Helga. Hálfdani konungi fell hugr til Helgu ok bað hennar, ok svá fekk hann hennar ok gat með henni son þann, sem margir menn hafa heyrt getit, er Haraldr hét enn hárfagri.

2. Fagrskinna 1: *faðir hennar var Sigurðr ormr í auga, sonr Ragnars loðbrókar.*

3. On the complex relation among these sources, see Rory McTurk, *Studies in Ragnars Saga Loðbrókar and Its Major Scandinavian Analogues* (Oxford: Society for the Study of Mediæval Languages and Literatures, 1991); Niels Lukman, "Ragnarr loðbrók, Sigifrid, and the Saints of Flanders," *Mediæval Scandinavia* 9 (1976): 7–50; Bjarni Guðnason, *Um Skjöldungasögu* (Reykjavík: Menningarsjoðs, 1963); and Jan de Vries, "Die Entwicklung der Sage von den Lodbrokssöhnen in den historischen Quellen," *Arkiv för Nordisk Filologi* 44 (1928): 117–63; idem, "Die historischen Grundlagen der Ragnarssaga Loðbrókar," *Arkiv för Nordisk Filologi* 39 (1923): 244–74. Heimskringla's handling of Ragnhild's lineage has been discussed by Joan Turville-Petre, "The Genealogist and History: Ari to Snorri," *Saga-Book of the Viking Society* 20 (1978–79): 20–23.

4. Cf. Ragnars Saga Loðbrókar 3 and Saxo Grammaticus, Gesta Danorum 9.252–53.

5. Cf. Ragnars Saga Loðbrókar 9, Flóamanna Saga 1, and the section of the Skjöldunga Saga preserved as Svíakonungatal Arngríms Lærða, found in Bjarni Guðnason, ed., *Danakonunga Sǫgur* (Reykjavík: Íslenzka Fornritafélag, 1982), 76–77. Both these sources name Sigurð Fafnir's-Bane as Aslaug's father, and the latter reads as follows:

> After many years of war in neighboring parts of Europe, the fame of Ragner's name and deeds grew. He went through a second set of vows, taking another wife upon the death of his first. This was Aslaug, whose father was the most celebrated fighter in Europe: Sigurð, who came from the kingdoms of Sweden. His epithet was Fafnir's Bane, which more or less means serpent- (or dragon-) killer. For Fafnir or Fophnyr (Greek ophis is not dissimilar) means serpent, snake, or dragon in Norwegian. From this marriage, Ragner begot five sons: Ívar, the firstborn, Hvitserk [White Shirt], Bjorn, and Rögnvald (who died as an adolescent, fighting in the army of his brothers), and Sigurð, born last of all.

> *Hinc postqvam multorum annorum bellis in finitimis Europæ partibus gestis nominis sui claritatem auxisset, ad secunda vota transiit, ducta in uxorem, priore demortua, Aslauga qvadam, cui pater fuerat celeberrimus Europæ pugil Sigvardus, Regibus Sveciæ oriundus; illi cognome Foffnisbane, qvasi serpenticidam dixeris. Foffnir enim vel Fophnyr (græco ofis non dissimile) Norvegis serpentem sive angvem significabat. Ex hoc conjugio filios qvinqve suscepit Ragnerus: Ivarum natu maximum; Witsercum; Biornonem et Raugnvaldum (qvi in adolescentia in fratrum exercitu pugnans occubuit) et Sigvardum ex reliqvis omnibus natu minimum.*

Saxo Grammaticus, Gesta Danorum 9.254, preserves Sigurð's epithet "Snake-in-the-Eye" (*Sywardus serpentini oculi*), but he attributes this to Óðinn's intervention and makes it an omen of Sigurð's "future ferocity" (*futuram juvenis sævitiam*).

6. Skjöldunga Saga, written at least two decades before Heimskringla, is cited by name at Ynglingasaga 29, and its account of the Danish royal dynasty recurs in the Saga of Olaf Tryggvason 9. Although the text has not survived in its original form, a Latin epitome prepared by Arngrimur Jonsson the Learned toward the end of the sixteenth century provides a good summary of its contents. On this text and its relation to Heimskringla, see Guðnason, ed., *Danakonunga Sögur*, esp. 30–36; idem, *Um Skjöldungasögu*, 70–95; and Jakob Benediktsson, "Icelandic Traditions of the Scyldings," *Saga-Book of the Viking Society* 15 (1954–57): 48–66. See also the Ágrip af Sögu Danakonunga, cited by Guðnasson, ed., *Danakonunga Sögur*, 325.

7. Hálfdan the Black's Saga 5: *Móðir Ragnhildar var þýrní, dóttir Klakk-Haraldz konungs af Jótlandi, systir þyri Danmarkarbótar, er átti Gormr inn gamli, er þá réð Danaveldi.*

8. Jomsviking Saga 2: *Haraldr hét jarl er réð fyrir Holtsetalandi; hann var kallaðr Klakk-Haraldr. Hann var vitr maðr. Jarl átti dóttur er þyri hét.* Hon var spǫk at viti, kvenna friðust at sjá, ok réð betr drauma en aðrir menn.* The version that served as a source for Heimskringla has not survived, but four other redactions of slightly later date are extant and agree on this passage.

9. Cf. "Tale of the Jomsvikings" (*Jómsvikinga þáttr*) 3 (Flateyjarbók 1.99).

10. Jutland is just across the straits from Vestfold and thus a highly plausible home for Hálfdan's bride. Holstein, much further to the south, might well supply a wife for the Danish king but would probably lie outside the sphere of activity and interest for a district king of Vestfold.

11. Saxo Grammaticus, Gesta Danorum 9.266–67.

12. Greater Saga of Olaf Tryggvason 63: *Klakk-Haraldr jarl var kallaðr vitrastr þeira manna, er þá váru í Danmǫrk.* Jomsviking Saga 2 and "Tale of the Jomsvikings" 3 (Flateyjarbók 1.99) refer to him more modestly as "a wise man." *Hann var vitr madr.*

13. Jomsviking Saga 2: "*því at hon er miklu vitrari en ek.*" Cf. "Tale of the Jomsvikings" 3 (Flateyjarbók 1.99). All the relevant texts establish a differential between the wisdom of father and daughter. Thus, for instance, the "Tale of the Jomsvikings" calls him a wise man (*vitr maðr*), but says she was wisest of all women (*allra kuenna vitruzst*). Similarly, the Greater Saga of Olaf Tryggvason 63 makes Klakk-Harald the wisest man in Denmark (*Klakk-Haraldr jarl var kallaðr vitrastr þeira manna, er þá váru í Danmǫrk*), while Thyri is the wisest women in all of the northern lands (*hafi verit mestr skǫrungr af konum á Norðrlǫndum*).

14. Historia Norwegiæ 12: *Gunnildam quandam malificam et iniquissimam, Gorms stultissimi Danorum regis filiam ac **Thyri mulieris prudentissimæ*** (emphasis added).

15. A. Walde and J. B. Hofmann, *Lateinisches etymologisches Wörterbuch* (Heidelberg: Carl Winter, 1938), 2: 378.

16. Jomsviking Saga 2: *Hon var spǫk at viti.*

17. Cleasby and Vigfusson, *Icelandic-English Dictionary*, 580, say of Old Norse *spakr* "wise = Gk. σωφός, Lat. *sapiens*; by the ancients the word is used with the notion of prophetic vision or second sight." It is derived from the verb *spá* "to spae (Scot.), prophesy, foretell," on which see further de Vries, *Altnordisches etymologisches Wörterbuch*, 531. The feminine substantive *spá*, derived from the same verb, means "a prophecy," and a host of compounds show the religio-mystical sense of this semantic group. Thus, from *spá*: *spá-domr*, "prophecy, divination"; *spáfarar*, "soothsayings, vaticination"; *spá-kona*, "prophetess"; *spá-mæli*, "prophetic words"; *Vǫluspá*, "prophecy of the Sibyl (*Vǫlva*)"; from *spakr*: *spak-frǫmuðr*, "oracle-framer, soothsayer, sage"; *spak-leikr*, "wisdom, prophecy"; *spak-mæli*, "wise saying, prophetic saying"; *spak-ráðugr*, "giving good advice." Cleasby and Vigfusson, *Icelandic-English Dictionary*, 580–81.

18. Jomsvikings Saga 2: *réð betr drauma en aðrir menn.* Cf. "Tale of the Jomsvikings" 3 (Flateyjarbók 1.99). On dreams in general, and royal dreams as a particularly powerful form of revelation, see Gabriel Turville-Petre, "Dream Symbols in Old Icelandic Literature," in *Festschrift Walter Baetke*, ed. Kurt Rudolph (Weimar: Bohlau, 1966), 343–54; idem, "Dreams in Icelandic Tradition," in *Nine Norse Studies* (London: Viking Society, 1972), 30–51; Alexander Argüelles, "Viking Dreams: Mythological and Religious Dream Symbolism in the Old Norse Sagas" (PhD diss., University of Chicago, 1994). Also relevant is Bernadine McCreesh, "Prophetic Dreams and Visions in the Sagas of the Early Icelandic Saints," in *Verbal Encounters: Anglo-Saxon and Old Norse Studies for Roberta Frank*, ed. Antonina Harbus and Russell Poole (Toronto: University of Toronto Press, 2005), 247–68.

19. Jomsvikings Saga 2–3; "Tale of the Jomsvikings" 3–4 (Flateyjarbók 1.99–101); Saxo Grammaticus, Gesta Danorum 9.266–67.

20. In place of the dreams of oxen from the sea, Saxo Grammaticus, Gesta Danorum 9.267, gives a dream of two birds. This is an omen pertaining to the fate of Gorm and Thyri's sons, corresponding to material found in Jomsvikings Saga 5 and the "Tale of the Jomsvikings" 8 (Flateyjarbók 1.105).

21. Cf. Genesis 41.1–4, 14–20, and 25–36.

22. Jomsvikings Saga 3; "Tale of the Jomsvikings" 4.

23. This tenth-century inscription reads as follows: "King Gorm established this monument for his wife Thyri Denmark's-savior." *Kurmr kunukr k[ar]þI kubl þusi a[ft] þurui kunu sina tanmarkar but.* Most literally, the epithet *Danmarkar-bót* identifies Thyri as someone who cured Denmark of its ills.

24. Fagrskinna 1:

> There was one strange thing about Hálfdan: he never dreamed. That thing he presented to the man called Thorleif the Prophetically-Gifted and he sought his counsel on what he could do. And Thorleif described what he did when he sought to know something: he went in a pigsty to sleep and then a dream never failed to come to him.

> *Með Hálfdani var kynligr einn hlutr; hann dreymði aldrigi. En þann hlut bar hann upp fyrir þann mann, er hét þorleifr spaki, ok leitaði ráða, hvat at því mætti gøra. Ok hann sagði, hvat hann gørði, at þá er hann forvitnaði nøkkurn hlut at vita, at hann fór í svinaból at sofa, ok brásk <honum þá eigi> draumr.*

Cf. Hálfdan the Black's Saga 7 and "Tale of Hálfdan the Black" 2 (Flateyjarbók 1.563).

25. Nora Chadwick, "Dreams in Early European Literature," in *Celtic Studies: Essays in Memory of Angus Matheson*, ed. James Carney and David Grene (London: Routledge and Kegan Paul, 1964), 41.

26. Hálfdan the Black's Saga 7: *honum sýndisk, at hann væri allra manna bezt hærðr ok var hár hans alt í lokkum, sumir síðir til jarðar, sumir í miðjan legg, sumir á kné, sumir í mjǫðum, sumir miðja síðu, sumir á háls, en sumir ekki meir en sprotnir upp ór hausi sem knýflar, en á lokkum hans var hvers kyns litr, en einn lokkr sigraði alla með fegrð ok ljósleik ok mikilleik.*

27. Ibid.: "He told Thorleif the dream, and he interpreted it thus: Many offspring would come from him and they would rule the lands with great distinction, but not all equally great. And one would come from his lineage that would be greater and higher than all." *þorleifi sagði hann þann draum, en hann þýddi svá, at mikill afspringr mynди af honum koma ok mynди sá lǫndum ráða með miklum veg ok þó eigi allir með jammiklum, en einn mynди sá af hans ætt koma, at ǫllum mynди meiri ok œðri.*

28. Ibid.: *ok hafa menn þat fyrir satt, at sá lokkr jartegnði Óláf konung inn helga.* Note the use of a generalized subject (*menn*) and the present tense (*hafa*). Cf. Fagrskinna 1 and "Tale of Hálfdan the Black" 2 (Flateyjarbók 1.563).

29. Thus, the other two variants conclude their discussion of Hálfdan's dream by saying of St. Olaf, "Among all Norway's kings, he is holier and more illustrious in heaven and on earth, as all men know." *er ǫllum Nóregs konungum er helgari ok bjartari í himnum ok á jǫrðu, svá at allir menn viti* (Fagrskinna 1; cf. "Tale of Hálfdan the Black" 3 [Flateyjarbók 1.563]).

30. Hálfdan the Black's Saga 6: *Ragnhildr drótning dreymði drauma stóra; hon var spǫk at viti.* Cf. Jomsvikings Saga 2, where similar phrasing is applied to Thyri Denmark's-Savior: "She

was prophetically gifted in her intellect." *Hon var spǫk at viti, kvenna friðust at sjá, ok réð betr drauma en aðrir menn.*

31. Hálfdan the Black's Saga 6: *Ragnhildr drótning dreymði drauma stóra; hon var spǫk at viti; sá var einn draumr hennar, at hon þóttisk vera stǫdd í grasgarði sínum ok taka þorn einn ór serk sér, ok er hon helt á, þá óx hann svá, at þat varð teinn einn mikill, svá at annarr endir tók jǫrð niðr ok varð brátt rótfastr, ok því næst var brátt annarr endir trésins hátt í loptit upp; því næst sýndisk henni treit svá mikit, at hon fekk varla sét yfir upp; þat var furðu digrt; inn nezti hlutr trésins var rauðr sem blóð, en þá leggrinn upp fagrgrœnn, en upp til limanna snjóhvítt; þar váru kvistir af trénu margir stórir, sumir ofarr, en sumir neðarr; limar trésins váru svá miklar, at henni þóttu dreifask um allan Nóreg ok enn víðara.*

32. Harald Fairhair's Saga 43: *kvistir ok limar trésins boðaði afkvæmi hans, er um alt land dreifðisk, ok af hans ætt hafa verit jafnan síðan konungar í Nóregi.* The notion that all subsequent kings descend from Harald Fairhair was probably a piece of later propaganda designed to legitimate the claims of Harald Hard-Ruler (r. 1047–66). This effectively sutured together certain disparate lines (including those of Olaf Tryggvason and St. Olaf), and constructed a sense of deeply rooted national unity. See further Claus Krag, "Norge som odel i Harald Hårfagres ætt," *Historisk Tidsskrift* 68 (1989): 288–301

33. Note, for example, Skaldskaparmál 69: "Hair is troped by calling it 'woods' naming it as some tree." *Hár er svá kent at kalla skóg eða viðar heiti nokkvoru.* Cf. Grímnismál 41; Gylfaginning 8; and the prologue to Snorri's Edda: "This is the second nature of the earth: each year grass and flowers grow on the earth, and in the same year they fall and wither. So also animals and birds grow hair and feathers, which also fall off each year." *Ǫnnur náttúra er sú jarðar, at á hverju ári vex á jǫrðunni gras ok blóm, ok á sama ári fellr þat year alt ok fǫlnar; svá ok dýr ok fuglar, at vex hár ok fjaðrar ok fellr af á hverju ári.*

34. For a similar reading of the difference between the two dreams, see Wolf, "Snorris Wege in die Vergangenheit," 274–78.

35. Hálfdan the Black's Saga 7: *Ragnhildr drótning ól son; var sá vatni ausinn ok nefndr Haraldr; hann var brátt mikill ok inn fríðasti; óx hann þar upp ok gerðisk brátt íþróttamaðr mikill, vel viti borinn; móðir hans unni honum mikit, en faðir hans minna.*

36. Barð's Saga 1: *Síðan vandi Dofri hann á alls kyns íþróttir ok ættvísi ok vígfimi, ok eigi var traust at hann næmi ekki galdra ok forneskju, svá at bæði var hann forspár ok margvís.* On the role of Dofri and other giants in this text, see Ármann Jakobsson, "History of the Trolls? Bárðarsaga As an Historical Narrative," *Saga-Book of the Viking Society* 25 (1998): 53–71; idem, "The Good, the Bad and the Ugly: Bárðarsaga and Its Giants," *Mediaeval Scandinavia* 15 (2005): 1–15.

37. Ibid.: *þá var þat á einni nótt, at Bárðr lá í sæng sinni, at hann dreymdi at honum þótti tré eitt mikit koma upp í eldstó fóstra síns, Dofra. þat var harla margkvistótt upp til limanna. þat óx svá skjótt, at þat hrökk upp í helisbjargit ok því næst út í gegnum hellisbjargit. þar næst var þat svá mikit, at brum þess þótti honum taka um allan Noreg, ok þó var á einum kvistinum fegrsta blóm, ok voru þó allir blómamiklir. Á einum kvistinum var gulls litr.*

38. The ultimate source for Ragnhild's dream is the one attributed to Astyages, king of Media and grandfather of Cyrus the Great, in Herodotus 1.108, which was reworked in the dream attributed to Alette, mother of William the Conqueror, in Wace's Roman de Rou 3.2823–68. In the former, Astyages sees a vine grow from the vagina of his daughter, Mandane, whom he has married off to a petty Persian noble. This vine grows so large as to cover all Asia, presaging the rise of the Persians under the soon-to-be-born Cyrus and the fall of the Medes. Two points that are clear in this dream have been significantly softened in Ragnhild's version: (1) the physical origin of the new dynasty founder in the most intimate parts of his mother's body, and (2) the

familial dynamics of the threat this child poses to the previous ruler. That Astyages is Cyrus's maternal grandfather, rather than his father, lessens the Oedipal aspects of the drama. On the relation of these texts, see Joan Turville-Petre, "A Tree Dream in Old Icelandic," *Scripta Islandica* 39 (1988): 17–19.

39. There is a significant manuscript variation on the wording of this sentence. Thus, one manuscript (AM 158), favored by the text's most recent editors, has *Var honum draumr sá ekki mjök skapfelldr* ("To him, this dream was not very pleasant"), stressing Barð's identity as a pagan. Another (AM 486 4to) has *Var honum draumr sá mjök skapfelldr* ("To him, this dream was very pleasant"), stressing the author's—or redactor's—identity as a Christian. For our purposes, this detail has no importance, however intriguing it may be.

40. Barð's Saga 1: *þann draum réð Bárðr svá, at í hellinn til Dofra mundi koma nokkr konungborinn maðr ok fæðast þar upp, ok sjá samr maðr mundi verða einvaldskonungr yfir Noregi. En kvistr sá inn fagri mundi merkja þann konung er af þess ættmanni væri kominn er þar yxi upp, ok mundi sá konungr boða annan sið en þá gengi. Var honum draumr sá ekki mjök skapfelldr. Hafa menn þat fyrir satt, at þat it bjarta blóm merkti Ólaf konung Haraldsson.*

41. Ibid.: *eptir draum þennan fóru þau Bárðr ok Flaumgerðr í burt frá Dofra. En litlu síðar kom þar Haraldr Hálfdánarson ok fæddist þar upp með Dofra jötun. Efldi Dofri hann síðan til konungs yfir Noregi eptir því sem segir í sögu Haralds konungs Dofrafostra.*

42. "Tale of Hálfdan the Black" 6 (Flateyjarbók 1.566): *En er Haralldr kom heim var hann til konungs tekinn yfir oll þau fylke er fadir hans hafde firir radit. sagde hann monnum sinum huar er hann hafde uerit þessa .v. uetr uar hann þa kalladr Haralldr Dofrafostri.* "Tale of Harald Fairhair" 2 (Flateyjarbók 1.569): *Eftir fall þessarra fiogurra hofdingea æignadizst Haralldr konungr Dofrafostri med krafti ok framkuemd Guthorms frænda sins Hringariki Heidmork Gudbrandzdali Hadaland þotnn Raumariki Uingulmork hinn nyrdra hlut.*

43. Barð's Saga 2:

King Shaggy Harald gained control of the realm in Norway. When he had accomplished this task, he was so powerful and imperious that there was not a man between Raumelf in the south and Finnabu in the north who was managing not to pay tribute to him, even those who burned the salt or those who worked the marches. When Barð heard these things, it seemed clear to him that he would no more escape these burdens of the king than had other men. He would rather forsake his kinsmen and native land than live under such a yoke of oppression as that to which, he heard, all the commons was now subject. Then he had the strong idea to seek another land.

Haraldr konungr lúfa efldist til ríkis í Noregi. Ok er hann var fullgjör í því starfi varð hann svá ríkr ok ráðgjarn, at sá skyldi engi maðr vera í milli Raumelfar suðr ok Finnabús norðr sá er nokkurs var ráðandi svá at eigi gildi honum skatt, jafn vel þeir sem saltit brenndu svá sem hinir er á mörkinni yrktu. En er Bárðr frétti þetta þóttist hann vita at hann mundi eigi heldr undan ganga þessum hans álögum en aðrir. Vildi hann heldr forláta frændr ok fóstrjarðir en lifa undir slíku ánauðaroki sem hann frétti at allr almúginn var þá undirgefinn. Kom honum þá helst í hug at leita annarra landa.

Chapter Seven

1. Barð's Saga 1: "A little while later, Harald Hálfdan's son came there and he was reared there by Dofri the giant. Dofri raised him to be king thereafter over Norway, as is told in the Saga of King Harald, Dofri's Foster Son." *En litlu síðar kom þar Haraldr Hálfdánarson ok fæddist*

þar upp með Dofra jötun. Efldi Dofri hann síðan til konungs yfir Noregi eptir því sem segir í sögu Haralds konungs Dofrafostra. The text seems to have circulated fairly widely and to have been influential. Harald is also identified as "Dofri's foster son" in the "Tale of Hálfdan the Black" 6 (Flateyjarbók 1.566); the "Tale of Harald Fairhair" 1–2 (Flateyjarbók 1.567–68); Vatnsdæla Saga 8; Flóamanna Saga 1; and the "Tale of Orm Storolfsson 1 (Flateyjarbók 1.521). For a discussion of these sources and of the tradition in general, see Finnur Jónsson, "Sagnet om Harald hårfagre som 'Dovrefostre,'" *Arkiv för Nordisk Filologi* 11 (1899): 262–67.

2. Kjalnesinga Saga 12–15; Illuga saga Tagldarbana 1–3. Latest of all is Henrik Ibsen's Peer Gynt, where the character anglophone readers know as "the Mountain King" or "the Troll King" actually bears the name Dovregubbe ("Old Man Dofri").

3. The literature is large and growing. It includes Hilda Ellis, "Fostering by Giants in Old Norse Saga Literature," *Medium Aevum* 10 (1941): 70–85; Lotte Motz, "Gods and Demons of the Wilderness: A Study in Norse Tradition," *Arkiv för Nordisk Filologi* 99 (1984): 175–87; idem, "Kingship and the Giants," *Arkiv för Nordisk Filologi* 111 (1996): 73–88; Gro Steinsland, *Det Hellige Bryllup og Norrøn Kongeideologi: En Analyse av Hierogami-myten i Skírnismál, Ynglingatal, Háleygjatal og Hyndluljóð* (Oslo: Solum, 1991); Riti Kroesen, "Ambiguity in the Relationship between Heroes and Giants," *Arkiv för Nordisk Filologi* 111 (1996): 57–71; and Lorenzo Lozzi Gallo, "The Giantess As Foster-Mother in Old Norse Literature," *Scandinavian Studies* 78 (2006): 1–20.

4. Whereas the literature cited in the previous note seems determined to file a brief on behalf of the giants' good qualities and constructive contributions, a more nuanced assessment of the productive but asymmetric and often tense dealings between gods and giants, dating to the events of creation and working out through cosmic history, has been offered by another body of scholarship, including Jón Hnefill Aðalsteinsson, "Gods and Giants in Old Norse Mythology," *Temenos* 26 (1990): 7–22; Torben A. Vestergaard, "Marriage Exchange and Social Structure in Old Norse Mythology," in *Social Approaches to Viking Studies*, ed. Ross Samson (Glasgow: Cruithne Press, 1991), 21–34; Margaret Clunies Ross, *Prolonged Echoes: Old Norse Myths in Medieval Northern Society*, vol. 1, *The Myths* (Odense: Odense University Press, 1994), esp. chap. 4, "Negative Reciprocity," 103–43; and Rasmus Tranum Kristensen, "Why Was Óðinn Killed by Fenrir? A Structural Analysis of Kinship Structures in Old Norse Myths of Creation and Eschatology," in *Reflections on Old Norse Myths*, ed. Pernille Hermann, Jens Peter Schjødt, and Rasmus Tranum Kristensen (Turnhout, Belgium: Brepols, 2007), 149–69. Most thorough of all is Katja Schulz, *Riesen: Von Wissenshütern und Wildnisbewohnern in Edda und Saga* (Heidelberg: Universitätsverlag Winter, 2004).

5. The pioneering article of Ellis, "Fostering by Giants," is thus dominated by her discussion of "the giantess fostermother" (70–79). Her chief example of a giant fosterfather is, in fact, Dofri, which she treats as a parallel case ("the youth of Haraldr Hárfagr," 79–83), not recognizing any of its more disquieting aspects that we will shortly consider. Ellis's uncritical view of the Dofri story has influenced much of the subsequent literature. Although Kroesen, "Ambiguity in the Relationship between Heroes and Giants," follows Ellis on Dofri (see 67–68), she is much more aware of the ominous undertones in giant-human relations. Gallo, "The Giantess As Foster-Mother," also provides a useful corrective by focusing exclusively on the relation of female giants and male humans, within which sexuality, seduction, and gender politics figure prominently. The relation of male giants and their male foster sons follows quite a different dynamic.

6. The fullest account of Ymir's fate is Gylfaginning 5–8. Eddic poems that refer to this myth

include Völuspá 3; Grímnismál 40–41; Vafþrúðmnismál 21; and Hyndluljóð 33. According to Gylfaginning 6, the gods' patriline begins with an autochthonous being named Buri, but their mother was the daughter of a giant. Ymir is thus their matrilineal ancestor.

7. Gylfaginning 8:

[Óðinn and his brothers] took Ymir and brought him in the middle of Ginnungagap and made the earth of him: of his blood, the sea and lakes; of his flesh, the earth was made; and mountains of his bones.

þeir tóku Ymi, ok fluttu í mitt Ginnungagap, ok gerðu af honum jǫrðina; af blóði hans sæinn og vǫtnin. Jǫrðin var gǫr af holdinu, en bjǫrgin af beinnunum.

Cf. Grímnismál 40–41 and Vafþrúðmnismál 21.

8. Gylfaginning 7:

The sons of Bor killed the giant Ymir, and when he fell, then so much blood ran from his wounds that with it they drowned all the race of frost giants, except one, who survived with his family. That one the giants call Bergelmir. He and his wife went up on his lúðr [?] and held on there, and the lineages of frost giants came from them.

Synir Bors drápu Ymi jǫtun. En er hann fell, þá hljóp svá mikit blóð or sárum hans at með því drektu þeir allri ætt hrímþursa nema einn komsk undan með sínu hýski. þann kalla jǫtnar Bergelmi. Hann fór upp á lúðr sinn ok kona hans ok helzk þar, ok eru af þeim komnar hrímþursa ættir.

9. Gylfaginning 8:

Of the blood which ran from his wounds and flowed freely, they made the sea there, with which they surrounded and secured the earth, and they laid the sea in a ring around it, and it will seem an impossibility to most men to cross over it. . . . [The world] is circular around the edge, and around it lies the deep sea. On the shore of the sea they gave lands for dwelling to the families of giants, and on the inner side of the earth they built a stronghold all around the world because of the hostility of the giants.

Af því blóði er ór sárum rann ok laust fór, þar af gerðu þeir sjá þann er þeir gerðu ok festu saman jǫrðina, ok lǫgðu þann sjá í hring útan um hana, ok mun þat flestum manni ófœra þykkja at komask þar yfir. . . . Hon er kringlótt útan, ok þar útan um liggr hinn djúpi sjár, ok með þeiri sjávar strǫndu gáfu þeir lǫnd til bygðar jǫtna ættum. En fyrir innan á jǫrðunni gerðu þeir borg umhverfis heim fyrir ófriði jǫtna.

10. On the spatial relations of gods and giants, see Motz,"Gods and Demons of the Wilderness"; Aron Gurevich, "Space and Time in the Weltmodell of the Old Scandinavian Peoples," *Mediaeval Scandinavia* 2 (1969): 42–53; Hastrup, *Culture and History in Medieval Iceland*, 145–51; and Ármann Jakobsson, "Where Do the Giants Live?," *Arkiv för Nordisk Filologi* 121 (2006): 101–12. On their ongoing enmity, see Ross, *Prolonged Echoes*; M. Ciklamini, "Óðinn and the Giants," *Neophilologus* 42 (1962): 145–58; and Ármann Jakobsson, "A Contest of Cosmic Fathers: God and Giant in Vafþrúðnismál," *Neophilologus* 92 (2008): 263–77.

11. "All-Father" (*Alfǫðr, Alfaðir*) is a standard epithet of Óðinn, occurring at Grímnismál 48; Helgaqviða Hundingsbana I 38; and elsewhere. The assertion that all the royal families of northern Europe descend from Óðinn is developed in detail in the prologue to Snorri's Edda

10–11. There is also reference to this tradition in Ynglingasaga 5 and 8. Most fully on this theme, see Anthony Faulkes, "Descent from the Gods," *Mediaeval Scandinavia* 11 (1978–79): 92–125.

12. On the way persistent demands for vengeance, beginning with Ymir's murder, build to the Ragnarök drama, see John Lindow, *Murder and Vengeance among the Gods: Baldr in Scandinavian Mythology* (Helsinki: Academia Scientiarum Fennica, 1997). The broader literature on the role of vengeance in the social, political, familial, and moral order is large, including Vilhelm Grønbech, *The Culture of the Teutons* (London: Oxford University Press, 1931) 1: 66–88; Byock, *Feud in the Icelandic Saga*; W. I. Miller, *Bloodtaking and Peacemaking*; and G. Nordal, *Ethics and Action in Thirteenth-Century Iceland*, 46–52 and 70–73.

13. Gylfaginning 45–47.

14. "Tale of Hálfdan the Black" 5 (Flateyjarbók 1.564): *æinn morgin snemma er menn koma til gullhussins sa þeir þar allmykinn jǫtun. þessi dolgr uar bade digr ok hárr.*

15. "Tale of Hálfdan the Black" 5 (Flateyjarbók 1.564–65): *Halfdan konungr spurde hann at nafnni en hann letzst Dofri hæita ok æiga hæima j fialle þui er uit hann er kent. Konungr spurde huort hann hefde stolit gulle hans. hann quad þat satt vera ok beiddizst þa grida ok baud at þrigillda honum aftr gullit. en konungr sagde at hann skyllde alldri gridum na ok þar bundinn bida þess er þing væri kuatt ok honum skyllde dœma þar hinn haduligazsta dauda. sagde hann ok at honum skyllde æinge biargir ueita ne mat gefa nema huerr at gerde skyllde lifit lata ok ongu odru firirkoma.*

16. "Tale of Hálfdan the Black" 5 (Flateyjarbók 1.565): *hann snidr fioturinn ok blybondin af Dofra. en er hann uar laus uordinn þakkade hann Haralldi lifgiofina ok hafde sig sidan af stad. batt hann ekki læinge sko sina ok lagde halann a bak ser ok setti j burtu suo at huorke sa af honum uedr ne reyk.*

17. "Tale of Hálfdan the Black" 6 (Flateyjarbók 1.565): *spurde konungr huerr þessa uerks munde sannr en Haralldr sagdizst Dofra leyst hafa. konungr vard uit þetta akafa ræidr suo at hann rak Haralld son sinn j burtu en kuezst eigi nenna at lata drepa hann. lagde hann þar suo rigt vid at honum skyllde einge biorg uæita bad hann þar nu hialp taka sem Dofri troll væri.*

18. "Tale of Hálfdan the Black" 6 (Flateyjarbók 1.566): *þa mællti Haralldr. þat er þo satt at segia **fostri minn** at fárr er fagr ef grætr þuiat mer synizst þu nu helldr bragdillr ok yfirlita mikill ok vertu katr þuiat mig sakar ekki* (emphasis added).

19. "Tale of Hálfdan the Black" 6 (Flateyjarbók 1.566): *þar var Haralldr .v. uetr ok skorti ekki þat er hafa þurfti. Dofri unni honum suo mikit at hann matti ekki j mot honum lata. mart kende Dofri honum j frǫdum. suo uande Dofri hann uit jþrottir. mikit gekzst Haralldr vid bæde vm uoxst ok afl.*

20. As signaled by the final sentence of Hálfdan the Black's Saga 7: "His mother loved [Harald] greatly, but his father less." *móðir hans unni honum mikit, en faðir hans minna.*

21. To cite one example, Heimskringla frequently handles this theme by describing an alternance between harsh and mild rulers, as when Eirik Bloodaxe is followed by Hákon the Good or Harald Hard-Ruler by Olaf the Gentle.

22. Gregory Bateson, *Naven: A Survey of the Problems Suggested by a Composite Picture of the Culture of a New Guinea Tribe Drawn from Three Points of View* (Stanford, CA: Stanford University Press, 1958).

23. "Tale of Hálfdan the Black" 6 (Flateyjarbók 1.566): *þat er sagt at æinn dag kom Dofri at male vid Haralld ok talade suo. nu þikiumzst ek hafa launat þer lifgiofina þuiat nu hefui ek komit þer til konungdomsins þuiat fadir þinn er daudr ok var ek þar ekki fiarre. nu skaltu fara heim ok taka vid riki þinu. legg ek þat til med þer at þu latir huorke skera hár þitt ne negl fyrr en þu verdr æinualldzkonungr yfir ollum Noregi. skal ek ok þer j lidsinne vera ok j bardogum med þer. mun þer þat at gagnni verda þuiat ek mun skęinuhættr uera saker þess at ek mun ekki audsærr vera. far þu nu heill ok uel ok gangi þer allt til tirs ok tima heidrs ok hamingiu æigi at sidr þott þu hafir hea mer*

verit. Fann þa miog a Dofra er þeir skildu. En er Haralldr kom heim var hann til konungs tekinn yfir oll þau fylke er fadir hans hafde firir radit. sagde hann monnum sinum huar er hann hafde uerit þessa .v. uetr uar hann þa kalladr Haralldr Dofrafostri.

24. Cleasby and Vigfusson, *Icelandic-English Dictionary*, 375. More fully, see Benveniste's discussion of the Gothic cognate *laun*, *Vocabulaire des institutions indo-européennes* 1: 166–69.

25. "Tale of Hálfdan the Black" 6 (Flateyjarbók 1.566): *fadir þinn er daudr **ok var ek þar ekki fiarre** (emphasis added).*

26. Ibid.: *ek mun skeinuhættr uera saker þess at ek mun ekki audsærr vera.*

27. "Tale of Harald Fairhair" 5 (Flateyjarbók 1.571) describes Dofri as having made good on his promise to provide Harald with battlefield aid by raining invisible blows on his enemies.

Thereafter, King Shaggy Harald took possession of all Trondheim and the main part of the land. Some had been willing to yield, some made it a gift of friendship, some gave consent, some yielded out of fear, some as the result of battles. And they all succumbed easily to him, due to his prowess, that of his champions, and a third factor was this: it seemed to men that Dofri assisted him in counsel and was apt to wound his enemies in battle. He took many men from the (enemy) troop and that was easy for him, because no one saw him in battle unless they were gifted with second sight.

Sidan æignnadizst Haralldr konungr lufa allan þrandheim ok allt megin landzsins sumt med villd eirra er att hofdu sumt med vingiofum sumt med radum sumt med otta sumt med bardogum. Ok fellu honum þeir aller lett sakir hraustleika sins ok kappa sinna ok þess hins þridea er monnum þotti sem Dofri yrde honum driugr j radum ok suo skæinuhættr j bardogum vinum hans ok kiore miog menn or flokki ok var honum þat hægt þuiat hann sa ongir menn j bardaga vtan þeir er ofresker voru.

28. Sophus Bugge, "Mythiske Sagn om Halvdan Svarte og Harald Haafagre," *Arkiv för Nordisk Filologi* 12 (1900): 1–37.

29. Grímnismál Prologue: *Frigg segir: "Hann er matníðingr sá, at hann qvelr gesti þiccia of-margir koma."*

30. Ibid.:

Frigg sent her maid, Fulla, to Geirröð. She told the king to beware, lest a magician attack him, one who had come into the land, and she said that he had a sign: that no dog was so fierce as to leap at him. And it was the greatest falsehood that Geirröð was not generous with food. And so he had that man seized whom no dog wanted to attack. He was in a blue cloak and was named Grímnir. He said nothing more about himself, although he was asked. The king had him tortured to make him speak and set him between two fires. He stayed there eight nights.

Frigg sendi escismey sína, Fullo, til Geirroðar. Hon bað konung varaz, at eigi fyrgerði hanóm fiolkunnigr maðr, sá er þar var kominn í land, oc sagði þat marc á, at engi hundr var svá ólmr, at á hann myndi hlaupa. Enn þat var inn mesti hégómi, at Geirroðr væri eigi matgóðr. Oc þó lætr hann handtaca þann mann, er eigi vildo hundar á ráða. Sá var í feldi blám oc nefndiz Grímnir, oc sagði ecci fleira frá sér, þótt hann væri at spurðr. Konungr lét hann pína til sagna oc setia milli elda tveggia, oc sat hann þar átta nætr.

31. Grímnismál prologue: *Geirroðr konungr átti son, tío vetra gamlan, oc hét Agnarr eptir bróður hans. Agnarr gecc at Grímni oc gaf hánom horn fult at drecca, sagði, at konungr gorði illa, er hann lét pína hann saclausan.*

32. Grímnismál 51–53:

You are drunk, Geirrod,	you have drunk too much;
Of much are you bereft,	you who have lost
The favor of Óðinn	and all the Einherjar.
I said much to you	and you followed little,
and your friends betray you.	
I see the sword	of my friend lying there,
all dripping with gore.	
Now may Ygg have	the sword-struck man killed in battle.
I know your life is short.	
Hostile are the Dísir—	now you can see Óðinn,
Approach me, if you are able!	

Qlr ertu, Geirroðr,   *hefr þú ofdruccit;*

Miclo ertu hnugginn,   *er þú ert míno gengi,*

qllom einheriom   *oc Óðins hylli.*

Fjqlð ec þér sagða,   *enn þú fát um mant,*

    oc þic véla vinir;

mæki liggia   *ec sé míns vinar*

    allan í dreyra drifinn.

Eggmóðan val   *nú mun Yggr hafa,*

    þitt veit ec líf um liðit;

úfar ro dísir—   *nú knáttu Óðin siá,*

    nálgaztu mic, ef þú megir!

33. Grímnismál epilogue: *Óðinn hvarf þá. Enn Agnarr var þar konungr lengi síðan.*

34. In adddition to Bugge's pioneer article, "Mytiske Sagn om Halvdan Svarte og Harald Haafagre," see also Moltke Moe, *Eventyrlige sagn i den ældre historie* (Christiania [Oslo]: Det Mallingske bogtrykkeri, 1906), 581–605 and 632–56; Wolf von Unwerth, *Untersuchungen über Totenkult und Óðinnverehrung bei Nordgermanen und Lappen* (Breslau: M. & H. Marcus, 1911), 130–34; Halvdan Koht, "Hadlands-Segnene i dei Norske Kongesogune," *Edda* 11 (1919): 85–94; Ólafia Einarsdóttir, "Harald Dovrefostre af Sogn," *Historisk Tidsskrift* 1 (1971): 131–66; and Klaus Böldl, "Königsmörder und Königsmacher: Samen in fundierenden Erzählungen des Mittelalters," in *Analecta Septentrionalia: Beiträge zur nordgermanischen Kultur- und Literaturgeschichte*, ed. Wilhelm Heizmann, Klaus Böldl, and Heinrich Beck (Berlin: Walter de Gruyter, 2009), 134–40. A convenient example of the relatively uncritical acceptance of Bugge's interpretation is found in de Vries, *Altgermanische Religionsgeschichte* 2: 88–89, where the author treats the Dofri episode as evidence for the presence of Óðinn at the Yule celebration of King Hálfdan, Dofri being utterly transparent to the god.

35. On the central role of feasting and hospitality in medieval Scandinavian ethics and society, see A. J. Gurevich, *Categories of Medieval Culture* (London: Routledge and Kegan Paul, 1985), 226–34 and 245–47; on generosity in general, Grønbech, *The Culture of the Teutons* 2: 54–76; Gurevich, *Historical Anthropology of the Middle Ages*, 177–89.

36. For all that the portrait of Dofri is sympathetic in many ways, the nouns used to denote him continually reassert his underlying evil nature. Along these lines, the "Tale of Hálfdan the Black" calls him "giant" (*jqtun*), "fiend" (*dolgr*), "troll" (*troll*), "monster" (*greppr*), "churl" (*karl*), while Barð's Saga adds "rock dweller" (*bergbúi*).

37. "Tale of Hálfdan the Black" 5 (Flateyjarbók 1.565): *hann **gerdizst** þa helldr hardlœitr ok miog harmþrunginn* (emphasis added).

38. It is not clear if Heimskringla made direct use of the *Saga of King Harald, Dofri's Foster Son or if it drew on the same oral traditions as did the lost text, but the latter seems more likely.

39. Hálfdan the Black's Saga 8: *Hálfdán konungr var á jólavist á Haðalandi. þar varð undarligr hlutr jólaaptan, þá er menn váru til borða gengnir, ok var þat allmikit fjǫlmenni, at þar hvarf vist ǫll af borðum ok alt mungát; sat konungr hryggr eptir, en hverr annarra sótti sitt heimili, en til þess at konungr mætti viss verða, hvat þessum atburð olli, þá lét hann taka Finn einn, er margfróðr var, ok vildi neyða hann til saðrar sǫgu ok píndi hann ok fekk þó eigi af honum. Finnrinn hét þannug mjǫk til hjálpar, er Haraldr var, sonr hans, ok Haraldr bað honum eirðar ok fekk eigi, ok hleypði Haraldr honum þó í brot at óvilja konungs ok fylgði honum sjálfr. þeir kómu þar farandi, er hǫfðingi einn helt veizlu mikla, ok var þeim at sýn þar vel fagnat, ok er þeir hǫfðu þar verit til várs, þá var þat einn dag, at hǫfðinginn mælti til Haraldz: "furðu mikit torrek lætr faðir þinn sér at, er ek tók vist nǫkkura frá honum í vetr; en ek mun þér þat launa með feginsǫgu. Faðir þinn er nú dauðr ok skaltu nú heim fara, muntu fá ríki þat alt, er hann hefir átt, ok þar með skaltu eignask allan Nóreg."*

40. The Finn is said to be "wise about many things" (*margfróðr*). Given derogatory stereotypes regarding those whom the sagas call Finns (more properly, those construed as barbarians to the north, including Saami), this is a relatively gentle way to signal magic knowledge and powers. Even so, any hint of magic has strong implications, since the discourse and category of magic served to identify the illicit knowledge and power through which actors normally consigned to subordinate positions were able to overcome their structural superiors. Above all, magic thus posed a threat to kings but also provided them with a way of explaining any incident in which they did not prevail as expected. See, most fully and perceptively, Nicolas Meylan, "How to Deal with Kings When You Are a Suet-Lander: Discourses of 'Magic' between Norway and Iceland" (PhD diss., University of Chicago, 2010).

41. Regarding stereotypes of the Finns and their importance for this narrative, see Asbjørn Nesheim, "Samisk trolldom," in *Kulturhistorisk Leksikon for Nordisk Middelalder* 15 (Copenhagen: Rosenkilde og Bagger, 1967), 104–67; Maj-Lis Holmberg, "Om Finland och övriga finnländer i den isländska fornlitteraturen," *Arkiv för Nordisk Filologi* 91 (1976): 166–91; Böldl, "Königsmörder und Königsmacher"; and Else Mundal, "The Perception of the Saamis and Their Religion in Old Norse Sources," in *Shamanism and Northern Ecology*, ed. Juha Pentikainen (Berlin: Mouton de Gruyter, 1996), 39–53; idem, "Coexistence of Saami and Norse Culture—Reflected in and Interpreted by Old Norse Myths," in *Old Norse Myths, Literature, and Society*, ed. Margaret Clunies Ross (Odense: Odense University Press, 2003), 346–55.

42. By law, theft of food was justified only when one was in need and hospitality had been refused. Otherwise, it constituted a crime punishable by outlawry. The relevant statute in Icelandic law is Grágás Ib 165. For a fuller discussion, see G. Nordal, *Ethics and Action in Thirteenth-Century Iceland*, 152–54.

Chapter Eight

1. Hálfdan the Black's Saga 8:

King Hálfdan was on a Yule visit in Haðaland. Something marvelous happened on Yule eve. When men had come to table and there were a great many people, all of the food and all the ale disappeared from the table.

Hálfdán konungr var á jólavist á Haðalandi. þar varð undarligr hlutr jólaaptan, þá er menn váru til borða gengnir, ok var þat allmikit fjǫlmenni, at þar hvarf vist ǫll af borðum ok alt mungát.

2. Ágrip 1: *En sjá er háttr á dauðdaga Hálfdanar. Hann þá veizlu á Haðalandi, en þá er hann fór þaðan í sleða, [þá drukk]naði hann í Rǫnd [í R]ykinvík, þar er nautabrunnr var.*

3. Historia Norwegiæ 10: *qui dum noctu per cujusdam stagni glaciem, quod Rond nominatur, iter ageret, cum curribus et equitatu magno a cena rediens in quandam scissuram, ubi pastores gregem suum adaquare solebant, improvide advectus sub glacie deperiit.*

4. Fagrskinna Appendix 2 (from the A-Text):

All wanted to rescue the king and a great number of drunken men assembled. The ice broke more and more widely and there was no help for the king from the drunken men. So the king perished there, along with Dagr the Wise, his father-in-law, and some twenty men with them.

þa vildu allir biargha kononge. oc þyrftiz þingat mykill fioldi druckinna manna. isinn brotnaðe þvi meir oc viðare. oc varð konongenom eighi meiri hiolp at drucknom monnom. enn sva at konongr tyndizk þar oc Daghr hinn froðe maghr hans. oc nocorir tyttughu menn með þeim.

Hálfdan the Black's Saga 9 also notes that "a great host" (*lið mikit*) died along with King Hálf-dan, without giving any details.

5. Fagrskinna Appendix 2 (from the A-Text): *þesse tiðendi þotto ollum monnum ill vera er til spurðu.*

6. The opening passages of Ágrip are lost, and what now stands as the first chapter contains three paragraphs: (1) A discussion of how Harald's epithet changed from "Shaggy" (*lúfa*) to "Fairhair" (*hárfagr*); (2) a self-identified excursus explaining the relation between the pagan Yule (dedicated to Óðinn) and its Christian counterpart (dedicated to Jesus); (3) an account of Hálfdan's death. It is generally understood that the excursus is motivated by a missing passage that locates the action at Hálfdan's Yule banquet in Haðaland, corresponding to Hálfdan the Black's Saga 8, which begins by specifying, "King Hálfdan was on a Yule visit in Haðaland" (*Hálfdán konungr var á jólavist á Haðalandi*).

7. Hálfdan the Black's Saga 9; and Fagrskinna Appendix 2 (from the A-Text).

8. Fagrskinna Appendix 2 (from the A-Text): *sva gerðiz eitthvert sinn til ugævo atburðr.*

9. Ibid.: *þat var um varit þann tima er isa tekr at læysa a votnum.*

10. Although Old Norse *brunnr* is conventionally translated as "well" or "spring," it actually denotes something a good deal more specific. As Bauschatz, *The Well and the Tree*, 16–19, pains-takingly established, a *brunnr* was the technical means through which human actors amplified a natural source of water, including a spring that bubbles up in a lake.

Springs rise almost exclusively in marshy land, usually lowlands. The source of the spring is usually quite hard to locate. Once it is found, it is isolated from the marsh by sinking shaftlike walls, most frequently wooden or rock, around it. The water then can rise clearly within it, free from contamination from its surroundings. Of course, a well does much the same thing at a deeper level. . . . The idea of the *brunn-* came then to include the enclosure, the water within it, and the powerful, active force that allows it to fill. (P. 17)

The *nauta-brunnr* in question was apparently sunk into Lake Rönd and kept open through the winter so that livestock could get fresh water there.

11. Hálfdan the Black's Saga 9: "It was spring, and there was an exceptionally sudden thaw." *þat var um vár; þá váru sólbráð mikil.* The phrase *sólbráð mikil* is unusual and holds particular interest. According to Cleasby and Vigfusson, *Icelandic-English Dictionary*, 77, the substantive *bráð* denotes "haste" but is used only in adverbial phrases and in numerous compounds. In the latter usage, it describes an action or entity as having an abrupt, unexpected, and violent character, as in *bráð-dauði* ("sudden death"), *bráð-fari* ("to travel in haste"), *bráð-fengr* ("hot, hasty"), *bráð-geðr* ("hot-tempered"), *bráð-kjörit* ("hastily chosen"), *bráð-mælt* ("hastily spoken"), *bráð-ræði* ("rashness"), *bráð-sjúkr* ("taken suddenly ill"), *bráða-sótt* ("a sudden illness, a plague"), *bráða-þeyr* ("a rapid thaw"). The text thus coins the compound *sól-bráð* ("hasty-sun") and adds the modifier *mikill* ("great, much") to describe a situation where the sun exerts its power much earlier and more intensely than would normally be expected.

12. Graphing these relations shows the extent to which Heimskringla exceeded all other variants in the attention it gave to the question of what caused the ice to break:

	Sun's Heat in Springtime	Ice Broken for Cattle Watering	Cattle Dung Attracts Sun's Rays and Generates Warmth
Historia Norwegiæ 10	–	+	–
Ágrip 1	–	+	–
Fagrskinna 1	–	+	–
Fagrskinna Appendix 2	+	–	–
"Tale of Hálfdan the Black" 7 (Flateyjarbók 1.566–67)	–	+	–
Hálfdan the Black's Saga 9	+	+	+

13. The form *mykr* appears in this passage only, and elsewhere Old Norse has *myki*. Both terms mean "dung, manure" and are cognate to Danish *møg* and English *muck*, terms with the same meaning. See further Cleasby and Vigfusson, *Icelandic-English Dictionary*, 440; and de Vries, *Altnordisches etymologisches Wörterbuch*, 397.

14. Hálfdan the Black's Saga 9:

> *Hálfdan svarti ók frá veizlu á Haðalandi, ok bar svá til leið hans, at hann ók um vatnit Rǫnd; þat var um vár; þá váru sólbráð mikil; en er þeir óku um Rykinsvík—þar hǫfðu verit um vetrinn nautabrunnar, en er mykrin hafði fallit á ísinn, þá hafði þar grafit um í sól-bráðinu—, en er konungr ók þar um, þá brast niðr íssinn, ok týndisk þar Hálfdan konungr ok lið mikit með honum.*

15. For recent studies of the cosmogonic myth, see Guðrún Nordal, *Tools of Literacy: The Role of Skaldic Verse in Icelandic Textual Culture of the Twelfth and Thirteenth Centuries* (Toronto: University of Toronto Press, 2001), 277–83; Ross, *Prolonged Echoes*, 1: 152–58; Rudolf Simek, *Religion und Mythologie der Germanen* (Darmstadt: Wissenschaftliche Gesellschaft, 2003), 173–75; and Kristensen, "Why Was Óðinn Killed by Fenrir?" Older views and literature are summarized in de Vries, *Altgermanische Religionsgeschichte*, 2: 362–66. Many years ago, I

sought to interpret Ymir and Auðhumla as inherited from a broad "Indo-European tradition," but I would now be more inclined to see a more fluid Eurasian continuum. See Bruce Lincoln, *Priests, Warriors, and Cattle: A Study in the Ecology of Religions* (Berkeley: University of California Press, 1981), 69–95; and idem, "Hegelian Meditations on 'Indo-European' Myths," *Papers from the Mediterranean Ethnographic Summer Seminar* 5 (2003): 59–76.

16. Gylfaginning 5 refers to the first elements of life as *kvikudropum* but also cites Vafþrúðnismál 31, which calls them "poison-drops" (*eitrdropar*). It is this which establishes Ymir—who came into being from those drops—as heinous *ab origine*, justifying Snorri's categorical pronouncement in the same chapter of Gylfaginning: "In no way may we acknowledge him a god. He was evil, as are all his kinsmen." *Fyr øngan mun játum vér hann guð. Hann var illr ok allir hans ættmenn.* Further on the significance of this term and image, see Frederik Stjernfelt, *Baldr og verdensdramet i den nordiske mytologi* (Copenhagen: Museum Tusculanum, 1990), 42–45.

17. Gylfaginning 5:

> Gangleri said: "How were things arranged before there were families or human folk multiplied?"
>
> Then High said: "When these rivers, which are called Elivágar, came so far from their source that a poisonous yeast accompanying them hardened like the slag that runs out of a fire. Then that became ice, and when the ice stopped and did not run, the vapor that was rising from the poison frosted over and it froze to the rime, and the rime increased in one layer over another all through Ginnungagap."
>
> Then Equally High said: "That part of Ginnungagap which looks to the north was filled with the weight and heaviness of ice and rime, and there was a vapor gusting inward from it. But the southern part of Ginnungagap lit up in the face of the sparks and embers that flew out of Muspellheim."
>
> Then Third said: "Just as the cold and all grim things come from Niflheim, so that which is near to Muspell was hot and bright. But Ginnungagap was as mild as windless air. And when the rime and the warm breeze met, it melted and dripped, and from these living drops, life quickened with the power of that which sent the heat. It had the bodily form of a man and he was named Ymir.

> *Gangleri mælti: "Hversu skipaðiz áðr en ættirnar yrði eða aukaðiz mannfólkit?"*
>
> *þá mælti Hár: "Ár þær er kallaðar eru Elivágar, þá er þær vóro svá langt komnar frá uppsprettunni at eitrkvika sú er þar fylgði, harðnaði svá sem sindr þat er renn ór eldinum, þá varð þat íss, ok þá er sá íss gaf staðar ok rann eigi, þá héldi yfir þannig úr þat er af stóð eitrinu ok fraus at hrími, ok iók hrímit hvert yfir annat allt í Ginnungagap."*
>
> *þá mælti Iafnhár: "Ginnungagap, þat er vissi til norðrsættar, fyltiz með þunga ok høf<ug>leik íss ok hríms, ok inn í frá úr ok gustr. En hinn syðri hlutr Ginnungagaps léttiz móti gneistum ok síum þeim er flugu ór Muspellsheimi."*
>
> *þá mælti þriði: "Svá sem kallt stóð af Niflheimi ok allir hlutir grimmir, svá var þat er vissi námunda Muspelli heitt ok lióst. En Ginnungagap var svá hlætt sem lopt vindlaust; ok þá er mœttiz hrímin ok blær hitans, svá at bráðnaði ok draup, ok af þeim kvikudropum kviknaði með krapti þess er til sendi hitann ok varð mannz líkanndi, ok var sá nefndr Ymir."*

18. Gylfaginning 6–7:

> *þá mælir Gangleri: "Hvar bygði Ymir eða við hvat lifði hann?"*
>
> *"Næst var þat, þá er hrímit draup, at þar varð af kýr sú er Auðhumla hét, en fjórar mjólkár runnu ór spenum hennar, ok fœddi hon Ymi."*

Þá mælir Gangleri: "Við hvat fæddisk kýrin?"

Hár segir: "Hon sleikti hrímsteinana, er saltir váru. Ok hinn fyrsta dag er hon sleikti steina kom ór steininum at kveldi manns hár, annan dag manns hǫfuð, þriðja dag var þar allr maðr. Sá er nefndr Búri. Hann var fagr álitum, mikill ok máttugr. Hann gat son þann er Borr hét. Hann fekk þeirar konu er Bestla hét, dóttir Bǫlþorns jǫtuns, ok fengu þau þrjá sonu. Hét einn Óðinn, annarr Vili, þriði, Vé. Ok þat er mín trúa at sá Óðinn ok hans bræðr munu vera stýrandi himins ok jarðar."

19. Gylfaginning 8:

Then Gangleri said: "What did Bor's sons do then, if you believe that they are gods?"

High One said: "There is not a little of that to tell. They took Ymir and brought him in the middle of Ginnungagap and made the earth of him: of his blood, the sea and lakes; of his flesh, the earth was made; and mountains of bones. They made rocks and stones of teeth and jawbones and of the bones which were broken."

Then Just-as-High said: "Of the blood which ran from his wounds and flowed freely, they made the sea there, with which they surrounded and secured the earth, and they laid the sea in a ring around it, and it will seem an impossibility to most men to cross over it."

Then Third said: "And they took up his skull, and made heaven of it, and set it up over the earth with its four corners, and under each corner they set a dwarf. These were called East, West, North, and South." Then they took sparks and embers which were moving freely and had been cast out of Muspellheim, and they set them in the middle of Ginnungagap, both above and below, to light heaven and earth."

þa svarar Gangleri: "Hvat hǫfðusk þá at Bors synir, ef þú trúir at þeir sé guð?"

Hár segir: "Eigi er þar lítit at segja. þeir tóku Ymi, ok fluttu í mitt Ginnungagap, ok gerðu af honum jǫrðina; af blóði hans sæinn og vǫtnin. Jǫrðin var gǫr af holdinu, en bjǫrgin af beinnunum; grjót ok urðir gerðu þeir af tǫnnum ok jǫxlum, ok af þeim beinum, er brotin váru."

þá mælir Jafnhár: "Af því blóði er ór sárum rann ok laust fór, þar af gerðu þeir sjá þann er þeir gerðu ok festu saman jǫrðina, ok lǫgðu þann sjá í hring útan um hana, ok mun þat flestum manni ófæra þykkja at komask þar yfir."

þá mælir þriði: "Tóku þeir ok haus hans ok gerðu þar af himin ok settu hann upp yfir jǫrðina með fjórum skautum, ok undir hvert horn settu þeir dverg. þeir heita svá: Austri, Vestri, Norðri, Suðri. þá tóku þeir síur ok gneista þá er lausir fóru ok kastat hafði ór Muspellsheimi, ok settu á miðjan Ginnungahimin bæði ofan ok neðan til at lýsa himin ok jǫrð."

This passage draws on Vafþrúðnismál 21; Grímnismál 40–41; Völuspá 5 and 11.

20. Gylfaginning 8:

ok með þeiri sjávar strǫndu gáfu þeir lǫnd til bygðar jǫtna ættum. En fyrir innan á jǫrðunni gerðu þeir borg umhverfis heim fyrir ófriði jǫtna, en til þeirar borgar hǫfðu þeir brár Ymis jǫtuns, ok kǫlluðu þá borg Miðgarð.

The poetic source cited in this passage, Grímnismál 41, specifies that the gods built the fortress of Miðgarð for the protection of humans: "Of [Ymir's] brows / the kind gods made / Miðgarð for the sons of men." *En ór hans brám / gerðu blíð regin / Miðgarð manna sonum.*

21. Hálfdan the Black's Saga, chap. 9:

Svá mikit gerðu menn sér um hann, at þá er þat spurðisk, at hann var dauðr, ok lík hans var flutt á Hringariki ok var þar til graptar ætlat, þá fóru ríkismenn af Raumaríki ok af Vestfold ok Heiðmǫrk ok beiddusk allir at hafa líkit með sér ok heygja í sínu fylki, ok þótti þat vera árvænt, þeir er næði. En þeir sættusk svá, at líkinu var skipt í fjóra staði, ok var hǫfuðit lagit í haug at Steini á Hringaríki, en hverir fluttu heim sinn hluta ok heygðu, ok eru þat alt kallaðir Hálfdanar-haugar.

22. The relation among these districts that constitute Hálfdan's realm can be graphed as follows:

	Location	Means of Acquisition	Order of Acquisition	Textual Reference
Vestfold	South	Patrilineal inheritance	First	Ynglingasaga 49
Raumariki	East	Conquest	First conquered	Hálfdan the Black's Saga 1–2
Heiðmark	North	Conquest	Second conquered	Hálfdan the Black's Saga 2
Hringariki	West	Marriage	Last	Hálfdan the Black's Saga 5

23. "Tale of Hálfdan the Black" 7 (Flateyjarbók 1.566–67). Within Hálfdan's realm, the situations of Vingulmark and Heiðmark are almost identical. Both are among the king's first conquests, but neither one was fully subjugated. According to Hálfdan the Black's Saga 1, only half of Vingulmark was taken, while chap. 2 recounts that after winning all of Heiðmark, Hálfdan generously decided to share the territory on equal terms with King Eystein, the kinsman he had just defeated.

24. Fagrskinna Appendix 2 speaks of this as the *ársæli konungs*, the marvelous, possibly also mystical and magic capacity of good kings in general and this king in specific to ensure good harvests every year, thereby securing the prosperity and well-being of his people. Hálfdan the Black's Saga 9 and "Tale of Hálfdan the Black" 7 make the same point with an adjective in the superlative degree, saying, "Of all kings, Hálfdan was most gifted in the power of prosperity." *Halfdan uar allra konunga ársælzstr.*

25. These themes have previously been explored by Marie Delcourt, "Le partage du corps royal," *Studi e Materiali di Storia delle Religioni* 34 (1963): 1–25; and François-Xavier Dillmann, "Pour l'étude des traditions relatives à l'enterrement du roi Halfdan le Noir," in *International Scandinavian and Medieval Studies in Memory of Gerd Wolfgang Weber*, ed. Michael Dallapiazza (Trieste: Parnaso, 2000), 147–56.

26. Gylfaginning 5: *Hann var illr ok allir hans ættmenn.*

27. The fullest discussion of his qualities comes in Hálfdan the Black's Saga 7, which emphasizes his wisdom and justice.

King Hálfdan was a wise man and a truthful man in fairness. He established the law and observed it himself, and he made others observe it so that overweening arrogance could not overthrow the laws. He himself made the penalties and arranged compensations for each man according to his birth and distinction.

Hálfdan konungr var vitr maðr ok sannendamaðr til jafnaðar ok setti lǫg ok helt sjálfr, ok lét aðra halda, svá at eigi mætti ofs steypa lǫgunum; hann gerði ok sjálfr saktal ok skipaði bótum hverjum eptir sínum burð ok metorðum.

Other passing references describe Hálfdan as powerful (*ríkr*, chap. 2), victorious (*hafði sigr*, chap. 2), and most possessed of the power to create prosperity (*allra konunga ársælstr*, chap. 9).

28. The sole other mention of this primordial cow occurs in the instructions for would-be poets at Skáldskaparmál 75/509, which probably depends on her appearance in Gylfaginning:

> A cow is called calf and
> Heifer and bovine
> And Auðhumbla—
> She is the noblest of cows.

> *Kýr heitir skirja*
> *Kvíga ok frenja*
> *Ok Auðhumbla:*
> *Hon er œzt kúa.*

29. All other proper names that appear in Gylfaginning 5–8 are taken from older Eddic poems that were known to—and cited by—Snorri. Thus, in the order of their appearance: Elivágar (Vafþrúðnismál 30–31, Hymiskviða 5), Ginnungagap (Völuspá 3), Muspellheim (Völuspá 51, Lokasenna 42), Niflheim (Vafþrúðnismál 43), Ymir (Vafþrúðnismál 20–21 and 28, Grímnismál 40–41, Völuspá in skamma 6, Hyndluljóð 33), Aurgelmir (Vafþrúðnismál 29–30), the first man and woman begotten by Ymir (Vafthrúðnismál 32–33), Buri (Völuspá 13 in the Hauksbók MS; NB, however, he appears in a list of dwarves), Bor (Völuspá 4, Völuspá in skamma 2), Bestla (Hávamál 140, Vellekla 4), Bölthorn (Hávamál 140), Óðinn (countless), Vili (Lokasenna 26), Vé (Lokasenna 26), Bergelmir (Vafthrúðnismál 28–29 and 34–35), dwarves named East, West, North, South (Völuspá 11), Sun, Moon, and Stars (Völuspá 5), Midgarð (Grímnismál 40–41).

30. Obviously, the comparison is stronger if Snorri was responsible for Heimskringla, as I take to be most likely. The analysis does not depend on this being so, however, for it is sufficient that whoever was responsible for chap. 9 in Hálfdan the Black's Saga was familiar with the cosmogonic narrative of Gylfaginning 5–8.

31. If Snorri was responsible for Heimskringla, as most experts believe, he would have been responsible for both innovations and for the implicit relation between them. Such an interpretation is extremely attractive, and I am inclined to think it is so. The argument here does not depend on this, however, and it is sufficient to assume that the Auðhumla narrative (whatever its origin and in whatever form it may have circulated) was known to the person(s) responsible for Heimskringla (whoever he or they might have been).

Chapter Nine

1. Theodricus Monachus, Historia de Antiquitate Regum Norwagiensium, 1:

In the year 858 from the incarnation of our Lord, Harald Fairhair, son of Hálfdan the Black, began his reign. For the first time he drove out all petty kings and alone gained kingship of all Norway for seventy years, and (then) he died.

Anno ab incarnatione Domini octigentesimo quinquagesimo octavo regnavit Haraldus pulchre-comatus, filius Halfdan nigri. Hic primum expulit omnes regulos et solus obtinuit regnum totius Norwagiæ annis septuaginta et defunctus est.

2. Historia Norwegiæ 11: *Haraldus comatus, ob decoram cæsariem sic cognominatus.*

3. Ágrip 2: *er maðrinn var snemma rǫskr ok risuligr vexti.*

4. Ibid.: *En þat var .x. vetr er hann barðisk áðr til lands en hann yrði allvaldskonungr at Nóregi, ok siðaði vel land sitt ok friðaði* (emphasis added).

5. The most important literature in the debate concerning whether the king's *hamingja* was a foundation of his sacred status includes Grønbech, *The Culture of the Teutons,* 127–74; Folke Ström, "Kung Domalde i Svitjod och 'kungalyckan,'" *Saga och Sed* 34 (1967): 52–66; and Peter Hallberg, "The Concept of *gipta, gæfa, hamingja* in Old Norse Literature," in *Proceedings of the First International Saga Conference* (London: Viking Society, 1973), 143–83, on the affirmative side; with Walter Baetke, *Yngvi und die Ynglinger: Eine quellenkritische Untersuchung über das nordische "Sakralkönigtum"* (Berlin: Akademie Verlag, 1964), 12–38; idem, "Christliches Lehngut in der Sagareligion," 345–49; Lennart Ejerfeldt, *Helighet, "karisma" och kungadöme i forngermansk religion* (Uppsala: Relgionshistoriska Institutionen i Uppsala, 1971); and Lars Lönnroth, "Dómaldi's Death and the Myth of Sacral Kingship," in *Structure and Meaning in Old Norse Literature,* ed. John Lindow, Lars Lönnroth, and Gerd Wolfgang Weber (Odense: Odense University Press, 1986), 73–93, on the negative side. Summaries of the debate are available in Rory McTurk, "Sacral Kingship in Ancient Scandinavia: A Review of Some Recent Writings," *Saga-Book of the Viking Society* 19 (1975–76): 157–69; and Olof Sundqvist, *Freyr's Offspring: Rulers and Religion in Ancient Svea Society* (Uppsala: Acta Universitatis Upsaliensis, Historia Religionum, 2002), 18–38.

6. Most broadly on the question of "sacred kingship," see Otto von Friesen, "Har det nordiska kungadomet sakralt ursprung?," *Saga och Sed,* 1932–34, 15–34; Jan de Vries, "Das Königtum bei den Germanen," *Saeculum* 7 (1956): 289–309; Otto Höfler, *Germanisches Sakralkönigtum,* vol. 1, *Der Runenstein von Rök und die germanische Individualweihe* (Tübingen: Max Niemeyer, 1952); idem, "Der Sakralcharakter des germanischen Königtums," in *La Regalità Sacra: Contributi al tema del VIII Congresso Internazionale di Storia delle Religioni, Roma, Aprile 1955,* (Leiden: E. J. Brill, 1959), 664–701; Ake V. Ström, "The King God and His Connection with Sacrifice in Old Norse Religion," in *La Regalità Sacra,* 702–15; Ejerfeldt, *Helighet, "karisma" och kungadöme;* Baetke, *Yngvi und die Ynglinger;* William A. Chaney, *The Cult of Kingship in Anglo-Saxon England* (Manchester: Manchester University Press, 1970); Hallberg, "The Concept of *gipta-gæfa-hamingja"*; Finn Fuglestad, "Earth-Priests, 'Priest-Chiefs,' and Sacred Kings in Ancient Norway, Iceland and West Africa: A Comparative Essay," *Scandinavian Journal of History* 4 (1979): 47–74; McTurk, "Sacral Kingship in Ancient Scandinavia"; idem, "Scandinavian Sacral Kingship Revisited," *Saga-Book of the Viking Society* 24 (1994–97): 19–32; Jens Peter Schjødt, "Det sakrale kongedømme i det førkristne Skandinavien," *Chaos* 13 (1990): 48–67; Eve Picard, *Germanisches Sakralkönigtum? Quellenkritische Studien zur Germania des Tacitus und aur altnordischen Überlieferung* (Heidelberg: Carl Winter, 1991); Claus Krag, *Ynglingatal og Ynglingesaga: En Studie i Historiske Kilder* (Oslo: Universitetsforlag, 1991); Gro Steinsland, *Den hellige kongen: Om religion og herskermakt fra vikingtid til middelalder* (Oslo: Pax, 2000); Klaus von See, *Königtum und Staat im skandinavischen Mittelalter* (Heidelberg: Carl Winter, 2002); Sundqvist, *Freyr's Offspring;* idem, "Aspects of Rulership Ideology in Early Scandinavia with Particular References to the Skaldic Poem Ynglingatal," in *Das frühmittelalterliche Königtum: Ideelle und religiöse Grundlagen,* ed. Franz-Reiner Erkens (Berlin: Walter de Gruyter), 87–124; Stefanie Dick, *Der Mythos vom "germanischen" Königtum* (Berlin: Walter de Gruyter, 2006). Although this is surely oversimplistic, one can perceive a heated political debate running through this literature, in which writers on the right, led by Otto Höfler, have claimed deep antiquity, great importance, and cultural continuity for "Germanic sacral kingship," which they take to be a religious valida-

tion of sovereign power and a hallmark of the uniquely Indo-European (aka "Aryan") capacity for state formation. Reacting to this formulation, which they take to be a dangerous mystification of ancient mystifications, writers on the left, led by Walter Baetke, have sought to minimize or deny most of the religious character imputed to the pre-Christian institution of kingship, while emphasizing the rational sociopolitical and economic bases of royal power.

7. Fagrskinna 2: *Haraldr sonr hans tók konungdóm eptir fǫður sinn Hálfdan svarta. Hann var þá œskumaðr at vetra tali, en fullkominn til mannanar allrar, þeirra er kurteisum konungi byrjaði at hafa. Hans hárvǫxtr var mikill með undarligum lit, því líkastr at sjá sem fagrt silki. Hann var allra manna fríðastr ok sterkastr ok svá mikill sem sjá má á legsteini hans, þeim er í Haugasundum er. Hann var spekimaðr mikill ok langsýnn ok ágjarn, hér með styrkði hann hamingja ok fyrirætlan, at hann skyldi vera yfirmaðr Norðmanna ríkis, er af hans ætt hefir tignazk þat land hér til ok svá mun vera jafnan. Hónum þýddusk gamlir menn með spekiráðum ok ásjá fyrirætlanar. Ungir drengir ok hreystimenn girndusk til hans fyrir sakar virðiligra fégjafa ok hirðprýði. . . . En þat var tíu vetr, er hann barðisk áðr til lands en hann yrði allvaldskonungr at Nóregi ok siðaði vel land sitt ok friðaði.*

8. "Tale of Harald Fairhair" 1 (Flateyjarbók 1.567). By introducing Guthorm immediately after Harald, this text makes the commander the referent of a passage elsewhere directed to the young king: "He was the most promising and strongest of all men, handsome, clearly a wise man and a great leader." *hann var allra manna uœnstr ok sterkaszstr fridr, synum uitr madr ok skorungr mikill.*

9. Harald Fairhair's Saga 1:

Harald took the kingship after his father. He was then ten years old. He was the greatest, strongest, and most handsome of all men, a wise man and a great leader.

Haraldr tók konungdóm eptir fǫður sinn; þá var hann x. vetra gamall; hann var allra manna mestr ok sterkastr ok fríðastr sýnum, vitr maðr ok skǫrungr mikill.

10. Egil's Saga 3: *Haraldr, sonr Hálfdanar svarta, hafði tekit arf eptir fǫður sinn í Vík austr; hann hafði þess heit strengt, at láta eigi skera hár sitt né kemba fyrr en hann væri einvaldskonungr yfir Nóregi; hann var kallaðr Haraldr lúfa. Síðan barðisk hann við þá konunga, er næstr váru, ok sigraði þá, ok eru þar langar frásagnir.*

11. Thus, Historia Norwegiæ 11; Fagrskinna 2; and "Tale of Harald Fairhair" 1 (Flateyjarbók 1.567).

12. Egil's Saga 3: *"þótt þetta vandræði hafi nú borit oss at hendi, þá mun eigi langt til, at sama vandræði mun til yðvar koma, því at Haraldr ætla ek at skjótt mun hér koma, þá er hann hefir alla menn þrælkat ok áþját, sem hann vill, á Norðmæri ok í Raumsdal. Munu þér inn sama kost fyrir hǫndum eiga, sem vér áttum, at verja fé yðvart ok frelsi ok kosta þar til allra þeira manna, er yðr er liðs at ván, ok vil ek bjóðask til með mínu liði móti þessum ofsa ok ójafnaði; en at ǫðrum kosti munu þér vilja taka upp þat ráð, sem Naumdælir gerðu, at ganga með sjálfvilja í ánauð ok gerask þrælar Haralds. þat þótti fǫður mínum vegr, at deyja í konungdómi með sæmð, heldr en gerask undirmaðr annars konungs á gamals aldri; hygg ek, at þér muni ok svá þykkja ok ǫðrum þeim, er nǫkkurir eru borði ok kappsmenn vilja vera."* Chap. 11 of Harald Fairhair's Saga contains a much less inflammatory, less ideological, and less sympathetic version of Sölvi Klofi's speech. Comparison of the two variants is revealing (synoptic table 9.2).

13. The distribution of epithets in Egil's Saga is interesting and instructive. Although the king is most often called King Harald (sixty-four times and used in almost every chapter where Harald is mentioned), he is referred to as Harald nineteen times, often in contexts that make

this feel curt and insulting. On two occasions, this occurs in skaldic poems by Kveld-Ulf's descendants (once in a poem of Skalla-Grim, quoted in chap. 27, and once in a poem of Egil's, quoted in chap. 59). Thrice he is called "Shaggy Harald," always in early chapters (3 and 6) and twice by Kveld-Ulf (the third occurrence is that of the authorial voice). In contrast, he is given his standard epithet, "Harald Fairhair" only five times, always in late chapters (22, 30, 50, 57, and 70), usually in historical retrospect of one sort or another.

14. Kveld-Ulf employs this epithet on this occasion and once more, when he observes that his predictions have been fulfilled (Egil's Saga 6): "'After that,' said Kveld-Ulf, 'things happened as I had anticipated and no one who fought against Shaggy Harald up north in Mæri traveled the victory-path.'" *"Eptir gekk þat," kvað Kveld-Úlfr, "er mér bauð hugr um, at þeir myndi engir sigrfǫr fara, er bǫrðusk við Harald lúfu norðr á Mæri."*

15. Egil's Saga 3: *"en hitt ætla ek mér allóskylt, at fara norðr á Mæri ok berjask þar ok verja land þeira. . . . Kveld-Úlfr mun heima sitja um þetta herhlaup, ok hann mun eigi herliði safna ok eigi gera sína þá heimanferð at berjask móti Haraldi lúfu, því at ek hygg, at hann hafi þar byrði gnóga hamingju, er konungr várr hafi eigi krepping fullan."*

16. "Tale of Harald Fairhair" 1 (Flateyjarbók 1.567): *At lidnum tiu uetrum alldrs Haralldz Halfdanarsonar er kalldr uar Dofrafostri tok hann konungdom yfir Hringariki Uestfolld Uingulmork ok Raumarike* (emphasis added).

17. Cf. "Tale of Hálfdan the Black" 7 (Flateyjarbók 1.566–67).

18. "Tale of Harald Fairhair" 1 (Flateyjarbók 1.567).

19. In stanza 4 of the Haraldskvæði of Thorbjorn Hornklofi, Harald is called *syni Hálfdanar*, just as he is called *filius Halfdan nigri* in Theodricus Monachus, Historia de Antiquitate Regum Norwagiensium, 1 or *sonr Hálfdanar svarta* in Egil's Saga, but the patronym *Hálfdánarson* is lacking in all texts of whatever age, save the two discussed here ("Tale of Harald Fairhair" 1 and Barð's Saga 1).

20. Barð's Saga 1: *En litlu síðar kom þar Haraldr Hálfdánarson ok fæddist þar upp með Dofra jötun. Efldi Dofri hann síðan til konungs yfir Noregi eptir því sem segir í sögu Haralds konungs Dofrafostra.*

21. These include "Tale of Orm Storolfsson" 1 (Flateyjarbók 1.521); "Tale of Hálfdan the Black" 6 (Flateyjarbók 1.565); "Tale of Harald Fairhair" 2 (Flateyjarbók 1.569); Kjalnesinga Saga 12–15; Barð's Saga 1; and Flóamanna Saga 1. Particularly interesting is Vatnsdæla Saga 7, where the D manuscript speaks of "Harald, who was called 'Shaggy'" (*Haraldr, er var kallaðar lúfa*), where the A and B manuscripts have "Harald, who was called 'Dofri's Foster Son' or 'Shaggy'" (*Haraldr, er var kallaðar Dofrafóstri eða lúfa*). For discussion of these sources, their dating and significance, see Jónsson, "Sagnet om Harald hårfagre som 'Dovrefostre.'"

22. Flóamanna Saga 1: *Son Hálfdanar svarta ok Ragnhildar var Haraldr er fyrst var kallaður Dofrafóstri, en þá Haraldr lúfa, en síðast Haraldr hinn hárfagri.*

23. The epithet *hárfagr* occurs in the first verse of the Haraldskvæði of Thorbjorn Hornklofi. "Shaggy" (*lúfa*) appears in a formulaic phrase used by two different authors, occuring in Haraldskvæði 10 and stanza 4 of an untitled poem about Harald written by Thjóðolf of Hvin ("Et digt om Harald hårfagre," in Jónsson, ed., *Den Norsk-Islandske Skjaldedigtning* 1.21).

24. Harald Fairhair's Saga 4: *ok því skýt ek til guðs, þess er mik skóp ok ǫllu ræðr.* Cf. the other variants listed in synoptic table 6.1: Fagrskinna 3; Fagrskinna Appendix 3 (from the A-Text); Egil's Saga 3; Greater Saga of Olaf Tryggvason 2 (Flateyjarbók 1.40); and "Tale of Harald Fairhair" 3 (Flateyjarbók 1.569).

25. Harald Fairhair's Saga 4: *aldri skal skera hár mitt né kemba, fyrr en ek hefi eignazk allan Nóreg.*

26. Fagrskinna 3: *svá vítt sem Nóregr er austr til marka ok norðr til hafs.*

27. "Tale of Hálfdan the Black" (Flateyjarbók 1.566): *þu latir huorke skera hár þitt ne negl* (emphasis added).

28. Harald Fairhair's Saga 4: *fyrr en ek hefi eignazk allan Nóreg með skǫttum ok skyldum ok forráði.*

29. Greater Saga of Olaf Tryggvason 2 (Flateyjarbók 1.40).

30. "Tale of Harald Fairhair" 3 (Flateyjarbók 1.569): "For that reason, he was then called 'Shaggy Harald'" (*þui uar hann þa kalladr Haralldr lufa*). Cf. Egil's Saga 3.2.

31. The patronym occurs in "Tale of Harald Fairhair" 1 (Flateyjarbók 1.567).

32. Harald Fairhair's Saga 23: "Earl Rögnvald cut his hair, which had previously been uncut and uncombed for ten years. At that time, they called him 'Shaggy Harald,' but thereafter Rögnvald gave a nickname to him and called him 'Harald the Fairhair.'" *þá skar Rǫgnvaldr jarl hár hans, en áðr hafði verit óskorit ok ókembt x. vetr. þá kǫlluðu þeir hann Harald lúfu, en síðan gaf Rǫgnvaldr honum kenningarnafn ok kallaði hann Harald inn hárfagra.*

33. Fagrskinna 3.: *Haralds hár var sítt ok flókit, fyrir þá sǫk var hann Lúfa kallaðr.* The same wording is found in Flateyjarbók 1.464.

34. For a variety of interpretive options, see E. R. Leach, "Magical Hair," *Journal of the Royal Anthropological Institute* 88 (1958): 147–64; J. M. Wallace-Hadrill, *The Long-Haired Kings, and Other Studies in Frankish History* (London: Methuen, 1962); and Dean Miller, "On the Mythology of Indo-European Heroic Hair," *Journal of Indo-European Studies* 26 (1998): 41–60.

35. Obviously, a good haircut is not the sole demand society makes and enforces. Submission to tonsorial standards is necessary but not sufficient to maintain one's status as a member in good standing. No society makes absolutely uniform tonsorial demands on all its members, and there is usually some latitude—perhaps also some debate—about what falls within the bounds of the acceptable.

36. Cristiano Grottanelli, The Enemy King Is a Monster: A Biblical Equation," *Studi Storico-Religiosi* 3 (1979): 5–36, reprinted in Grottanelli, *Kings and Prophets*, 47–72.

37. Sahlins, *Islands of History*, esp. 73–103; idem, "The Stranger-King Or Elementary Forms of the Political Life," *Indonesia and the Malay World* 36 (2008): 177–99; idem, "The Alterity of Power and Vice Versa, with Reflections on Stranger Kings and the Real-Politics of the Marvellous," in *History: From Medieval Ireland to the Post-modern World*, ed. Anthony McElligott, Liam Chambers, Clara Breathnach, and Catherine Lawless (Dublin: Irish Academic Press, 2011), 63–101.

38. Max Gluckman, "Rituals of Rebellion in South and South-East Africa," in *Order and Rebellion in Tribal Africa* (New York: Free Press of Glencoe, 1963), 110–36; Bruce Lincoln, "Ritual, Rebellion, Resistance: Rethinking the Swazi Ncwala," in *Discourse and the Construction of Society* (New York: Oxford University Press, 1989), 53–74.

39. Fagrskinna 3: *Hér eptir siðaðisk landit, guldusk skattar et øfra sem et ýtrsa. Nú er hann orðinn fullgǫrr maðr um afl, vǫxt ok ráðagerð. Hár hans var sítt ok flókit; fyrir þá sǫk var hann lúfa kallaðr. þá skar Rǫgnvaldr jarl á Møri hár hans ok gaf hónum nafn ok kallaði Harald enn hárfagra. þá var hann meirr en tvítøgr at aldri. Hann átti margt barna, ok af hans ætt eru komnir allir Nóregskonungar. þat var tíu vetr, er hann barðisk til lands áðr en hann yrði einvaldskonungr at <Nóregi>. Hann friðaði vel land sitt <ok siðaði>.* Only one other Norwegian work in prose

mentions the term "Shaggy." This is Ágrip 1, which introduces the term only to discard it, with no mention of the deeds Harald accomplished when this was his epithet.

He was then called "Shaggy Harald," because the man was then not fair-haired. But thereafter, he changed his name and was called Harald Fairhair, because he was the most handsome and best haired of men.

var hann þá kallaðr [Haral]dr lúfa, því at maðrinn var þá eigi [hárfa]gr. En síðan b[rey]ttisk nafn hans ok var kallaðr Haraldr h[á]rfagri, því at manna va[r hann listuligastr ok hærðr bezt.

40. Most beautiful, poignant, and perfect of all are Walter Benjamin's theses "On the Concept of History," in *Selected Writings*, vol. 4, *1938–1940*, ed. Howard Eiland and Michael W. Jennings (Cambridge, MA: Belknap Press of Harvard University Press, 2003), 389–400. Especially relevant are theses 3, 4, 6, 7, and 14.

Chapter Ten

1. Cf. synoptic table 7.3. The texts in question are Fagrskinna 3; Fagrskinna Appendix 3 (from the A-Text); Harald Fairhair's Saga 4; Egil's Saga 3; Greater Saga of Olaf Tryggvason 2 (Flateyjarbók 1.40); and "Tale of Harald Fairhair" 3 (Flateyjarbók 1.569). The only exception is "Tale of Hálfdan the Black" 6 (Flateyjarbók 1.566), which does not credit Harald with having said or sworn anything, only as acting on instructions he received from Dofri the Giant.

2. On the ritual performance of *heitstrenging*, see de Vries, *Altgermanische Religionsgeschichte* 1: 457 and 504–5. The collocation of verb plus noun indicates the act through which a solemn vow (*heit*) is bound or made fast (*strengja*). For references and fuller discussion, see Cleasby and Vigfusson, *Icelandic-English Dictionary*, 252, 253, and 598. De Vries does not take note of oaths sworn at weddings, as evidenced in Hœnsa-Thóris Saga 12.

3. See, for instance, the descriptions of the succession of Harald Gormsson to the Danish throne after the death of Gorm the Old, as recounted in Jómsvikinga Saga 5 and Jómsvíkinga þáttr 9 (Fláteyjarbók 1.106).

4. Most extensively, see Ottar Grønvik, *The Words for "Heir," "Inheritance" and "Funeral Feast" in Early Germanic* (Oslo: Universitetsforlaget, 1982); along with Cleasby and Vigfusson, *Icelandic-English Dictionary*, 133. For the English *arval* (also attested in the forms *arvall, arvell,* and *arvill*), see *The Oxford English Dictionary* (Oxford: Oxford University Press, 1971), 476. Cognates also exist in Old Danish *arveöl* and Old Swedish *arföl*.

5. Ynglingasaga 36:

Ingjald, King Önund's son, was king at Uppsala. The Uppsala kings were the highest kings in Sweden when there were many district kings, ever since Óðinn was chief in Sweden. Those who had their seat at Uppsala were sole rulers over all the empire of the Swedes until Agni died, when the realm first came to be divided as an inheritance among brothers, as has previously been written. Thereafter, the realm and the kingdom have been dispersed within families.

Ingjaldr, sonr Qnundar konungs, var konungr at Upsqlum. Upsala-konungar váru œztir konunga í Svíþjóð, þá er þar váru margir heraðskonungar, frá því er Óðinn var hǫfðingi í Svíþjóð; váru einvaldzhǫfðingjar þeir, er at Upsqlum sátu, um alt Svíaveldi, til þess er

Agni dó, en þá kom ríkit fyrst í brœðraskipti, svá sem fyrr er ritit, en síðan dreifðisk ríki ok konungdómr í ættir.

6. Ynglingasaga 36: *þat var siðvenja í þann tíma, þar er erfi skyldi gera eptir konunga eða jarla, þá skyldi sá, er gerði ok til arfs skyldi leiða, sitja á skǫrinni fyrir hásætinu alt þar til er inn væri borit full, þat er kallat var Bragafull; skyldi sá þá standa upp í móti Bragafulli ok strengja heit, drekka af fullit síðan; síðan skyldi hann leiða í hásæti, þat sem átti faðir hans; var hann þá kominn til arfs allz eptir hann.*

7. As its name suggests, the Bragafull is a strongly marked ritual implement. Thus, Old Norse *full* does not denote a simple cup, but a goblet filled with drink and raised for a toast in ceremonial contexts, i.e., the conjunction of a marked vessel, marked drink, and marked act of speech. In compounds, the term almost always appears alongside the name of the god (in the genitive case) to whom a ritual toast is directed, e.g., *Óðins-full, Njarðar-full, Freys-full*, the goblets drunk in honor of Óðinn, Njörð, and Frey, respectively (Cleasby and Vigfusson, *Icelandic-English Dictionary*, 177). The sole exception is the word that concerns us: *Braga-full* (or *Bragar-full*, as it appears in some manuscripts), where the first element is formed from the masculine adjective *bragr* "the best, foremost," thus: "the toast-drink devoted to the best," presumably the king or, better yet, the line of kings to whom the prince pledges his troth before taking his place among them (Cleasby and Vigfusson, *Icelandic-English Dictionary*, 75–76). On the ritual nature of this vessel and its use in oath-swearing ceremonies, see Klaus Düwel, *Das Opferfest von Lade* (Vienna: Karl M. Halosar, 1985), 84–89.

8. Cf., above all, Jómsvíkinga Saga 26, where King Sveinn explains: "I know that men perform oath-swearings at such feasts for the sake of their fame" (*Konungr mælti: 'þat veit ek menn gøra at veizlum slíkum at hafa fram heitstrengingar til ágætis sér*). Hœnsa-Thóris Saga 12 is also relevant.

9. Stanzas from the Ynglingatal are quoted in most later chapters (twenty-eight of forty) of the Ynglingasaga. Heimskringla's Prologue describes the nature and importance of this text as a source for historical writing.

> Thjodolf the Wise, of Hvin, was a skald of Harald the Hairfair. He also composed the poem about King Rögnvald the Highly Honored that is called Ynglingatal. . . . The biography of the Ynglings was first written according to Thjodolf's tale, and therewith was augmented according to the tales of wise men.

> *þjóðólfr inn fróði ór Hvini var skáld Haraldz ins hárfagra; hann orti ok um Rǫgnvald konung heiðumhæra kvæði þat, er kallat er Ynglingatal. . . . Eptir þjóðólfs sǫgn er fyrst ritin æfi Ynglinga ok þar við aukit eptir sǫgn fróðra manna.*

10. Ynglingatal actually ends with the reign of Rögnvald the Highly Honored (*Rǫgnvaldr heiðumhæri*), Thjodólf's patron at the time the poem was written, from whom Hálfdan the Black apparently usurped the throne. Heimskringla is at pains to normalize Hálfdan's accession and to suture him onto the Yngling line, but it leaves clear clues of what actually happened. See further the critical discussion of Joan Turville-Petre, "The Genealogist and History."

11. Much has been written on the ways Ynglingasaga expanded on Ynglingatal. See, inter alia, Beyschlag, *Die Konungasögur*, 21–111; Joan Turville-Petre, "On Ynglingatal," *Medieval Scandinavia* 10 (1978–79): 48–67; Marlene Ciklamini, "Ynglingasaga: Its Function and Its Appeal," *Medieval Scandinavia* 8 (1975): 86–99; and Jon Gunnar Jørgensen, "Ynglinga saga mellom

fornaldersaga og kongesaga," in *Fornaldarsagaerne: Myter og virkelighed; Studier i de oldislandske fornaldarsögur Norðurlanda*, ed. Agneta Ney, Ármann Jakobsson, and Annette Lassen (Copenhagen: Museum Tusculanums Forlag, 2009), 49–59. Heimskringla attributes Ynglingatal's composition to Thjoðólf of Hvín, which would place it in the latter half of the ninth century, and this has generally been accepted, following the analysis of Walter Åkerlund, *Studier över Ynglingatal* (Lund: H. Ohlsson, 1939). This was challenged, however, by Krag, *Ynglingatal og Ynglingasaga*, who saw the poem as an archaizing composition of the twelfth century whose actual date of composition was revealed by kennings that showed knowledge of the four-element theory (earth, air, fire, water) that entered Scandinavia only after conversion. Krag's argument has been much discussed (for an English summary, see McTurk, "Scandinavian Sacral Kingship Revisited," 25–27), and its weaknesses have been pointed out, inter alia, by Bjarne Fidjestøl, review of *Ynglingatal og Ynglingasaga, Maal og Minne*, 1994, 191–99; Jørn Sandnes, review of *Ynglingatal og Ynglingasaga, Historisk Tidsskrift* 73 (1994): 229–31; Preben Meulengracht Sørensen, "The Sea, The Flame, and the Wind," 223–25; Olof Sundqvist, "Aspects of Rulership Ideology," 87–93; and Dagfinn Skre, "The Dating of Ynglingatal," in *Kaupang in Skiringssal*, ed. Dagfinn Skre (Oslo: Museum of Cultural History, 2007), 407–29. The ninth-century date thus remains reasonably certain.

12. Manuscripts vary on this word. Jónsson, ed., *Den Norsk-Islandske Skjaldedigtning* 1: 13 prefers *siallgætastr* ("most unusual"), but *sangeyrvazir* and *sangerazir* ("most fitting") are also attested, and it is this sense that informs Heimskringla in its depiction of popular attitudes toward Ingjald.

13. Thjoðólf of Hvín, Ynglingatal 27–28:

> *Ok Ingjald*
> *ifjǫrvan trað*
> *reyks rǫsuðr*
> *á Ræningi,*
> *þás er húsþjófr*
> *hyrjar leistum*
> *goðkynning*
> *í gǫgnum sté.*
> *Ok sá urðr*
> *allri þjóðu*
> *sanngǫrvastr*
> *með Svíum þótti,*
> *es hann sjalfr*
> *sínu fjǫrvi*
> *frœknu fyrstr*
> *of fara skyldi.*

14. Historia Norwegiæ 9 reads as follows: "After that, his son Ingjald, who was fearful beyond measure, was elevated to king. At that time, Ívar Widefathomer was causing fear to many. He burned that one (Ingjald) in his banquet hall, together with all his retinue." *Post istum filius suus Ingialdr in regem sublimatur, qui ultra modum timens. Ivarum cognomine withfadm regem tunc temporis multis formidabilem se ipsum cum omni comitatu suo cenaculo inclusos igne cremavit.* Note that Ívar Widefathomer is depicted as Ingjald's conqueror, not his successor. He comes from a different lineage, and the text goes on to follow Ingjald's line, not Ívar's.

15. Ynglingasaga 34: *annan dag eptir lét Svipdagr taka hjarta ór vargi ok steikja á teini, ok gaf síðan Ingjaldi konungssyni at eta, ok þaðan af varð hann allra manna grimmastr ok verst skaplundaðr.* For other examples of men being turned fierce by eating significant parts of wild animals, see Hrólf Kraki's Saga 20 and 23.

16. Ynglingasaga 36: *En þá er Ingjaldr tók ríkit ok konungdóm, váru margir heraðskonungar, sem fyrr er ritit. Ingjaldr konungr lét búa veizlu mikla at Upsǫlum ok ætlaði at erfa Ǫnund konung, fǫður sinn; hann lét búa sal einn, engum mun minna eða óvegligra, en Upsalr var, er hann kallaði vii.-konungasal; þar váru í gǫr hásæti. Ingjaldr konungr sendi menn um alla Svíþjóð ok bauð til sín konungum ok jǫrlum ok ǫðrum merkismǫnnum; til þess erfis kom Algautr konungr, mágr Ingjaldz, ok Yngvarr konungr af Fjaðryndalandi ok synir hans tveir, Agnarr ok Álfr, Sporsnjallr konungr af Næríki, Sigverkr konungr af Áttundalandi; Granmarr konungr af Suðrmannalandi var eigi kominn. þar var vi. konungum skipat í inn nýja sal; var þá eitt hásæti autt, þat er Ingjaldr konungr hafði búa látit. Ǫllu liði því, er til var komit, var skipat í inn nýja sal. Ingjaldr konungr hafði skipat hirð sinni ok Ǫllu liði sínu í Upsal.*

17. Ibid.: *Nú var svá hér gǫrt, at þá er Bragafull kom inn, stóð upp Ingjaldr konungr ok tók við einu miklu dýrshorni; strengði hann þá heit, at hann skyldi auka ríki sitt hálfu í hverja hǫfuðátt eða deyja ella, drakk af síðan af horninu. Ok er menn váru druknir um kveldit, þá mælti Ingjaldr konungr til Fólkviðar ok Hulviðar, sona Svipdags, at þeir skyldu vápnask ok lið þeira, sem ætlat var, um kveldit; þeir gengu út ok til ins nýja sals, báru þar eld at, ok því næst tók salrinn at loga, ok brunnu þar inni vi. konungar ok lið þeira alt, ok þeir, er út leituðu, þá váru skjótt drepnir; eptir þetta lagði Ingjaldr konungr undir sik ǫll þessi ríki, er konungar hǫfðu átt, ok tók skatta af.*

18. The account of Ynglingasaga 38, is carefully crafted to show Granmar as more committed to the truce than Ingjald, and to foreshadow the latter's betrayal.

> Now, when things had gone thus for a long while, friends of both kings brought it about that they reconciled. The kings arranged a meeting with each other, met and made peace among themselves: King Ingjald, King Granmar, and King Hjörvard, Granmar's son-in-law. And the peace should hold among them as long as the three kings lived. This was bound by oaths and pledges. The following spring, King Granmar went to Uppsala to sacrifice, as was the custom toward summer, so that there would be peace. But divination showed that he had not long to live, and he went home to his realm.

> *Nú er langar hríðir hafði þannug fram farit, kómu vinir beggja því við, at þeir sættusk, ok lǫgðu konungar stefnu með sér ok hittusk ok gerðu frið millum sín, Ingjaldr konungr ok Granmarr konungr ok Hjǫrvarðr konungr, mágr hans; skyldi friðr sá standa millum þeira, meðan þeir lifði iii. Konungar; var þat bundit eiðum ok tryggðum. Eptir um várit fór Granmarr konungr til Upsala at blóta, sem siðvenja var til, móti sumri, at friðr væri; fell honum þá svá spánn, sem hann myndi eigi lengi lifa; fór hann þá heim í ríki sitt.*

19. Ynglingasaga 39.

20. Ibid.: *þat er sǫgn manna, at Ingjaldr konungr dræpi xii. konungra ok sviki alla í griðum; hann var kallaðr Ingjaldr inn illráði; hann var konungr yfir mestum hlut Svíþjóðar.*

21. Ynglingasaga 40: *þau gerðu fólk alt dauðadrukkit, síðan létu þau leggja eld í hǫllina; brann þar hǫllin ok alt fólk, þat er inni var, með Ingjaldi konungi.*

22. Ynglingasaga 41:

> Ívar Widefathomer subdued all of Sweden. He also possessed all of Denmark , a large portion of Saxony, all of eastern Europe, and a fifth part of England. Thereafter, the

Danish kings and the Swedish kings—those who have sole [i.e., monarchic] power—
came from his family. After Ingjald the Wicked, the domain of Uppsala was lost to the
Yngling line, as far as one can trace the dynasty.

*Ívarr viðfaðmi lagði undir sik alt Svíaveldi; hann eignaðisk ok alt Danaveldi ok mikinn
hlut Saxlandz ok alt Austríki ok inn v. hlut Englandz. Af hans ætt eru síðan komnir Da-
nakonungar ok Svíakonungar, þeir er þar hafa einvald haft. Eptir Ingjald illráða hvarf
Upsala-veldi ór ætt Ynglinga þat er langfeðgum mætti telja.*

23. Ynglingasaga 42: *þvíat allr múgr Svía hljóp upp með einu samþykki at rækja ætt Ingjaldz
konungs.*

24. Cf. Historia Norwegiæ 9.32 and "Af Upplendinga Konungum" 1 (from Hauksbók).

25. Historia Norwegiæ 9.30–31: *Post istum filius suus Ingialdr in regem sublimatur. Qui ultra modum timens Iuarum cognomine Withfadm, regem tunc temporis multis formidabilem, se
ipsum cum omni comitatu suo cenaculo inclusos igne cremauit.* The variant of Hervarar Saga 15
is similar:

> Ívar Widefathomer invaded Sweden with his army, as in told in the Kings' Saga. King
> Ingjald the Wicked dreaded his army and burned himself, with all his retinue, in the
> town that is called Rœning. Ívar Widefathomer placed all of Sweden under his rule.

> *Ivarr inn viðfaðmi kom með her sinn i Sviaveldi, sem segir i konunga sogum, en Ingjaldr
> konungr inn illraði hraeddist her hans ok brenndi sik sjalfr inni með allri hirð sinni a þeim
> bæ, er a Raeningi heitir, Ivarr inn viðfaðmi lagði undir sik allt Sviaveldi.*

26. On the self-conscious founding of the Icelandic commonwealth as a society based on
law and opposed to kingship, see Magnus Olsen, "Með lǫgum skal land byggja," *Maal og Minne,*
1946, 75–88; Hastrup, *Culture and History in Medieval Iceland,* 7–13, 205–37; Byock, *Medieval
Iceland,* 51–76; and Tomasson, *Iceland: The First New Society.*

Chapter Eleven

1. Ari Thorgilsson, Íslendingabók Appendix I; Historia Norwegiæ 10; Fagrskinna 1; Ynglingasaga 48–49; Hálfdan the Black's Saga 1–2; "Tale of Hálfdan the Black" 1 (Flateyjarbók 1.562).
Joan Turville-Petre, "The Genealogist and History," has discussed some of the intricacies in
Heimskringla's handling of Hálfdan and the pains it takes to construe him as a legitimate heir
to the Yngling throne, but there is more to say.

2. Harald Fairhair's Saga 8; Egil's Saga 3; "Tale of Harald Fairhair" 6 (Flateyjarbók 1.571–72),
on which see Elisabeth Vestergaard, "A Note on Viking Age Inaugurations," in *Coronations:
Medieval and Early Modern Monarchic Ritual,* ed. János M. Bak (Berkeley: University of California Press, 1990), 121–22.

3. Haraldskvæði 10, which is quoted at Fagrskinna 3; Harald Fairhair's Saga 18; and "Tale of
Harald Fairhair" 7 (Flateyjarbók 1.574), with minor variations.

> *Leiddisk þá fyr Lúfu
> landi at halda
> hilmi inum halsdigra,
> holm lézk sér <at> skjaldi;
> slógusk und sessþiljur,*

> *es sárir vǫru,*
> *létu upp stjǫlu stúpa,*
> *stungu í kjǫl hǫfðum.*

The line *Leiddisk þá fyr Lúfu* appears to be formulaic, as it recurs in an untitled poem that is cited in "Tale of Harald Fairhair" 7 (Flateyjarbók 1.574). A fragment of skaldic verse quoted by Jónsson, ed., *Den Norsk-Islandske Skjaldedigtning* 1.21, shows that the story of how Harald changed his name from "Shaggy" to "Fairhair" as part of his consolidation of kingship already was part of the poetic tradition.

> Then was the prince
> called "Shaggy,"
> who of the people
> . . . grew.
> Well was he called
> with the title of King
> Harald Fairhair
> . . . thereafter.
>
> *þa var lofðungr*
> *lufa kallaðr*
> *er i fylkis*
> *l . . . cár oxv*
> *vallt var kallaðr*
> *með konongs nafne*
> *Haraldr harfagri*
> *. . . . . mir siðan.*

4. Ágrip 1: *[Var] hann þá einn tekinn til [konungs], var hann þá kallaðr [Haral]dr lúfa, því at maðrinn var þá eigi [hárfa]gr. En síðan b[rey]ttisk nafn hans ok var kallaðr Haraldr h[á]rfagri, því at manna va[r hann listuligastr ok hærðr bezt.* Both Theodricus Monachus, Historia de Antiquitate Regum Norwagiensium, 1; and Historia Norwegiæ 9 introduce Harald as "Fairhair" (*Haraldus pulchre-comatus* in the former, *Haraldus comatus* in the latter), but both scrupulously avoid any mention of his prior "Shaggy" incarnation.

5. Fagrskinna 3:

> King Harald swore a vow that he would not cut his hair until he had subdued [i.e., made tributary] all the inland valleys, as well as the outlying headlands as far as Norway goes east to the marches and north to the sea. After that, there were many battles for a long while.
>
> *þá strengir Haraldr konungr heit, at eigi skal skera hár hans áðr en hann hefir skatt af hverjum uppdal sem af útnesi, svá vítt sem Nóregr er austr til marka ok norðr til hafs. Hér eptir gørask orrostur margar langar hríðir.*

6. Fagrskinna Appendix 3 (from the A-Text):

> King Harald . . . swore a vow, swearing on his head that he would have no wife in Norway, save Ragna, and with this measure as well—that he would make all men in Norway his subjects.

Haraldr konungr . . . strengði hann þegar heit ok sór við hofuð sitt, at hann skyldi enga eigna konu eiga í Nóregi nema Rǫgnu ok þó með þeim hætti, at hann gørði alla menn at þegnum sér í Nóregi.

7. Thus, for instance, the speech of Sölvi Klofi cited in Egil's Saga 3 and Harald Fairhair's Saga 11, discussed above in chap. 9.

8. Fagrskinna Appendix 3 (from the A-Text): *hann gørði alla menn at **þegnum** sér í Nóregi* (emphasis added).

9. Theodricus Monachus, Historia de Antiquitate Regum Norwagiensium, prologue: *Domino et patri suo, viro reverendissimo Augustino Nidrosiensi archiepiscopo Theodricus humilis peccator debitæ servitutis subjectionem et orationum suffragia. Operæ pretium, duxi, vir illustrissime, pauca hæc de antiquitate regum Norwagiensium breviter annotare, et prout sagaciter perquirere potuimus ab eis, penes quos horum memoria præcipue vigere creditur, quos nos Islendinga vocamus, qui hæc in suis antiquis carminibus percelebrata recolunt. Et quia pæne nulla natio est tam rudis et inculta, quæ non aliqua monumenta suorum antecessorum ad posteros transmiserit, dignum putavi hæc, pauca licet, majorum nostrorum memoriæ posteritatis tradere. Sed quia constat nullam ratam regalis stemmatis successionem in hac terra extitisse ante Haraldi pulchre-comati tempora, ab ipso exordium fecimus.*

10. Similarly high praise for the historical reliability of Icelandic informants and of their poetic tradition is voiced by Saxo Grammaticus and Svend Aggesen in the prologues to their works on Danish history.

11. See Charlton T. Lewis and Charles Short, *A Latin Dictionary* (Oxford: Clarendon Press, 1962), 1535, on *re-colō;* Alfred Ernout and Antoine Meillet, *Dictionnaire etymologique de la langue latine* (Paris: Klincksieck, 1951), 236–38, on *colō.*

12. Theodricus Monachus, Historia de Antiquitate Regum Norwagiensium, 1: *Anno ab incarnatione Domini octingentesimo quinquagesimo octavo regnavit Haraldus pulchre-comatus, filius Halfdan nigri. Hic primum expulit omnes regulos et solus obtinuit regnum totius Norwagiæ annis septuaginta et defunctus est.*

13. Ibid.: *Hunc numerum annorum Domini, investigatum prout diligentissime potuimus ab illis, quos nos vulgato nomine Islendinga vocamus, in hoc loco posuimus: quos constat sine ulla dubitatione præ omnibus aquilonaribus populis in hujusmodi semper et peritiores et curiosiores extitisse. Sed quia valde difficile est in hujusce ad liquidum veritatem comprehendere, maxime ubi nulla opitulatur scriptorum auctoritas.*

14. Regarding the situation of Theodricus's patronage, the immediate context in which he wrote, and the ways in which he tried to connect Norwegian history to paradigms taken from classical, biblical, and continental sources, see further Sverre Bagge, "Theodricus Monachus," *Scandinavian Journal of History* 14 (1989): 113–33.

15. The poem, titled Snæfriðardrápa ("Praise-Poem on Snæfrið's Death") is cited at Flateyjarbók 1.582, where it is identified as King Harald's composition. It is also found in Jónsson, *Den Norsk-Islandske Skjaldedigtning* 1.5. On the Snæfrið narrative, see Moe, *Eventyrlige sagn i den ældre historie*, 632–56; Ólafur Halldórsson, "Snjófriðar drápa," in *Afmælisrit Jóns Helgasonar*, ed. Jakob Benediktsson et al. (Reykjavík: Heimskringla, 1969), 217–30; Else Mundal, "Kong Harald hårfagre og samejenta Snøfrid: Samefolket sin plass i den norske riksamlinsmyten," *Nordica Bergensia* 14 (1997): 39–53; and Rudolf Simek, "Lust, Sex and Domination: *Skírnismál* and the Foundation of the Norwegian Kingdom," in *Sagnaheimur: Studies in Honouur of Hermann Pálsson*, ed. Ásdis Egilsdóttir and Rudolf Simek (Vienna: Fassbaender, 2001), 229–46.

16. The incident is recounted at Ágrip 3–4; Heimskringla 25; and Flateyjarbók 1.582–83. All

lines descending from Harald Fairhair via his other wives having been exhausted, the line of his sons by Snæfrið, which had previously been excluded from the kingship, put Harald Hard-Ruler (*Haraldr Hardráðr*) on the throne in 1045. Alternatively, one might imagine this claim of descent was fabricated *ex post facto*. In either event, critics of the new king, whose epithet signals his reputation as a tyrant, could develop aspects of the Snæfrið story to turn opinion against him, forcing his supporters to respond with other variants still. This dynamic could also play out during the reign of any subsequent king, since all rulers thereafter traced their lineage to Harald Hard-Ruler and through him back to Harald Fairhair, but always via Snæfrið.

17. *Ágrip* 4: *Seig hón svá í ǫsku, en konungr steig til vizku ok hugði af heimsku, stýrði síðan ríki sínu ok styrkði; gladdisk hann af þegnum sínum, ok þegnar af hónum, en ríkit af hvǫru tveggja, ok sat at Nóregi einvaldskonungr sex tøgu vetra síðan.* Cf. Harald Fairhair's Saga 25, which follows Ágrip, and the less reassuring variant of Flateyjarbók 1.582–83.

18. Fagrskinna 2 cites the poetic evidence of Haraldskvæði 14–15 to take note of the fact that Harald kept jesters and jugglers (*leikurum ok trúðum*) as part of his royal retinue, something noted by no other source.

19. Fagrskinna Appendix 3 (from the A-Text).

20. Gustav Indrebø, *Fagrskinna* (Christiana [Oslo]: Avhandlinger fra Universitets historiske Seminar, 1917), 277–84; Bjarni Einarsson, ed., *Ágrip af Nóregskonunga Sǫgum: Fagrskinna— Nóregs Konunga Tal* (Rekjavík: Íslenzk Fornritafélag, 1984), cxxiii and cxxvii–cxxxi.

21. Hákon Hákonarson's Saga 329:

In his illness, King Hákon first had Latin books read to him. But then it seemed much trouble to him to ponder over how to interpret that [language]. Then he had Norse books read to him night and day, first the sagas of holy men. And when he finished with them, he had the Konungatal ["Catalogue of Kings"] read to him from Hálfdan the Black, and thereafter all the kings of Norway, one after the other.

Í sóttinni lét hann fyrst lesa sér Látinu-bækr. En þá þótti hónum sér mikil mœða í, at hugsa þar eptir hversu þat þýddi. Lét hann þá lesa fyrir sér Norænu-bækr, nætr ok daga; fyrst Heilagra-manna-sögur; ok er þær þraut, lét hann lesa sér Konungatal frá Hálfdani Svarta, ok síðan frá öllum Noregs-konungum, hverjum eptir annan.

Two pieces of evidence strongly suggest that Fagrskinna was the text in question. First, Fagrskinna opens with Hálfdan the Black, as described here. Second, according to its two surviving medieval manuscripts, the proper title of this text was *Nóregs Konungatal* ("Catalogue of Norway's Kings") or *Ættartal Noregskonunga* ("Catalogue of the Lineage of Norway's Kings"), closely matching what is said of King Hákon's text. The title Fagrskinna ("Fair Parchment") was given to it by Danish bibliographers of the seventeenth century, based on the good condition of the vellum on which their manuscript was written and to distinguish it from another one stored nearby that they dubbed *Morkinskinna* ("Rotten Parchment").

22. The argument, summarized by Finlay, *Fagrskinna*, 1–2, runs as follows: (1) King Sverri (r. 1184–1202), Hákon's grandfather, arranged for the saga that bears his name to be written under his close personal supervision, as is reported in the saga's first chapter, which states: "The beginning of this book is written following the book that Abbot Karl Jónsson first wrote and King Sverri himself sat over him and advised what he should write" (*er þat upphaf bókarinnar er ritat er eptir þeiri bók er fyrst ritaði Karl ábóti Jónsson, en yfir sat sjálfr Sverrir konungr, ok réð fyrir hvat rita skyldi*). (2) Fagrskinna ends its account in 1177, the year of Sverri's accession, and thus seems to have been designed as a complement to Sverri's Saga. (3) Fagrskinna was written

shortly after Hákon's accession in 1217, apparently with Sverri's Saga as a model. (4) It thus seems a reasonable inference that King Hákon selected an author and gave clear instructions to him, patterning himself after Sverri.

23. The precise identity of the "Agnellus" to whom the text is addressed has not been established, but the name itself ("Lamb") and the tone of the prologue make clear he was a worthy of the church, who supervised its author's labors. The key sentence reads: "However much others, having read my writing, may declare it unpolished with rhetorical charm and further, caught up in rough barbarisms, do you, Agnellus, who have rightly been set over me as my instructor, accept it with joy, as befits a friend." *Tu igitur, o Agnelle, iure didascalico mi prelate, utcumque alii ferant hec mea scripta legentes non rhetorico lepore polita, immo scrupulosis barbarismis implicita, gratanter, ut decet amicum, accipito.*

24. Historia Norwegiæ Prologue: *nichil a me de uetustatis serie nouum uel inauditum assumpserim, sed in omnibus seniorum asserciones secutus.*

25. de Vries, *Altnordisches etymologisches Wörterbuch*, 459 and 467.

26. Cleasby and Vigfusson, *Icelandic-English Dictionary*, 508.

27. Bruce Lincoln, *Theorizing Myth: Narrative, Ideology, and Scholarship* (Chicago: University of Chicago Press, 1999), 209.

28. Bonaparte's maxim is frequently misquoted, but what he is actually supposed to have said is *"Elle est impossible au moment même des évènements, dans la chaleur des passions, et si, plus tard, on trouve un accord, c'est que les intéressés et les contradicteurs ne sont plus. Qu'est alors la vérité historique ? Une fable convenue."* The passage is found in the Comte de Las Cases record of his conversations with Napoleon in his final exile, Emmanuel-Auguste-Dieudonné Marius Joseph de Las Cases, *Mémorial de Ste. Hélène*, republished under a variety of titles, usually without a date of publication being listed. Fittingly enough, the emperor was offering a variant of observations previously made by others, including Fontenelle and Voltaire. The latter, for instance, wrote in his *Jeannot et Colin*, *"Toutes les histoires anciennes, comme le disait un de nos beaux esprits, ne sont que des fables convenues."*

29. These are the closing words to Ford's classic western *The Man Who Shot Liberty Valance* (1962).

Coda

1. On the notion of a society against the state, see the classic work of Pierre Clastres, *Society against the State: The Leader As Servant and the Humane Uses of Power among the Indians of the Americas*, trans. Robert Hurley (New York: Urizen Books, 1977); and, more recently, James C. Scott, *The Art of Not Being Governed: An Anarchist History of Upland Southeast Asia* (New Haven, CT: Yale University Press, 2009).

2. Mikhail Bakhtin, *Rabelais and His World* (Bloomington: Indiana University Press, 1984).

3. Antonio Gramsci, *Prison Notebooks*, ed. and trans. Joseph A. Buttigieg and Antonio Callari (New York: Columbia University Press, 1992–).

4. Walter Benjamin, "On the Concept of History," in *Selected Writings*, ed. Michael W. Jennings (Cambridge, MA: Belknap Press of Harvard University Press, 1996–2003), 4: 389–400.

5. I think most immediately of Scott, *The Art of Not Being Governed*, but in truth all his books have been an inspiration, even when he mistakenly understands himself to be locked in debate with Gramsci: *Weapons of the Weak: Everyday Forms of Peasant Resistance* (New Haven, CT: Yale University Press, 1985); *Domination and the Arts of Resistance: Hidden Transcripts* (New

Haven, CT: Yale University Press, 1990); *Seeing like a State: How Certain Schemes to Improve the Human Condition Have Failed* (New Haven, CT: Yale University Press, 1998); *Two Cheers for Anarchism: Six Easy Pieces on Autonomy, Dignity, and Meaningful Work and Play* (Princeton, NJ: Princeton University Press, 2012). Also relevant is the classic work of Clastres, *Society against the State.*

Bibliography

Primary Sources

Ágrip: Bjarni Einarsson, ed. In *Ágrip af Nóregskonunga Sögum [ok] Fagrskinna—Nóregs Konunga Tal*, 3–54. Reykjavík: Íslenzka Fornritafélag, 1984.

———: M. J. Driscoll, ed. *Ágrip af Nóregskonungasǫgum*. London: Viking Society for Northern Research, 1995; 2d ed., 2008.

Ágrip af Sögu Danakonunga: Bjarni Guðnason, ed. In *Danakonunga Sögur*, 323–36. Reykjavík: Íslenzka Fornritafélag, 1982.

Barð's Saga: Jón Skaptason and Phillip Pulsiano, eds. and trans. *Bárðar Saga*. New York: Garland Publishing, 1984.

Eddic Poems: See Poetic Edda.

Egil's Saga: Sigurður Nordal, ed. *Egils Saga Skalla-Grímssonar*. Reykjavík: Íslenzka Fornritafélag, 1933.

Fagrskinna: Bjarni Einarsson, ed. In *Ágrip af Nóregskonunga Sögum [ok] Fagrskinna—Nóregs Konunga Tal*, 57–373. Reykjavík: Íslenzka Fornritafélag, 1984.

———: Alison Finlay, trans. *Fagrskinna, a Catalogue of the Kings of Norway: A Translation with Introduction and Notes*. Leiden: E. J. Brill, 2004.

———: Gustav Indrebø, ed. *Fagrskinna*. Christiana [Oslo]: Avhandlinger fra Universitets historiske Seminar, 1917.

Flateyjarbók: *Flateyjarbok: En Samling af Norske Konge-Sagaer med indkudte minre fortællinger om Begivenheder i og udenfor Norge*. 3 vols. Christiania (Oslo): P. T. Mallings Forlagsboghandel, 1860. Citations indicate volume and pages.

Flóamanna Saga: Finnur Jónsson, ed. *Flóamannasaga*. Copenhagen: Samfund til udgivelse af Gammel Nordisk Litteratur, 1932.

Frostathing Law: Rudolf Keyser, P. A. Munch, et al. *Norges Gamle Love indtil 1387*. 5 vols. Christiania (Oslo), 1846–95.

———: Laurence M. Larson, trans. *The Earliest Norwegian Laws: Being the Gulathing Law and the Frostathing Law*. New York: Columbia University Press, 1935.

Grágás: Vilhjalmar Finsen, ed. *Grágás, Islændernes Lovbog i Fristatens Tid*. 4 vols. Copenhagen: Brødrene Berlings, 1870.

———: Andres Dennis, Peter Foote, and Richard Perkins, trans. *Laws of Early Iceland: Grágás*. 2 vols. Winnipeg: University of Manitoba Press, 1980–2000.

Gregory of Tours. *History of the Franks*: Rudolf Buchner, ed. *Gregorii Episcopi Turonensis: Historiarum Libri Decem*. 2 vols. Darmstadt: Wissenschaftliche Buchgesellschaft, 1967.

Gulathing Law: Rudolf Keyser, P. A. Munch, et al., eds. *Norges Gamle Love indtil 1387*. 5 vols. Christiania (Oslo), 1846–95.

————: Laurence M. Larson, trans. *The Earliest Norwegian Laws: Being the Gulathing Law and the Frostathing Law*. New York: Columbia University Press, 1935.

Gylfaginning: Anthony Faulkes, ed. *Snorri Sturluson, Edda: Prologue and Gylfaginning*. Oxford: Clarendon Press, 1982.

Hákon Hákonarson's Saga: Gudbrand Vigfusson, ed. *Icelandic Sagas and Other Historical Documents Relating to the Settlements and Descents of the Northmen on the British Isles*. Vol. 2, *Hakonar Saga and a Fragment of Magnus Saga*. London: Eyre and Spottiswood, 1887.

Heimskringla: Finnur Jónsson, ed. *Snorri Sturluson, Heimskringla: Nóregs Konunga Sögur*. Copenhagen: G. E. C. Gads Forlag, 1911.

Historia Norwegiæ: In *Monumenta Historica Norvegiæ: Latinske Kildeskrifter til Norges Historie i Middelalderen*, edited by Gustav Storm, 69–124. Christiania (Oslo): A. W. Brøgger, 1880.

————: Inger Ekrem and Lars Boje Mortensen, eds. *Historia Norwegie*. Translated by Peter Fisher. Copenhagen: Museum Tusculanum Press, 2003.

Hœnsa-Thóris Saga: Andreas Heusler, ed. *Zwei Isländer-Geschichten*. Berlin: Weidmann, 1897.

Hungrvaka: In *Kristni saga, þáttr þorvalds ens viðfǫrla, þáttr Ísleifs biskups Gizurarsonar, Hungrvaka*, Altnordische Saga-Bibliothek, vol. 11, edited by Bernhard Kahle. Halle: Niemeyer, 1905.

Íslendingabók: Wolfgang Golther, ed. *Ares Isländerbuch*. Altnordische Saga-Bibliothek, vol. 1. Halle: Max Niemeyer, 1892.

Íslendinga Saga: In *Sturlunga Saga* , edited by Jón Jóhannesson, Magnús Finnbogason, and Kristján Eldjárn, 1: 229–534. Reykjavík: Sturlunguútgáfan, 1946.

Jómsvíkinga Saga: N. F. Blake, ed. and trans. *The Saga of the Jomsvikings*. London: Thomas Nelson and Sons, 1962.

Kjalnesinga Saga: Jóhannes Halldórsson, ed. *Kjalnesinga Saga*. Reykjavík: Íslenzka Fornritafélag, 1959.

Kristni Saga: In *Kristni saga, þáttr þorvalds ens viðfǫrla, þáttr Ísleifs biskups Gizurarsonar, Hungrvaka*, Altnordische Saga-Bibliothek, vol. 11, edited by Bernhard Kahle. Halle: Niemeyer, 1905.

Landnámabók: Det Kongelige Nordiske Oldskrift-Selskab, *Landnámabók I–III: Hauksbók, Sturlubók, Melabók*. Copenhagen: Thieles Bogtrykkeri, 1900.

————: Jakob Benediktsson, ed. *Skarðsárbók: Landnámabók*. Reykjavík: Háskóli Íslands, 1958.

Orkneyinga Saga: Alexander Taylor, ed. and trans. *The Orkneyinga Saga*. Edinburgh: Oliver and Boyd, 1938.

————: Finnbogi Guðmundsson, ed. *Orkneyinga Saga*. Íslenzk Fornrit, vol. 34. Reykjavík: Íslenzka Fornritafélag, 1965.

Paulus Diaconus. *History of the Langobards*: Wolfgang F. Schwarz, ed. and trans. *Paulus Diaconus, Geschichte der Langobarden*. Darmstadt: Wissenschaftliche Buchgesellschaft, 2009.

Poetic Edda: Gustav Neckel, ed. *Edda: Die Lieder des Codex Regius nebst verwandten Denkmälern*. 4th ed. Edited by Hans Kuhn. Heidelberg: Carl Winter, 1962.

————: Dronke, Ursula, ed. and trans. *The Poetic Edda*. Vol. 2, *Mythological Poems*. Oxford: Clarendon Press, 1997.

Saga of Ragnar Shaggy-Breeches: Magnus Olsen, ed. *Volsunga Saga ok Ragnars Saga Loðbrókar*. Copenhagen: S. L. Møller, 1906–8.

Saints' Sagas: C. R. Unger, ed. *Heilagra manna sögur: Fortællinger og legender om hellige mænd og kvinder; Efter gamle hanskrifter.* 2 vols. Christiana: B. M. Bentzen, 1877.

Saxo Grammaticus: Petrus Erasmus Müller, ed. *Saxonis Grammatici, Historica Danica.* Copenhagen: Gyldendal, 1839.

Skaldic poems: Finnur Jónsson, ed. *Den Norsk-Islandske Skjaldedigtning.* 3 vols. Copenhagen: Rosenkilde og Bagger, 1967.

Skáldskaparmál: Finnur Jónsson, ed. *Edda Snorra Sturlusonar.* Copenhagen: Gyldendalske Boghandel, 1931.

—————: Anthony Faulkes, ed. *Snorri Sturluson, Skáldskaprmál,* 2 vols. London: Viking Society for Northern Research, 1998.

Skjöldunga Saga: Bjarni Guðnason, ed. *Danakonunga Sögur.* Reykjavík: Íslenzka Fornritafélag, 1982.

Sturlungasaga: Jón Jóhannesson, Magnús Finnbogason, and Kristján Eldjárn, eds. *Sturlunga Saga.* 2 vols. Reykjavík: Sturlunguútgáfan, 1946.

Tacitus, *Germania*: Rudolf Much, ed. *Die Germania des Tacitus.* 3rd ed. Revised by Herbert Jankuhn and edited by Wolfgang Lange. Heidelberg: Carl Winter, 1967.

Tacitus, *Histories*: C. H. Moore, ed. and trans. *Tacitus.* Vols. 2 and 3. Cambridge, MA: Harvard University Press, 1925–31.

Theodricus Monachus, *Historia de Antiquitate Regum Norwagiensium*: In *Monumenta Historica Norvegiæ: Latinske Kildeskrifter til Norges Historie i Middelalderen,* edited by Gustav Storm, 1–68. Christiania (Oslo): A. W. Brøgger, 1880.

—————: David and Ian McDougall, trans. and annotations, *Theodoricus Monachus: Historia de Antiquitate Regum Norwagiensium: An Account of the Ancient History of the Norwetian Kings.* Introduction by Peter Foote. London: Viking Society for Northern Research, 1998.

Vatnsdæla Saga: Finnur Jónsson, ed. *Vatnsdælasaga.* Copenhagen: J. Jørgensen, 1934.

Ynglingatal: In *Den Norsk-Islandske Skjaldedigtning.* 3 vols. edited by Finnur Jónsson, 1: 7–15. Copenhagen: Rosenkilde og Bagger, 1967.

Secondary Literature

Aðalbjarnarson, Bjarni. 1937. *Om de Norske Kongers Sagaer.* Oslo: Det Norske Videnskaps Akademi.

Aðalsteinsson, Jón Hnéfill. 1990. "Gods and Giants in Old Norse Mythology." *Temenos* 26: 7–22.

Adler, Eve. 2003. *Vergil's Empire: Political Thought in the Aeneid.* Oxford: Rowman and Littlefield.

Africa, Thomas W. 1970. "The One-Eyed Man against Rome: An Essay in Euhemerism." *Historia* 19: 528–38.

Åkerlund, Walter. 1939. *Studier över Ynglingatal.* Lund: H. Ohlsson.

Andersson, Theodore M. 1985. "Kings' Sagas (*Konungasögur*)." In *Old Norse-Icelandic Literature: A Critical Guide,* edited by Carol Clover and John Lindow, 197–238. Ithaca, NY: Cornell University Press.

—————. 1994. "The Politics of Snorri Sturluson." *Journal of English and Germanic Philology* 93: 55–78.

—————. 1999. "The King of Iceland." *Speculum* 74: 923–34.

—————. 2008. "From Tradition to Literature in the Sagas." In *Oral Art Forms and Their Passage into Writing,* edited by Else Mundal and Jonas Wellendorf, 7–17. Copenhagen: Museum Tusculanum Press.

Argüelles, Alexander. 1994. "Viking Dreams. Mythological and Religious Dream Symbolism in the Old Norse Sagas." PhD diss., University of Chicago.

Baetke, Walter. 1964. *Yngvi und die Ynglinger: Eine quellenkritische Untersuchung über das nordische "Sakralkönigtum."* Berlin: Akademie Verlag.

———. 1973. "Christliches Lehngut in der Sagareligion." In *Kleine Schriften: Geschichte, Recht und Religion in germanischem Schriftum*, 319–50. Weimar: Hermann Böhlaus Nachfolger.

Bagge, Sverre. 1987. *The Political Thought of the King's Mirror*. Odense: Odense University Press.

———. 1989. "Theodricus Monachus." *Scandinavian Journal of History* 14: 113–33.

———. 1991. *Society and Politics in Snorri Sturluson's Heimskringla*. Berkeley: University of California Press.

———. 2005. "Christianization and State Formation in Early Medieval Norway." *Scandinavian Journal of History* 30: 107–34.

———. 2008. "Division and Unity in Medieval Norway." In *Franks, Northmen, and Slavs: Identities and State Formation in Early Medieval Europe*, edited by Ildar Garipzanov, Patrick Geary, and Przemyslaw Urbanczyk, 145–66. Turnhout, Belgium: Brepols.

———. 2010. *From Viking Stronghold to Christian Kingdom: State Formation in Norway, c. 900–1350*. Copenhagen: Museum Tusculanum Press.

Bakhtin, Mikhail. 1984. *Rabelais and His World*. Bloomington: Indiana University Press.

Bandle, Oskar. 1993. "Tradition und Fiktion in der Heimskringla." In *Snorri Sturluson: Kolloquium anläßlich der 750; Wiederkehr seines Todestages*, edited by Alois Wolf, 27–47. Tübingen: Gunter Narr Verlag.

Bateson, Gregory. 1958. *Naven: A Survey of the Problems Suggested by a Composite Picture of the Culture of a New Guinea Tribe Drawn from Three Points of View*. Stanford, CA: Stanford University Press.

Bauschatz, Paul. 1982. *The Well and the Tree: World and Time in Early Germanic Culture*. Amherst: University of Massachusetts Press.

Benediktsson, Jakob. 1954–57. "Icelandic Traditions of the Scyldings." *Saga-Book of the Viking Society* 15: 48–66.

———. 1955. "Hvar var Snorri nefndur höfundur Heimskringlu?" *Skírnir* 129: 118–27.

Benjamin, Walter. 2003. "On the Concept of History." In *Selected Writings*, vol. 4, *1938–1940*, edited by Howard Eiland and Michael W. Jennings, 389–400. Cambridge, MA: Belknap Press of Harvard University Press.

Benveniste, Émile. 1969. *Le vocabulaire des institutions indo-européennes*. Paris: Éditions de Minuit.

Berger, Alan J. 1980. "The Sagas of Harald Fairhair." *Scripta Islandica* 31: 14–29.

———. 1999. "Heimskringla and the Compilations." *Arkiv för Nordisk Filologi* 114: 5–15.

Berman, Melissa. 1982. "Egils saga and Heimskringla." *Scandinavian Studies* 54: 21–50.

Bessone, Luigi. 1972. *La rivolta batavica e la crisi del 69 d.C.* Turin: Accademia delle Scienze di Torino.

Beyschlag, Siegfried. 1950. *Die Konungasögur: Untersuchungen zur Königssaga bis Snorri*. Copenhagen: Einar Munksgaard.

Böldl, Klaus. 2009. "Königsmörder und Königsmacher: Samen in fundierenden Erzählungen des Mittelalters." In *Analecta Septentrionalia: Beiträge zur nordgermanischen Kultur- und Literaturgeschichte*, edited by Wilhelm Heizmann, Klaus Böldl, and Heinrich Beck, 125–50. Berlin: Walter de Gruyter.

Boulhosa, Patricia Pires. 2005. *Icelanders and the Kings of Norway; Mediaeval Sagas and Legal Texts.* Leiden: E. J. Brill.

Bourdieu, Pierre. 1998. *Practical Reason.* Stanford, CA: Stanford University Press.

Brink, Stefan. 2005. "*Verba Volant, scripta manent?* Aspects of Early Scandinavian Oral Society." In *Literacy in Medieval and Early Modern Scandinavian Culture,* edited by Pernille Hermann, 77–135. Odense: University Press of Southern Denmark.

Bruder, Reinhold. 1974. *Die germanische Frau im Lichte der Runeninschriften und der antiken Historiographie.* Berlin: de Gruyter.

Brunt, P. A. 1960. "Tacitus on the Batavian Revolt." *Latomus* 19: 494–517.

Bugge, Sophus. 1900. "Mytiske Sagn om Halvdan Svarte og Harald Haafagre." *Arkiv för Nordisk Filologi* 12: 1–37.

Byock, Jesse. 1982. *Feud in the Icelandic Saga.* Berkeley: University of California Press.

———. 1988. *Medieval Iceland.* Berkeley: University of California Press.

Chadwick, Nora. 1964. "Dreams in Early European Literature." In *Celtic Studies: Essays in Memory of Angus Matheson,* edited by James Carney and David Grene, 33–50. London: Routledge and Kegan Paul.

Chaney, William A. 1970. *The Cult of Kingship in Anglo-Saxon England.* Manchester: Manchester University Press.

Ciklamini, Marlene. 1962. "Óðinn and the Giants." *Neophilologus* 42: 145–58.

———. 1975. "Ynglingasaga: Its Function and Its Appeal." *Medieval Scandinavia* 8: 86–99.

———. 1978. *Snorri Sturluson.* Boston: Twayne.

Clastres, Pierre. 1977. *Society against the State: The Leader As Servant and the Humane Uses of Power among the Indians of the Americas.* Translated by Robert Hurley. New York: Urizen Books.

Cleasby, Richard, and Gudbrand Vigfusson. 1957. *An Icelandic-English Dictionary.* 2d ed. Oxford: Clarendon Press.

Coirault-Neuberger, Sylvie. 2007. *Le roi juif: Justice et raison d'état dans la Bible et le Talmud.* Paris: L'Harmattan.

Cunliffe, Marcus. 1962. "Parson Weems and George Washington's Cherry Tree." *Bulletin of the John Rylands Library* 45: 58–96.

Delcourt, Marie. 1963. "Le partage du corps royal." *Studi e Materiali di Storia delle Religioni* 34: 1–25.

Deliyannis, Deborah Mauskopf, ed. 2003. *Historiography in the Middle Ages.* Leiden: E. J. Brill.

Dick, Stefanie. 2006. *Der Mythos vom "germanischen" Königtum.* Berlin: Walter de Gruyter.

Dillmann, François-Xavier. 2000. "Pour l'étude des traditions relatives à l'enterrement du roi Halfdan le Noir." In *International Scandinavian and Medieval Studies in Memory of Gerd Wolfgang Weber,* edited by Michael Dallapiazza, 147–56. Trieste: Parnaso.

Dronke, Ursula. 1992. "Völuspá and Sibylline Traditions." In *Latin Culture and Medieval Germanic Europe,* edited by Richard North and Tette Hofstra, 3–23. Groningen: Egbert Forsten.

Düwel, Klaus. 1985. *Das Opferfest von Lade.* Vienna: Karl M. Halosar.

Ebel, Else. 1993. *Der Konkubinat nach altwestnordischen Quellen: Philologische Studien zur sogenannte "Friedelehe."* Berlin: de Gruyter.

Egilsson, Sveinbjörn. 1931. *Lexicon Poeticum Antiquæ Linguæ Septentrionalis: Ordbog over det Norsk-Islandske Skjaldesprog.* 2nd ed. with Finnur Jónsson. Copenhagen: S. L. Møller.

Einarsdóttir, Ólafia. 1971. "Harald Dovrefostre af Sogn." *Historisk Tidsskrift* 1: 131–66.

Einarsson, Stefán. 1957. *A History of Icelandic Literature.* Baltimore: Johns Hopkins University Press.

Ejerfeldt, Lennart. 1971. *Helighet, "karisma" och kungadöme i forngermansk religion.* Uppsala: Relgionshistoriska Institutionen i Uppsala.

Elias, Norbert. 1983. *The Court Society.* New York: Pantheon.

Ellehøj, Svend. 1965. *Studier over den Ældste Norrøne Historieskrivning.* Copenhagen: Einar Munksgaard.

Ellis, Hilda. 1941. "Fostering by Giants in Old Norse Saga Literature." *Medium Aevum* 10: 70–85.

Ernout, Alfred, and Antoine Meillet. 1951. *Dictionnaire etymologique de la langue latine.* Paris: Klincksieck.

Faulkes, Anthony. 1978–79. "Descent from the Gods." *Mediaeval Scandinavia* 11: 92–125.

Feist, Sigmund. 1939. *Vergleichendes Wörterbuch der Gotischen Sprache.* Leiden: E. J. Brill.

Fidjestøl, Bjarne. 1994. Review of *Ynglingatal og Ynglingasaga. Maal og Minne*, 1994, 191–99.

Frank, Roberta. 1984. "Viking Atrocity and Scaldic Verse: The Rite of the Blood-Eagle." *English Historical Review* 99: 332–43.

Frazer, James George. 1911. *The Golden Bough.* 3rd ed. 12 vols. London: Macmillan.

Friesen, Otto von. 1932–34. "Har det nordiska kungadomet sakralt ursprung?" *Saga och Sed*, pp. 15–34.

Fuglestad, Finn. 1979. "Earth-Priests, 'Priest-Chiefs,' and Sacred Kings in Ancient Norway, Iceland and West Africa: A Comparative Essay." *Scandinavian Journal of History* 4: 47–74.

Gallo, Lorenzo Lozzi. 2006. "The Giantess As Foster-Mother in Old Norse Literature." *Scandinavian Studies* 78: 1–20.

Geary, Patrick. 2003. *The Myth of Nations: The Medieval Origins of Europe.* Oxford: Oxford University Press.

Glauser, Jürg. 1998. "Vom Autor zum Kompilator: Snorri Sturlusons *Heimskringla* und die nachklassischen Sagas von Olav Tryggvason." In *Snorri Sturluson: Beiträge zu Werk und Rezeption*, edited by Hans Fix, 34–43. Berlin: de Gruyter.

Gluckman, Max. 1963. "Rituals of Rebellion in South and South-East Africa." In *Order and Rebellion in Tribal Africa*, 110–136. New York: Free Press of Glencoe.

Gramsci, Antonio. 1992–, *Prison Notebooks*, ed. and trans. Joseph A. Buttigieg and Antonio Callari. New York: Columbia University Press.

Grønbech, Vilhelm. 1931. *The Culture of the Teutons.* London: Oxford University Press.

Grønvik, Ottar. 1982. *The Words for "Heir," "Inheritance" and "Funeral Feast" in Early Germanic.* Oslo: Universitetsforlaget.

Grottanelli, Cristiano. 1979. The Enemy King Is a Monster: A Biblical Equation." *Studi Storico-Religiosi* 3: 5–36.

———. 1999. *Kings and Prophets: Monarchic Power, Inspired Leadership, and Sacred Text in Biblical Narrative.* New York: Oxford University Press.

Guðnason, Bjarni. 1963. *Um Skjöldungasögu.* Reykjavík: Menningarsjóðs.

Gunnes, Erik. 1974. "Rex iustus et iniustus." In *Kulturhistoriskt Lexikon för Nordisk Medeltid*, 14: 154–56. Malmö: Allhems förlag.

Gurevich, Aron. 1969. "Space and Time in the Weltmodell of the Old Scandinavian Peoples." *Mediaeval Scandinavia* 2: 42–53.

———. 1978. "The Early State in Norway." In *The Early State*, edited by Henri J. M. Claessen and Peter Skalník, 403–23. The Hague: Mouton.

———. 1985. *Categories of Medieval Culture.* London: Routledge and Kegan Paul.

———. 1992. *Historical Anthropology of the Middle Ages.* Chicago: University of Chicago Press.

Hallberg, Peter. 1962. *Snorri Sturluson och Egils saga Skallagrímssonar: Ett försök till språklig författarbestämning*. Reykjavík: Menningarsjóður.

———. 1973. "The Concept of *Gipta, Gæfa, Hamingja* in Old Norse Literature." In *Proceedings of the First International Saga Conference*, 143–83. London: Viking Society.

Halldórsson, Ólafur. 1969. "Snjófriðar drápa." In *Afmælisrit Jóns Helgasonar*, edited by Jakob Benediktsson et al., 217–30. Reykjavík: Heimskringla.

Haraldsdóttir, Kolbrún. 1991. "Hvenær var Egils saga rituð?" In *Yfir Íslandsála: Afmælisrit til heiðurs Magnúsi Stefánssyni sextugum*, edited by Gunnar Karlsson and Helgi Þorláksson, 131–45. Reykjavík: Sögufræðslusjóður.

———. 1998. "Der Historiker Snorri: Autor oder Kompilator?" In *Snorri Sturluson: Beiträge zu Werk und Rezeption*, edited by Hans Fix, 97–108. Berlin: Walter de Gruyter.

Hardie, Philip. 1986. *Virgil's Aeneid: Cosmos and Imperium*. Oxford: Clarendon Press.

Hastrup, Kirsten. 1985. *Culture and History in Medieval Iceland*. Oxford: Clarendon Press.

Helle, Knut. 1981. "Norway in the High Middle Ages." *Scandinavian Journal of History* 6: 161–89.

Hines, John. 1992. "Kingship in Egil's Saga." In *Introductory Essays on Egil's Saga and Njals Saga*, edited by John Hines and Desmond Slay, 15–32. London: Viking Society.

Hoffmann, Erich. 1975. *Die heiligen Könige bei den Angelsachsen und den skandinavischen Völkern*. Neumünster: Wachholtz.

Höfler, Otto. 1952. *Germanisches Sakralkönigtum*. Vol. 1, *Der Runenstein von Rök und die germanische Individualweihe*. Tübingen: Max Niemeyer.

———. 1959. "Der Sakralcharakter des germanischen Königtums." In *La Regalità Sacra: Contributi al tema del VIII Congresso Internazionale di Storia delle Religioni, Roma, Aprile 1955*, 664–701. Leiden: E. J. Brill.

Holmberg, Maj-Lis. 1976. "Om Finland och övriga finnländer i den isländska fornlitteraturen." *Arkiv för Nordisk Filologi* 91: 166–91.

Hosking, Geoffrey, and George Schöpflin, eds. 1997. *Myths and Nationhood*. New York: Routledge.

Ishida, Tomoro. 1977. *The Royal Dynasties in Ancient Israel: A Study on the Formation and Development of Royal-Dynastic Ideology*. Berlin: W. de Gruyter.

Jackson, Tatiana N. 1984. "On Snorri Sturluson's Creative Activity: The Problem of Writer Intrusion into the Narrative." *Arkiv för Nordisk Filologi* 99: 107–25.

Jakobsson, Ármann. 1997. *Í Leit að Konungi: Konungmynd Íslenskra Konungasagna*. Reykjavík: Háskólaútgáfan.

———. 1998. "History of the Trolls? Bárðar Saga As an Historical Narrative." *Saga-Book of the Viking Society* 25: 53–71.

———. 2005. "The Good, the Bad and the Ugly: Bárðar Saga and Its Giants." *Mediaeval Scandinavia* 15: 1–15.

———. 2006. "Where Do the Giants Live?" *Arkiv för Nordisk Filologi* 121: 101–12.

———. 2008. "A Contest of Cosmic Fathers: God and Giant in Vafþrúðnismál." *Neophilologus* 92: 263–77.

Jakobsson, Sverrir. 1997. "Myter om Harald Hårfagre." In *Sagas and the Norwegian Experience: Preprints for the 10th International Saga Conference*, 597–610. Trondheim: Center for Middelalderstudier.

———. 2002. "'Erindringen om en mægtig Personlighed': Den norsk-islandske historiske tradisjon om Harald Hårfagre i et kildekritisk perspective." *Historisk Tidsskrift* 81: 213–30.

Jochens, Jenny. 1987. "The Politics of Reproduction: Medieval Norwegian Kingship." *American History Review* 92: 327–49.

———. 1987. "The Female Inciter in the Kings' Sagas." *Arkiv för Norsk Filologi* 102: 100–119.

———. 1995. *Women in Old Norse Society.* Ithaca, NY: Cornell University Press.

Jones, Gwyn. 1984. *A History of the Vikings.* 2d ed. Oxford: Oxford University Press.

Jónsson, Finnur. 1899. "Sagnet om Harald hårfagre som 'Dovrefostre.'" *Arkiv för Nordisk Filologi* 11: 262–67.

———. 1924. "Snorri Sturluson i Norge." *Historisk Tidsskrift* 5: 116–22.

Jørgensen, Jon Gunnar. 1995. "Snorre Sturlesons fortale paa sin chronicke": Om kildene til opplysningen om *Heimskringlas* forfatter." *Gripla* 9: 45–62.

———. 2009. "Ynglinga saga mellom fornaldersaga og kongesaga." In *Fornaldarsagaerne: Myter og virkelighed; Studier i de oldislandske fornaldarsögur Norðurlanda*, edited by Agneta Ney, Ármann Jakobsson, and Annette Lassen, 49–59. Copenhagen: Museum Tusculanums Forlag.

Karlsson, Stefan. 1979. "Islandsk bogeksport til Norge i middelalderen." *Maal og Minne*, 1979, 1–17.

Karras, Ruth. 1990. "Concubinage and Slavery in the Viking Age." *Scandinavian Studies* 62: 141–62.

Kauffmann, Friedrich. 1902. *Balder: Mythus und Sage nach ihren dichterischen und religiösen Elementen untersucht.* Strassburg: Karl Trübner.

Kern, Fritz. 1956. "The Limitation of the Monarch by Law." In *Kingship and Law in the Middle Ages*, trans. S. B. Chrimes. Oxford: Basil Blackwell.

Kjartansson, Helgi Skúli. 2006. "English Models for King Harald Fairhair?" In *The Fantastic in Old Norse / Icelandic Literature: Sagas and the British Isles; Preprint Papers of the 13th International Saga Conference*, 359–64. Durham: Centre for Medieval and Renaissance Studies.

Knudsen, Gunnar, Marius Kristensen, and Rikard Hornby. 1936–40. *Danmarks Gamle Personnavne.* Copenhagen: G. E. C. Gad.

Koht, Halvdan. 1919. "Hadlands-Segnene i dei Norske Kongesogune." *Edda* 11: 85–94.

———. 1921. "Sagaenes opfatning av vår gamle historie." In *Innhogg og utsyn i Norsk Histori*, 76–91. Oslo: H. Aschehoug.

———. 1955. *Harald Hårfagre og Rikssamlinga.* Oslo: Aschehoug.

Krag, Claus. 1989. "Norge som odel i Harald Hårfagres ætt." *Historisk Tidsskrift* 68: 288–301.

———. 1991. *Ynglingatal og Ynglingasaga: En Studie i Historiske Kilder.* Oslo: Universitetsforlag.

———. 2003. "The Early Unification of Norway." In *The Cambridge History of Scandinavia*, vol. 1, *Prehistory to 1520*, edited by Knut Helle, 411–20. Cambridge: Cambridge University Press.

Kreutzer, Gert. 1994. "Das Bild Harald Schönhaars in der altisländischen Literatur." In *Studien zum Altgermanischen: Festschrift für Heinrich Beck*, edited by Heiko Uecker, 443–61. Berlin: Walter de Gruyter.

Kristensen, Rasmus Tranum. 2007. "Why Was Óðinn Killed by Fenrir? A Structural Analysis of Kinship Structures in Old Norse Myths of Creation and Eschatology." In *Reflections on Old Norse Myths*, edited by Pernille Hermann, Jens Peter Schjødt, and Rasmus Tranum Kristensen, 149–69. Turnhout, Belgium: Brepols.

Kristjánsson, Jónas. 1977. "Egilssaga og Konungasögur." In *Sjötíu Ritgerðir: Helgaðar Jakobi Benediktssyni*, edited by Einar Pétursson and Jónas Kristjánsson, 449–72. Reykjavík: Stofnun Árnamagnússonar.

———. 1988. *Eddas and Sagas*, trans. Peter Foote. Reykjavík: Hið íslenska bókmenntafélag.

Kroesen, Riti. 1996. "Ambiguity in the Relationaship between Heroes and Giants." *Arkiv för Nordisk Filologi* 111: 57–71.

Lange, Gudrun. 1989. *Die Anfänge der islandisch-norwegischen Geschichtsshreibung*. Reykjavík: Bókaútgáfa Menningarsjóðs.

Leach, E. R. 1958. "Magical Hair." *Journal of the Royal Anthropological Institute* 88: 147–64.

Lehman, Paul. 1936–37. *Skandinavens Anteil an der lateinischen Literatur und Wissenschaft des Mittelalters: Sitzungsberichte der Bayerischen Akademie der Wissenschaften, Philosophisch-historisch Abteilung*.

Lewis, Charlton T., and Charles Short. 1962. *A Latin Dictionary*. Oxford: Clarendon Press.

Lincoln, Bruce. 1981. *Priests, Warriors, and Cattle: A Study in the Ecology of Religions*. Berkeley: University of California Press.

———. 1986. *Myth, Cosmos, and Society*. Cambridge, MA: Harvard University Press.

———. 1989. "Ritual, Rebellion, Resistance: Rethinking the Swazi Ncwala." In *Discourse and the Construction of Society*, 53–74. New York: Oxford University Press.

———. 1994. *Authority: Construction and Corrosion*. Chicago: University of Chicago Press.

———. 1999. *Theorizing Myth: Narrative, Ideology, and Scholarship*. Chicago: University of Chicago Press.

———. 2001. "Intertextual Silence and Veiled Critique: Snorri on Harald Fairhair and Váli Höðr's-Slayer." In *Kontinuität und Brüche in der Religionsgeschichte: Festschrift for Anders Hultgård*, edited by Michael Stausberg, 485–91. Berlin: Walter de Gruyter.

———. 2003. "Hegelian Meditations on 'Indo-European' Myths." *Papers from the Mediterranean Ethnographic Summer Seminar* 5: 59–76.

———. 2006. "Kings, Cowpies, and Creation: Intertextual Traffic between 'History' and 'Myth' in the Writings of Snorri Sturluson." In *Old Norse Religion in Long-Term Perspectives: Origins, Changes, and Interactions*, edited by Anders Andrén, Kristina Jennbert, and Catharina Raudvere, 381–88. Lund: Nordic Academic Press.

Lindow, John. 1997. *Murder and Vengeance among the Gods: Baldr in Scandinavian Mythology*. Helsinki: Academia Scientiarum Fennica.

Linville, James Richard. 1998. *Israel in the Book of Kings: The Past As a Project of Social Identity*. Sheffield: Sheffield Academic Press.

Lönnroth, Lars. 1964. "Tesen om de två kulturerna: Kritiska studier i den isländska sagaskrivningens sociala forutsättningar." *Scripta Islandica* 15: 83–97.

———. 1965 *European Sources of Icelandic Saga-Writing: An Essay Based on Previous Studies*. Stockholm: Akademisk Avhandling.

———. 1969. "The Noble Heathen: A Theme in the Sagas." *Scandinavian Studies* 41: 1–29.

———. 1976. "Ideology and Structure in Heimskringla." *Parergon* 15: 16–29.

———. 1986. "Dómaldi's Death and the Myth of Sacral Kingship." In *Structure and Meaning in Old Norse Literature*, edited by John Lindow, Lars Lönnroth, and Gerd Wolfgang Weber, 73–93. Odense: Odense University Press.

Louis-Jensen, Jonna. 1997. "Heimskringla: Et værk af Snorri Sturluson?" *Nordica Bergensia* 14: 230–45.

Lukman, Niels. 1976. "Ragnarr loðbrók, Sigifrid, and the Saints of Flanders." *Mediæval Scandinavia* 9: 7–50.

Lunden, Kåre. 1995. "Was There a Norwegian National Identity in the Middle Ages?" *Scandinavian Journal of History* 20: 19–33.

————. 1997. "Overcoming Religious and Political Pluralism: Interactions between Conversion, State Formation and Change in Social Infrastructure in Norway, c. AD 950–1260." *Scandinavian Journal of History* 22: 83–97.

McCreesh, Bernadine. 2005. "Prophetic Dreams and Visions in the Sagas of the Early Icelandic Saints." In *Verbal Encounters: Anglo-Saxon and Old Norse Studies for Roberta Frank*, edited by Antonina Harbus and Russell Poole, 247–68. Toronto: University of Toronto Press.

McTurk, Rory. 1975–76. "Sacral Kingship in Ancient Scandinavia: A Review of Some Recent Writings." *Saga-Book of the Viking Society* 19: 139–69.

————. 1991. *Studies in Ragnars Saga Loðbrókar and Its Major Scandinavian Analogues*. Oxford: Society for the Study of Mediæval Languages and Literatures.

————. 1994–97. "Scandinavian Sacral Kingship Revisited." *Saga-Book of the Viking Society* 24: 19–32.

Meylan, Nicolas. 2010. "How to Deal with Kings When You Are a Suet-Lander: Discourses of "Magic" between Norway and Iceland." Ph.D. diss., University of Chicago.

Miller, Dean. 1998. "On the Mythology of Indo-European Heroic Hair." *Journal of Indo-European Studies* 26: 41–60.

Miller, William Ian. 1990. *Bloodtaking and Peacemaking: Feud, Law, and Society in Saga Iceland*. Chicago: University of Chicago Press.

Minnis, A. J. 1988. *Medieval Theories of Authorship*. Aldershot: Wildwood House.

Moe, Moltke. 1906. *Eventyrlige sagn i den ældre historie*. Christiania (Oslo): Det Mallingske bogtrykkeri.

Mortensen, Lars Boje. 2006. "Sanctified Beginnings and Mythopoietic Moments: The First Wave of Writing on the Past in Norway, Denmark, and Hungary." In *The Making of Christian Myths in the Periphery of Latin Christendom (c. 1000–1300)*, edited by Lars Boje Mortensen, 247–73. Copenhagen: Museum Tusculanum Press.

Motz, Lotte. 1984. "Gods and Demons of the Wilderness: A Study in Norse Tradition." *Arkiv för Nordisk Filologi* 99: 175–87.

————. 1996. "Kingship and the Giants." *Arkiv för Nordisk Filologi* 111: 73–88.

Müllenhoff, Karl. 1887–1900. *Deutsche Altertumskunde*. 5 vols. Berlin: Weidman.

Müller, Reinhard. 2004. *Königtum und Gottesherrschaft: Untersuchungen zur alttestamentlichen Monarchiekritik*. Tübingen: Mohr Siebeck.

Mundal, Else. 1992. "Snorri og Völuspá." In *Snorrastefna*, edited by Úlfar Bragason, 180–92. Reykjavík: Stöfnun Sigurðar Nordals.

————. 1996. "The Perception of the Saamis and Their Religion in Old Norse Sources." In *Shamanism and Northern Ecology*, edited by Juha Pentikainen, 39–53. Berlin: Mouton de Gruyter.

————. 1997. "Kong Harald hårfagre og samejenta Snøfrid: Samefolket sin plass i den norske riksamlinsmyten." *Nordica Bergensia* 14: 39–53.

————. 2003. "Coexistence of Saami and Norse Culture—Reflected in and Interpreted by Old Norse Myths." In *Old Norse Myths, Literature, and Society*, edited by Margaret Clunies Ross, 346–55. Odense: Odense University Press.

Naumann, Hans. 1938. "Der König und die Seherin." *Zeitschrift für deutsche Philologie* 63: 347–58.

Neckel, Gustav. 1920. *Die Überlieferungen vom Gotte Balder*. Dortmund: Wilhelm Ruhfus.

Nedkvitne, Arnved. 2004. *The Social Consequences of Literacy in Medieval Scandinavia*. Turnhout, Belgium: Brepols.

Nesheim, Asbjørn. 1967. "Samisk trolldom." In *Kulturhistorisk Leksikon for Nordisk Middelalder* 15: 104–67. Copenhagen: Rosenkilde og Bagger.

Nordal, Guðrún. 1998. *Ethics and Action in Thirteenth-Century Iceland.* Odense: Odense University Press.

———. 2001. *Tools of Literacy: The Role of Skaldic Verse in Icelandic Textual Culture of the Twelfth and Thirteenth Centuries.* Toronto: University of Toronto Press.

Nordal, Sigurður. 1920. *Snorri Sturluson.* Reykjavík: n.p.

Nordenfalk, Carl. 1982. *The Batavians' Oath of Allegiance: Rembrandt's Only Monumental Painting.* Stockholm: Nationalmuseum.

Nordenstreng, Rolf. 1924. "Guden Vali." In *Festskrift tillägnad Hugo Pipping*, 392–94. Helsingfors: Mercator.

O'Donaghue, Heather. 2005. *Skaldic Verse and the Poetics of Saga Narrative.* Oxford: Oxford University Press.

Ólason, Vésteinn. 1968. "Er Snorri höfundur Egils sögu?" *Skirnir* 142: 48–67.

Olsen, Magnus. 1946. "Með lǫgum skal land byggja." *Maal og Minne*, 1946, 75–88.

Pomathios, Jean-Luc. 1987. *Le pouvoir politique et sa représentation dans l'Éneide de Virgile.* Brussels: Collection Latomus.

Picard, Eve. 1991. *Germanisches Sakralkönigtum? Quellenkritische Studien zur Germania des Tacitus und aur altnordischen Überlieferung.* Heidelberg: Carl Winter.

Quinn, Judy. 2000. "From Orality to Literacy in Medieval Iceland." In *Old Icelandic Literature and Society*, edited by Margaret Clunies Ross, 30–60. Cambridge: Cambridge University Press.

Radcliffe-Brown. 1952. *Structure and Function in Primitive Society.* Glencoe, IL: Free Press.

Ross, Margaret Clunies. 1983. "Snorri Sturluson's Use of the Norse Origin-Legend of the Sons of Fornjótr in His *Edda*." *Arkiv för Norsk Filologi* 98: 47–66.

———. 1994. *Prolonged Echoes: Old Norse Myths in Medieval Northern Society.* Vol. 1, *The Myths.* Odense: Odense University Press.

Rossum, J. A. van. 1992. "Julius Civilis en het Germaanse gevaar." *Lampas* 25: 184–97.

Sahlins, Marshall. 1985. *Islands of History.* Chicago: University of Chicago Press.

———. 2008. "The Stranger-King Or Elementary Forms of the Political Life." *Indonesia and the Malay World* 36: 177–99.

———. 2011. "The Alterity of Power and Vice Versa, with Reflections on Stranger Kings and the Real-Politics of the Marvellous." In *History: From Medieval Ireland to the Post-modern World*, edited by Anthony McElligott, Liam Chambers, Clara Breathnach, and Catherine Lawless, 63–101. Dublin: Irish Academic Press.

Sandnes, Jørn. 1994. Review of *Ynglingatal og Ynglingasaga.* *Historisk Tidsskrift* 73: 229–31.

Sandvik, Gudmund. 1955. *Hovding og Konge i Heimskringla.* Oslo: Akademisk Forlag.

Schach, Paul. 1971. "Symbolic Dreams of Future Renown in Old Icelandic Literature." *Mosaic* 4: 51–73.

Schjødt, Jens Peter. 1990. "Det sakrale kongedømme i det førkristne Skandinavien." *Chaos* 13: 48–67.

Schröder, Franz Rolf. 1924. *Germanentum und Hellenismus.* Heidelberg: Carl Winter.

Schulz, Katja. 2004. *Riesen: Von Wissenshütern und Wildnisbewohnern in Edda und Saga.* Heidelberg: Universitätsverlag Winter.

Scott, James C. 1985. *Weapons of the Weak: Everyday Forms of Peasant Resistance.* New Haven, CT: Yale University Press.

————. 1990. *Domination and the Arts of Resistance: Hidden Transcripts.* New Haven, CT: Yale University Press.

————. 1998. *Seeing like a State: How Certain Schemes to Improve the Human Condition Have Failed.* New Haven, CT: Yale University Press.

————. 2009. *The Art of Not Being Governed: An Anarchist History of Upland Southeast Asia.* New Haven, CT: Yale University Press.

————. 2012. *Two Cheers for Anarchism: Six Easy Pieces on Autonomy, Dignity, and Meaningful Work and Play.* Princeton, NJ: Princeton University Press.

See, Klaus von. 1960. "Der Skalde Torf-Einar." *Beiträge zur Geschichte der deutschen Sprache und Literatur* 82: 31–43.

————. 1961. "Studien zum Haraldskvæði." *Arkiv för Nordisk Filologi* 76: 96–111.

————. 2002. *Königtum und Staat im skandinavischen Mittelalter.* Heidelberg: Carl Winter.

Sigurðsson, Gisli. 2004. *The Medieval Icelandic Saga and Oral Tradition.* Cambridge, MA: Harvard University Press.

Simek, Rudolf. 2001. "Lust, Sex and Domination: *Skírnismál* and the Foundation of the Norwegian Kingdom." In *Sagnaheimur: Studies in Honour of Hermann Pálsson,* edited by Ásdis Egilsdóttir and Rudolf Simek, 229–46. Vienna: Fassbaender.

————. 2003. *Religion und Mythologie der Germanen.* Darmstadt: Wissenschaftliche Gesellschaft.

Skånland, Vegard. 1966. "The Year of King Harald Fairhair's Access to the Throne according to Theodoricus Monachus." *Symbolae Osloenses* 41: 125–28.

Skre, Dagfinn. 2007. "The Dating of Ynglingatal." In *Kaupang in Skiringssal,* edited by Dagfinn Skre, 407–29. Oslo: Museum of Cultural History.

Smalley, Beryl. 1974. *Historians in the Middle Ages.* London: Thames and Hudson.

Smith, Anthony D. 1999. *Myths and Memories of the Nation.* Oxford: Oxford University Press.

————. 2003. *Chosen Peoples: Sacred Sources of National Identity.* Oxford: Oxford University Press.

Sørensen, Preben Meulengracht. 2001. "The Sea, the Flame, and the Wind: The Legendary Ancestors of the Earls of Orkney." In *At fortælle Historien/Telling History: Studier i den gamle nordiske litteratur/Studies in Norse Literature,* 221–30. Trieste: Edizioni Parnaso.

Spiegel, Gabrielle. 1997. *The Past As Text: The Theory and Practice of Medieval Historiography.* Baltimore: Johns Hopkins University Press.

Steinsland, Gro. 1991. *Det Hellige Bryllup og Norrøn Kongeideologi: En Analyse av Hierogami-myten in Skírnismál, Ynglingatal, Háleygjatal og Hyndluljóð.* Oslo: Solum.

————. 2000. *Den hellige kongen: Om religion og herskermakt fra vikingtid til middelalder.* Oslo: Pax.

Stjernfelt, Frederik. 1990. *Baldr og verdensdramet i den nordiske mytologi.* Copenhagen: Museum Tusculanum.

Storm, Gustav. 1873. *Snorre Sturlassons Historieskrivning: En kritisk Undersögelse.* Copenhagen: B. Lunos bogtrykkeri.

Ström, Ake V. 1959. "The King God and His Connection with Sacrifice in Old Norse Religion." In *La Regalità Sacra: Contributi al tema del VIII Congresso Internazionale di Storia delle Religioni, Roma, Aprile 1955,* 702–15. Leiden: E. J. Brill.

Ström, Folke. 1967. "Kung Domalde i Svitjod och 'kungalyckan.' " *Saga och Sed* 34: 52–66.

Sundqvist, Olof. 2002. *Freyr's Offspring: Rulers and Religion in Ancient Svea Society.* Uppsala: Acta Universitatis Upsaliensis, Historia Religionum.

———. 2005. "Aspects of Rulership Ideology in Early Scandinavia with Particular References to the Skaldic Poem Ynglingatal." In *Das frühmittelalterliche Königtum: Ideelle und religiöse Grundlagen*, edited by Franz-Reiner Erkens, 87–124. Berlin: Walter de Gruyter.

Tomasson, Richard. 1980. *Iceland: The First New Society*. Minneapolis: University of Minnesota Press.

Tómasson, Sverrir. 1989. "'Sǫguljóð, skrǫk, háð": Snorri Sturluson's Attitude to Poetry." In *Úr Dölum til Dala: Guðbrandur Vigfússon Centenary Essays*, edited by Rory McTurk and Andrew Wawn, 317–27. Leeds: Leeds Texts and Monographs.

Toorn, M. C. van den. 1959. *Zur Verfasserfrage der Egilssaga Skallagrímssonar*. Cologne: Böhlau Verlag.

Turville-Petre, Gabriel. 1966. "Dream Symbols in Old Icelandic Literature." In *Festschrift Walter Baetke*, edited by Kurt Rudolph, 343–54. Weimar: Bohlau.

———. 1972. "Dreams in Icelandic Tradition." In *Nine Norse Studies*, 30–51. London: Viking Society.

Turville-Petre, Joan. 1978–79. "On Ynglingatal." *Medieval Scandinavia* 10: 48–67.

———. 1978–79. "The Genealogist and History: Ari to Snorri." *Saga-Book of the Viking Society* 20: 7–23.

———. 1988. "A Tree Dream in Old Icelandic." *Scripta Islandica* 39: 12–20.

Unwerth, Wolf von. 1911. *Untersuchungen über Totenkult und Óðinnverehrung bei Nordgermanen und Lappen*. Breslau: M. & H. Marcus.

Urban, Ralf. 1985. *Der "Bataveraufstand" und die Erhebung des Iulius Classicus*. Trier: Verlag Trier Historische Forschungen.

Vestergaard, Elisabeth. 1990. "A Note on Viking Age Inaugurations." In *Coronations: Medieval and Early Modern Monarchic Ritual*, edited by János M. Bak, 119–24. Berkeley: University of California Press.

Vestergaard, Torben Anders. 1988. "The System of Kinship in Early Norwegian Law." *Mediaeval Scandinavia* 12: 160–93.

———. 1991. "Marriage Exchange and Social Structure in Old Norse Mythology." In *Social Approaches to Viking Studies*, edited by Ross Samson, 21–34. Glasgow: Cruithne Press.

Volkmann, Hans. 1964. *Germanische Seherinnen in römischen Diensten*. Krefeld: Scharpe Verlag.

Vries, Jan de. 1923. "Die historischen Grundlagen der Ragnarssaga Loðbrókar." *Arkiv för Nordisk Filologi* 39: 244–74.

———. 1928. "Die Entwicklung der Sage von den Lodbrokssöhnen in den historischen Quellen." *Arkiv för Nordisk Filologi* 44: 117–63.

———. 1942. "Harald Schönhaar in Sage und Geschichte." *Beiträge zur Geschichte der deutschen Sprache* 66: 55–116.

———. 1956. "Das Königtum bei den Germanen." *Saeculum* 7: 289–309.

———. 1970. *Altgermanische Religionsgeschichte*. 3d ed. 2 vols. Berlin: Walter de Gruyter.

———. 1977. *Altnordisches etymologisches Wörterbuch*. Leiden: E. J. Brill.

Walde, A., and J. B. Hofmann. 1938. *Lateinisches etymologisches Wörterbuch*. Heidelberg: Carl Winter.

Wallace-Hadrill, J. M. 1962. *The Long-Haired Kings, and Other Studies in Frankish History*. London, Methuen.

Walser, Gerold. 1951. *Rom, das Reich, und die fremden Völker*. Baden-Baden: Verlag für Kunst und Wissenschaft.

Wanner, Kevin. 2008. *Snorrri Sturluson and the Edda: The Conversion of Cultural Capital in Medieval Scandinavia.* Toronto: University of Toronto Press.

Weber, Gerd Wolfgang. 1987. "*Intellegere historiam*: Typological Perspectives of Nordic Prehistory (in Snorri, Saxo, Widukind and Others)." In *Tradition og historieskrivning: Kilderne til Nordens ældste historie*, edited by Kirsten Hastrup and Preben Meulengracht Sørensen, 95–141. Århus: Aarhus Universitetsforlag.

Weems, M. L. 1800. *A History of the Life, Death, Virtues, and Exploits of General George Washington: Faithfully taken from authentic documents.* Philadelphia: Bioren.

West, Ralph. 1980. "Snorri Sturluson and Egils Saga: Statistics of Style." *Scandinavian Studies* 52: 163–93.

Whaley, Diana. 1991. *Heimskringla: An Introduction.* London: Viking Society for Northern Research.

———. 2000. "A Useful Past: Historical Writing in Medieval Iceland." In *Old Icelandic Literature*, edited by Margaret Clunies Ross, 161–202. Cambridge: Cambridge University Press.

Wolf, Alois. 1993. "Snorris Wege in die Vergangenheit und die Besonderheiten altisländischer Mündlichkeit und Schriftlichkeit." In *Snorri Sturluson: Kolloquium anläßlich der 750; Wiederkehr seines Todestages*, edited by Alois Wolf, 267–93. Tübingen: Gunter Narr Verlag.

Wright, Neil. 1995. *History and Literature in Late Antiquity and the Early Medieval West: Studies in Intertextuality.* Aldershot: Variorum.

Index

The letter *f* following a page number denotes a figure.